Health and Economic Growth

Health and Economic Growth

Findings and Policy Implications

edited by Guillem López-Casasnovas, Berta Rivera, and Luis Currais

The MIT Press
Cambridge, Massachusetts
London, England

MIT Press books may be purchased at special quantity discounts for business or sales promotional use. For information, please email special_sales@mitpress.mit.edu or write to Special Sales Department, The MIT Press, 55 Hayward St., Cambridge, MA 02142.

This book was set in Palatino on 3B2 by Asco Typesetters, Hong Kong and was printed and bound in the United States of America.

Library of Congress Cataloging-in-Publication Data

Economía y salud. English
Health and economic growth : findings and policy implications / edited by Gullem López-Casasnovas, Berta Rivera, and Luis Currais.
   p. cm.
Includes bibliographical references and index.
ISBN 0-262-12276-6 (hc : alk. paper)
1. Medical economics. 2. Medical policy. 3. Economic growth. 4. Macroeconomics.
I. López i Casasnovas, Guillem, 1955– . II. Rivera, Berta. III. Currais, Luis. IV. Title.
RA410.E28713   2005
338.4′73621—dc22   2004062534

10 9 8 7 6 5 4 3 2 1

To our children,
Julia, Clara, Francesc, Diego, and Claudia,
Our capital

Contents

Preface

Guillem López-Casasnovas

Health and Economic Growth is the result of an excellent initiative by two Spanish health economists, my colleagues Berta Rivera and Luis Currais, both of whom are Research Fellows at the Economics and Health Research Center at Universitat Pompeu Fabra and members of the Economics Faculty at the University of A Coruña in Galicia.

In preparing the preface to this volume I have become aware of the growing interest in this field and its importance as the chosen leitmotiv for the International Health Economics Association Conference, which I will have the honor to chair in Barcelona in 2005.

This book is a collection of essays by the foremost researchers in health economics and growth, and is readily accessible to readers with no background in the field. It emphasizes the relevance of devoting time, financial resources, and effort to the improvement of health and social welfare. This requires not only an investment in health care, but also in public health policies, sanitation, nutrition, and other sectors that interact with health. The relative weight of each of these factors or investment priorities are intimately linked to the part of the world being contemplated; so investing in health should not be envisaged as simply pledging funds for higher health care spending in a broad, non-selective fashion. Health investment also involves devoting attention to a wider range of strategies that are mid- and long-term in their outlook and that aim to improve the population's human and social capital. Such strategies may require a greater focus on medical research in the developed world. It will also require striving toward innovation, changing practices, and improving human capital in the clinical management arena in an attempt to augment its effectiveness and efficiency in the real world.

The first component of investment (research and development) in real terms is, to a great extent, influenced by markets and the willingness of wealthy countries to pay. This is the case even when it leads to minor breakthroughs and adds value for health. From time to time however, research investment generates positive externalities worldwide. Semi- and less-developed countries can benefit from important innovations in health care, even if they have not made any financial contribution. Some benefits are certainly limited due to patent protection. Neverthe- less, even in this case, they may benefit from price discrimination and be able to have access to better health care. A greater social responsibil- ity by the pharmaceutical industry may help considerably to improve health in less developed countries.

The second component of investment (fighting poverty and im- proving human and social conditions) is undoubtedly linked to educa- tion and workforce strategies. This involves the need to enlarge our perspectives and to open minds from within and outside the health care system. This is not always an easy task when public policies are designed.

The findings of the impact of health on economic growth and the analysis of the different dimensions of their connections will contribute to a deeper understanding of the benefits of investing in health. This understanding is highly significant for economic policymaking and should help to contribute to human and socioeconomic development.

Acknowledgments

This volume has been made possible with the help and support of various individuals and institutions to whom we would like to express our gratitude.

A big thank you goes to all of the authors who have, from the outset, tackled this project with much enthusiasm and have contributed unstintingly. The fact that this book has seen the light of day at all is due in no small part to the confidence and initiative shown by Vicente Ortun, Director of the Health Economic Series of the CRES-UPF (the Economics and Health Research Center at Universitat Pompeu Fabra), and by Ruben Suarez-Berenguela, Economic Advisor of the Pan American Health Organization (PAHO). We would also like to express our thanks for the financial support provided by the PAHO and the Merck Foundation to the CRES-UPF. The editorial viability of this book is due to the professionalism of Elizabeth Murry at The MIT Press who helped coax the project to fruition. Preparation of the manuscript was aided by Bruno Casal of the University of A Coruña, whose help was invaluable. Finally, a special thanks to Howard Carter, for his technical support, efficiency, and dedication.

Introduction: The Role Health Plays in Economic Growth

Guillem López-Casasnovas,
Berta Rivera, and Luis Currais

1 A Preliminary Overview of Health and Economic Growth

The evolution of economic growth theory has become inextricably linked to the evolution of economics itself, at least insofar as that discipline provides an explanation for the wealth of nations. Many of the elements that form the basis of modern economic growth theory have their origins in the work of classical economists such as Adam Smith ([1776] 1937), David Ricardo ([1817] 1951), and Thomas Malthus ([1798] 1986). It wasn't until much later that Frank Ramsey (1928), Allyn Young (1928), and Joseph Schumpeter (1934) developed the basic approaches of competitive behavior and equilibrium dynamics, the role of increasing returns and economic progress, and the effects of technological progress through invention, innovation, and entrepreneurship.

The next important contributions were those of Solow (1956) and Swan (1956), whose work formed what has become known as the neoclassical growth model. This model gave rise to a wide-ranging literature on economic growth that in turn fueled the debate on the capital–production relationship and the properties that determine market equilibrium. Taking as a starting point the intertemporal optimization approach of Ramsey, the contributions of Cass (1965) and Koopmans (1965) effectively transformed the neoclassical growth model into a tool capable of analyzing optimal consumer behavior. However, the limitations of the neoclassical model in explaining long-term growth along with the persistent interest of economists in short-term phenomena led to a dearth of ideas during the 1970s, a situation that began to change only in the second half of the 1980s.

The exogeneity of technological progress in the neoclassical model and the difficulty of explaining long-term economic growth because of diminishing returns to capital has limited the analytical capacity of the neoclassical model and its empirical verification. The ever-widening gap between rich and poor economies has thus led researchers to look for new theories that they feel might explain this dynamic. As a result, a new family of theories has emerged that seems better equipped to explain long-term growth. Central to these models is the idea that technology is endogenous to the growth process. Since technology determines economic growth in an endogenous way, these are known as endogenous growth models. The first of these models was published by Romer (1986) and Lucas (1988). The concept of technology in these models depends on economic factors such the capital–labor relationship. An increase in this ratio explains not only an increase in income but also the ability to maintain high levels of growth in the long term.

From the early 1990s, various studies have attempted to identify the determinants of economic growth. Many variables have been tested, but only a few have been accepted as being statistically significant in explaining growth. The role of human capital is now almost universally regarded as being indispensable in this respect. Sustained growth depends on levels of human capital whose stocks increase as a result of better education, higher levels of health, and new learning and training procedures. Without a labor force with some minimal levels of education and health, a country is incapable of maintaining a state of continuous growth.

The effects of human capital variables imply that the investment rate tends to increase as levels of education and health rise. Because these variables evolve systematically according to levels of economic development, such changes may be linked to increases in the investment rate. Thus, low levels of human capital represent a barrier to development, which impedes competitiveness. Any attempt to reduce the gap between the rich and poor worlds must therefore incorporate a better understanding of the mechanisms that underlie the process of human capital formation.

Right up until the second half of the 1990s, the role of human capital was, in the main, linked to education, although a few authors had already recognized the importance of other factors such as health and nutrition. In a groundbreaking analysis, Mankiw, Romer, and Weil (1992) cite the importance of considering not only education, but also health and nutrition in a broader analysis of human capital. Yet there was a delay of several years before the link between economic growth and health became widely accepted as a significant issue of economic inquiry. Fogel (1994), Barro and Sala-i-Martín (2004), and Barro (1996) were among the first in examining the relationship between economic growth and health, and their research has subsequently given rise to a substantial store of work focusing on the link between wealth and health.[1]

Good health is a crucial component of overall well-being. However, improvements in health status may be justified on purely economic grounds. Good health raises levels of human capital, and this has a positive effect on individual productivity and on economic growth rates. Better health increases workforce productivity by reducing incapacity, debility, and the number of days lost to sick leave, and increases the opportunities an individual has of obtaining better paid work. Further, good health helps to forge improved levels of education by increasing levels of schooling and scholastic performance. There is also an important positive spillover effect in that the resources that would otherwise be used for preventative health treatments are freed for alternative uses or in cushioning the effects of other negative externalities such as poverty within the nation.

To gain a more adequate understanding of the accumulation process driving health human capital and wealth, it is essential to ascertain how the causal relationship between the two works. The main difficulty in any approach to this task lies in the possible existence of endogeneity between health and wealth. Although good health may be considered a form of human capital that has a beneficial effect on productivity, income also influences health in a positive way. The capacity to generate higher earnings facilitates an increase in the consumption of health-related goods such as adequate food or medicine. There is also an indirect effect on individual health via the improvements inherent in changes in lifestyle, a more intensive participation in the work place, and higher levels of education, all of which promote higher health levels through increases in income.[2] The nature of this feedback would yield biased and inconsistent estimates of the structural parameters when it comes to carrying out estimates of the impact that health has on economic growth.[3]

Over the last few years, a large body of literature has provided evidence supporting the thesis that health exerts a positive effect on wealth. In analytical terms, several theoretical models have been developed that attempt to describe the accumulation process of health and economic growth. According to the basic set-up, the income earner does not decide on the amounts of money a household will save or invest in human or physical capital. On the other hand, in models in which individuals attempt to maximize their utility, investment in human capital may have a direct impact on those individuals carrying out that investment both for themselves or their children. Such lines of research have led to models that, by considering the specific characteristics of consumption and production in a given economy, are capable of assessing the direct and indirect influence that individual health and education investment decisions have on present and future generations. The positive effect of health on economic growth is thus identified either in exogenous growth models during the transition to the steady state or in endogenous growth models, each within the context of intertemporal optimization.

In the empirical literature, macro and micro studies have analyzed whether different health indicators are positively linked to different dimensions of economic growth. On a macroeconomic level, both within-country and cross-country analyses measure the effects of different inputs on total economic output. These inputs include human capital that is given jointly as a combination of health and education. But studies such as these come up against specification problems that arise by attempting to simultaneously analyze health and education due to the aggregate effects of health or to reverse causation. On a microeconomic level, many studies have focused on the impact of health on wages. Different health indicators are used and range from anthropometric measures such as weight, height, body mass index (BMI), and measures based on surveys that report factors such as self-assessed health status, whether the individual is suffering from a particular chronic illness, or whether their main activity is impaired or limited. These lines of research are based on the idea that healthier workers are less susceptible to disease, more alert, more energetic, and consequently more productive and command higher earnings. The main problems in these kinds of analyses are typically derived from measurement errors when it comes to capturing the individual's health status, heterogeneity of the variables, and the possible feedback among them.

In addition to individual research important international, organizations have set in motion their own initiatives to verify and measure the extent of the relationship between health and the accumulation of wealth. The Commission on Macroeconomics and Health spent two years analyzing the impact of health on development in an attempt to examine the channels through which health-related investments might have a positive impact on economic growth and equity in developing countries. Two other important research projects were directed by the Pan American Health Organization and the Inter-American Development Bank. Both focused on Latin America and the Caribbean. The former dealt with the impact of health on long-term economic growth and the latter on the impact of health on household productivity. The Pan American Health Organization is currently carrying out phase II of its Health and Economic Growth project. This undertaking looks at the relationship between the persistence of poverty and inequalities and human capital accumulation, and variations in economic growth and social development. These initiatives, besides generating an enormous amount of high quality research, have served to fill a void in the existing literature.[4]

2   Investing in Health

The literature on health economics and economic growth has shown the importance of improving the health of populations as a means of reducing poverty and inequality in less developed countries (LDCs). In fact, when we take into account the increase in life expectancy, "freely imported," at least in part, from the developed world, a new picture emerges: the inequalities between the rich and poor worlds would have been far greater in the absence of improvements in health were it not for the significant reduction of the burden of disease that has already taken place.

A World Health Report published in 2003 emphasizes the magnitude of the work to be done: the gap in life expectancies between rich and poor countries is widening. Today a baby born in Japan can expect to live for 82 years, and will probably spend 92 percent of that time in good health. In Sierra Leone, however, average life expectancy at birth is a mere 34 years, more than five (16%) of which are spent in ill health, and this miserable scenario is similar in Angola and Afghanistan. Rather nearer to the West, life expectancy in Russia is 59 years, and in Turkey 61 years. While AIDS is the main killer in Africa, heart disease and other noncommunicable conditions are taking their toll elsewhere.

Indeed, for LDCs, investing in health often provides a means of escaping from the poverty trap. Public health and epidemiological programs help to short-circuit the vicious circle characteristic of poverty and ill health by creating complementarities within other forms of human capital, such as education or sustainable fertility rates for families.

Indeed, it is well documented how increases in life expectancy affect parental decisions to invest in their children's education by lowering the expected losses from infant mortality. As a result, women may reduce birth rates since the rate at which the family labor needs to be replaced declines. This, in itself, increases per-capita income. In addition, a more highly educated, healthier population is more productive, and contributes a national income that is shared among a less impoverished populace.

In this sense, a greater emphasis on improving health tends to shift a society's production frontier and the creation of wealth thus becomes a real possibility. Once survival is ensured and per-capita income increases, new types of consumer goods will be supplied to meet new kinds of demand, creating a true consumer economy. According to preferences for higher-income elasticity goods, quality of life aspects reach the citizens' shopping baskets as evidence of the general health improvement of the population.

In the developing world, investing in health is synonymous with higher labor productivity. Even under decreasing marginal returns, fighting obesity, alcohol abuse, smoking, drug addiction, and lack of exercise improves industrial output, lowers absenteeism, and reduces losses of human capital (and social investment opportunities) for the economy. Needless to say, society itself is spared a huge amount of pain and suffering, and resources that would otherwise be spent on chronic health conditions can be spent on other aspects of community welfare.

When planning a global strategy for health investment, either by devoting international aid to LDCs or by increasing money spent on health finance, *targeting* should not be the exception but the norm. Indeed, aid needs to focus on selective population groups, such as the family members who are responsible for the household group (women, income earners, young parents with dependants), as the World Bank does when designating its priorities according to the global burden of disease. Less accessible, isolated areas need to be prioritized too. Public health and primary care, together with basic education and health prevention, should be paramount. They may not be instrumental in saving lives at the individual level, but their externalities and indirect benefits mean that they are a valuable investment. Public resources first need to be concentrated to insure against the catastrophic consequences of illness, just the opposite of most of our national health public systems, which are rather good on full coverage for minor acute health problems, and much less for chronic conditions and mental health. Public solidarity funds should at the margin provide more benefits to more needy portions of the population. This recommendation is at odds with the idea of universalism and free, equal access to health care.

Investing in health cannot be identified, as we have commented here, with higher health care (public) expenditure. Investing in health and health care spending are not the same thing. Investment in health requires an all-embracing strategy aimed at addressing health population targets as a means of closing the gap between efficacy in the laboratory of ideas, and effectiveness in the real world.

3   Scope and Structure

Recently, the field of health economics has given rise to an increasing amount of research focused on the relationship between health levels and economic growth. The growing interest shown both by fellow researchers and students in the overlapping areas that affect the relationship between health status and economic growth has been the primary stimulus to the preparation of this volume.

This book is a practical, wide-ranging work of reference that marries the fields of health economics and growth theory. As such, it is aimed at researchers, students, and professors of undergraduate and graduate courses in economics, health sciences, social sciences, and public affairs, together with all those simply interested in the most recent and innovative lines of economic research.

We aim to explore the mechanisms by which a population's health status affects a country's economic performance in terms of economic growth and social development. This book looks at the impact of health on economic growth and development, and analyzes the nature and magnitude of the economic outcomes of investing in health. It gives scope to the most recent initiatives in the field both on a theoretical and empirical level. Theoretical analyses attempt to decipher the complex relationship between endogenous growth, health, and demographics. From an empirical viewpoint, there is an attempt to assess the incentives for investing in health. In this sense, this volume deals with health indicators, nutrition, income distribution, poverty traps, and HIV/AIDS, and brings together many of the lines of research that have come to the fore in recent years within the fields of growth and health.

The volume is divided into five parts, each of which deals with a distinct facet of the relationship between health and economic growth. As the main lines of study are closely linked in many cases, there is a certain overlapping theme that serves to highlight the interconnectedness of all of the elements in the field. At the same time, the proximity of each part allows the reader to have access to a cross-section of contributions according to specific areas of individual interest. The chapters identify a set of dynamic relationships that exist between income, human capital, and demographic change. Knowledge of these relationships is essential to an insight into the processes of social and economic development at the heart of much human progress. In a world in which the socioeconomic differences between nations are becoming increasingly pronounced at an alarming rate, it is imperative to reach a deeper, more rigorous understanding of the causes of these changes and to be able to analyze the dynamics that underlie them.

The first set of essays presented in part I, entitled "Health, Human Capital, and Economic Growth," focuses on economic growth theory and the channels through which health human capital generates both higher income and individual well-being. Models of economic growth have been extended to include the importance of health as a human capital input. All these initiatives are a product of advances in both theoretic economic modeling and improvements in the quality of data. This section presents three distinct endogenous economic growth models that shed light on the way that health affects economic growth.

In chapter 1, "Health, Human Capital, and Economic Growth: A Schumpeterian Perspective," Peter Howitt sets up a simple model of innovation-based Schumpeterian growth theory that contains different channels through which an improvement in a population's health affects a country's long-run growth performance. With one possible exception these effects all work in the same direction. Specifically, they raise the productivity and per-capita GDP—both relative to the world technology leaders—of a country that is sufficiently well off to be growing at the same rate as those world technology leaders. The effects that are new to Schumpeterian theory are those that work through the equilibrium rate of innovation, especially those that impinge directly on creativity and coping skills. In this respect, this chapter underscores the importance of recent research showing the beneficial effects that early childhood health and maternal health have on these critical dimensions of human capital.

In chapter 2, "Health as a Principal Determinant of Economic Growth," Adriaan van Zon and Joan Muysken develop an endogenous growth model where the provision of health services influences an economy's rate of growth. Since growth is produced using labor services that have alternative uses, increasing health activities may also imply lowering output and possibly growth. At the same time good health is necessary to be productive at all. Hence there is a direct trade-off between the health state of the population and growth performance. The authors add a stylized demographical and epidemiological module to the Lucas model that enables us to distinguish between care activities and cure activities. The chapter illustrates how changes in the rate of morbidity and the rate of mortality influence the optimum allocation of scarce (labor) resources over its various uses that include care, cure, final output production, and human capital accumulation activities.

The first part ends with "Health's Contribution to Economic Growth in an Environment of Partially Endogenous Technical Progress," by Dean T. Jamison, Lawrence J. Lau, and Jia Wang. The authors focus on the differences across countries in their rates of technical progress and explore some potential determinants of this variation. The chapter relaxes the assumption of exogeneity of technical progress in order to asses its potential determinants. In particular, they analyze health among other potential endogenous sources of technical progress using multilevel techniques. The chapter concludes that health does indeed have a positive effect on income but does not change the rate of technological progress. In contrast, education has a positive effect on income and on technical progress, but the magnitude of the latter is shown to be small.

In part II, entitled "Macroeconomics, Development, and Health," the authors identify the role of health as being central to long-term economic development, economic growth, and a reduction in levels of poverty. Higher life expectancies and low levels of disease tend to stimulate growth through accelerating the demographic transition, promoting investments in human capital, increasing household savings, and by augmenting domestic and foreign investment and greater social and macroeconomic stability. The four chapters that follow analyze the impact of health on development, economic growth, and equity. The authors recommend health measures designed to minimize poverty and maximize economic development in developing countries.

They place a special emphasis on the effects of child health and nutrition and how these affect life outcomes.

Chapter 4, by Xavier Sala-i-Martín, is "On the Health-Poverty Trap," which analyzes a predicament in which poor health generates poverty and vice versa. Both health and economic growth are presented as key factors underlying three basic human rights: life, liberty, and the pursuit of happiness. This chapter argues that health and growth are not simply fundamental determinants of human welfare, but are in fact so closely interrelated that it is impossible to generate economic growth in the developing world without solving the central health problems faced by these countries, and that it will not be possible to improve health without generating economic growth. Sala-i-Martín suggests micro- and macrointerventions aimed at promoting health, and points to poverty reduction as indispensable to fostering growth.

In "Human Development Traps and Economic Growth," chapter 5, David Mayer-Foulkes examines macroeconomic evidence that supports the idea that, nowadays, there are prolonged transitions taking place that are characterized by barriers to human development in the form of nutrition and health, and barriers to productivity growth. This chapter presents a model in which human development interacts with technological change and is characterized by a sequence of market failures. The existence of dynamic, intergenerational, human development traps makes economic growth slower, stratified, and transitional. The author presents a microeconomic study of Mexico that finds evidence for an economywide, intergenerational, low-human-capital trap consistent with the model. Mayer-Foulkes concludes that the effects found for early childhood development on the acquisition of education, and therefore on adult income, are commensurate with the historical and macroeconomic impact of nutrition and health on economic growth.

In chapter 6, "Health, Education, and Economic Development," Edward Miguel analyzes the effects of child health and nutrition on determining life outcomes in underdeveloped countries and examines the use of public policies to break the cycle of poverty. This chapter presents a series of recent randomized evaluations in less developed countries that provide compelling evidence of a causal link between child health gains and educational outcomes. Evidence from a school-based nongovernmental organization deworming project in Kenya and from a project providing dietary iron supplements in India, indicates that health gains lead to substantial improvements in school attendance. Edward Miguel shows that both child health shocks and parental death have a large impact on education and development across a range of African, Asian, and Latin American settings.

In chapter 7, "Nutrition, Malnutrition, and Economic Growth," Harold Alderman, Jere R. Behrman, and John Hoddinott examine the potential channels through which nutrition and health may affect economic growth. This chapter first assesses the extent of malnutrition in developing countries. It then surveys microevidence relating to the productivity impact of improved nutrition in those countries, from conception through infancy and childhood into adolescence and adulthood. These gains are evidenced by increases in cognitive development, physical stature, and strength; earlier school enrollment and more consistent attendance; and adult productivity. There is a consequent saving in resources that otherwise would go toward battling disease and other problems related to malnutrition. The study supports the use of nutritional policy to attain better food distribution goals through helping individuals from poor families become more productive over the life cycle.

The next part, "Human Capital, Health, and Demography," covers demographic and epidemiological transitions. The links between a population's human capital levels and fertility and mortality rates are crucial to the formulation of social and economic policies that are capable of guaranteeing development, combating misery, and ensuring human dignity. Infirmity and illness associated with maternity and early infancy, unwanted pregnancies, illiteracy, and discrimination against women are all linked to high fertility levels and elevated population growth. Without addressing these symptoms sustained economic growth is practically impossible. Chapters 8 and 9 provide models that analyze demographic and epidemiological growth processes.

Chapter 8, "On Epidemiologic and Economic Transitions: A Historical View," by Suchit Arora, reexamines some of the key milestones of the epidemiologic transition. It discusses long-term trends (based on annual data) of disease-driven mortality in the United Kingdom between 1850 and 1994. The author has compiled a data set that helps delineate the epidemiologic transition for the United Kingdom and uses that framework as a means of analyzing the potential benefits and pitfalls of this kind of data for human-capital-based theories of long-term economic growth. The usual approach to this problem is via life expectancy variables. The chapter attempts to delve deeper by commenting on how the eradication of diseases has contributed to the continuous rise of life expectancy since the beginning of the nineteenth century, along with a look at those diseases that have impeded its progress since then. The attempt therefore is to move away from summary measures such as life expectancy and aggregate mortality toward more microlevel trends that drive life expectancy itself. The author concludes that the consequences of health-related improvements have determined important intergenerational effects in the population. In the nineteenth century, for example, the emergence of human capital, particularly in the form of better health, influenced the behavior of economic growth permanently.

In chapter 9, "Economic Growth, Health, and Longevity in the Very Long Term: Facts and Mechanisms," Olivier F. Morand proposes a simple framework that integrates health investments with a standard growth model where physical and human capital are the combined engines of growth. The author explores the relationship between economic growth and health through a theoretical model characterized by the existence of two growth regimes separated by an epidemiological transition. The model shows how a health transition can help countries switch from a neoclassical growth regimen to a modern growth regimen. It suggests that health policies in developing countries can have important consequences for long-term growth as well as the immediate well-being of the population. Measuring the returns to health investment simply in terms of increasesd life expectancy would underestimate the true returns to health expenditures since it ignores the consequent effects on education. Policies aimed at generating economic growth should combine education and health policies as rising life expectancies result in increased educational investment and longer periods of schooling.

Part IV is entitled "Productivity, Labor Markets, and Health" and discusses how better health affects productivity and wages in labor market outcomes. Health as a form of human capital influences the wage levels of individuals and their capacity to generate sustained income over time. Poor health tends to handicap the poor far more than the well off, and this is particularly true when it comes to labor market opportunities. An insight into the nature and depth of the links between health and labor outcomes provides an important channel through which to formulate and carry out policies aimed at optimizing labor efficiency. The following two chapters aim to quantify the labor market returns that a positive health status induces.

In chapter 10, "Productive Benefits of Health: Evidence from Low-Income Countries," T. Paul Schultz analyzes various survey indicators of adult nutrition and health status as determinants of individual wages and labor productivity in low-income countries. The chapter argues that the major complexity posed by health is that indicators which represent health are multifaceted and are not always adequately justified by their correspondence with mortality, morbidity, and quality of life. Survey indicators of health status may be heterogeneous, or a combination of exogenous measurement error and genetic components on the one hand, and an endogenous or human capital component on the other. In this sense, although there are no definitive methods for distinguishing between human capital and genetic variation in health outcomes, alternative mappings of health status such as height, access to community health services, parental socioeconomic characteristics, and ethnic categories may be suggestive.

Chapter 11, by Berta Rivera and Luis Currais, "Individual Returns to Health in Brazil: A Quantile Regression Analysis," explores the links between health indicators and labor productivity at different levels of earnings distribution in Brazil. Economic inequality in Brazil is among the highest in the world and this is reflected in the relative access and utilization of health services as well as in the health conditions of individuals across income groups. The authors use extensions of instrumental variables techniques to carry out a quantile regression on a sample of workers to estimate the returns of health at different quantiles of the conditional distribution of wages. The chapter analyzes whether there is individual heterogeneity in returns to health or if there are constant returns for all workers.

Given the economic and social ramifications of AIDS, this pandemic warrants special consideration. The final part of the volume, entitled "Quantity of Life and the Welfare Costs of AIDS," discusses the effects of the disease on populations, specifically on the quantity of life and well-being of individuals, and also assesses future perspectives in terms of incentives for developing new treatments. AIDS is a particularly devastating disease, and in underdeveloped countries it is by far the most deadly, the most economically damning, and the surest barrier to growth. According to the World Health Organization (2001), 3 million people died of AIDS in the year 2000 and a staggering 2.4 million of these deaths were in sub-Saharan Africa. The number of children in Africa that have been orphaned by the disease has reached 12 million and predictions point to a figure of 40 million by the end of 2010.

Chapter 12, "The Economic Cost of AIDS in Sub-Saharan Africa: A Reassessment," by Tomas J. Philipson and Rodrigo R. Soares, reviews the value-of-life methodology, and describes how it can be used to assess the evolution of welfare across countries when changes in health are a significant dimension. It then applies this methodology to estimate the welfare cost of AIDS in sub-Saharan Africa. More than 70 percent of the population afflicted by AIDS in the world is in Africa, and the vast majority of those are in the sub-Saharan region. The chapter uses AIDS death statistics from UNAIDS and life tables from the World Health Organization to estimate counterfactual mortality rates that would be observed if AIDS did not exist. It then uses the marginal willingness-to-pay approach from the value-of-life methodology to estimate the welfare loss from the changes in mortality rates brought about by the AIDS epidemic. The results indicate that the welfare cost of AIDS in sub-Saharan Africa is on the order of $800 billion, or equivalent to one year of aggregate production for the whole region. This value eclipses any available estimate of the direct financial cost of AIDS.

In chapter 13, "Profits and People: On the Incentives of Business to Get Involved in the Fight against AIDS," David Bloom and Jaypee Sevilla discuss the motivation for private firms to play an active role in the struggle against HIV/AIDS. The authors suggest that there is a considerable gap between the potential and actual contributions of firms toward the global effort against AIDS. This disparity is not due to any lack of business know-how, but rather an inherent difference between the interests of business, making profits, and those of society at large. Economic theory provides a way of thinking about possible solutions in order to improve business participation in the fight against AIDS. The general principle is that one ought to build a public-private partnership capitalizing on the relative strengths and comparative advantages of states and business enterprises. This chapter argues that states are the natural designers of such alliances. And because of their skill in mobilizing resources, innovation, marketing, and distribution, businesses can carry out the work agreed upon.

Notes

1. Among them, Schultz 1997, Strauss and Thomas 1998, Rivera and Currais 1999, Bloom and Canning 2000, Bhargava et al. 2001, Case 2001, Mayer-Foulkes 2001, Weil 2001, and van Zon and Muysken 2001.

2. The effects of causality can also be observed through the economic impacts generated by maternity and fluctuations in the levels of women entering the labor market, a dynamic that may have secondary impacts on education.

3. The existence of a feedback effect between these two variables is documented in a wide number of studies. See, for instance, Wheeler 1980, Bherman 1990, Currais and Rivera 1999, Adams et al. 2003, and Meer, Miller, and Rosen 2003.

4. Some of these results can be found in Savedoff and Schultz 2000, Pan American Health Organization 2001, and World Health Organization 2001.

References

Adams, P., M. Hurd, D. McFadden, A. Merril, and T. Ribeiro. 2003. Healthy, Wealthy, and Wise? *Journal of Econometrics* 112: 3–56.

Barro, R. 1996. Health and Economic Growth. Unpublished paper.

Barro, R., and X. Sala-i-Martín. 2004. *Economic Growth,* second edition. Cambridge, Mass.: The MIT Press.

Bhargava, A., D. T. Jamison, L. J. Lau, and C. J. L. Murray. 2001. Modelling the Effects of Health on Economic Growth. *Journal of Health Economics* 20 (3): 423–440.

Bherman, J. 1990. The Action of Human Resources and Poverty on One Another: That We Have Yet to Learn. World Bank Living Standards Measurement Study. Working paper no. 74, The World Bank, Washington, D.C.

Bloom, D. E., and D. Canning. 2000. The Health and Wealth of Nations. *Science* 287: 1207–1209.

Case, A. 2001. Health, Income, and Economic Development. Paper presented at ABCDE Conference, The World Bank (May), Washington, D.C.

Cass, D. 1965. Optimum Growth in an Aggregative Model of Capital Accumulation. *Review of Economic Studies* 32 (July): 233–240.

Currais, L., and B. Rivera. 1999. Economic Growth and Health: Direct Impact or Reverse Causation? *Applied Economic Letters* 6 (11): 761–764.

Fogel, R. W. 1994. Economic Growth, Population Theory, and Physiology: The Bearing of Long-Term Process on the Making of Economic Policy. *American Economic Review* 84 (3): 369–395.

Koopmans, T. 1965. On the Concept of Optimal Economic Growth. In *The Econometric Approach to Development Planning.* Amsterdam: North Holland.

Lucas, R. 1988. On the Mechanics of Economic Development. *Journal of Monetary Economics* 22 (1): 3–42.

Malthus, T. R. 1986 (1798). *An Essay on the Principle of Population.* London: W. Pickering.

Mankiw, G., D. Romer, and D. Weil. 1992. A Contribution to the Empirics of Economic Growth. *Quarterly Journal of Economics* 107 (2): 407–437.

Mayer-Foulkes, D. 2001. The Long-Term Impact of Health on Economic Growth in Latin America. *World Development* 29 (6): 1025–1033.

Meer, J., D. Miller, and H. Rosen. 2003. Exploring the Health–Wealth Nexus. Working paper no. 9554, National Bureau of Economic Research, Cambridge, Mass.

Pan American Health Organization (PAHO). 2001. Investing in Health. Scientific and Technical Publication no. 582, Washington, D.C.: Pan American Health Organization.

Ramsey, F. 1928. A Mathematical Theory of Saving. *Economic Journal* 38: 534–559.

Ricardo, D. 1951 (1817). *On the Principles of Political Economy and Taxation.* Cambridge: Cambridge University Press.

Rivera, B., and L. Currais. 1999. Income Variation and Health Expenditure: Evidence for OECD Countries. Review of Development Economics 3 (3): 258–267.

Romer, P. 1986. Increasing Returns and Long-Run Growth. *Journal of Political Economy* 94 (5): 1002–1037.

Savedoff, W. D., and T. P. Schultz. 2000. *Wealth from Health: Linking Social Investments to Earnings in Latin America.* Washington, D.C.: Inter-American Development Bank.

Schultz, T. P. 1997. Assessing the Productive Benefits of Nutrition and Health: An Integrated Human Capital Approach. *Journal of Econometrics* 77 (1): 141–158.

Schumpeter, J. 1934. *The Theory of Economic Development.* Cambridge, Mass.: Harvard University Press.

Smith, A. 1937 (1776). *An Inquiry into the Nature and Causes of the Wealth of Nations.* New York: Random House.

Solow, R. 1956. A Contribution to the Theory of Economic Growth. *Quarterly Journal of Economics* 70 (1): 65–94.

Strauss, J., and D. Thomas. 1998. Health, Nutrition, and Economic Development. *Journal of Economic Literature* 36 (2): 766–817.

Swan, T. 1956. Economic Growth and Capital Accumulation. *Economic Record* 32 (November): 334–361.

Weil, D. 2001. Accounting for the Effect of Health on Economic Growth. Unpublished paper.

Wheeler, D. 1980. Basic Needs Fulfillment and Economic Growth: A Simultaneous Model. *Journal of Development Economics* 7: 435–451.

World Health Organization (WHO). 2001. *Macroeconomics and Health: Investing in Health for Economic Development.* Report of the Commission on Macroeconomics and Health. Washington, D.C.: World Health Organization.

World Health Organization (WHO). 2003. *The World Health Report: Shaping the Future.* Washington, D.C.: World Health Organization.

Young, A. 1928. Increasing Returns and Economic Progress. *Economic Journal* 38 (December): 527–542.

Zon, A. H. van, and J. Muysken. 2001. Health and Endogenous Growth. *Journal of Health Economics* 20 (2): 169–185.

I

Health, Human Capital, and Economic Growth

1

Health, Human Capital, and Economic Growth: A Schumpeterian Perspective

Peter Howitt

At the start of the twenty-first century, the gap in living standards between rich and poor nations is large and rising. The developing world suffers persistent poverty, while the developed world enjoys growing prosperity. According to Maddison (2001) the ratio of per-capita GDP in the richest group of nations to per-capita GDP in the poorest grew from 11 in 1950 to 19 in 1998.[1] The same ratio between Mayer's (2002) richest and poorest convergence groups grew by a factor of 2.6 from 1960 to 1995. This situation is undesirable, and probably unsustainable. The challenge to economists is to find remedies that will close the gap by raising the growth rates of poor countries.

Useful prescription depends on accurate diagnosis. Why has the growth performance of poor countries been so disappointing? Among the many causal factors that economists have proposed, poor health stands out as a likely candidate. Although life expectancy has increased dramatically in developing countries over the past 60 years, many people in poor countries still face shocking health conditions. The average rate of mortality for children under the age of 5 is 84 deaths per 1000 in developing countries. Over a billion people in low- and middle-income countries lack access to safe water.[2] Sub-Saharan Africa has been ravaged by AIDS, malaria, and tuberculosis. That health conditions such as these are likely to play a strong causal role in the growth process is confirmed by the time-series analysis of Arora (2001).

Different theories of economic growth produce different answers to the question of how health conditions affect a country's per-capita GDP over time (Barro and Barro 1996). For example, the neoclassical growth theory of Solow (1956) and Swan (1956) implies that in the long run only the level of per-capita GDP will be affected, not the growth rate, which is determined by the global rate of technological progress. The first generation of endogenous growth models, in which the rate of technological progress varies from country to country depending on local economic conditions, predicts a permanent effect on the growth rate.

The purpose of this chapter is to show how the question might be answered from the most recent vintage of endogenous growth theories, namely the "Schumpeterian" growth theory that Philippe Aghion and I, among others, have been developing (for example, Aghion and Howitt [1998]; Howitt [2000]; Howitt and Mayer-Foulkes [2002]). This recent theory differs from neoclassical theory in assuming that technological progress is endogenous and can vary from country to country. But it is also unlike the first generation of endogenous growth theories because it takes into account the process of international technology transfer, which makes the rate of technological progress in each country depend on global as well as local conditions.

The structure of the chapter is as follows. Section 1 below presents an introduction to the main ideas of Schumpeterian theory. Section 2 lays out a simple formal model. Section 3 discusses how health conditions impinge on the growth process according to this model. Section 4 concludes with a brief summary.

1 Schumpeterian Growth Theory

The basic ideas of endogenous growth theory are quite simple. The first is that technological progress is the driving force behind long-run growth. This proposition follows inescapably from the fact of diminishing returns. That is, if people continued to produce the same products, of the same quality, using the same means of production and the same procedures, with no growth in knowledge, then sustained growth in per-capita output would require sustained growth in the amount of capital used per worker. But beyond some point, increases in capital per worker would eventually reduce its marginal product to zero. This force would eventually reduce a country's growth rate (that is, the growth rate of its per-capita GDP) to zero. The only force that can prevent this eventual stagnation is increasing productivity, coming from new products, processes, and markets—that is, technological progress.

So far we are in agreement with neoclassical growth theory. Endogenous growth theory departs from neoclassical theory, however, in emphasizing that technological progress is itself an economic process, with economic determinants, much like the process of capital accumulation. The first version of endogenous growth theory was the so-called *AK* theory, which did not make an explicit distinction between capital accumulation and technological progress. In effect it just lumped together the physical capital whose accumulation is studied by neoclassical theory and the intellectual capital that is accumulated when technological progress is made. When this aggregate bundle of different kinds of capital is accumulated there is no reason to think that diminishing returns will drag its marginal product down to zero because part of that accumulation is the very technological progress needed to counteract diminishing returns.

Schumpeterian growth theory goes beyond *AK* by distinguishing explicitly between physical and intellectual capital, and between saving, which makes physical capital grow, and innovation, which makes intellectual capital grow. It supposes that technological progress comes from innovations carried out by firms motivated by the pursuit of profit, and that it involves what Schumpeter called "creative destruction." That is, each innovation is aimed at creating some new process or product that gives its creator a competitive advantage over its business rivals; it does so by rendering obsolete some previous innovation; and it is in turn destined to be rendered obsolete by future innovations.

Recent versions of Schumpeterian theory also assume that the rate of technological progress in one country depends not only on innovations in that country but also on technology spillovers resulting from innovations in other countries. In this way it takes into account the international diffusion of technology, or what is sometimes known as "technology transfer." It therefore recognizes what Gerschenkron (1952) called the "advantage of backwardness." That is, a country that lags behind the world's technology leaders has the advantage of being able to advance just by making use of inventions that have already been made elsewhere, without having to break new ground.

The advantage of backwardness is a strong force toward the convergence of growth rates, for it tends to make a country's rate of technological progress greater the larger the gap separating it from the global technological frontier, thus tending to stabilize the gap. The fact that the gap between rich and poor nations continues to grow into the twenty-first century as it has since the early nineteenth century suggests however that there are countervailing forces at work on the evolution of the gap. In Schumpeterian theory the countervailing force comes from two additional factors.

The first of these additional factors is the necessity to make techno-logical investments if one is to take advantage of technology transfer. Technologies developed in one country are typically not available to be taken off the shelf and used without further modification in another country. This is partly because much technological knowledge is what Polanyi (1958) calls "tacit," and cannot be codified. Thus adopters must spend time and other resources learning and experimenting before they can master what has been mastered elsewhere. It is also partly because of what Evenson and Westphal (1995) call "circumstantial sensitivity." That is, because of differences in climate, available raw materials, skills, customs, preferences, regulations, and so on, what works in one country will often not work in another.

The other additional factor is increasing complexity. As technology develops, the size of investment needed in order to transfer it to any given country tends to grow, because it becomes harder to master and to modify. For example, new technologies are often embedded in physical capital. As the capital becomes more advanced it involves more complex interdependencies, so that changing one component in response to local conditions may imply a long and unpredictable series of further changes before the technology will again work properly.

These two additional factors create a disadvantage of backwardness, because as a country falls further behind the technological frontier, its income falls relative to the size of investments that must be made in order to keep drawing on foreign technology at the same rate. This disadvantage is constantly fighting Gerschenkron's advantage, and Schumpeterian theory helps us understand why in some countries the advantage prevails, allowing the country eventually to grow at the same rate as the technology leaders, with a stable proportional income gap, while in other countries the disadvantage prevails, causing the country to grow indefinitely at a lower rate than the technology leader, with an ever increasing proportional gap.

Two observations are in order concerning the relevance of Schumpeterian theory to the situation of very poor countries. First, unlike neoclassical theory, the theory attributes differences in growth rates between rich and poor countries to differences in rates of productivity growth rather than to differences in rates of factor accumulation. This is consistent with a large number of recent empirical studies. For example, Easterly and Levine (2001) estimate that about 60 percent of the cross-country variation in growth rates of per-capita GDP is attributable to differences in productivity growth, and Klenow and

Rodríguez-Clare (1997) estimate that in their sample about 90 percent of the variation is attributable to differences in productivity growth.

Second, Cohen and Levinthal (1989) and Griffith, Redding, and Van Reenen (2001) present evidence that technology investments, in the form of R&D expenditures, are indeed an important ingredient in the technology transfer process, at least between developed countries. Although developing countries do not conduct formal R&D on a significant scale, nonetheless the investments that they make in adapting and implementing foreign technologies share many of the analytical characteristics of R&D in an economic model. Specifically, like R&D these implementation investments are costly, they make use of ideas developed elsewhere through technology spillovers of the sort that Griliches and others have shown to be very important, and they become increasingly expensive as the technology frontier advances.[3] Thus, for example, the role of technology investments in the diffusion of agricultural technology through the developing world during the "green revolution" that Evenson and Westphal (1995) describe is much like the role of R&D in Griliches's (1958) celebrated account of the diffusion of hybrid corn technology in the United States.

2   A Formal Model

In this section I construct a simple formal model illustrating the main ideas of Schumpeterian theory. The model ignores many details that would be important in applications, in the aim of providing a simple framework that allows us to see the various channels through which health can influence a country's long-run growth rate.

Consider the situation of a single country in a world of many. This country produces final output using capital, skills, and a variety of intermediate products that in turn are produced by capital and skills. The model of this economy can be described by the following eight equations:

$$Y = \psi F(K, AS(1 - \varepsilon)), \tag{1}$$

$$dK/dt = \sigma Y - \delta K, \tag{2}$$

$$dL/dt = \eta L, \tag{3}$$

$$dS/dt = \lambda \varepsilon L - \phi S, \tag{4}$$

$$R = \rho Y, \tag{5}$$

$$dA/dt = v(A^* - A), \tag{6}$$

$$dA^*/dt = g^*A^*, \tag{7}$$

$$v = \mu R/(A^*L), \tag{8}$$

where the endogenous variables are:

Y Final output (GDP)

K Capital stock

S Stock of skills

A Aggregate productivity

L Labor force (and population)

R Technology-investment expenditures

v Rate of innovation

A^* Global technology frontier

and the parameters (all of them defined to be positive valued) are:

ψ Productive efficiency

ε School attendance ($\varepsilon < 1/2$)

σ Saving rate ($\sigma < 1$)

δ Depreciation rate

η Population growth rate

λ Learning efficiency

ϕ Skill-adjusted death rate

ρ Research intensity ($\rho < 1$)

g^* Frontier growth rate

μ Research efficiency

The first four equations constitute a neoclassical Solow–Swan model of growth through factor accumulation, augmented to include the accumulation of skills as well as physical capital. Equation (1) represents the country's reduced-form aggregate production function, where F exhibits constant returns, concavity, and the usual Inada boundary conditions. The fraction $1 - \varepsilon$ of skills are applied to production rather than to learning, and technological progress is represented by growth in the labor-augmenting productivity variable A. Equations (2) and (3) describe net investment and population growth as in the original

Solow–Swan model assuming a given saving rate σ, a given depreciation rate δ and a given population growth rate η. Equation (4) indicates that the economy's net investment of skills equals gross skill investment minus depreciation. Gross skill investment consists of the number of people engaged in the learning process, multiplied by a learning-efficiency parameter. Depreciation occurs through death of people embodying skills. As in the original Solow–Swan model these first four equations imply that in the long run the country's per-capital GDP (Y/L) will grow at the rate of technological progress $(dA/dt)/A$.

The next four equations endogenize the rate of technological progress, assuming that the country spends a given fraction of its GDP on technology investments. This fraction ρ is referred to as the country's "research intensity." Equation (6) indicates how technological progress depends on both the domestic rate of innovation v and the country's "distance to the frontier." It is similar to the technological progress function postulated by Nelson and Phelps (1966) and highlights the role of innovation in determining what Nelson and Phelps call a country's "absorptive capacity." This equation captures Gerschenkron's advantage of backwardness because the annual increase in the productivity variable A is the product of the frequency of technological innovations v and the gap $(A^* - A)$ between domestic productivity and the global technology frontier.

Equation (7) indicates that the frontier grows at the given rate g^*. This and (6) together imply that if the country were to maintain a constant innovation rate v then its productivity would eventually grow at the same proportional rate as the global frontier, so that its economic growth rate (that is, the growth rate of its per-capita GDP) would converge in the long run to the global growth rate g^*.

Whether or not the country is *able* to maintain a constant innovation rate is one of the central questions to be determined by the model. The reason this is problematic is the above-mentioned disadvantage of backwardness, which is captured in the equation (8) representing the technology of innovation. According to this equation the country's rate of innovation is proportional to its technology investments but also inversely proportional to the global technology frontier. Thus the further behind it falls the slower will be the pace of innovations.

Note that equation (8) also makes the rate of innovation inversely proportional to the size of population. This assumption nullifies the "scale" effect that would otherwise make more populous nations grow faster because they have more innovators.[4] In more detailed accounts this assumption follows from a "product proliferation" effect whereby a larger population leads to more ideas for new products, which spreads quality-improving innovations over a broader range of products thereby diluting their aggregate effectiveness.[5]

These eight equations can be simplified by the following process of elimination to result in a simple two-dimensional dynamical system. Note first that the population-growth equation (3) and the skill-investment equation (4) together imply that the stock of skills per worker used in manufacturing $(S(1 - \varepsilon)/L)$ will converge in the long run to:

$$s = \frac{\lambda \varepsilon (1 - \varepsilon)}{\phi + \eta}, \tag{9}$$

independently of the other forces in the model. At the expense of missing some short-run dynamics, I will simplify the analysis by assuming that this convergence has already taken place.

Next, from (1)–(4) using (9), the law of motion governing the evolution of the capital stock per effective worker $(k \equiv K/AL)$ can be written as:

$$dk/dt = \sigma \psi F(k, s) - (\delta + \eta + g)k, \tag{10}$$

which is precisely the fundamental differential equation of the Solow–Swan model, where $g \equiv (dA/dt)/A$ is the rate of technological progress.

Define $a \equiv A/A^*$ as the country's relative productivity. In the long run the proportional income gap between this country and the world's technology leaders will be proportional to a. It follows directly from (7) and the definition of a that:

$$da/dt = a(g - g^*) \tag{11}$$

and it follows from (1), (5), (6), and (8) that:

$$g = \mu \rho \psi F(k, s)(1 - a). \tag{12}$$

Substituting this expression for g into (10) and (11) yields a system of two differential equations in the two dynamic variables k, the capital stock per effective worker, and a, the country's relative productivity. The behavior of this two-dynamical system is illustrated in figures 1.1 and 1.2.

In figure 1.1, the curve labeled K depicts the steady-state value of the capital stock per effective worker as a function of the country's relative

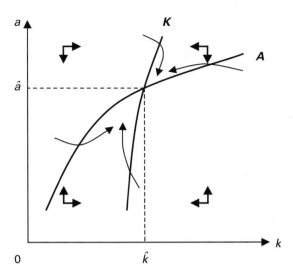

Figure 1.1
The dynamics of a country in the first convergence group, with a steady-state growth
rate equal to g*, the growth rate of the global technology frontier.

productivity.[6] It is upward sloping because according to (12) the larger
the country's relative productivity, given k, the slower will be its rate
of technological progress (that is, as a grows the country loses some
of its advantage of backwardness). As in the Solow–Swan model, a
slower rate of labor-augmenting technological progress g will imply
a higher steady-state capital stock per effective worker because it
reduces the rate at which this adjusted capital stock is diluted by
growth in efficiency units. Anywhere to the left of this curve k will be
increasing, and anywhere to the right k will be decreasing.

The curve labeled A in figure 1.1 depicts the steady-state value of the
country's relative productivity as a function of the capital stock per
effective worker.[7] It is upward sloping because according to (12) the
larger the country's capital stock per effective worker, given a, the
more income it will have to finance technology investments and hence
the faster will be its rate of technological progress, which will lead to a
higher steady-state relative productivity. Anywhere above the curve a
will be decreasing, and anywhere below a will be increasing.

It is easy to verify that the K curve is steeper than the A curve
at the point of intersection $(\hat{k}, \hat{a})$.[8] Therefore this point of intersection defines a unique stable long-run equilibrium. Every trajectory will
end up being trapped in a region, either where both variables are

increasing or where both are decreasing, in which all paths lead monotonically to the steady state $(\hat{k}, \hat{a})$.

Per-capita GDP in the country described by figure 1.1 will grow at the same rate g^* as the global technology frontier in the long run, because its relative productivity $a = A/A^*$ has stabilized at a positive level, which is only possible if the growth rate of the numerator (the rate of domestic technological progress g that will be the long-run rate of economic growth) is the same as the growth rate of the denominator (which is g^*). However, there is no guarantee that the two curves A and K will intersect in the positive quadrant as depicted in figure 1.1. On the contrary, it is possible that the K curve could lie everywhere to the left of the A curve, as shown in figure 1.2. In this case, the unique stable steady state is the point $(\hat{k}, \hat{a}) = (\hat{k}, 0)$ where the K curve intersects the horizontal axis.

The country described by figure 1.2 will not grow as fast as the global frontier, because even if its relative productivity falls to zero, the advantage that this extreme backwardness conveys on its ability to grow is outweighed by the disadvantage of backwardness described above. Instead its growth rate will be determined endogenously by local conditions according to equation (12):

$$\hat{g} = \mu\rho\psi F(\hat{k}, s) < g^*. \tag{13}$$

The country's per-capita GDP will fall forever relative to that of countries with a positive steady-state relative productivity.

Thus according to Schumpeterian theory countries will divide into two convergence groups, depending on the local conditions defined by the parameters of the model. Each country in the first convergence group, described by figure 1.1, will end up with a growth rate equal to g^*, the growth rate of the global technology frontier. The relative gap between it and the richest countries in the world will not grow forever but will eventually stabilize. Its relative productivity, and hence its relative per-capita GDP, will be endogenously determined in the long run by local conditions.

Each country in the second convergence group, described by figure 1.2, will end up with a growth rate that is strictly less than g^*, the growth rate of the global technology frontier. Its long-run growth rate will be determined endogenously in the long run by local conditions. The relative gap between it and the richest countries in the world will grow forever, without stabilizing. Its relative productivity, and hence its relative per-capita GDP, will fall asymptotically to zero.

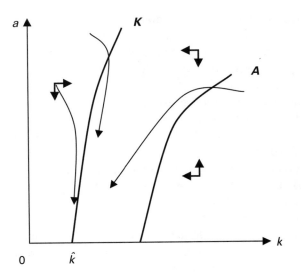

Figure 1.2
The dynamics of a country in the second convergence group, with an endogenous steady-state growth rate strictly less than g^*, the growth rate of the global technology frontier.

3 The Effect of Health on a Country's Long-Run Growth Path

The state of health in a country will affect its growth path through various channels, in a way that depends on local conditions. The nature of these effects will depend on which convergence group the country belongs to. For example, a small parameter change in a country in group 1 will affect the long-run level of per-capita GDP relative to the world's technology leaders, without affecting its long-run growth rate, whereas the same change in a country in group 2 will affect its long-run growth rate. Moreover, a large parameter change can shift the country from one convergence group to another. This section identifies six different channels through which population health impinges on growth and analyzes their effects.

Productive Efficiency
Healthier workers are more productive for a variety of reasons—increased vigor, strength, attentiveness, stamina, creativity, and so forth. This means that when health improves the country can produce more output with any given combination of skills, physical capital,

and technological knowledge. One way to think about this effect is to treat health as another component of human capital, analogous to the skill component. In the formal model above the effect would be represented by an increase in the efficiency parameter ψ that multiplies the production function in equation (1).

For a country in the first convergence group an increase in health working through this channel would have no long-run effect on growth, but it would have a positive effect on the long-run level of relative per-capita GDP. Not only would there be the direct effect that raises GDP for any given combination of factor inputs but this parameter change would also lead to a higher level of capital per effective worker, exactly as in the Solow–Swan model. In addition, there would be another effect that goes beyond what the Solow–Swan model would predict. That is, because the country is now more productively efficient it will end up with a higher relative productivity level a, which will further raise its relative per-capita GDP.

More specifically, the steady-state capital stock per effective worker $\hat{k}$ of a country in group 1 is the solution to the familiar neoclassical steady-state equation:

$$\sigma \psi F(k,s) = (\delta + \eta + g^*)k, \tag{14}$$

its steady-state relative productivity is:

$$\hat{a} = 1 - \frac{g^*}{\mu \psi \rho F(\hat{k},s)} \tag{15}$$

and its steady-state relative per-capita GDP is:

$$\hat{y} = \psi F(\hat{k},s)\hat{a}, \tag{16}$$

which will be increased directly by the increase in ψ, by the resulting increase in $\hat{k}$ that can be derived from equation (14), and also by the resulting increase in $\hat{a}$ that can be derived from equation (15).

For a country in the second convergence group, the improvement in health will raise the steady-state growth rate, through two channels. First, because the economy is now more productive it will have more income out of which to finance technology investments. For a given research intensity this means a higher rate of innovation, which will raise the country's steady-state rate of technological progress (which is also its rate of economic growth) even if there is no change in its capital stock per effective worker $\hat{k}$. Second, because the increase in productive efficiency will tend to raise $\hat{k}$ this will give a further boost to growth by further raising the income out of which to finance technology investments.

In addition, if the increase in productive efficiency is large enough it will shift the country from the second convergence group to the first, allowing it finally to stabilize the relative gap in living standards that separates it from the world's technology leaders.

These effects on a country in convergence group 2 can be seen with the aid of figure 1.3, in which the curves K and G represent the two steady-state conditions:

$$\sigma\psi F(k,s) = (\delta + \eta + g)k, \tag{17}$$

$$g = \mu p\psi F(k,s). \tag{18}$$

The first is the familiar neoclassical steady-state condition for k, and the second is the steady-state growth equation (13) already presented above. The K curve is downward sloping for the same reason that the K curves in figures 1.1 and 1.2 are upward sloping, namely because of the diluting effect on k of an increase in the steady-state rate of technological progress. The G curve is upward sloping because of the effect of increased capital on the country's ability to finance growth-enhancing technology investments.

An increase in the productivity parameter ψ will shift both curves up in figure 1.3. The upward shift of the G curve is the direct growth effect of productive efficiency described above and the upward shift of the K curve is the indirect effect that works through capital accumulation. Both effects work to raise the steady-state growth rate. Moreover, if the increase in productive efficiency is large enough to raise the intersection point of the two curves in figure 1.3 above the horizontal line at g^*, then the country will now join the first convergence group, and will eventually grow at the same rate as the world's technology leaders.

Life Expectancy
Increases in life expectancy have a direct effect on the steady-state average skill level of the population, by affecting the skill-adjusted death rate ϕ that constitutes the effective depreciation rate of aggregate skills, and hence affecting the steady-state level of skills per effective worker s, according to equation (9) above. The sign of this effect depends on its demographic incidence. If the increase in life expectancy works

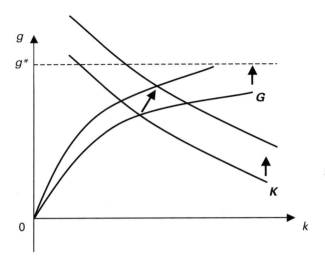

Figure 1.3
The effects of an improvement in health, working through enhanced productive efficiency, on a country in the second convergence group.

primarily through prolonging the lifetime of productive workers who
have already formed most of their skills, then ϕ will decrease, leading
to an increase in s. But if it works primarily through a reduction in infant mortality then ϕ may actually increase, because the average age of
the population will be reduced and the average death will destroy a
larger fraction of the existing stock of skills.

Suppose first that the increase in life expectancy reduces the skill-
adjusted death rate and hence raises s. Then it will affect the country's
growth path exactly like an increase in productive efficiency, except
that in this case it works by raising the education component of human
capital per effective worker instead of the health component. Thus for
a country in the first convergence group relative per-capita income
will be raised through three separate channels. In terms of equation
(16) there is the direct effect of increasing s, the indirect effect that
works through the induced increase in $\hat{k}$ and the indirect effect that
works through the induced increase in $\hat{a}$. For a country in the second
convergence group the effect will be to raise growth through two
channels—the direct effect of having more income with which to
finance technology investments, and the indirect effect that works
through increased capital accumulation, which also raises the income
with which to finance technology investments. If the increase in life

expectancy is large enough this will raise the country up to the first convergence group, allowing it to overcome the disadvantage of backwardness and to stabilize the relative gap in living standards that separates it from the world's technology leaders.

Of course if the effect on infant mortality is the dominant one, and the skill-adjusted death rate increases, then all of the above effects will be reversed. In this case it is possible for a country that was in the first convergence group to fall back into the second group, no longer able to overcome the disadvantage of backwardness with its relative income falling to zero. This effect may help to account for the fact that so many poor countries that appeared to be growing as fast as the developed world in the early and mid-twentieth century have had such disappointing growth performances since then.

In a more detailed working out of the theory, the effects of an increase in life expectancy would go beyond the direct effect on the parameter ϕ. In particular, by lengthening the time horizon over which the return to saving and to education can be earned, an increase in life expectancy is likely to raise the saving rate σ and the enrolment rate ε. The increase in the saving rate will work much like the increase in productive efficiency studied above. For a country in the first convergence group it will raise relative income by increasing the steady-state capital stock per effective worker, as in neoclassical theory, and also by the positive effect on the country's relative productivity induced by the increased capital accumulation. A country in the second group will enjoy an increase in growth, because of a rightward shift of the K curve in figure 1.3, which induces more growth by raising the income out of which technology investments are financed. If large enough, the increase in saving will allow the country to shift into the first convergence group with a growth rate equal to that of the world's technology leaders.

All of the effects of an increased saving rate will be reinforced by the increase in the enrollment rate, which works by changing the steady-state level s of skills per effective worker, with exactly the same effects as a decrease in the skill-adjusted death rate ϕ as described above.

Learning Capacity
Health plays an important role in determining the rate of return to education. Children who are well nourished, vigorous, and alert will gain more from a given amount of education than will children who are malnourished and suffering the debilitating effects of disease. In terms

of our formal model this effect shows up as an increase in the learning-efficiency parameter λ. The effects are the same as the above-analyzed effects of an increase in the attendance rate ε and a decrease in the skill-adjusted depreciation rate ϕ. In all cases the parameter change works by raising the steady-state level s of skills per effective worker. For a country in the first convergence group relative per-capita income will be raised through three channels. In terms of equation (16) there is the direct effect of increasing s, the indirect effect that works through the induced increase in $\hat{k}$ and the indirect effect that works through the induced increase in $\hat{a}$. For a country in the second convergence group the effect will be to raise growth through two channels—the direct effect of having more income with which to finance technology investments and the indirect effect that works through capital accumulation that also raises the income with which to finance technology investments. If the increase in learning efficiency is large enough this will raise the country up to the first convergence group.

In addition to these effects, anything that raises the steady-state level of skills is likely to have a further effect that works through the country's innovation technology. That is, to the extent that innovation is a more skill-intensive activity than production, we would expect that the increase in learning efficiency would induce an increase in the research-efficiency parameter μ, and that it would also lead the country to allocate a larger fraction of its resources to the activity of innovation, which would mean an increase in the research-intensity parameter ρ.

Both of these additional parameter changes would work in the same way, because only the product $\rho\mu$ matters for determining the steady-state values of a, k, and g. Thus for a country in the first convergence group the combined increase in the efficiency and intensity of research would raise the steady-state value of relative productivity, through equation (15), which would raise the country's relative per-capita income according to equation (16). For a country in the second convergence group the growth curve G in figure 1.3 would shift up, resulting in a higher steady-state growth rate, which if large enough would allow the country to join the first convergence group and stabilize the relative gap in living standards separating it from the world's technology leaders.

These same additional effects would follow also from the increase in life expectancy studied above, in the case where it led to an increase in skills per effective worker.

Creativity

One of the benefits of good health, especially good childhood health and good maternal health, is that it tends to make a person more creative.[9] Just as a healthier person will be more efficient in producing goods and services, so will the person be more efficient in producing new ideas. In other words, one of the effects that one would expect to come from an improvement in the state of health in a country is an increase in the research-efficiency parameter μ that affects the country's ability to generate innovations. As discussed above this would also likely raise the equilibrium research intensity ρ, and the combined effect of the two increases would be to raise relative productivity and relative per-capita income in a country in the first convergence group, and to raise steady-state growth in a country in the second convergence group, possibly allowing it to join the first group.

Coping Skills

Another benefit of improved childhood health and maternal health is that young people develop a better ability to cope with stress, and hence to adapt to the frequently disruptive and stressful effects of rapid technological change.[10] One simple way to capture this effect in the above model would be to make the productive efficiency parameter ψ a decreasing function of the rate of technological progress g, and to suppose that improved health shifts this function, resulting in more productivity for any given value of g. The long-run effect of this shift would again be an increase in relative per-capita GDP for a country in group 1, an increase in growth for a country in group 2, and a shift of some countries from group 2 to group 1.

In more elaborate versions of Schumpeterian theory the ability of workers to adapt to technological change can be shown also to raise the equilibrium research intensity ρ.[11] The idea is that when workers are more adaptable, then innovators will face a bigger payoff from creating fundamentally different new technologies to which workers will have to adjust. One could also imagine various labor-market and political-economy channels through which this might work. For example, unions whose members have an especially hard time coping with new technologies will be especially prone to bargain for featherbedding contracts that make it difficult for a firm to implement new processes; such contracts obviously discourage process innovations. Likewise voters who lack coping skills will tend to support politicians promising to protect such unions and promising to use other means of blocking disruptive technological progress.

Taking these effects into account implies that an improvement in health that raises the coping skills of a population will affect a country's growth path by raising the research-intensity ρ. This would reinforce the effects of improved coping skills that work through productive efficiency, for as we saw above, the long-run effect of increased research intensity would also be an increase in relative per-capita GDP for a country in group 1, an increase in growth for a country in group 2, and a shift of some countries from group 2 to group 1.

Inequality

Empirically, there is a strong negative correlation between various indicators of population health and measures of income inequality.[12] Although the causal interpretation of this correlation is still an open research question, many measures that increase population health will also result in reduced inequality because their main impact will be on the least privileged members of society and on those for whom poor health would otherwise make them relatively less well off.

Reduced income inequality is likely to have a positive impact on a country's growth path. The main effect that has been analyzed extensively in the growth literature works through credit-market imperfections and school attendance.[13] That is, in some countries even though there might be a high rate of return to education many people are unable to take advantage of this high rate because of financial constraints. A reduction in inequality, even if it leaves average income unchanged, will raise the fraction of people able to finance an education and will lengthen the years of schooling of those able to afford some. This effect works even in countries with widely available public education systems involving no tuition costs, because for many parents the main economic cost of sending a child to school is the income that the child would otherwise have earned for the family.

Thus by reducing income inequality an improvement in population health will impact on the above formal model through an increase in the school attendance parameter ε. As we saw above, the long-run effect of increased school attendance would also be an increase in relative per-capita GDP for a country in group 1, an increase in growth for a country in group 2, and a shift of some countries from group 2 to group 1.

Moreover, according to much sociological and epidemiological research on the health effects of SES gradients, there is likely to be a positive feedback effect of reduced inequality on health.[14] This effect has been challenged on empirical grounds by Deaton (2003), but there is no reason to think that there will be a negative feedback effect. Thus if there is any feedback at all it will probably serve to amplify all of the positive effects of improved health on growth and relative income identified in this section of the paper.

4 Conclusions

In summary, we have laid out a simple version of recent Schumpeterian growth theory that allows us to identify and analyze six different channels through which an improvement in a country's population health will impact its long-run growth performance. With one possible exception these effects all work in the same direction. Specifically, they will raise the productivity and per-capita GDP (both relative to the world technology leaders) of a country that is sufficiently well off to be growing at the same rate as the world technology leaders, they will raise the growth rate of per-capita GDP in a country whose growth rate is below that of the technology leaders, and they will allow some countries finally to stabilize the relative gap in living standards that separates them from the technology leaders. The one possible exception is an increase in life expectancy, which can work so as to reduce average skill levels in the population if it operates mainly by reducing the rate of infant mortality.

The main effects that Schumpeterian theory brings out and that were not present in either neoclassical growth theory or the earlier (AK) version of endogenous growth theory are those that work through the equilibrium rate of innovation. The effects on creativity and coping skills are especially important. In this respect, Schumpeterian theory underscores the importance of recent research showing the beneficial effects that early childhood health and maternal health have on these critical dimensions of human capital.

Acknowledgments

I thank Adrienne Lucas and my discussants Tim Lane and Luis Riveros for helpful comments. Stylianos Michalopoulos provided valuable research assistance. I also thank the Pan American Health Organization for financial support.

Notes

1. The richest group was the "Western offshoots": Australia, Canada, New Zealand, and the United States. The poorest was Africa.

2. These facts are drawn from Stern forthcoming.

3. See Griliches 1984, 1998.

4. Jones 1995.

5. Young 1998 and Howitt 1999.

6. That is, the solution k to the equation: $\sigma\psi F(k,s) - (\delta + \eta + \mu\rho\psi F(k,s)(1-a))k = 0$.

7. That is, the solution a to the equation: $\mu\rho\psi F(k,s)(1-a) = g^*$.

8. $(da/dk)|_K = -g_k/g_a + (\sigma\psi F_k - (\delta + \eta + g))/kg_a = -g_k/g_a + (\sigma\psi F_k - \sigma\psi F/k)/kg_a > -g_k/g_a = (da/dk)|_A$, where the subscripts denote partial derivatives evaluated at the steady state, and the function g is defined by equation (12).

9. The neural pathways involved in this connection are discussed at some length by McCain and Mustard (1999, chap. 1).

10. This benefit is emphasized by McCain and Mustard (1999).

11. See Aghion and Howitt 1996 and 1998, chap. 6.

12. The evidence is surveyed critically by Deaton (2003).

13. Galor and Zeira 1993; Aghion, Caroli, and García-Peñalosa 1999.

14. Wilkinson 1996, 2000.

References

Aghion, P., E. Caroli, and C. García-Peñalosa. 1997. Inequality and Economic Growth: The Perspective of the New Growth Theories. *Journal of Economic Literature* 37: 1615–1660.

Aghion, P., and P. Howitt. 1996. Research and Development in the Growth Process. *Journal of Economic Growth* 1: 49–73.

———. 1998. *Endogenous Growth Theory*. Cambridge, Mass.: The MIT Press.

Arora, S. 2001. Health, Human Productivity, and Long-Term Economic Growth. *Journal of Economic History* 61 (3): 699–749.

Barro, R. J., and J. R. Barro. 1996. Three Models of Health and Economic Growth. Unpublished paper.

Cohen, W. M., and A. Daniel Levinthal. 1989. Innovation and Learning: The Two Faces of R&D. *Economic Journal* 99: 569–596.

Deaton, A. 2003. Health, Inequality, and Economic Development. *Journal of Economic Literature* 41: 113–158.

Easterly, W., and R. Levine. 2001. It's Not Factor Accumulation: Stylized Facts and Growth Models. *World Bank Economic Review* 15: 177–219.

Evenson, R. E., and E. Larry Westphal. 1995. Technological Change and Technology Strategy. In *Handbook of Development Economics* vol. 3A, edited by Jere Behrman and T. N. Srinivasan. Amsterdam: Elsevier, pp. 2209–2299.

Galor, O., and J. Zeira. 1993. Income Distribution and Macroeconomics. *Review of Economic Studies* 60: 35–52.

Gerschenkron, A. 1952. Economic Backwardness in Historical Perspective. In *The Progress of Underdeveloped Areas*, edited by Bert F. Hoselitz. Chicago: University of Chicago Press.

Griffith, R., S. Redding, and J. Van Reenen. 2001. Mapping the Two Faces of R&D: Productivity Growth in a Panel of OECD Industries. Unpublished.

Griliches, Z. 1958. Research Cost and Social Returns: Hybrid Corn and Related Innovations. *Journal of Political Economy* 66: 419–431.

———. 1984. *R&D, Patents, and Productivity.* Chicago: University of Chicago Press.

———. 1998. *R&D and Productivity: The Econometric Evidence.* Chicago: University of Chicago Press.

Howitt, P. 1999. Steady Endogenous Growth with Population and R&D Inputs Growing. *Journal of Political Economy* 107: 715–730.

———. 2000. Endogenous Growth and Cross-Country Income Differences. *American Economic Review* 90: 829–846.

Howitt, P., and D. Mayer-Foulkes. 2002. R&D, Implementation, and Stagnation: A Schumpeterian Theory of Convergence Clubs. Working paper no. 9104 (August), National Bureau of Economic Research, Cambridge, Mass.

Jones, C. I. 1995. R&D-Based Models of Economic Growth. *Journal of Political Economy* 103: 759–784.

Klenow, P. J., and A. Rodríguez-Clare. 1997. The Neoclassical Revival in Growth Economics: Has It Gone Too Far? In *NBER Macroeconomics Annual*, edited by Ben Bernanke and Julio Rotemberg. Cambridge, Mass.: The MIT Press, pp. 73–103.

Maddison, A. 2001. *The World Economy: A Millennial Perspective.* Development Centre Studies. Paris: OECD.

Mayer, D. 2002. Divergence Today. Working Paper, Centro de Investigación y Docencia Económicas (CIDE).

McCain, M. N., and F. Mustard. 1999. *Reversing the Real Brain Drain: Final Report of the Early Years Study.* Toronto: Government of Ontario.

Nelson, R., and E. S. Phelps. 1966. Investment in Humans, Technological Diffusion, and Economic Growth. *American Economic Review* 56: 69–75.

Polanyi, M. 1958. *Personal Knowledge: Towards a Post-Critical Philosophy.* Chicago: University of Chicago Press.

Solow, R. M. 1956. A Contribution to the Theory of Economic Growth. *Quarterly Journal of Economics* 70: 65–94.

Stern, N. Forthcoming. *Growth and Empowerment: Making Development Happen.* Cambridge, Mass.: The MIT Press.

Swan, T. W. 1956. Economic Growth and Capital Accumulation. *Economic Record* 32: 334–361.

Wilkinson, R. 1996. *Unhealthy Societies: The Affliction of Inequality.* London: Routledge.

Wilkinson, R. 2000. *Mind the Gap: Hierarchies, Health, and Human Evolution.* London: Weidenfeld and Nicolson.

Young, A. 1998. Growth without Scale Effects. *Journal of Political Economy* 106: 41–63.

2

Health as a Principal Determinant of Economic Growth

Adriaan van Zon and Joan Muysken

For a long time economists have tended to ignore health as both a relevant factor of production and an important determinant of economic growth. The widely observed positive relationship between health expenditures and economic growth was considered only as the result of a strong positive income effect. Gradually, however, more and more economists have come to recognize that the relationship between health and economic growth is not only demand driven, but that health itself is an important determinant of economic growth. The latter has been recognized mainly on the basis of empirical cross-country studies, starting with developing economies (see Strauss and Thomas 1998 for an overview) and later covering Western economies (Knowles and Owen 1995; Barghava et al. 2001; McDonald and Roberts 2002; Webber 2002). However, until now only a few attempts have been made to present a coherent account of the causal links between health and economic growth.

A pioneering analytical study in this field is Grossman 1972, followed by, for example, Muurinen 1982, Forster 1989, Ehrlich and Chuma 1990, Johansson and Lofgren 1995, and Meltzer 1997. However, these studies focus on the provision of health services from a microeconomic demand perspective, ignoring the positive productivity feedbacks of population health at the macrolevel as an additional argument in favor of such services. Furthermore, this line of research does not recognize the possible interaction between health and the process of knowledge accumulation as the driving force behind economic growth.

Our model recognizes explicitly that economic growth is driven by knowledge accumulation in the tradition of Lucas (1988), and as such is based on labor services supplied by healthy people. The health state of the population at the aggregate level (i.e., the share of healthy people in the population) determines the extent to which potential labor services embodied in the population can be used effectively. Moreover, knowledge accumulation requires the spending of "healthy hours," wherein the embodiment of knowledge can take hold in individual people. These two positive effects of health on economic performance are recognized explicitly by Bloom and Canning (2000), who mention two other impacts: improvements in longevity that will increase savings (for retirement) and hence facilitate investment; and the occurrence of a "demographic dividend" due to the decline in infant mortality, which creates an increase in the working-age population. Since we want to use our model to focus on developments in the West, this demographic dividend is less relevant. Instead, we recognize explicitly that an aging population may become a drag on the economy because older people do require greater amounts of care from the health sector although they have ceased to be productive.[1]

Apart from care activities, a significant part of health activities take the form of cure in hospitals or by general practitioners, prevention activities, and so on. The important distinction between cure and care activities from a modeling point of view is that cure activities may change the health state of the population, whereas care activities do not. Because both activities take up scarce resources, but their impact on the population is principally different, we distinguish explicitly between both types of activities in our model.

A complicating factor is that at the aggregate level health production, both cure and care, takes place under decreasing returns to scale. Baumol (1967), for instance, takes the health sector as an example of a sector that permits "only sporadic increases in productivity" because "there is no substitute for the personal attention of a physician ...," as opposed to human capital accumulation activities, which give rise to "technologically progressive activities in which innovations, capital accumulation, and economies of large scale make for a cumulative rise in output per man hour."[2] In terms of our growth model, this implies that we assume the generation of health services to be characterized by decreasing returns, whereas human capital accumulation generally is modeled using increasing returns.[3]

The increase in demand for both cure and care, together with the declining productivity in the provision of cure and care, explain the dramatic increase in health costs over recent decades. Table 2.1 shows that in most Western countries health expenditures more than doubled their share in GDP during the past 40 years. Moreover, there is a fall in

Table 2.1
Health expenditure and aging population in selected Western economies, 1960–2000.

	Total expenditure on health, % GDP			Population aged 65 years and over—% of total population		
	1960	1990	2000	1960	1990	2000
Australia	4.1	7.8	8.9	8.5	11.1	12.4
France		8.6	9.3	11.6	14.0	16.1
Germany	6.2[a]	8.5	10.6			16.4
Italy		8.0	8.2	9.3	14.9	18.1
Japan	3.0	5.9	7.6	5.7	12.1	17.4
United Kingdom	4.5[a]	6.0	7.3	11.7	15.7	15.9
United States	5.0	11.9	13.1	9.2	12.5	12.0

Note: [a] Figure for 1970.
Source: OECD health statistics.

the productive base of the economy due to the aging population of the West, as one can see from the increase in the share of the population aged 65 and over in table 2.1.[4] These developments are the cause of our strong interest in the relationship between health and economic growth.

It follows from the observations above that our model should recognize the following principles: (1) health care and cure both use and produce resources for economic growth, directly with respect to goods production, indirectly with respect to knowledge production; (2) any activity depending on the input of labor hours will be negatively affected by a decrease in the health state of the population. Cure activities therefore regulate the level at which activities can be performed, including human capital accumulation activities; (3) cure and care activities are substitutes at the macro level, in that a higher level of cure activity reduces the share of nonhealthy people in the population, thus reducing their need for care.

In a previous paper (van Zon and Muysken 2001), we did not distinguish between cure and care activities, and we had a fixed population by assumption, forcing us to drop demographical issues from the outset. In this chapter, however, we want to see what the implications of changes in demographical and epidemiological parameters, such as the rates of mortality and morbidity, are likely to be for long-term steady-state growth. To this end we depart slightly from the notion of a health index used in van Zon and Muysken 2001, which "corrects" the effective supply of labor measured in efficiency units, by instead using as health index the fraction of the population that is healthy enough to provide productive labor services. By implication, the complement of this healthy subpopulation is the part of the total population that cannot provide these services because of ill health and/or old age. This enables us to introduce population dynamics into the Lucas framework, resulting from endogenous decisions regarding the provision of health services, next to exogenous developments in mortality and morbidity. Since the standard intertemporal utility function used in endogenous growth theory has both the numbers of heads and consumption per head as positive arguments, and since the health state of the population influences the net growth rate of the population, a link between health activities and the population growth rate can be said to provide a direct link between health activities and growth.

Apart from the direct link between health and growth decisions, there is an indirect link that is similar to the impact of education on economic growth. Investments in health, together with investments in education, determine the amount of effective labor services relative to the physical units of labor available that represent potential labor services. The resulting flow of labor services then has to be distributed over the various productive uses of available "healthy" time, that is, the production of final output, the rendering of health services in order to maintain the health state of the population, and the accumulation of productive knowledge. By regulating the provision of health and education services, one is able to influence the choice between consumption now and consumption in the future and hence the (steady-state) growth rate of the economy.

In order to be able to present our health and endogenous growth model, we will first reiterate the most important features of the Lucas model in the following section. To introduce endogenous population growth, we have constructed a very simple and stylized epidemiological and demographical module that is described in section 2. Section 3 then shows how the results obtained from this module are integrated with the original Lucas model and presents the formal results obtained for the modified model. Section 4 illustrates these results through a numerical analysis that we have performed in order to show how growth and the allocation of health care resources react to changes in the system parameters. Then, in section 5, we show what the growth and health implications of this model are for Western economies. Finally, section 6 contains some conclusions.

1   The Lucas Growth Model Revisited

We focus on the Lucas model without spillovers from individual knowledge accumulation to the macrolevel, because these spillovers only strengthen the role of knowledge accumulation for endogenous growth, rather than being a condition sine qua non for growth. The Lucas model then consists basically of a standard intertemporal utility function, a standard neoclassical Cobb–Douglas production function exhibiting labor-augmenting technical change, and a production function for the efficiency of labor that is driven by the accumulation of knowledge. The latter process takes time that cannot be used to produce current output, but it leads to additional future output due to the higher efficiency of labor. This represents an intertemporal trade-off between consumption possibilities now and in the future, which Lucas solves through an intertemporal utility-maximization approach in the form of an optimum control problem.

The original Lucas model can now be summarized as follows:

$$Y = A \cdot ((1 - w) \cdot e \cdot P)^{\alpha} \cdot K^{1-\alpha}. \tag{1}$$

In equation (1), Y represents output, A is a (constant) productivity parameter, P is the size of the population, K is the capital stock and e is the average efficiency per worker, and $1 - w$ is the fraction of labor time allocated to final output production. Consequently, w is the fraction of time per worker allocated to knowledge accumulation. Finally, $1 - \alpha$ is the partial output elasticity of capital. A and α are fixed parameters, w will be a fixed variable in the steady state, and e, P, Y, and K will be growing in the steady state at fixed proportional rates of growth.

Savings, that is, final output not consumed, are invested, and disregarding depreciation, the capital stock will accumulate in accordance with:

$$dK/dt = Y - c \cdot P, \tag{2}$$

where c is consumption per head, and t represents time.

The production function for "new" productive knowledge that manifests itself in the form of efficiency increases of labor, is given in equation (3) below, where δ_e is a fixed parameter that measures the productivity of the learning process:

$$de/dt = \delta_e \cdot e \cdot w. \tag{3}$$

Note that equation (3) implies that a constant allocation of labor time w implies in turn a constant growth rate of efficiency per worker e. It is obvious that a higher value of w will result in more consumption (possibilities) in the future and less consumption now.

Lucas models the trade-off between present and future consumption by a standard constant intertemporal elasticity of substitution utility function:

$$U = \int_0^\infty e^{-\rho t} \cdot P \cdot (c^{1-\theta} - 1)/(1 - \theta)\, dt. \tag{4}$$

In equation (4), ρ is the rate of discount and $1/\theta$ is the intertemporal elasticity of substitution. Note that now $\rho - \hat{P}$ acts as a kind of effective discount rate for the flow of utility coming out of the development over time of consumption per head.[5]

In the optimum w is chosen to maximize intertemporal utility U, subject to equations (1)–(3). The solution of the optimal control problem is then given by:

$$\hat{e} = \frac{\delta_e + \hat{P} - \rho}{\theta}, \tag{5}$$

$$w = \frac{\delta_e + \hat{P} - \rho}{\delta_e \cdot \theta}.^{[6]} \tag{6}$$

The steady-state growth rate of consumption, output, and capital per head in this Lucas economy is given by the growth rate of the efficiency of labor defined in equation (5). This economy grows fast if the productivity of the learning process is relatively high, and/or if the intertemporal elasticity of substitution is high. It grows slower if the effective rate of discount $\rho - \hat{P}$ rises, as one would expect, since the benefits from postponing consumption now take the form of increased future consumption that is valued less if the rate of discount rises. The allocation of time to knowledge accumulation w rises with an increase in the productivity of the learning process and with an increase of the intertemporal elasticity of substitution. In both cases it becomes more profitable (utilitywise) to invest more in future consumption; in the former case because the returns to investment have gone up, and in the latter case because the valuation of future rewards for current sacrifices in terms of consumption foregone has increased.

It should strike one as odd, although Lucas does not comment on it, that the growth rate of consumption per head rises with the rate of growth of the number of heads. But the underlying reason is very simple and has to do with the nonrivalrous nature of human capital per person in Lucas's model. Since the total human capital stock is the product of human capital per person and the number of persons, Lucas's and our specification implies that a larger future population raises the productivity of current human capital accumulation activities, the results of which will be "shared" in a nonrival way among the individuals of this larger population.[7] Given the specification of equation (3), a growing population then "ought" to allocate more resources to human capital accumulation, and consumption per head should grow faster than with a nongrowing population.

2   Health Extensions to the Lucas Model

Health enters the intertemporal decision framework in three different ways. First, a fall in the average health level of the population may be expected to cause a fall of the amount of effective labor services that the population can supply. Second, the generation of health takes scarce resources that have alternative uses (like the production of output or human capital), and third, good health may be expected to influence utility directly. As we have mentioned above, this direct link consists of the relation between the net growth rate of the population and the endogenously determined level of health activities. We elaborate this below.

2.1   The Demographical and Epidemiological Module

We distinguish between two health states that the population can be in. People are either healthy in which case they belong to the group of healthy people H, or they are not healthy and belong to the group of nonhealthy people S—the latter group also includes elderly, inactive people. We have for the total population $P = H + S$. The health state of an individual can change either through exogenous causes or through health activities. Such a change is represented by a flow between the two different states, as depicted in figure 2.1.

As figure 2.1 shows, we assume that all people are born healthy (B is an inflow in H), and only healthy people reproduce, at a given rate ι. In addition, healthy people don't die (D is an outflow of S). They will do so only if they get sick first. People can move from the healthy state into the nonhealthy state at a given morbidity rate μ_S, that is, a fraction μ_S of all healthy people at a certain moment in time will

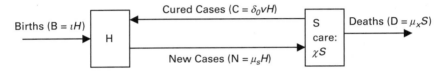

Figure 2.1
Stock-flow diagram of the population.

become ill, or otherwise nonactive (i.e., the flow N from H to S). A given fraction μ_X of all nonhealthy people will die and so leave the population. The number of nonhealthy people that switches to the healthy state (i.e., the flow C from S to H) is assumed to be proportional to the level of cure activities as given by $v \cdot H$. The factor of proportion is a given parameter called δ_0. The parameters are all positive and smaller than unity, except for δ_0, which can be greater than 1. Apart from the resources spent on the flow out of S to H, care resources need to be spent on the individuals that stay in S (cf. equation [13] below). The set of assumptions above can be summarized as follows:

$$dS/dt = N - C - D = \mu_S \cdot H - \delta_0 \cdot v \cdot H - \mu_X \cdot S, \tag{7}$$

$$dH/dt = B + C - N = \iota \cdot H + \delta_0 \cdot v \cdot H - \mu_S \cdot H. \tag{8}$$

Equations (7) and (8) show how the number of healthy and nonhealthy people changes over time, and therefore how the population itself changes. Defining $h = H/P$, it follows that $S/P = (1 - h)$, and therefore we have from equations (7) and (8):

$$\hat{P} = \frac{dP/dt}{P} = \frac{dH/dt + dS/dt}{P} = (B - D)/P = \iota \cdot h + (-\mu_X) \cdot (1 - h). \tag{9}$$

Equation (9) defines the net growth rate of the population P as the weighted average of the growth rates of healthy and nonhealthy people. One sees immediately that for $\iota > \mu_X$ an increase in h will lead to an increase in population growth, as might be expected.

2.2 Cure Activities in the Steady State: The Aggregate Health Production Function

Our assumption that the number of nonhealthy people that are cured is proportional to the level of cure activities as given by $v \cdot H$ is at the base of the aggregate health production function. The implication for the growth rate of the fraction of healthy people in the population can be found using equations (8) and (9), which yield:

$$\hat{h} = \hat{H} - \hat{P} = (\iota - \mu_S) + \delta_0 \cdot v - (\iota + \mu_X) \cdot h + \mu_X. \tag{10}$$

This equation shows, as one might expect, that a higher effort by the health sector, that is, a higher value of v, yields a stronger health growth. However, the higher average health level also represents a drag to this growth because of its positive impact on population growth. Following the line taken in van Zon and Muysken 2001, we will concentrate on the steady-state properties of the health cure activities, where we expect a constant value of v.

An interesting property of differential equation (10) is that it has a stable equilibrium in the steady state, since $\iota + \mu_X > 0$. As a consequence, for any given positive value of v, the health level h will converge to h^*. The latter can be obtained by setting the growth rate of h as given by equation (10) equal to zero:

$$\hat{h} = 0 \Rightarrow h^* = \frac{\delta_0}{\iota + \mu_X} \cdot v + 1 - \frac{\mu_S}{\iota + \mu_X} \equiv \varsigma_0 \cdot v + \varsigma_1 \equiv h(v), \tag{11}$$

where $\varsigma_0 = \delta_0/(\iota + \mu_X)$ and $\varsigma_1 = 1 - \mu_S/(\iota + \mu_X)$. Equation (11) defines the steady-state health level as a function of v and the parameters defined above. As in van Zon and Muysken (2001), we will use equation (11) as the aggregate health production function for the steady state. Since it is well-documented that the provision of health services takes place under conditions of decreasing returns (see, e.g., Johansson and Lofgren 1995 and Or 2000), we assume that $\varsigma_0, \varsigma_1 > 0$. This ensures that the average health productivity h/v falls with an increase in v, and leads to Baumol's law at the macro level in the case of health services, as we mentioned before.

The requirement $\varsigma_1 > 0$ implies $\mu_S < \iota + \mu_X$, from which it follows that the steady-state health level in the absence of care activities is still positive, that is, not everybody is ill. A final restriction follows from the linear nature of the health production function, to ensure that h^* does not exceed 1. One sees immediately that this puts a maximum v^{max} on the share of the cure activities in total employment, such that $v < v^{max} = \mu_S/\delta_0$ should hold.[8]

It follows from equation (11) for a given value of v, that the steady-state health level of the population h^* depends positively on the "cure productivity" δ_0, as one might expect. It is also positively related to ι

and μ_X, first of all because h increases if ι increases by construction, and second because $(1 - h)$ decreases (hence h increases) if μ_X increases. Finally, h^* decreases if μ_S increases, as it should.

Substituting equation (11) into equation (9), we get the steady-state population growth rate:

$$\hat{P} = \delta_0 \cdot v + \iota - \mu_S \equiv \eta_0 \cdot v + \eta_1, \tag{12}$$

where $\eta_0 = \delta_0$, $\eta_1 = \iota - \mu_S$. Comparison with equation (8) shows that this equals the growth rate of the number of healthy people in the population, so that h does indeed remain fixed in the steady state. The stability of equation (10) ensures that this will be the case in the long run.

Equation (12) shows that as v comes close enough to $v^{\max}$, that is, $v^{\max} - v < \iota/\delta_0$, the steady-state population P will be growing. Moreover, as one might expect, the growth rate of the population depends positively on the "cure" productivity δ_0, positively on the birth rate and negatively on the rate of morbidity, for given values of v.

2.3 Adding Care Activities
Unfortunately, not every nonhealthy person can be cured. We assume that nonhealthy people need care and will be cared for. At each moment in time this costs healthy labor resources that are proportional to the number of people that are ill or otherwise inactive, with a factor of proportion χ. Let these resources be a fraction u of the healthy population. Then we have:

$$u \cdot h \cdot P = \chi \cdot (1 - h) \cdot P \Rightarrow u = \chi \cdot (1 - h(v))/h(v). \tag{13}$$

Since it follows from equation (11) that u depends negatively on v, equation (13) shows that there is a direct trade-off between u and v. This represents the notion that a low value of v lowers h and therefore raises the proportion of sick people in the population and hence the need for care activities.

3 Model Modifications and Formal Growth Results

Given the assumptions regarding the use of health resources for the cure and care purposes outlined above, the Lucas production structure is modified as follows:

$$Y = A \cdot ((1 - u - v - w) \cdot e \cdot h \cdot P)^\alpha \cdot K^{1-\alpha}, \tag{14}$$

$$dK/dt = Y - c \cdot P, \tag{15}$$

$$de/dt = \delta_e \cdot e \cdot h \cdot w. \tag{16}$$

The difference with equations (1)–(3) is that we recognize that resources used for care and cure cannot be used for production. Moreover, only healthy hours (measured in efficiency units) are used in final goods production and in human capital accumulation.

In addition to equations (14)–(16), we add the macrohealth production function given by equation (11), and the demand for care activities defined in equation (13).[9] Finally we add the endogenous link between cure activities v and the growth rate of the population $\hat{P}$ as given by equation (12). Hence the full model consists of equations (11)–(16).

A description of all the first-order conditions of the model is presented in the appendix to this chapter. Here we concentrate on a description of the main results. The solution to the optimum control problem is obtained for the steady state, that is, the situation where the control variables u, v, w, and the real interest rate are constant.[10] Moreover, we focus on comparative steady states disregarding transitional dynamics.

The solution of the model results in the following equation for the optimum growth rate of consumption per head:

$$\hat{c} = \{\delta_e \cdot (1 - v - u) \cdot h(v) + \eta_0 \cdot v + \eta_1 - \rho\}/\theta. \tag{17}$$

This is identical to the Lucas endogenous growth results as given by equation (5), except for the term $(1 - u - v) \cdot h(v)$, which represents the fraction of healthy working hours available for activities outside the health sector.[11] Since Lucas doesn't have a health sector, the same fraction in the Lucas model is 100 percent, in which case equation (17) is reduced to equation (5).

Using equations (11) and (13), equation (17) can be rewritten as a quadratic function of v:

$$\hat{c} = \{-v^2 \cdot \delta_e \cdot \varsigma_0 + v \cdot (\eta_0 + \delta_e \cdot (\varsigma_0 - \varsigma_1 + \varsigma_0 \cdot \chi))$$
$$+ \delta_e \cdot (\varsigma_1 - (1 - \varsigma_1) \cdot \chi) - \rho\}/\theta. \tag{18}$$

Equation (18) describes a parabolic relationship between consumption growth and cure activities v. It increases in v through its impact on population growth and the positive impact of cure activities on productivity. However, the diminishing returns to health production

and the increasing absorption of employment necessary for cure and
care activities will eventually take over. Hence consumption growth
reaches a maximum for $v^* = (\eta_0 + \delta_e \cdot (\varsigma_0 - \varsigma_1 + \varsigma_0 \cdot \chi))/(2 \cdot \delta_e \cdot \varsigma_0)$ and
decreases for higher values of v. The parabolic growth equation is
depicted in figure 2.2.

As the appendix shows, the solution of the model also yields a second relation between the optimum growth rate and the volume of
cure activities v, which is derived from the dynamic constraint regarding the optimal development over time of the population. Unfortunately, this gives rise to an implicit relation between the growth rate of
consumption per head and v that is strongly nonlinear and precludes
finding an analytical solution.[12] However, the function can be solved
numerically and for plausible parameter values it depicts a negative
relationship between the growth rate and v, which is also depicted in
figure 2.2. Part of the explanation for the downward sloping relation
is that more cure activities (a higher value for v) increase population
growth, as in equation (12), and hence a lower value of consumption
growth is required to achieve the same utility, as in the intertemporal
utility function shown in equation (4). In general, however, v contributes through many channels to the valuation of population growth.
It contributes positively through its impact on the steady-state health
level of the population, but current output and investment levels are
negatively affected by increases in v (because of the reallocation of
resources this entails). Hence it depends on the specific parameter
values whether a negative relative steep relation with a unique equilibrium solution will arise. Since we found that this is the case for plausible parameter values, we will use that curve to illustrate the working
of our model.

In van Zon and Muysken 2001 we could provide convincing arguments for the location of the equilibrium point E to the right of the
top of the parabolic growth curve.[13] Lack of analytical tractability precludes us from coming up with any nonnumerical arguments here. The
outcomes we present below, however, resemble the general situation
depicted in figure 2.2, as well as in van Zon and Muysken 2001.

4   A Numerical Analysis of the Link between Health and Growth

Although it is not possible to provide a full analytical solution of
the model, with some reasonable a priori parameter values one can obtain a graphical impression of the two relations between the growth

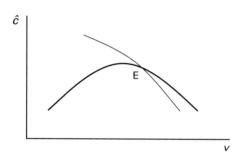

Figure 2.2
The growth and health trade-offs.

Table 2.2
Parameter values.

"Lucas" Parameter	Value	Health Parameter	Value	Implied Structural Parameter	Value
θ	0.5000	χ	0.1000		
α	0.7500	η_0	0.0100	δ_0	0.0100
ρ	0.0500	η_1	0.0050	μ_S	0.0089
δ_e	0.1000	ς_0	0.4500	μ_X	0.0083
		ς_1	0.6000	ι	0.0139

rate of consumption per head and the level of cure activities, as illustrated in figure 2.2. The underlying parameter values have either a priori reasonable values, or they are calibrated such that the growth outcomes as well as the general behavior of the system seem reasonable. Nonetheless, there is an arbitrary element in the presentation of the results below, since the nonlinearity of the system does allow for multiple equilibria and a host of other computational problems. We leave this for future scrutiny, however. Suffice it to say here that the model does generate qualitatively the same results as in van Zon and Muysken 2001, although we now have an endogenously evolving population. The parameter values are presented in table 2.2.

The first column of table 2.2 shows the standard parameters of the Lucas model, of which the numerical values are roughly similar to those used in van Zon and Muysken 2001.[14] Since the health sector is modeled somewhat differently, we chose new parameter values for the health parameters, which are presented in the fourth column of table 2.2.

The values for the health parameters from column 3 in table 2.2 first were constrained to obtain reasonable results for the structural parameters shown in columns 5 and 6 of the table. The steady-state share of healthy persons $h = 0.65$ implies a birth rate relative to the entire population close to 0.9 percent, and a death rate that is somewhat low at 0.3 percent. These numbers result in a population growth rate equal to 0.63 percent. These outcomes have all the right orders of magnitude.[15] Next the health parameters were calibrated in order to obtain reasonable values for the growth rate of consumption per head of about 2 percent, and for the allocation of labor time over its various uses, that is, care and cure between 10 and 15 percent, whereas u should be twice as small as v, human capital accumulation w of about 30 percent, and the remainder (over 55%) on final output production. The figure on human capital accumulation is in line with Lucas's (1988, pp. 26–27) finding that 28 percent of total working time is spent on human capital formation. The care and cure figures are based on the situation in the Netherlands, where the share of health expenditures in GDP has now risen above 10 percent, due to the present lack of economic growth and the ever increasing costs of health care.[16] In addition to this, the distribution of total health costs between care and cure activities is roughly equal to 35 percent and 65 percent, respectively.[17] The precise steady-state outcomes are listed in the second column of table 2.3, labeled SSV. Inspection of table 2.3 shows that the fraction of time spent on health activities, in total about 18 percent, is a bit high, as is the time spent on human capital accumulation—roughly a third of one's life. Nonetheless, none of the variables seem a priori to be wildly off—which fits our illustrative purpose. Moreover, the parameter restrictions on the model that we formulated in the previous section are all satisfied.[18]

Table 2.3
Parameter elasticities of health and growth performance.

1	SSV	θ	a	ρ	δ_e	χ	μ_s	μ_x	l	δ_0
$\hat{c}$	0.020	−1.27	0.08	−4.97	5.61	−0.40	−5.18	1.62	4.09	0.08
u	0.311	−0.60	0.15	−0.12	0.54	0.88	0.79	0.10	0.21	−1.49
v	0.657	2.45	−0.60	0.49	−2.10	0.42	3.98	−2.69	−4.65	4.76
w	0.126	−1.45	0.14	−4.99	4.45	−0.43	−5.05	1.66	4.19	−0.44
$1-u-v-w$	0.489	0.34	0.05	2.93	−2.25	0.07	2.01	−0.36	−1.42	−0.76
h	0.052	0.21	−0.05	0.04	−0.18	0.04	−0.26	−0.04	−0.07	0.54
$\hat{p}$	0.006	0.49	−0.12	0.10	−0.42	0.09	−0.62	−0.54	1.28	1.26

The remaining entries in table 2.3 are the elasticities of the steady-state equilibrium values for the system variables in the first column with respect to changes in the system parameters. We calculated these elasticities by changing the parameter under consideration by 10 percent, after which we were able to calculate the relative change in the system variables given in the first column. Such a parameter change results in a shift of both curves in figure 2.2.[19] The shift in the parabolic curve is relatively easy to retrace given equation (18), but that in the downward sloping curve can be determined only numerically.

From the table we can conclude that it reproduces the results found in van Zon and Muysken 2001; raising θ and ρ lowers growth and tips the allocation balance in favor of activities that stimulate current utility rather than future utility, that is, final output production and health production (because of its positive impact on current productivity levels). Parameter changes that affect the productivity of the health sector directly through δ_0 and χ, or in a broad sense through the compound parameters η_0, η_1, ζ_0, and ς_1, also work in the same way as in van Zon and Muysken 2001. Except perhaps for changes in the rate of mortality, the results obtained for the other structural parameters are plausible a priori. We will further elaborate the results on mortality in the next section where we analyze the decrease in mortality that drives the aging of the population in Western economies.

From the parameter elasticities in table 2.3 we make five observations that illuminate the workings of our model. First, as might be expected from our discussion in equation (13), we observe a trade-off between cure and care activities. Our results show that, as a rule, u and v move in opposite directions, indicating that there exists a structural trade-off between both. In fact, that trade-off is underlined by the exception to the rule provided by the results regarding the sensitivity to changes in χ. A rise in the latter parameter implies that the care intensity of nonhealthy people rises, which increases the marginal benefits from cure activities. This positive second order effect on u does not entirely remove the increased need for care due to a rise in χ, however. The observation that for an increase in the morbidity rate we observe a positive change in both u and v can be explained in a similar way, as we elaborate in the next section.

Second, there is a very robust trade-off between cure and human capital accumulation. It is these activities that have relatively strong intertemporal effects through their impact on the growth rate of the population, and on the growth rate of human capital per person.[20]

Interestingly, there is a positive correlation between changes in v and $1 - u - v - w$, suggesting that a change in v is primarily countered by an opposite change in u and w. Apparently, the rise in v raises the marginal product of labor in final output production more than proportionally (i.e., both through the rise in $h(v)$ and through the fall in $1 - u - v - w$, ceteris paribus).

Third, an increase in productivity in education or cure activities does not lead to an increased share of labor available for production, that is, substitution effects outweigh the corresponding income effects. Note that this finding is consistent with the observed positive correlation between productivity increases in the health sector and the increased share of health expenditures in GDP (Glied 2003).

Fourth, it is interesting to note that a rise in the productivity of cure activities, even though the equilibrium is on the downward sloping part of the parabolic curve, does give rise to a double dividend, since both the steady-state level of health, and the rate of growth of consumption per head are positively affected, whereas in all other cases a negative correlation exists between the impact on growth and the impact on the steady-state health level of some parameter change. So, health seems to be a substitute for growth.

Finally, a decrease in the relevance of the future in deciding what to do now (either a rise in θ or in ρ), causes a rise in the steady-state growth rate of the population, through a reallocation of human capital accumulation time to cure and production activities. It is equally interesting to notice that cure activities rise much faster than the allocation of labor time to final output production, because cure activities positively influence the availability of labor time for all activities. However, there is a countereffect resulting from the observation that a decrease in the discount rate will result in higher growth and less resources used up in cure activities. Since such a decrease is consistent with increased longevity (Becker and Mulligan 1997), this might point to a positive feedback between longevity and economic growth.

In conclusion we may state that the comparative steady-state analysis we have performed here seems to generate a priori plausible results that are in line with the results by van Zon and Muysken (2001), even though the steady-state population growth rate itself now depends on care and cure activities. The question we will address in the next section is how we might interpret the changes observed in Western economies, that is, the aging of the population, into corresponding changes in terms of our model, and see what the comparative steady-state growth implications will be.

5   Growth Impacts of Demographical Changes

The reason we want to have a look at the burden of an aging population from an endogenous growth perspective is that these effects can be significant in principle but are routinely overlooked when using the standard apparatus for such exercises. Jacobzone, Cambois, and Robine (2000), for instance, use a simple extrapolation scheme to obtain an estimate of the share of health spending in GDP by multiplying the current share with the relative increase over time in the dependency ratio as compared to its current value. The numerator of the dependency ratio is a direct indicator of the projected increase in health demand, whereas the denominator is a direct indicator of the projected increase in the productive base of the economy. However, such a mechanistic extrapolation scheme is incomplete and overly optimistic, certainly in the long run, since a rise in the dependency ratio through an increase in longevity and the allocative adjustments this entails may act as a break on economic growth, as our sensitivity analysis in section 4 has indicated.

Because care activities seem to be especially insensitive to labor-augmenting technical change, Baumol's law holds strongly here. The need to supply care to the older generation when they need it will therefore inevitably lead to a changing distribution of labor time in favor of health care, and so will add a significant growth dimension to the level of problems caused by an aging population. That this growth dimension may indeed be significant, follows directly from the relative sensitivity of the growth responses to changes in demographical and epidemiological parameters on the one hand (see table 2.3), as well as the significance per se of the demographic changes expected for the future that ultimately drive changes in the dependency ratio over the long term.[21] At this stage, however, we can only illustrate the existence of a case in favor of a general equilibrium growth perspective in medical spending decision making, rather than providing a complete numerical defense, although, as stated above, the circumstantial evidence seems to be strong.

So far, we have described our model in terms of a population that can be in two different health states, that is, healthy and nonhealthy. However, from an economic perspective the distinguishing feature between people in these two states is that they differ in terms of production and consumption activities. Nonhealthy persons do not produce anything, whereas they do consume final output and health services. Healthy persons, on the other hand, consume only final output. In addition they produce both output and health services. Furthermore, they accumulate human capital. It does not take a giant leap of the imagination to see that the consequences of a permanent change in the composition of the population in terms of active and inactive people in favor of the inactive due to an aging of the population will resemble those of a change in the composition of the population in our model in favor of nonhealthy people, ceteris paribus. We analyze these consequences below by mimicking a more or less autonomous drift in the composition of the population in favor of inactivity by manipulating the demographical and epidemiological parameters of our model. We also evaluate what our model has to say about the growth effects of policy actions aimed at reducing the dependency ratio.[22]

5.1   Growth Effects of an Aging Population

In the context of our model, an ageing population can be mimicked by a rise of the propensity to stay in S once one is in S. The latter can be linked directly to a fall in the rate of mortality μ_X. Since that leads to a rise in the average age of the population, and since older people generally require more care than younger people, this would also imply an increase in χ. At the same time one would also have to lower the productivity δ_0 of curing activities, since one cannot normally be cured of inactivity due to old age.

We are now able to infer, albeit in a fairly impressionistic way, what an aging population may mean for growth. The growth effects of changes in the parameters μ_X, χ, and δ_0 all work in the same direction. A fall in mortality reduces the growth rate, and so does an increase in care intensity and a decrease in cure productivity. Hence growth of the economy will be affected in an unambiguously negative way. The effects on the steady-state health level are less clear cut, although it seems likely that the limited positive effects of a decrease in mortality and an increase in care intensity are more than balanced by the negative effect of a drop in cure productivity δ_0. The negative growth effects are mirrored by a net decrease in w, but it is hard to say how the reallocation of resources will affect their distribution among v, u, and $1 - u - v - w$. It is equally hard therefore to conclude what will happen to the health sector as a whole. It is clear, though, that the balance of activities will shift in favor of cure and of current output production, thus diminishing the rate of growth due to the ageing of the population. This finding is in line with the one for a constant population by van Zon and Muysken (2001), who indicated that an aging population would lead to a fall in the overall productivity of the health sector. In the current model too, a fall in the productivity of health activities, either through a fall in δ_0 or an increase in χ, leads to a definite fall in growth performance.

5.2   Growth Effects of Early Retirement

The effects of a decrease in the dependency ratio by raising the (early) retirement age could be captured by lowering the rate of morbidity μ_s to mimic a decreased flow from the active state to the inactive state, increasing χ to mimic the fact that early retired people require less care on average than older retired people, and to increase δ_0 in order to mimic the rise in the responsiveness of the inactive population to cure activities.[23] A decrease in the rate of morbidity has a very large positive effect on the rate of growth of consumption per head (see table 2.3). The negative impact on growth of an increase in care intensity is of a relatively limited size, however, whereas the rise in δ_0 with a rise in the retirement age has positive but equally limited growth effects. The positive growth effect of the decrease in morbidity that mimics the postponement of early retirement is thus likely to dominate. As with the aging of the population, the net effect on health activities is unclear. Nonetheless, increasing the retirement age almost certainly helps to counter the negative growth effects of an aging population. In fact, if the difference in the sensitivity to changes in the rate of mortality and in the rate of morbidity is as significant as shown in table 2.3, then we may even expect that discouraging early retirement would stimulate growth more than an aging of the population would depress it. From an economic perspective this also makes sense, since early retirement moves active people into inactivity, thus reducing the productive human capital base of the economy, whereas an aging population only raises the ratio of inactive versus active people without reducing the absolute number of inactive people.

6   Conclusions

Having a good health care system and being cared for in a decent manner at old age comes at a cost in terms of current consumption and growth possibilities foregone: intergenerational decency comes at a price. Acknowledging this is but part of the solution to the problem of financing health activities that are generally perceived as a continuously growing burden on Western economies due to an aging population that increases the demand for care and cure per head, but also the number of heads, ceteris paribus. It is the very nature of these care and cure activities that call for a growing share of GDP for the health sector, due to Baumol's law.

By incorporating Baumol's law in our model, we have shown that steady-state growth situations are still possible, even though they are influenced by population dynamics. Different steady-state growth situations can arise for different structural parameter combinations. Therefore, policy actions directly affecting those parameters (for instance through the productivity of cure and care activities) may have an equally direct impact on health production, and hence also on growth performance. To some extent we can choose between different health and growth futures.

In addition to these health productivity promoting actions that would increase the effective availability of scare labor resources, other types of policy actions may prove to be at least as effective. Our results suggest that an increase in the retirement age may be effective in promoting growth and sustaining high levels of health.

Of course, in this chapter we have concentrated on the promotion of health as a prerequisite for growth, but the ultimate source of growth in this model is still technical change. Nonetheless, our model has been built on the basic principle that good health is instrumental in realizing the productivity potentials provided by ever improving production technologies. From the sensitivity analyses above, we have seen that growth performance is highly sensitive to changes in the productivity of human capital accumulation activities (i.e., δ_e), which are at least as important for growth as changes in morbidity rates, mortality rates, and so on. Indeed, the results obtained from our model suggest that it may be wise to include the growth effects of health spending decision making in economic policy analysis, since an exclusive focus on cutting current health costs rather than focusing on the intertemporal effects of health activities too, may have severe negative effects for long-run growth performance, simply because having good health is necessary for any individual to realize his or her productive potential. And although underachievement with respect to the provision of health services has a direct negative effect on welfare, it is perhaps even more important to consider that it negatively affects the productive base of the economy and the economy's potential for growth.

Appendix

The Hamiltonian of the revised Lucas model can be written as:

$$H = e^{-\rho t} P c^{1-\theta}/(1-\theta) + \lambda_e \cdot w \cdot \delta_e \cdot (\varsigma_0 \cdot v + \varsigma_1)$$
$$\cdot e + \lambda_P \cdot P \cdot (\eta_0 \cdot v + \eta_1) + \lambda_K (A((1-u-v-w) \cdot e$$
$$\cdot (\varsigma_0 \cdot v + \varsigma_1) \cdot P)^{\alpha} K^{1-\alpha} - c \cdot P), \tag{A.1}$$

where c, u, v, and w are the control variables, K, e, and P are the state variables, and where we have used equations (11), (12), and (14)–(16). λ_K, λ_e, λ_P are the costate variables of K, e, and P. They measure the marginal value (in terms of integral utility) of an additional unit of the respective stock at a certain time. By substituting equation (13) into equation (A.1), u can be dropped as a direct control variable. The first-order conditions with respect to the remaining control variables are:

$$\frac{\partial H}{\partial c} = e^{-\rho t} c^{-\theta} \cdot P - \lambda_K \cdot P = 0, \tag{A.2}$$

$$\frac{\partial H}{\partial v} = \lambda_K \partial Y/\partial v + \lambda_e \partial (de/dt)/\partial v + \lambda_P \cdot \partial (dP/dt)/\partial v = 0, \tag{A.3}$$

and

$$\frac{\partial H}{\partial w} = \lambda_K \partial Y/\partial w + \lambda_e \partial (de/dt)/\partial w = 0. \tag{A.4}$$

Equation (A.2) gives rise to the familiar growth $\hat{c} = (-\hat{\lambda}_K - \rho)/\theta$. Equations (A.3) and (A.4) state that on an optimum path, total utility at some point in time cannot be improved on by shifting resources between their alternative uses. The dynamic constraints state that on an optimum path total utility cannot be improved on by shifting resources that can be accumulated (the state variables) over time, that is, by changing the rate of investment, human capital accumulation, and the rate of growth of the population. This will be the case if the valuation of an additional unit of a stock falls by exactly the same amount as the direct contribution of that additional unit to current utility (this includes the impact of that additional unit on future stocks and the contribution of future utility to total utility as captured by the costate variables). We therefore have as dynamic constraints:

$$d\lambda_X/dt + \partial H/\partial X = 0 \quad \forall \ X = K, e, P. \tag{A.5}$$

Equations (A.5) give rise to a set of differential equations in the co-state variables. Since equations (A.2)–(A.4) must hold for all t, the time derivatives of equations (A.2)–(A.4) must also be equal to zero. These results can be substituted into the system given by equation (A.5). Using equation (A.5) for $X = K, e$ in combination with the constraints of equations (A.2)–(A.4) as well as equations (11), (12), and (14)–(16), and assuming a fixed allocation of labor time, we arrive at equation (18). Using equation (A.5) for $X = P$ and using the same set of constraints as before, we end up with an implicit relation between the growth rate of per-capita consumption and v. The latter relation is obtained by using some intermediate results from the previous step, notably the results $\hat{c} = \hat{e}$, $\hat{c} = (r - \rho)/\theta$, $\hat{K} = \hat{e} + \hat{P}$, and $\hat{\lambda}_P = \hat{e} - r$. In addition to that, we use the investment constraint to solve for consumption $c = (K/P) \cdot (r/(1 - \alpha) - \hat{K})$. Likewise, we use the production function to relate K/P to the real rate of interest, and given the intermediate results above, to $\hat{e}$ again. The resulting link between c on the one hand and $\hat{e}$ and v on the other is used to substitute for c. In addition, w is substituted for by using equation (16), again giving rise to an expression containing both $\hat{e}$ and v. All these manipulations lead to a strongly nonlinear implicit relation between $\hat{e}$ and v, in which location and shape in the $\hat{e}$, v-plane depend very much on the particular parameter values chosen or observed.

Further technical details are available on request in the form of a mathematica notebook.

Notes

1. While Bloom and Canning (2000, n. 1) argue that "Eventually, the large-sized cohorts will pass through the age distribution as surely as a pig that has been swallowed by a python," we focus on the problem of what happens to the Western python if the pig keeps growing on its way through.

2. Baumol 1967, pp. 416, 423, and 415, respectively. It is these differences in productivity that are the cause of Baumol's disease.

3. Decreasing returns in health services are used in Forster 1989, Ehrlich and Chuma 1990, and Johansson and Lofgren 1995. Increasing returns in human capital generation appear in the growth models mentioned above.

4. This picture is enforced by the projections presented in Jacobzone, Cambois, and Robine (2000), who show that for the OECD the age dependency ratio (percentage of persons aged 65 and over as a percentage of the working-age population) increased from 14.1 in 1960 to 20.6 in 2000 and will further increase to 32.7 in 2030.

5. And we require $\rho - \hat{P} > 0$, which is a necessary (but not sufficient) condition for the integral in equation (4) to converge.

6. The proportional growth rate of a variable x is denoted by $\hat{x}$.

7. If, instead, the absolute human capital stock as such would accumulate in accordance with (3) rather than average human capital per person, and if human capital per person would be equal to the human capital stock thus accumulated per head of the population, then one can easily verify that the growth rate of the population would drop out of equations (5) and (6).

8. An alternative interpretation of this requirement is that it ensures that the growth of the healthy population does not exceed the birth rate, that is, $\hat{H} \leq \iota$, as can be seen from equation (8); in a steady-state growth situation, the growth rate of H cannot be permanently higher than the birth rate.

9. Consistent with the notion of Baumol's law at the micro level, we do not assume labor augmenting technical progress in the health sector.

10. If the latter is not the case, then the standard optimization result for the rate of growth of consumption per head to be constant under a constant intertemporal elasticity of substitution (CIES) function would not hold.

11. Note that the term $\eta_0 \cdot v + \eta_1$ in equation (17) represents population growth.

12. See the appendix for further details.

13. In this model E can be anywhere, which is not necessarily a bad thing, certainly for economies that have a point of intersection to the left of the top. If these economies could somehow shift the downward sloping curve upwards, then they could experience a double dividend, i.e., higher growth and higher health.

14. There we used $\theta = 0.5$, $a = 0.65$, $\rho = 0.075$, and $\delta_e = 0.114$ resulting in a growth rate of 0.026. The somewhat different values for θ and ρ follow from the interaction with the different health structure of the present model in the calibration process.

15. The figure for h seems too low, but we will later on reinterpret this number as the share of active people in the population, rather than the share of healthy people in the population.

16. The cost share is admittedly a very rough indicator of the labor share, but Baumol's law suggests that the 10 percent would be a lower estimate for the volume share of labor.

17. See www.rivm.nl/kostenvanziekten for information about the costs of illness in the Netherlands in 1999. The distribution of total costs over different forms of cure and care suggests that care activities took on 36 percent of total costs in 1999.

18. That is, μ_s is smaller than $\iota + \mu_x$, and v is smaller than $v^* = \delta_0/\mu_s$.

19. We also calculated the parameter elasticities for a drop in the parameters by 10 percent. These gave qualitatively identical results, and numerically nearly identical results that are therefore not presented here.

20. This is in line with what we found in van Zon and Muysken 2001. Our finding that v and u are negatively correlated, is in contrast with microeconomic analysis, which suggests a positive correlation—cf. Fuchs 1982 and Bloom and Canning 2000. The latter

point out that first of all an increase in health induces a higher productivity of learning (a modern variant of "mens sana in corpore sano") and second, induces more investment in human capital through the potential of higher returns.

21. The dependency ratios from table 2.1 are expected to more or less double between 2000 and 2030, certainly for the Netherlands (see OECD 2003).

22. At present, the Dutch government considers a rise in the retirement age as part of the solution to decreasing the financial burden of an aging population.

23. A higher fraction of inactivity is now due to ill health.

References

Barro, R. J. 1996. Determinants of Economic Growth: A Cross-Country Empirical Study. Working paper no. 5698, National Bureau of Economic Research.

Baumol, W. J. 1967. Macroeconomics of Unbalanced Growth: The Anatomy of Urban Crisis. *American Economic Review* 57 (3): 415–426.

Becker, G. S., and C. B. Mulligan. 1997. The Endogenous Determination of Time Preference. *Quarterly Journal of Economics* 112 (3): 729–758.

Bhargava, A., D. T. Jamison, L. J. Lau, and C. J. L. Murray. 2001. Modeling the Effects of Health on Economic Growth. *Journal of Health Economics* 20 (3): 423–440.

Bloom, D. E., and D. Canning. 2000. The Health and Wealth of Nations. *Science* 287: 1207–1209.

Ehrlich, I., and H. Chuma. 1990. A Model of the Demand for Longevity and the Value of Life Extension. *Journal of Political Economy* 98: 761–782.

Forster, B. A. 1989. Optimal Health Investment Strategies. *Bulletin of Economic Research* 41: 45–57.

Fuchs, V. R. 1982. Time Preference and Health: An Exploratory Study. Working paper no. 0539, National Bureau of Economic Research, Cambridge, Mass.

Glied, S. 2003. Health Care Costs: On the Rise Again. *Journal of Economic Perspectives* 17 (2): 125–148.

Grossman, M. 1972. On the Concept of Health Capital and the Demand for Health. *Journal of Political Economy* 80 (2): 223–255.

Jacobzone, S., E. Cambois, and J. M. Robine. 2000. Is the Health of Older Persons in OECD Countries Improving Fast Enough to Compensate for Population Ageing? *OECD Economic Studies* 30: 14–190.

Johansson, P. O., and K. G. Lofgren. 1995. Wealth from Optimal Health. *Journal of Health Economics* 14: 65–79.

Knowles, S., and D. P. Owen. 1995. Health Capital and Cross-Country Variation in Income per Capita in the Mankiw–Romer Weil Model. *Economics Letters* 48: 99–106.

Lucas, R. E. 1988. On the Mechanics of Economic Development. *Journal of Monetary Economics* 22: 3–42.

McDonald, S., and J. Roberts. 2002. Growth and Multiple Forms of Human Capital in an Augmented Solow Model: A Panel Data Investigation. *Economics Letters* 74 (2): 271–276.

Meltzer, D. 1997. Accounting for Future Costs in Medical Cost-Effectiveness Analysis. *Journal of Health Economics* 16: 33–64.

Muurinen, J. M. 1982. Demand for Health: A Generalised Grossman Model. *Journal of Health Economics* 1: 5–28.

Muysken, J., I. H. Yetkiner, and T. Ziesemer. 2003. Health, Labour, Productivity and Growth. In *Growth Theory and Growth Policy*, edited by H. Hagemann and S. Seiter. London: Routledge, pp. 187–205.

OECD. 2003. *Health Data 2003: A Comparative Analysis of 29 Countries.* Paris: OECD.

Or, Z. 2000. Determinants of Health Outcomes in Industrialised Countries: A Pooled, Cross-Country, Time-Series Analysis. *OECD Economic Studies* 30: 53–77.

Strauss, J., and D. Thomas. 1998. Health, Nutrition, and Economic Development. *Journal of Economic Literature* 36 (2): 766–817.

Warshawsky, M. J. 1999. An Enhanced Macroeconomic Approach to Long-Range Projections of Health Care and Social Security Expenditures as a Share of GDP. *Journal of Policy Modeling* 21 (4): 413–426.

Webber, D. J. 2002. Policies to Stimulate Growth: Should We Invest in Health or Education? *Applied Economics* 34 (13): 1633–1643.

Zon, A. H. van, and J. Muysken. 2001. Health and Endogenous Growth. *Journal of Health Economics* 20 (2): 169–185.

3 Health's Contribution to Economic Growth in an Environment of Partially Endogenous Technical Progress

Dean T. Jamison, Lawrence J. Lau, and Jia Wang

Much of the existing growth literature models growth rates of per-capita GDP over a substantial period—often measured in decades—as a function of initial conditions in a country and aspects of the country's policy regime, investments, and institutional characteristics during the period. Barro (1997, pp. 7–8) observed that this class of models precludes assessment of the role of the generation and diffusion of new technology even though technical change is widely viewed as central to long-run growth (e.g., by Easterly and Levine [2000]). Indeed, as Bernard and Jones (1996) have pointed out, much of the empirical literature at least implicitly assumes that technical progress is exogenous at a rate that is constant across countries. Our primary purpose in this chapter is to relax this assumption in order to assess potential determinants of the rate of technical progress. Our second purpose is to assess the nature and magnitude of health's contribution to economic growth.[1]

Within an aggregate production function framework, we use multi-level modeling techniques to assess human capital, geographical, and policy-related determinants of how much and why the rate of technical progress differs from one country to another. We find that the rate of technical progress (from either the diffusion or the generation of new technologies) varies markedly across countries and is related to both geographical and policy variables. In this sense technical progress can be viewed as partially (but only partially) endogenous. Some previous work has relaxed the assumption of homogeneity across countries in long-term rates of technical progress (e.g., Boskin and Lau 1990, 2000; Dougherty and Jorgenson 1996; and Lee, Pesaran, and Smith 1997) and found great heterogeneity. We build on this work and extend it with an exploratory assessment of reasons for cross-country variation in rates of technical progress.

A growing literature—perhaps beginning with Myrdal (1952)—provides insight into the nature and magnitude of health's effects on development.[2] A second purpose of this chapter is to add to that literature by estimating the magnitude of the effect of improved health on GDP per capita using data from 53 countries over the period 1965 to 1990. The chapter provides estimates of the contribution of better health—as measured by improvements in adult survival rates (for males)—by incorporating health into a meta (or aggregate) production function framework and by decomposing growth to assess the component due to mortality decline. This is within the spirit of augmentation of the Solow growth model along lines initiated by Mankiw, Romer, and Weil (1992), but extended to assess whether health's effects operate through changing output levels directly or through affecting the rate of technical progress.

In what follows we first review available evidence on health's contribution to economic growth, which can in principle arise either from shifting the level of productivity or from facilitating technical progress (or both). After discussing methods, we then turn to our main findings on determinants of outcome levels and of the rate of technical progress. In a final brief section we use these results to decompose growth into its sources, including improvements in health, technical progress, and the component of technical progress that we identify as endogenous. A brief annex uses more recently available data to update the analysis to the year 2000.

1 Background: Health and Economic Growth

The World Bank's world development report for 1993, *Investing in Health*, begins by summarizing the enormous and unprecedented gains in health in the second half of the twentieth century:

In 1950 life expectancy in developing countries was forty years; by 1990 it had increased to 63 years. In 1950 twenty-eight of every 100 children died before their fifth birthday; by 1990 the number had fallen to 10. Smallpox, which killed more than 5 million annually in the early 1950s has been eradicated entirely.[3]

The contribution to human welfare of this transformation may be difficult to value in monetary terms, but it is certainly huge.[4] To the extent that improved health is an ultimate objective of development, that objective is being well met. Health improvements contribute, moreover, to other development objectives. Ill health reduces learning and school attendance; it increases absenteeism and lowers productivity at work; it may lead to premature retirement and in other ways decrease the ratio of a country's working population to its nonworking population; it attenuates incentives to acquire education or to invest in physical capital; and, as Bloom and Sachs (1998, p. 13) have argued, widespread ill health in a country may create an adverse climate for international trade and foreign direct investment.

Studies of the effects of health on income growth or productivity divide naturally into three categories. The first comprises historical case studies that may be more or less quantitative. The second comprises studies at the individual or household level; these "micro" studies involve either household surveys that include one or more measures of health status along with extensive other information or they involve an assessment of the impact of specific diseases (or disease-control programs). The third category—into which the present study falls— utilizes cross-national data to assess the impact of measures of health at the national level on income, income growth rates, or investment rates.

Robert Fogel and his collaborators have initiated an assessment of the health and nutrition status of populations in a series of studies on the economic history of Europe. Health status serves both as an indicator of population welfare and, in some of the studies, as a determinant of economic growth rates. Fogel (1997) provides an overview with extensive references to the relevant literature. From this literature Fogel concludes that health and nutrition improvements may have accounted for between 20 and 30 percent of Britain's GDP growth rate of about 1.15 percent per person per year in the 200-year period of 1780–1979.

Studies at the individual and household level are, increasingly, corroborating the historical findings. Strauss and Thomas (1998) provide a major review and Savedoff and Schultz (2000) overview methods used in the household studies and summarize findings of a recent analyses from five Latin American countries. Illustrative studies include econometric work from West Africa (Schultz and Tansel 1997), from Mexico (Knaul 2000), from China (Liu et al. 2003) and from Vietnam (Laxminarayan 2004). Rather different in approach are an epidemiological study of the consequences of disability in the Netherlands

(Stronks et al. 1997) and assessments of the interplay between disability and public assistance in the United States (Burkhauser, Haveman, and Wolfe 1993; Brady, Meyers, and Luks 1998).

Cross-country studies of the impact of health on income levels and growth rates go back at least to the first of the World Bank's world development reports (WDRs) on poverty (World Bank 1980; Hicks 1979; Wheeler 1980). Findings were suggestive of the importance of health but not definitive. Work undertaken by two of the present authors (Jamison and Lau) as background for the World Bank's WDR *Investing in Health* (1993, p. 21) found stronger effects of health using better data and an aggregate production function methodology. More recent studies have examined the effects of life expectancy circa 1965 on economic growth in the subsequent 15 to 25 years (Barro 1997; Sachs and Warner 1997; Bloom and Williamson 1998). These studies consistently found strong positive direct effects as well as indirect ones operating through rates of investment in physical capital or demographic profiles of populations. Meltzer (1992) reviewed and extended the literature on the effects of mortality levels on investments in education and concluded that those effects may be substantial. Bhargava et al. (2001) assessed the effects of initial health status on growth over a shorter period (5 years) in a panel of countries and likewise found strong effects, but only in low-income countries. An intriguing recent finding suggests that high levels of malaria morbidity may have a substantial growth retarding effect even when controlling for life expectancy (Gallup and Sachs 2001).

Issues of data quality and causality will continue to place caveats on findings of cross-country studies such as those just described and those reported in this paper. Easterly et al. (1993) point to the volatility of growth performance of countries relative to their basic characteristics and suggest that much variation may be due to luck or exogenous shocks (e.g., in terms of trade) rather than to levels of education, say, or adequacy of economic policy. This is a useful caution, but recent work with better data and a broader range of determining variables (e.g., Bloom and Williamson 1998; Boskin and Lau 2000) does suggest that the cross-country data contain lessons for policy. The lessons are far more credible, though, when corroborated by microeconomic studies, as is increasingly the case concerning the impact of better health (Strauss and Thomas 1998; World Health Organization 2001).

In what follows we extend the cross-country literature on health's effects to an aggregate production function framework that allows assessment of potential determinants of cross-country variation in the rate of technical progress. This allows us to test the hypothesis that health's effect on economic outcomes results from its role in explaining why some countries' rates of technical progress are high (versus its role in changing the level of productivity).

2   Methods

In order to model income level in a panel data set we used the meta-production function approach as developed by Lau and his coworkers in a series of studies of the sources of economic growth in both high-income and East Asian countries.[5] For an overview of their methods and findings, see Lau 1996 and Boskin and Lau 1990, 2000. Within the metaproduction function framework alternative estimation procedures can be used to analyze panel data across countries. If data are available for many time points for a sufficient number of countries, the flexibility of the transcendental logarithmic (translog) production function allows estimation of critical country-specific parameters (e.g., rates of technical progress) and also allows separation of the level and bias of technical progress from scale effects. Boskin and Lau (2000) apply the translog specification to 40 years of annual data from the G-5 countries. They find substantial significance in different rates of technical progress for determining long-term differences in growth rates across the large high-income countries and that technical progress is both physical and human capital augmenting (and, therefore, significantly endogenous in that it is affected by countries' savings rates and educational investments).

Our analysis includes many developing countries in a much larger sample of countries than was studied by Boskin and Lau. This limits data availability to five-year intervals and precludes use of the highly data intensive translog formulation. In this paper we instead estimate a Cobb–Douglas or variants of a Cobb–Douglas specification. In order to allow, however, for cross-country variation in technical progress (or diffusion), as a critical source of variation in rates of long-term growth, we explore use of a multilevel modeling technique, specifically, version 5 of the hierarchical linear modeling (HLM) technique developed by Bryk and Raudenbusch (1992).[6] This maximum-likelihood procedure allows us to model country-specific intercepts and the associated complex error structure. This specification of HLM is similar to a generalized least squares (GLS) estimated random effects model when we

impose a common production function across countries (while allowing the intercept to vary). We also employ a more generalized HLM
procedure that allows estimation of country-time interactions (i.e., of
country-specific technical progress in a Cobb–Douglas framework)
and, central to the purposes of this paper, it allows us to explore potential determinants of this cross-country variation in technical progress.
(Temple [1999] points to parameter heterogeneity in general as a major
problem to be dealt with in the empirical growth literature. We address it explicitly only in connection with technical progress.)

Most of the previous literature has used specifications that impose
common coefficients across countries, but as explained in the introduction, we believe that important sources of cross-country differences
in income growth result not only from different investment rates but,
even more significantly, from *persistent* differences in the characteristics
of countries. Our work is thus in the spirit of Hall and Jones (1997,
1999) who observe that it "is the fixed effect itself that we are trying to
explain" (1997, p. 174). Our work generalizes theirs in also seeking to
model persistent country differences in the rate of acquiring and using
new technologies.[7] In order to capture this phenomenon, our aggregate
production function is given by equation (1) supplemented with equations (3) and (4), which are estimated simultaneously with equation
(1), and seek to explain the country-specific intercepts (β_{0i}) and rates
of technical progress (β_{1i}) in equation (1):

$$lypc_{it} = \beta_{0i} + \beta_{1i}time_t + \beta_2 lkpc_{it} + \beta_3 med_{it} + \beta_4 lasr_{it} + \beta_5 ltfr_{it} + \varepsilon_{it}, \qquad (1)$$

where the variables and coefficients signify

$lypc_{it}$ the natural log of average per-capita GDP in country i over a
5-year period from $t - 2$ to $t + 2$ ($\mu = 8.27$, $\sigma = 0.94$);

$time_t$ the number of years lapsed since 1965 ($t - 1965$);

$lkpc_{it}$ the natural log of average per-capita physical capital in country i
over a 5-year period from $t - 2$ to $t + 2$ ($\mu = 8.93$, $\sigma = 1.35$);

med_{it} the average number of years of education in the male population, aged 15 and over, of country i at time t ($\mu = 6.12$, $\sigma = 2.60$);

$lasr_{it}$ the natural log of the male survival rate in country i at time t
($\mu = 6.62$, $\sigma = 0.16$);[8]

$ltfr_{it}$ the natural log of the total fertility rate in country i at time t
($\mu = 1.22$, $\sigma = 0.54$);

β_{0i} the country-specific intercept for country i;

β_{1i} the effect of "technical progress" in increasing income per capita in country i;

β_2 the elasticity of income with respect to per-capita physical capital;

β_3 the responsiveness of per-capita income with respect to changes in male education;

β_4 the elasticity of income with respect to adult male survival rate;

β_5 the elasticity of income with respect to total fertility rate; and

ε_{it} unexplained residual for country i at time t, assumed to be normally distributed with mean 0.

The working paper version of this chapter provides definitions, sources, and further discussion of the variables.

Assuming a common intercept and time coefficient for all countries (i.e., assume $\beta_{0i} = \beta_{0j}$ and $\beta_{1i} = \beta_{1j}$ for all i, j), equation (1) has the model specification for an ordinary least squares (OLS) regression. To make the above equation similar to a random-effects regression, to be estimated by generalized least squares, one can supplement equation (1) with:

$$\beta_{0i} = \gamma_{00} + \mu_{0i}, \tag{2}$$

where μ_{0i} is assumed to be normally distributed with the mean zero and uncorrelated with the unexplained residual for the country ε_{it}, in other words, the covariance between them is zero $[Cov(\mu_{0i}, \varepsilon_{it}) = 0]$. This allows estimation of country-specific intercepts since the random variable μ_{0i} is the deviation of country i's mean from the overall mean. To model potential *determinants* of the country intercept we can use the random-intercept specification in HLM:

$$\beta_{0i} = \gamma_{00} + \gamma_{01} tropics_i + \gamma_{02} coastal_i + \mu_{0i}. \tag{3}$$

The right-hand-side variables chosen here denote the fraction of a country's land area situated within the geographical tropics (*tropics*; $\mu = 0.41$, $\sigma = 0.47$) or within 100 km from the seacoast or an ocean-navigable waterway (*coastal*; $\mu = 0.54$, $\sigma = 0.36$), respectively.

HLM provides a practical Bayesian algorithm for modeling potential determinants of coefficients on other variables and, because of the central importance of technical progress, we modeled its coefficient (i.e., the coefficient on time) as a function of *tropics*, *coastal*, and *open6590* (the fraction of years between 1965 and 1990 the country was deemed to have an open economy; $\mu = 0.54$, $\sigma = 0.45$). Specifically,

$$\beta_{1i} = \gamma_{10} + \gamma_{11} tropics_i + \gamma_{12} coastal_i + \gamma_{13} open6590_i + \mu_{1i}.^9 \qquad (4)$$

The actual estimated values of the parameters indicate, for example, to illustrate the interpretation of equations (3) and (4), that tropical countries' income levels are shifted downward (γ_{01} is negative). We consistently found little effect of *coastal* in equation (3) or of *tropics* in equation (4) and, in the next section, we report only results from more parsimonious specifications that delete those variables from the relevant equations.

3 Statistical Results

Tables 3.1 and 3.2 report the main results of our analysis using an estimate of an aggregate production function for 53 countries based on data at 5-year time intervals between 1965 and 1990. Table 3.1 presents the basic estimates of aggregate production functions. Table 3.2 goes beyond table 3.1 by reporting on our estimates of the magnitude of selected determinants of why countries differ in their levels of productivity and rates of technical progress.[10] (The annex table augments the analysis reported in the text by extending, for a subsample of 48 countries, the period of observation to the year 2000 and by using a more recently available data series.)

As indicated previously, most of the models reported in this paper are estimated by maximum likelihood using the HLM algorithm, and model 2 in table 3.1 reports the HLM results. To relate the HLM approach to those more frequently used in economics, models 3 and 4 convey results from using fixed effects (model 3) and random effects (model 4) with the same specifications. These are estimated with generalized least squares (GLS) using the STATA package. These basic models follow much of the literature in maintaining the assumption that technical progress proceeds at the same rate across all countries (i.e., there is a single coefficient on *time*). In these models, estimated technical progress is actually negative—with a magnitude of around -0.8 percent per annum—strongly suggesting an underlying heterogeneity (given, for example, the finding of Boskin and Lau [2000] concerning the central (positive) role of technical progress in explaining growth in the G-5 economies). The HLM algorithm for computing standard errors of estimates of coefficients generally results in larger values than does GLS hence the reported t-ratios are smaller in model 2 than in models 3 and 4. Estimated coefficients, however, are virtually

Table 3.1
Determinants of income levels: the effects of physical capital, health, education, geography, and technical progress (53 countries with 316 observations).

Independent Variable	Model					
	1	2[a]	3[a]	4[a]	5	6
I. Time-invariant determinants of income level:						
Constant	8.27	2.23	2.55	2.25	2.96	2.63
	(65.72)	(1.61)	(1.90)	(7.98)	(2.00)	(1.71)
tropics					−0.258	−0.449
					(1.84)	(3.36)
II. Time-varying determinants of income level:						
lkpc		0.40	0.40	0.40	0.38	0.41
		(8.17)	(12.25)	(14.90)	(7.58)	(12.05)
med		0.027	0.014	0.027	0.022	0.035
		(1.33)	(0.79)	(1.81)	(1.16)	(2.61)
lasr		0.465	0.41	0.462	0.38	0.32
		(1.98)	(2.02)	(2.61)	(1.55)	(1.41)
ltfr		−0.53	−0.47	−0.53	−0.49	−0.15
		(4.80)	(6.82)	(8.66)	(4.01)	(2.15)
time (common coefficient		−0.008	−0.006	−0.008	−0.006	
assumed for all countries)		(4.46)	(2.41)	(5.09)	(2.65)	
time (average of country-						−0.001
specific coefficients)						(0.67)
Model Statistics						
Within-country variance reduction[b]		73%			73%	89%
Between-country variance reduction[b]		89%			90%	83%
Number of parameters estimated	3	8			9	11
Deviance[c]	285	−175			−181	−295
Within country R-square			73%	73%		
Between country R-square			88%	89%		

[a] Estimation in model 2 uses HLM's maximum likelihood algorithm. Models 3 and 4 are the equivalent specifications in STATA, cross-sectional time-series regression, using generalized-least-squares. Model 3 shows the fixed-effect results and model 4 has the random-effect results.

[b] The variance reduction numbers indicate the percentage of the between- or within-country variance found in model 1 that is explained with the indicated model. Based on model 1, 8% of the variance in the dependent variable is within-country and 92% is between-country.

[c] "Deviance" is twice the negative log-likelihood value associated with the maximum likelihood parameter estimates. The larger the deviance, the poorer the fit.

Table 3.2
Determinants of income levels and rates of technical progress (53 countries with 316 observations).

	Model				
Independent Variable	7	8	9	10	11
I. Time-invariant determinants of income level:					
Constant	2.19	1.55	1.37	4.67	20.07
	(1.38)	(0.98)	(0.83)	(16.65)	(5.15)
tropics	−0.46	−0.39	−0.41	−0.40	−0.32
	(3.59)	(3.26)	(3.10)	(3.32)	(2.49)
II. Time-varying determinants of income level:					
lkpc	0.41	0.38	0.40	0.40	−2.06
	(12.45)	(11.86)	(12.64)	(13.39)	(3.85)
med	0.03	0.04		0.04	0.03
	(2.56)	(2.90)		(3.00)	(2.33)
lasr	0.38	0.50	0.55		−2.40
	(1.63)	(2.13)	(2.21)		(3.95)
ltfr	−0.10	−0.04	−0.09	−0.04	−0.11
	(1.58)	(0.78)	(1.66)	(0.79)	(1.79)
lkpc * lasr					0.38
					(4.65)
III. Determinants of technical progress:					
constant (common across countries)	−0.008	−0.012	−0.014	−0.051	−0.005
	(2.28)	(3.83)	(3.45)	(0.96)	(2.16)
coastal	0.013	0.009	0.007	0.007	
	(2.93)	(2.40)	(2.22)	(1.73)	
open6590		0.017	0.014	0.016	
		(5.97)	(4.71)	(5.01)	
med65			0.001		
			(1.98)		
lasr65				0.006	
				(0.76)	
Model Statistics					
Within-country variance reduction[a]	89%	90%	89%	90%	89%
Between-country variance reduction[a]	83%	83%	82%	81%	86%
Number of parameters estimated	12	13	13	13	12
Deviance[b]	−305	−329	−323	−324	−313

[a] The variance reduction numbers indicate the percentage of the between- or within-country variance found in model 1 that is explained with the indicated model. Based on model 1, 8% of the variance in the dependent variable is within-country and 92% is between-country.

[b] "Deviance" is twice the negative log-likelihood value associated with the maximum likelihood parameter estimates. The larger the deviance, the poorer the fit.

the same in all three models as would be expected. The elasticity of output with respect to physical capital is 0.40 with a tiny standard error; this remains virtually unchanged in all our specifications, included those reported in the annex table. The elasticity with respect to the adult male survival rate or *asr* is about 0.45, which is statistically significant but only marginally so.

Models 5 and 6 add the geographical variable *tropics* and return to HLM with its maximum likelihood estimation procedure. Model 5 continues to maintain the assumption that the rate of technical progress is constant across countries whereas model 6 relaxes that assumption. Model 6 achieves a markedly better overall fit to the data (the deviance value drops from −181 to −295), and its better overall explanatory power has the effect of changing the (now *average*) rate of technical progress almost to zero, which is consistent with the findings of Kim and Lau (1994) for East Asian Countries. Figure 3.1 illustrates the huge variation across countries in the rate of technical progress (or diffusion) as estimated from model 6 and underscores the importance of treating technical progress as a country-specific variable. Note that in model 6

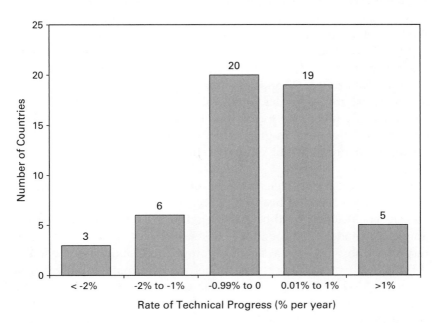

Figure 3.1
Country-specific variation in the annual rate of technical progress.

the estimated effects of *asr* and *tfr* are much reduced from models 2 and 5. The further exploration of sources of technical progress reported in table 3.2 continues to suggest that the adverse effect of a high *tfr* on income levels is modest, but an important health effect reappears and is robust with respect to alternative specifications. (Bloom and Williamson [1998] concluded that population growth affects economic growth principally when the dependent and working-age populations have different growth rates. In light of their research finding, we included the total fertility rate (*tfr*) in the model to proxy the character-istics of the country's age structure; countries with high *tfr* will tend to have a high ratio of dependent to working-age population which, in the production function formulation, should adversely affect per-capita output levels.)

Models 7 through 11 in table 3.2 convey our main results. Results for each model are divided into three categories: time-invariant deter-minants of income level, time-varying determinants of income level, and determinants of the country-specific rate of technical progress. The time-invariant determinants of income level consist of: an intercept term that is common to all countries (γ_{00} in equation 3); an effect due to *tropics*, that is, a measure of the extent to which being tropical affects the level of a country's income; and a third country-specific "fixed" ef-fect (μ_{0i} in equation 3) that is not reported in table 3.2. Being fully in the tropics (*tropics* = 1) is estimated to result in a downward shift in in-come *level* of between 27 and 37 percent, depending on the model, rela-tive to an otherwise similar country from entirely outside the tropics. As previously noted, we found the variable *coastal* to have its effects only through technical progress whereas *tropics* has no estimated effect on technical progress but only the effect on income level reported here.[11]

The next category of determinants consists of time-varying ones for each country—levels of health, fertility, education, and physical capi-tal. The coefficients are to be interpreted in the standard way, for ex-ample, in models 7 through 10 the elasticity of income level with respect to physical capital stock is found to be about 0.4.[12] Models 7 through 10 vary in how they model the determinants of technical progress. Model 11 explores the possibility of interaction between the health of a population and physical capital levels. The findings are of a strong interaction and one that has the effect of markedly increasing the estimated impact of health on income. Model 11 is on the whole less satisfactory in terms of fit than our other models, and we report it principally to pose questions for further analysis. It does suggest that our estimates of the contribution of health improvements to economic growth, reported in the final section, are likely to be conservative.

The third block of coefficients in table 3.2 shows our estimates of the effects of several factors likely to be influencing the rate of technical progress (or diffusion). Model 7 reports on a single determinant, *coastal*, and model 8 adds *open6590* as an additional determining variable. The inclusion of *open6590* reduces the estimated effect of *coastal* by about 30 percent but *coastal* nonetheless remains quantitatively important and statistically significant. Model 9 retains both of these variables but changes how education is modeled by including the initial education level, *med65*, as a determinant of technical progress rather than having *med* be a time-varying determinant of income as in models 7 and 8.[13] Each of these three variables is, in different ways, capturing an element of contact with the outside world. Coastal nations' access to ocean trade greatly reduces the cost and ease of commerce (Radelet, Sachs, and Lee 1997). Open economic policies likewise facilitate knowledge transfer, allow the realization of comparative advantage, and create competitive pressures for innovation. More educated populations, as Schultz (1993, chapter 3) and others have stressed, enjoy economic advantage at least as much from their ability to adapt to change (deal with "disequilibria") as from simply producing more from a given input list. Models 7 to 10 strongly suggest that the gains from contact with the world are indeed dynamic ones, involving as they do quantitatively important driving forces for technical change.

For our purposes in the remainder of this paper we will focus on model 8, which leaves education as a time-varying determinant of income level. Our results concerning health are insensitive to this choice although an analysis concerned with the long-term effects of education might choose to focus on model 9. In contrast to the case with education, our explanation of alternative specifications (e.g., model 10) suggests that the effect of health is on *levels* of income. To put this slightly differently, although education potentially can be viewed as a (weak) endogenous source of technical progress, health's effects do not appear to be an endogenous source of technical progress.

In model 8, a country's rate of technical progress is determined from an element that is common across countries (-0.012 or γ_{10} from equa tion [4]), from how coastal and open it is by way of the relevant coef cients on those variables and by a remaining country-specific effect (from equation [4]). We include geographical variables in our analy in light of recent findings strongly suggestive that tropical and isolated countries face additional barriers to growth (Sachs and Warner 1997; Bloom and Williamson 1998). These same studies provide empirical support for the importance of open economies, as do several more specific studies (e.g., Edwards 1998; Frankel and Romer 1999). Hence our inclusion of openness (*open6590*). The important point to note about determinants of technical progress is how strong are the effects both of being coastal and of having open economic policies. Other things equal, an inland Bolivia would have an annual rate of technical progress 0.9 percent less per year than, say, a highly coastal Jamaica. At least some component of technical progress is, clearly, best viewed as exogenous.[14]

The difference between fully closed and fully open trade policies is even more substantial—about 1.7 percent per year (in model 8).[15] Although OLS regressions predicting growth rates that we have estimated show an even more substantial effect of open policies on growth, it needs to be remembered that those models fail to distinguish between effects on levels and effects on growth rates, and in particular they assume all effects are on growth. Such models (e.g., Romer 1989; Sachs and Warner 1997) are therefore incapable of ascribing the estimated coefficients unequivocally to growth effects but are nonetheless valuable in identifying main effects. Our empirical analysis concludes that technical progress includes a substantial endogenous component with respect to policies on economic openness. (Important parts of the residual country-specific element of technical progress, μ_{1i}, may also, of course, be endogenous.)

Of all the time-varying determinants of income in model 8 only *tfr* has an estimated impact that is statistically insignificant, although in some of the other models its coefficient is notably larger and significant. Allowing technical progress to be country specific seems to be capturing some of the effects of *tfr*. That said, given the magnitude of fertility decline in many countries during the period being analyzed, even a small coefficient can still lead to an explanation of a noticeable amount of a country's growth between 1965 and 1990.

The annex table reports results from a specification equivalent to model 8 but that uses data at ten-year intervals for the period 1960 to 2000 (and data drawn from somewhat more recent sources). For the most part the annex table results confirm the findings from model 10 that we have just discussed. The exceptions are:

(1) the estimated magnitude of the adverse effect of being in the tropics on the level of output is reduced to 25 percent of its level with the original data set and becomes insignificant;

(2) the estimated effects of health and of education are reduced, and the health variable switches to insignificant;

(3) the estimated effects of physical capital and total fertility rates become more substantial; and

(4) the effects on technical progress of being coastal and of economic openness become less substantial (while remaining highly statistically significant).

Finally, we note that the annex table also reports the results of estimating model 11, which includes the interaction term between physical capital and adult survival. The calculated elasticity of output with respect to adult survival in model 11 is about 0.7, substantially higher than in model 8. It remains this high with parameters estimated from the augmented data set.

4 Conclusions

One purpose of this chapter was to examine health's contribution to economic growth and, for that reason, using model 8, we assessed how much of economic growth between 1965 and 1990 could be attributed to changes in health. The average adult survival rate increased from 707 per thousand in 1965 to 796 in 1990. The estimated resulting increase in the level of 1990 income would then imply, on average, a contribution of 0.23 percent per year from better health to the income growth rate during this period. This was about 11 percent of growth overall. Annex table 1.2 in the working paper version of this chapter reports decomposition results for all the countries we analyzed along with basic data on each country's income growth rates and adult male survival rates.

Countries with initially high levels of *asr* typically realized a much more modest contribution to their growth rates from health improvements than did countries with an initially lower *asr*. In these countries *asr* improvements resulted in gains in growth rates estimated at 0.1 percent per annum or less. In Honduras, Bolivia, and Thailand, to take examples of a more major effect, health improvements added about half a percent to the annual per-capita income growth. This finding of diminishing returns is consistent with that of Bhargava et al. (2001) but should be interpreted with some caution for several reasons. First, lack of data on morbidity or disability required use of mortality rates as a proxy for overall health conditions, but it is plausible that morbidity declines may be significant determinants of income growth, only partially correlated with mortality decline and, in particular, that they might lag mortality decline. Second, health improvements above age 60 are likely to be important (for example, in influencing the age of retirement) and may show scope for significant improvement well after *asr* has reached near-maximum levels (in the low 900s). The instrumental value of health improvements for income growth is limited by (very slowly changing) upper bounds on health. But the limit is probably reached less rapidly than our analysis, taken literally, would suggest.

The major purpose of this paper was to estimate empirically the difference across countries in their rates of technical progress and to explore some potential determinants of this variation. In particular we explored health among other potential endogenous sources of technical progress and concluded that health's effects on outcomes were unlikely to be through this mechanism. Education's effects, in contrast, were plausibly in part through technical progress but the magnitude of that effect was small. Policies of economic openness, in contrast, were found to have a major impact on the rate of technical progress.[16] Many of our parameters are estimated with only modest precision, and alternative models could be defended. Yet all variants of our models showed major differences across countries in rates of technical progress and that openness of the economy was a powerful predictor of these differences.

The working paper version of this chapter reports (in its annex table 1.3) results of a decomposition of growth into its constituents for 47 of the countries in our sample (using model 8 of table 3.2). The final two columns show the effect of technical progress overall and of the component of technical progress due to economic openness. On average, for the countries in our sample, for the period 1965–1990, technical progress was positive, but only slightly so, and accounted for only 4.5 percent of all growth. This low total for technical progress comprised, however, a strong positive component due to actual openness (relative to none) counterbalanced by a negative component due to everything else. The average value of *open6590* was 0.5 and its coefficient in model 10 is 0.017 implying about a 0.85 percent increment in the annual rate of technical progress for the average country relative to a closed country. This results in openness being responsible for about 37 percent of the observed average growth rate of 2.3 percent per annum. Country-specific decompositions should be viewed only as suggestive, but they do give a broad picture of the importance of alternative sources of growth. Increases in physical capital stocks dominate (accounting for 67% of total growth) but both educational improvements (14%) and health improvements (11%) are important, and relatively much more so in some countries.[17]

Our findings point to the importance of investment—in physical capital, education, and health—for affecting per-capita GDP in the medium term. They point to the importance of cross-country variation in rates of technical progress in explaining long-term differences in growth rates, and to the value of increasing economic openness for increasing the rate of technical progress. Understanding the reasons why, for much of the world, technical progress (after controlling for economic openness) is negative is a major challenge posed by our research.

Appendix: Updating the Analysis to the Year 2000

In order to update the findings of an earlier draft of this chapter, we constructed a new data set that covers the time period between 1960 and 2000. We made a number of changes to our existing data in both sources and data definition; annex 2 of the working paper version of the chapter describes these changes fully (see note 1). Most significantly, for the education variable, instead of using Barro and Lee's (1996) total number of years of education for the male population aged 15 and over, we used Cohen and Soto's (2001) education numbers for the population between ages 15 and 64. The variable is at 10-year intervals from 1960 to 2000, which gives us only 5 observations per country rather than the 6 that we have with Barro and Lee. The descriptive information and sources for this newly constructed data set are reported in annex table 2.1 of the working paper. As indicated there, these new data cover 48 out of the 53 countries that are in our original data.

The annex table to this chapter reports the HLM results repeating the analysis for models 8 and 11 using the extended data set (reported in the annex table as models 8a and 11a). The original models 8 and 11, from table 3.2, are also reported there for comparison. We found that our existing models with the new data set are yielding broadly similar patterns of findings although, obviously, there are some changes in the magnitude of coefficients, as discussed at the end of section 4 in the text.

Annex Table
Determinants of income levels and rates of technical progress, 1960–2000.

Independent Variable	53 Countries		New: 48 countries 1960–2000	
	8	11	8a	11a
I. Time-invariant determinants of income level:				
Constant	1.55	20.07	3.28	19.41
	(0.98)	(5.15)	(4.57)	(5.65)
Tropics	−0.39	−0.32	−0.09	0.00
	(3.26)	(2.49)	(1.12)	(0.03)
II. Time-varying determinants of income level:				
ln physical capital per capita	0.38	−2.06	0.48	−1.84
	(11.86)	(3.85)	(13.06)	(3.78)
Adult education level	0.04	0.03	0.03	0.02
	(2.90)	(2.33)	(2.06)	(1.71)
ln adult survival rate	0.50	−2.40	0.14	−2.38
	(2.13)	(3.95)	(1.26)	(4.63)
ln total fertility rate	−0.04	−0.11	−0.17	−0.16
	(0.78)	(1.79)	(2.66)	(2.69)
interaction of ln physical capital per capita and ln adult survival rate		0.38		0.36
		(4.65)		(4.95)
III. Determinants of technical progress:				
constant (common across countries)	−0.012	−0.005	−0.002	−0.00003
	(3.83)	(2.16)	(1.17)	(0.03)
Coastal	0.009		0.004	
	(2.40)		(2.41)	
Open6590	0.017		0.006	
	(5.97)		(3.63)	
Model Statistics				
Within-country variance reduction[a]	90%	89%	87%	88%
Between-country variance reduction[a]	83%	86%	86%	87%
Number of parameters estimated	13	12	13	12
Deviance[b]	−329	−313	−105	−120

Note: Models 8a and 11a show the results from the data set extended to the year 2000, for which there were 5 fewer countries with data availability. For ease of comparison, models 8 and 11 for the 53-country data set are reproduced here from Table 3.2.

[a] The variance reduction numbers indicate the percentage of the between- or within-country variance found in model 1 that is explained with the indicated model. Based on model 1, 8% of the variance in the dependent variable is within-country and 92% is between-country.

[b] "Deviance" is twice the negative log-likelihood value associated with the maximum likelihood parameter estimates. The larger the deviance, the poorer the fit.

Acknowledgments

We received valuable comments from participants—particularly David Bloom, David Canning, Jeffrey Sachs, and Peter Timmer—in a seminar at the Harvard Center for International Development (CID) in April 1998 and at the World Health Organization (WHO) Director-General Transition Workshop at CID in June of 1998 where an early version of this chapter was presented. We are also indebted to Alok Bhargava, William Easterly, Bengt Muthen, Jennifer Ruger, and Christopher Spohr for valuable discussions. Christopher Murray and Lant Pritchett provided useful reminders concerning the caveats that must be attached to cross-country analyses and the data on which they are based. John Gallup provided us with several of the geographic and economic policy variables from the data base assembled at CID. Working Group 1 of the WHO Commission on Macroeconomics and Health and the Fogarty International Center of the U.S. National Institutes of Health (NIH) supported preparation of this chapter.

Notes

1. This chapter was commissioned by the WHO and the NIH and for this reason we pay particular attention to health's effects on growth. An expanded version of the chapter appears as Working Paper no. 10 of the Disease Control Priorities Project, Bethesda, Maryland: Fogarty International Center, U.S. National Institutes of Health, February 2004 (http://www.fic.nih.gov/dcpp/wps/wp10.pdf).

2. A number of reviews conclude there to be an important effect of health on economic development. See Bloom and Canning 2000, World Health Organization 2001, and Ruger, Jamison, and Bloom 2001. A major recent review of the determinants of growth treats health's role only in passing, however, and conveys skepticism about its importance (Temple 1999).

3. See World Bank 1993, p. 1.

4. Although monetary valuation of health gains may be difficult, Nordhaus (2003) has used published estimates of the "value of a statistical life" to generate estimates of the contribution of mortality decline to the rate of improvement of overall economic welfare in the United States (or "full income"). He concluded that the magnitude of the contribution in recent decades was about the same as the welfare gain resulting from growth in the output of goods and services. Jamison, Sachs, and Wang (2001) utilized similar methods to conclude that the economic impact of the AIDS epidemic in Africa is far greater than is typically estimated through assessment of its impact on GDP per person. Bloom, Canning, and Jamison (2004) provide a brief overview of the literature (mostly very recent) on health and full income.

5. Islam (1995) develops methods for analyzing economic growth in a panel of countries with an emphasis on accounting for country fixed effects. Mayer et al. (2001) report

results from Latin America using Islam's approach. Lee, Pesaran, and Smith (1997) extend Islam's work by allowing for country-specific rates of technical progress and additionally provide a succinct account (1998) of the similarities and differences between their approach and his. Kreuger and Lindahl (2001) extend the work of Lee et al. in a different way by allowing for heterogeneity in the coefficient of education on growth.

6. Kreft and de Leeuw (1998) provide a more general and introductory account of multi-level modeling and Raudenbusch et al. (1999) document the software package that we use.

7. Easterly (2001, chap. 3) and Easterly and Levine (2000) place the role of technical progress and diffusion more centrally than we do. Factor accumulation rates, particularly of physical capital, vary enormously across countries and the resultant differences in growth rates over periods of decades are, in our view, more significant than implied by Easterly. That said, this chapter supports Easterly's perspective by providing empirical evidence for the central role of variation in the rates of technological change in explaining cross-country differences in long-run growth rates and levels of income.

8. Demographers increasingly refer to 45q15 (the probability of dying between ages 15 and 60, assuming continuation of the prevailing age-specific mortality rates) as the "adult mortality rate," which is usually expressed per thousand. The adult survival rate asr is 1000 minus the adult mortality rate. Bhargava et al. (2001) found asr to be a (somewhat) better predictor of growth rates than life expectancy, and Meltzer (1992) earlier used a related measure of adult survival, the expected number of productive years lived per adult. These measures correlate highly with one another.

9. Note that adding country indicator variables to the right-hand side of equation (1) along with interaction terms between those indicators and other variables would, from an algebraic perspective, be equivalent to the utilization of supplementary equations (3) and (4). Estimation of such a specification is unworkable. Edwards (1998) approaches this question in a somewhat different way by first calculating total factor productivity growth using coefficients estimated in a random-effects model, then using that result as the dependent variable in separate regressions.

10. Before turning to our results, however, we note that the working paper version of this chapter reported growth equations in a form more closely related to much of the literature, that is, it reports predictors of countries' growth rates between 1965 and 1990 in terms of conditions in 1965 and other variables. More elaborate variants of these models appear in the literature with extensive discussions (e.g., Barro 1997; Sachs and Warner 1997). Our purpose in generating these comparisons was twofold. First, versions of these models that were estimated on the same set of countries as the models reported here indicate that our variables behave more or less as they are reported to do in the published literature, including the openness and geographical variables. Second, availability of data on the value of a country's physical capital stock per capita limits the number of countries in our analysis to 53, but this variable is not used in the growth prediction literature. Checking our results in a larger group of 80 countries suggests that there was no important relevant selection bias in getting to our 53-country sample.

11. Most models in literature by the nature of their specification *assume* that *tropics* has its effect on the growth rate rather than level of income. When growth rate prediction models specify convergence to a long-term (country-specific) steady state, however, the long-term estimated effect of *tropics* is not greatly different than our estimate. For example, Radelet, Sachs, and Lee (1997, p. 14) find a 47 percent reduction in steady-state income from being tropical relative to our finding of a 27–37 percent reduction. Hall and

Jones (1999) find "distance from the equator" to be their strongest predictor of long-term economic success, and the adverse effect of an equatorial location to be much stronger than our findings suggest.

12. We explored whether the physical capital elasticity was related to initial levels of physical capital and concluded that this was unlikely.

13. The relatively slow change over time within a country of *med* suggests the plausibility of modeling it either way. Over the 25 years considered here, the dynamic effect of education (model 9) would have less effect on end-of-period income than would modeling its effect on income levels (models 7 or 8). Over a longer time period, however, if education did indeed affect technical progress, the effect through technical progress would be more significant. (Model 9 could also be modified to include both the initial level of education, *med65*, and its average level over subsequent years as determinants of the rate of technical progress.) Temple (1999) has noted that in many circumstances there will be little quantitative difference in results resulting from modeling levels or growth rates. This would appear to be the case with *med*.

14. Easterly and Levine (1997) have found strong (adverse) effects of ethnolinguistic diversity on both the level and the growth rate of income. This would be another potential exogenous determinant of technical change and another example of how factors impeding economic interactions (either within a country or with the outside world) could adversely affect the rate of technical progress.

15. Frankel and Romer (1999, pp. 390–391) use geographical instruments to assess directly the impact of the share of trade in national income to productivity change. They find strong effects.

16. The economic openness variable no doubt proxies for other aspects of the economic policy in addition to international openness per se. Indeed Hall and Jones (1997) use this variable as one of two components of their social infrastructure construct.

17. Boskin and Lau (2000) and Dougherty and Jorgenson (1996), in decompositions for the G-5 countries, found technical progress followed by physical capital accumulation to be principal sources of growth. The average contribution of technical progress reported for the G-7 countries in annex table 1.3 of the working paper version is 22 percent of total per-capita income growth—far above the 4.5 percent for the sample as a whole but substantially less than estimated by Boskin and Lau or Dougherty and Jorgenson. This results from several factors (in addition to the possibility of differences resulting from somewhat differently constructed data sets). One is that Boskin–Lau separate out a negative effect due to the oil price shock of the early 1970s that, if not separated out, would have reduced their estimates of the contribution of technical progress. Second, and probably more important, their more powerful estimation procedures allow them to identify technical progress as capital augmenting and it is likely that our estimates of a high proportion of growth due to physical capital investments embodies part of what they are able to attribute to capital-augmenting technical change.

References

Barro, R. J. 1997. *Determinants of Economic Growth*. Cambridge, Mass.: The MIT Press.

Barro, R. J., and J. W. Lee. 1996. International Measures of Schooling Years and Schooling Quality. *American Economic Review* 86: 218–223.

Bernard, A. B., and C. I. Jones. 1996. Technology and Convergence. *Economic Journal* 106: 1037–1044.

Bhargava, A., D. T. Jamison, L. J. Lau, and C. J. L. Murray. 2001. Modeling the Effects of Health on Economic Growth. *Journal of Health Economics* 20 (3): 423–440.

Bloom, D. E., and D. Canning. 2000. The Health and Wealth of Nations. *Science* 290: 1207–1209.

Bloom, D. E., D. Canning, and D. T. Jamison. 2004. Health, Wealth, and Welfare. *Finance and Development* 41 (March): 10–15.

Bloom, D. E., and J. D. Sachs. 1998. Geography, Demography, and Economic Growth in Africa. *Brookings Papers on Economic Activity* 2: 1–65.

Bloom, D. E., and J. Williamson. 1998. Demographic Transitions and Economic Miracles in Emerging Asia. *World Bank Economic Review* 12: 419–455.

Boskin, M. J., and L. J. Lau. 1990. Post-War Economic Growth in the Group-of-Five Countries: A New Analysis. Working paper no. W3521, National Bureau of Economic Research, Cambridge, Mass.

———. 2000. Generalized Solow-Neutral Technical Progress and Postwar Economic Growth. Working paper no. 8023, National Bureau of Economic Research, Cambridge, Mass.

Brady, H., M. Meyers, and S. Luks. 1998. The Impact of Child and Adult Disabilities on the Duration of Welfare Spells. Paper presented at the Seminars in Aging, Development, and Population, Santa Monica, California: RAND Corporation.

Bryk, Anthony S., and S. W. Raudenbusch. 1992. *Hierarchical Linear Models: Application and Data Analysis Methods*. Newbury Park, Calif.: Sage Publications.

Burkhauser, R., R. Haveman, and B. Wolfe. 1993. How People with Disabilities Fare When Public Policies Change. *Journal of Policy Analysis and Management* 12: 251–269.

Cohen, D., and M. Soto. 2001. Growth and Human Capital: Good Data, Good Results. Technical paper no. 179, OCED Development Centre, Paris.

Dougherty, C., and D. W. Jorgenson. 1996. International Comparisons of the Sources of Growth. *American Economic Review (Papers and Proceedings)* 86: 25–29.

Easterly, W. 2001. *The Elusive Quest for Growth*. Cambridge, Mass.: The MIT Press.

Easterly, W., and R. Levine. 1997. Africa's Growth Tragedy: Policies and Ethnic Divisions. *Quarterly Journal of Economics* 112: 1203–1250.

———. 2000. It's Not Factor Accumulation: Stylized Facts and Growth Models. Unpublished paper. The World Bank.

Easterly, W., M. Kremer, L. Pritchett, and L. Summers. 1993. Good Policy or Good Luck? Country Growth Performance and Temporary Shocks. *Journal of Monetary Economics* 32: 1–25.

Edwards, S. 1998. Openness, Productivity, and Growth: What Do We Really Know? *Economic Journal* 108: 383–398.

Fogel, R. W. 1997. New Findings on Secular Trends in Nutrition and Mortality: Some Implications for Population Theory. Chap. 9 in *Handbook of Population and Family Economics*, vol. 1A, edited by M. Rosenzweig and O. Stark. Amsterdam: Elsevier, pp. 433–481.

Frankel, J. A., and D. Romer. 1999. Does Trade Cause Growth? *American Economic Review* 89: 379–399.

Gallup, J. L., and J. D. Sachs. 2001. The Economic Burden of Malaria. *American Journal of Tropical Medicine and Hygiene* 64 (supplement): 85–96.

Hall, R. E., and C. I. Jones. 1997. Levels of Economic Activity Across Countries. *American Economic Review (Papers and Proceedings)* 87: 173–177.

———. 1999. Why Do Some Countries Produce So Much More Output per Workers Than Others? *Quarterly Journal of Economics* 114: 83–116.

Handa, S., and M. Neitzert. 1998. Chronic Illness and Retirement in Jamaica. Living Standards Measurement Study. Working paper no. 131, The World Bank, Washington, D.C.

Hicks, N. L. 1979. Growth vs. Basic Needs: Is There a Trade-Off? *World Development* 7: 985–994.

Islam, N. 1995. Growth Empirics: A Panel Data Approach. *Quarterly Journal of Economics* 110: 1127–1170.

Jamison, D. T., J. Sachs, and J. Wang. 2001. The Effect of the AIDS Epidemic on Economic Welfare in Sub-Saharan Africa, 1960–2000. CMH Working paper no. WG1: 13. World Health Organization, Commission on Macroeconomics and Health, Geneva.

Jamison, D. T., M. E. Sandbu, and J. Wang. 2004. Why Has Infant Mortality Decreased at Such Different Rates in Different Countries? Working paper no. 14 (February), Disease Control Priorities Project (DCPP), Bethesda, Maryland.

Kim, J. I., and L. J. Lau. 1994. The Sources of Economic Growth of East Asian Newly Industrialized Countries: Some Further Evidence. *Journal of the Japanese and International Economies* 8: 235–271.

Knaul, F. M. 2000. Health, Nutrition, and Wages: Age at Menarche and Earnings in Mexico. In *Wealth from Health*, edited by W. D. Savedoff and T. P. Schultz. Washington, D.C.: Inter-American Development Bank, pp. 35–70.

Kreft, I., and J. de Leeuw. 1998. *Introducing Multilevel Modeling*. London: Sage Publications.

Krueger, A. B., and M. Lindahl. 2001. Education for Growth: Why and for Whom? *Journal of Economic Literature* 39: 1101–1136.

Lau, L. J. 1996. The Sources of Long-Term Economic Growth: Observations from the Experience of Developed and Developing Countries. In *The Mosaic of Economic Growth*, edited by R. Landau, T. Taylor, and G. Wright. Stanford, Calif.: Stanford University Press, pp. 63–91.

Laxminarayan, R. 2004. Does Reducing Malaria Improve Household Living Standards? *Tropical Medicine and International Health* 9: 267–272.

Lee, K., M. H. Pesaran, and R. Smith. 1997. Growth and Convergence in a Multi-Country Empirical Stochastic Growth Model. *Journal of Applied Econometrics* 12: 357–392.

———. 1998. Growth Empirics: A Panel Data Approach—A Comment. *Quarterly Journal of Economics* 113 (1): 319–323.

Liu, G. G., W. H. Dow, A. Z. Fu, and J. Akin. 2003. Income Growth in China: On the Role of Health. Paper presented at the Fourth World Congress of the International Health Economics Association (IHEA), San Francisco.

Mankiw, N. G., D. Romer, and D. N. Weil. 1992. A Contribution to the Empirics of Economic Growth. *Quarterly Journal of Economics* 107: 407–437.

Meltzer, D. O. 1992. Mortality Decline, the Demographic Transition, and Economic Growth. Ph.D. dissertation, Department of Economics, The University of Chicago.

Myrdal, G. 1952. Economic Aspects of Health. *Chronicle of the World Health Organization* 6: 203–218.

Nordhaus, W. 2003. The Health of Nations: The Contributions of Improved Health to Living Standards. In *Measuring the Gains from Health Research: An Economic Approach*, edited by K. M. Murphy and R. H. Topel. Chicago: University of Chicago Press, pp. 9–40.

Radelet, S., J. Sachs, and J.-W. Lee. 1997. Economic Growth in Asia. Development discussion paper no. 609, Harvard Institute for International Development, Cambridge, Mass.

Raudenbusch, S., A. Bryk, Y. F. Cheong, and R. Congdon. 1999. *HLM5: Hierarchical Linear and Nonlinear Modeling*. Lincolnwood, Ill.: Scientific Software International.

Romer, P. M. 1989. What Determines the Rate of Growth and Technological Change? Working paper no. 279, Policy, Planning, and Research, The World Bank, Washington, D.C.

Ruger, J. P., D. T. Jamison, and D. E. Bloom. 2001. Health and the Economy. In *International Public Health*, edited by M. H. Merson, R. E. Black, and A. J. Mills. Gaithersburg, Maryland: Aspen Publishers, pp. 617–666.

Sachs, J., and A. Warner. 1997. Fundamental Sources of Long-Run Growth. *American Economic Review (Papers and Proceedings)* 87: 184–188.

Savedoff, W. D., and T. P. Schultz. 2000. Earnings and the Elusive Dividends of Health. In *Wealth from Health*, edited by W. D. Savedoff and T. P. Schultz. Washington, D.C.: The Inter-American Development Bank, pp. 1–34.

Schultz, T. P. 1993. *Origins of Increasing Returns*. Oxford: Blackwell.

Schultz, T. P., Jr., and A. Tansel. 1997. Wage and Labor Supply Effects of Illness in Côte d'Ivoire and Ghana: Instrumental Variable Estimates for Days Disabled. *Journal of Development Economics* 53 (2): 251–286.

Strauss, J., and D. Thomas. 1998. Health, Nutrition, and Economic Development. *Journal of Economic Literature* 36 (2): 766–817.

Stronks, K., H. Van de Mheen, J. Van den Bos, and J. P. Mackenbach. 1997. The Interrelationship between Income, Health, and Employment Status. *International Journal of Epidemiology* 26: 592–599.

Temple, J. 1999. The New Growth Evidence. *Journal of Economic Literature* 37: 112–156.

Wheeler, D. 1980. Basic Needs Fulfillment and Economic Growth. *Journal of Development Economics* 7: 435–451.

World Bank. 1980. *Poverty and Human Development: World Development Report 1980.* Washington, D.C.: The World Bank.

World Bank. 1993. *Investing in Health: World Development Report 1993.* Washington, D.C.: The World Bank.

World Bank. 2002. *World Development Indicators.* Washington, D.C.: The World Bank.

World Health Organization (WHO). 2001. *Macroeconomics and Health: Investing in Health for Economic Development.* Geneva: World Health Organization.

II

Macroeconomics,
Development, and Health

4   On the Health-Poverty Trap

Xavier Sala-i-Martín

It's not terrorism. Nor it is global warming. The biggest problem, the largest human tragedy in the world today is the health debacle suffered by the citizens of Africa. More than one third of the citizens in some regions of southern Africa are infected with the HIV virus. Tens of millions of people are expected to die of malaria, AIDS, or tuberculosis during the next couple of decades. This human tragedy is magnified by the fact that Africa is also the poorest continent of the world. And this is not a coincidence: low income tends to cause poor health and poor health, in turn, tends to cause low income. This two-way circle of causation generates a trap that one may well call the health-poverty trap. A trap that has tragic consequences because poverty cannot be eradicated without dealing with the health issues of the poor, and these health problems, in turn, will not be fully solved until poverty is eradicated. In other words, health and poverty form a vicious circle from which it may be very difficult to escape.[1]

In the first section of the chapter, we describe the mechanisms through which poverty affects health. In the second section, we show how poor health affects the level of income and the growth rate of the entire economy. The third section argues that solutions must be global in the sense that they need to address health and poverty simultaneously and sketches policies that should be undertaken by the governments of the poor nations as well as the donors of the rich world.

1 Poverty Affects Health

Poverty affects health through many different channels. First, and most obviously, poor people (and poor countries) do not have the material resources, the money necessary to buy health care: they cannot afford prevention before the disease appears and they cannot afford doctors and drugs once they have been infected. Thus, poor people are more likely to be unhealthy. Moreover, poor people are more likely to be malnourished, are more likely to have an insufficient caloric and protein intake and, as a result, are more likely to be immunodeficient and vulnerable to infectious diseases. Thus, what is a small epidemic in a relatively rich town or country ends up being a large pandemic in a poor society.

Second, the fact that poor citizens cannot afford drugs reduces the incentives that pharmaceutical corporations are given to devote R&D resources to poor people's diseases. The profits that such products might generate are unlikely to cover large R&D outlays. The decision to invest in R&D relates the present discounted value of all future profits to the cost of R&D. If the interest is constant, r, then the present discounted value of all future profits is the ratio

$$\frac{\pi}{r} = \frac{(P - mc)X}{r}, \tag{1}$$

where the expected profit flow, π, is equal to the sales price of the vaccine, P, minus the marginal cost of production, mc, times the quantity of units sold, X.[2] The current system of patents gives the inventor the monopoly right to produce the invented product. Since the demand for vaccines is likely to be downward sloping, the quantity of units sold, X, will depend negatively on the price charged by the inventor. The pharmaceutical firm will decide to invest in R&D and try to invent the vaccine if

$$\frac{(P - mc)X}{r} > \eta, \tag{2}$$

where η is the R&D cost. If the only potential customers have low levels of income (as is certainly the case today with the potential users of vaccines that prevent malaria, AIDS, or tuberculosis), then the amount of units, X, of the vaccine that will be sold at the monopolistic price, P, is likely to be small. Thus, it is less likely that the firm will devote resources to R&D of this vaccine. It follows that this firm will devote most of their financial effort to discover solutions to the health problems of the rich. This is why, today, the resources devoted to research on colon cancer, baldness, obesity, or erectile dysfunction are vastly superior to those devoted to find a vaccine or a cure for malaria. In fact, over the last quarter century, about 1 out of every 100 products patented by the pharmaceutical industry is related to tropical diseases (and tropical countries tend to be the poorest countries in the world).[3]

Third, poor people are more likely to live in massively overcrowded areas without clean water and sanitation or in distant rural areas, also without clean water and sanitation. As a result, they have a larger propensity to have diarrhea, cholera, or typhoid fever. According to the UN's children's fund, diarrhea is one of the three main causes of child mortality (the other two are malnutrition and respiratory infections).[4]

Fourth, poor people are more likely to live far away from doctors and hospitals, making it very expensive to seek help when problems arise. Thus, poor people are more likely to go untreated and, therefore, to suffer from worse health.

Fifth, poor people are more likely to have less education and hence understand the need to seek doctors or other kinds of help. It has been widely documented that one of the key determinants of child mortality is the literacy of mothers.[5] Educated mothers, for example, understand the need for hand washing, for the use of soap, for the need to drink of clean water. One important cause of neonatal tetanus in sub-Saharan Africa for example, is the use of rusty scissors or knives when cutting the umbilical cord.[6] Very simple education, therefore, can reduce the incidence of neonatal tetanus substantially.

Sixth, poor (and uneducated) young girls are more likely to be unable to refuse sex with rich and powerful men, which makes them vulnerable to the spread of venereal diseases or AIDS.[7] Although AIDS started as an "American" disease in 1981, it is now mainly concentrated in the poorest continent: 75 percent of the global population infected by the HIV virus live in sub-Saharan Africa, especially Southern Africa. UNAIDS 2000 reports that in Botswana 20 percent is infected, in Swaziland 25 percent, in Lesotho 24 percent, in South Africa 20 percent, and in Namibia 20 percent. For the same countries, the fraction of HIV-positive pregnant females are 43 percent, 30 percent, 30 percent, 19 percent, and 26 percent, so millions of babies are likely to be infected at birth.[8]

In sum, there is a variety of mechanisms that explain how poverty and economic underdevelopment cause poor health. But the causation also goes in the other direction. The importance of this other channel is understood by growth economists, whose theoretical and empirical models increasingly incorporate "health" as a fundamental determinant of the process of economic growth and development. We deal with this second channel in the next section.

2   Health Affects Poverty

In one of most recent broad empirical studies of the determinants of
economic growth, Gernot Doppelhoffer, Ronald Miller, and Xavier
Sala-i-Martín incorporate dozens of potential factors into their econometric analysis of robust estimators.[9] Most of them have been proposed by economists. Others have been incorporated by political
scientists, sociologists, and general observers worldwide: from technology to openness, to macroeconomic stability, to the rule of law,
to democracy, to religion. Although intuitive at first, many of these factors turn out not to be robustly correlated with growth. One of the
elements that seem to be robustly correlated with growth is human
capital. Human capital is the input associated with the human body:
strength, brainpower, and native ability are elements that suggest a
direct link between the human body and productivity. Education can
also help improve human skills and, therefore, productivity and economic growth.

Another important component of human capital emphasized by the
fathers of the concept, Theodore W. Schultz and Gary S. Becker, is
health.[10] The interesting empirical result is that health is the most important component of human capital when it comes to its relation to
aggregate economic growth. For example, Doppelhofer et al. (2004)
find life expectancy at birth to be one of the robust determinants of
growth: countries that had a larger life expectancy in the 1960s are
countries that grew the fastest over the following four decades. They
find also that malaria prevalence is an important (negative) determinant of growth: countries with a larger fraction of population affected
by malaria tend to grow less, and this is true even after taking into account that these countries are likely to be in Africa (with all the negative growth implications that that tends to have). Elsa V. Artadi and
Xavier Sala-i-Martín show that the growth rate of a malaria-free Africa
would be 1.25 percentage points higher.[11] In addition, if African life
expectancy were at OECD levels, its growth rate would go up by an
additional 2.07 points. In other words, if Africa enjoyed health levels
similar to those of developed industrial countries, its overall growth
rate would be 3.32 percentage points larger. This empirical evidence,
therefore, suggests that people's incomes and their growth rates are
affected fundamentally by the aggregate health status of the region in
which they live. It also suggests the existence of a trap: poor economies

tend to grow less because they have poor health, and they tend to have poor health because they are poor.

Although the empirical analysis shows that health has important effects on the aggregate rate of economic growth, it does not fully describe the mechanisms through which this effect operates. Economic theory helps us understand these potential mechanisms. Indeed, theory suggests that health may affect growth through a large variety of channels. An easy way to organize these thoughts is to use an aggregate production function of the type generally used by macroeconomists:

$$Y = AF(K, hL), \tag{3}$$

where Y is output or product, A is an efficiency parameter, $F(\ )$ is a production function, K is physical capital, L is labor and h is the "quality of labor," or human capital. The process of economic growth is the process of continuous increases in aggregate output. A simple analysis of the production function displayed in equation (3) suggests that GDP growth can occur only if there are increases in the levels of efficiency, A, in the aggregate level of physical capital, K, or the quality or quantity of labor, hL. In this section we show that health affects growth through each and every one of these factors.

2.1 Effects on Human Capital

The obvious and most direct relation between health and aggregate growth is through the effect of health on the labor productivity term, h: unhealthy citizens have less productive bodies, so the same amount of hours of work delivers less product. Sick children weigh less, are shorter, and have lower brain capacity. Deficits in iron and vitamin A are found to be associated with deficits in brainpower, and all of this tends to lower future productivity and wages. An immediate implication of this is that unhealthy individuals are more likely to be poor and their incomes are more likely to experience low growth rates. This effect is compounded by shorter life expectancy: poor individuals work fewer years and, therefore, are likely to earn lower lifetime wages.

This direct mechanism is important, but it is not the only one. A second channel through which health affects the productivity and growth of a family's, a society's, or a nation's income is through its effects on education and training, which is another component of h, human capital. Here, too, there are various operating channels. First, sick children tend to miss school more often so they get less education, which again, tends to make them poorer in the future. Edward Miguel and Michael Kremer's recent studies of schools in Kenya report interesting effects.[12] They randomly selected schools for treatment with deworming drugs—drugs against hookworm, roundworm, whipworm, and schistosomiasis. The results show that children in treated schools reduced their absenteeism by one quarter, with gains being especially large among the youngest children. The paper also shows untreated kids in treated schools tended to show lower absenteeism, which is thought to be an externality resulting from social norms: absenteeism is seen as socially bad if few people miss class. A drawback of the paper is that it fails to find any relation between deworming and academic test scores, which might be more a sign of the poor quality of education than of the small effects of health improvements on human capital.

Another channel through which health affects education is through the incentives of firms to train their workers: training tends to be directed away from the workers that have a higher probability of being sick. For example, Engel (2003) finds that African companies located in areas with high HIV/AIDS prevalence tend to reduce the amount of training they give to young workers and, instead, invest more on the training of older employees. The reason is that young workers are more likely to be infected and, therefore, the expected rate of return that firms get for the investment of their training is lower.

A fourth effect operates through the Beckerian quality–quantity of children trade-off.[13] Parents who know that their children are very likely to die early will tend to have many kids in order to end up with some adult descendants. The problem is that budget constraints cause the amount of resources devoted to each child to be lowered. As a result, each child ends up with lower education and human capital. Using the jargon of the human capital literature, parents substitute away from quality of children into quantity of children. To the extent that education is an essential determinant of the process of economic development, poor health tends to have an adverse effect on it.

A fifth effect of health on education operates through the incentives to educate and invest in health improvements. The rate of return to education is the present discounted value of all future wage differentials that educated people get relative to uneducated people

$$ROR = \sum_{t=0}^{N} \frac{(w_t^E - w_t^{NE})}{(1 + r)^t}, \tag{4}$$

where ROR is the rate of return to education, N is life expectancy, r is the interest rate, w^E is the wage rate of an educated citizen, and w^{NE} is the wage rate of a noneducated person. Notice that low life expectancy tends to reduce the rate of return and, as a result, the incentives to educate and accumulate human capital. For example, imagine that one more year of schooling gives a 15 percent higher initial wage (a number similar to what is found in the labor literature that estimates the rate of return to schooling). Imagine also that, following the endogenous growth literature, education also allows for a higher growth of wages, say 2 percent rather than 1 percent. Finally, consider a real interest rate is 1 percent. If the working life expectancy, N, is 20 years, then the overall rate of return to one year of schooling would be 32 percent. That is, the present discounted value of lifetime income of a person with one more year of education would be 1.32 times that of a person with one less year. If the working life expectancy were 50 years instead, the rate of return would be 55 percent.

The rate of return displayed in equation (4) assumes that poor and rich citizens have the same life expectancy. If rich people happen to enjoy a higher life expectancy, then the rate of return is much higher. For example, imagine that the working life expectancy is 50 years for the rich and 20 years for the poor, then the rate of return to education is 387 percent.

Finally, health has effects on the education of children through the death of parents. The process of education requires many inputs: teachers, materials, student's time, schools, and so on. One of the most important inputs of this process is parental (and especially maternal) time. The guidance, financial protection, support, and even knowledge provided by parents is key in the process of educating the children. A big problem is that the recent AIDS pandemic has left more than 14 million orphans in Africa alone. These children have to grow up without the guidance and without the financial protection and moral support supplied by parents. We should remember that these children tend to live in countries with very weak governments and without welfare. Thus, public schooling and public protection are out of the question for them. Among their feasible alternatives (which include child prostitution, enrollment as child soldiers, or concubines of soldiers in some war), work is the most attractive. As a result, their education opportunities are greatly reduced.

2.2 Effects on Health

The complementarity between health and schooling exists also between different kinds of health investments. Dow, Phillipson, and Sala-i-Martín (1999) argue that, since individuals cannot die twice, competing risks imply that individuals will not waste resources on causes that are not the most immediate, but will make health investments so as to equalize cause-specific mortality.[14] Analyzing data from one of the most important public health programs ever introduced, the Expanded Program on Immunization (EPI) of the United Nations in Malawi, Tanzania, Zambia, and Zimbabwe, they find evidence for the existence of such complementarities, involving causes that are not biomedically, but behaviorally, linked. In particular, they find that if using the tetanus vaccine simply reduces death, then it should decrease mortality by 1 percent. However, they estimate declines significantly larger. They also estimate larger birthweights and lower mortality rates six months down the road, phenomena for which there is no direct medical pathway. Their conclusion is that when mothers observe lower probability of infant death due to neonatal tetanus vaccination, their reaction is a superior investment in other kinds of health. This is another example of how input complementarities have potentially large effects on incentives.

2.3 Effects on Physical Capital

The third set of channels through which health affects output, income, productivity, and ultimately, growth, operates through the accumulation of physical capital, K. Citizens who expect to live long after retirement tend to have strong incentives to save and invest (this is what macroeconomists call life-cycle savings). If life expectancy happens to be close to sixty years of age, people do not expect to live many years in retirement and, as a result, their incentives to save are greatly reduced.[15] Thus, through its adverse effect on life expectancy, poor health will tend to reduce national savings and investment.

A second effect on physical capital comes from the complementarities across inputs. If human capital is complementary to physical capital, then there is little incentive to invest in physical capital when human capital is low. For example, firms do not want to invest in countries where the labor force is unhealthy, uneducated, or untrained (and we have already argued that unhealthy citizens will tend to have less education and training). Multinational corporations are pulling out of Botswana, even though this has been the most successful country in Africa over the last four decades. The reason is that the spread of AIDS forces firms to train several workers for every position since trained workers are likely to be infected in the near term and firms cannot afford not to have a trained person in every position.[16] This, of course, increases the training costs substantially and reduces profitability. The result is that firms find it unprofitable to remain in Botswana and decide to leave the country. AIDS reduces corporate profits in another important way: absenteeism to attend funerals. Funeral absenteeism is reaching such proportions that many firms have had to restrict their workers to attending only the funerals of their most direct relatives.

The effect of health on physical capital can also be found through public investment: governments of countries with widespread epidemics see their budgets so stressed by health outlays that they have had to stop investing in physical infrastructures. Public capital slowly deteriorates and this reduces the rate of return of complementary private physical capital (e.g., the rate of return to a truck depends on the quality of the road). This in turn, lowers the incentives to invest in both human and physical capital.

A third channel is found in what can very well be called a "private poverty trap." Many poor citizens who live in countries where there is no public health or where private insurance is hard to get, are often forced to spend their life savings in an attempt to cure a member of the family that falls ill. Sometimes, this forces the children out of school and into the labor force and, therefore, the health problem ends up affecting the wealth of the family and the ability to earn income in the future.

2.4   Effects on Aggregate Efficiency

Finally, health has a direct effect on efficiency, the term that we labeled A in the production function reported in equation (3). The aggregate efficiency of the economy depends on the business activities that citizens decide to undertake. Sometimes, the choice is affected by the health conditions of the region in which they live.

A simple model of a health-poverty trap   One example of this effect can be found in Ethiopia, where there are many wealthy regions irrigated by lakes. People can choose to live in these fertile areas but there is a problem: mosquitoes. In particular, the mosquito *anopheles gambiae* that transmits the plasmodium protozoa that cause malaria. Mosquitoes tend to live near lakes. In tropical regions, mosquitoes live sufficiently long so as to have time to transmit the plasmodium. This is not the case in nontropical zones, which explains why malaria exists only in tropical areas of the world. In countries like Ethiopia, living near the lakes means suffering a high risk of infection. The alternative is to move to drier land where there are no mosquitoes and, therefore, lower the risk of getting malaria. The problem is that these drier regions are less fertile. This choice also tends to lead to another kind of poverty trap. An easy way to analyze this phenomenon is through a simple model of economic growth.[17] Imagine that a nation has access to two production functions. One is depicted in equation (3), where the productivity level, A, is assumed to be very low. The other production function is given by a linear technology with high productivity:

$$Y = BK, \tag{5}$$

where $B > A$. In order to use the productive technology represented by equation (5), a fixed cost, F, has to be paid (this could be identified with the eradication of malaria, for example). Graphically, we depict these two production functions (in per-capita terms) in figure 4.1.

Notice that the more efficient technology does not start at the origin because, in order to use it, we need to pay the fixed cost F. Thus, it

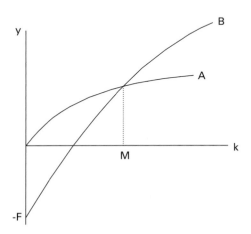

Figure 4.1
The model with different production functions.

intersects the vertical axis at $-F$, as shown in figure 4.1. For low levels of capital, the nonproductive technology given by equation (3) delivers more output. For economies with capital per person above M, the more productive production function delivers more output. Knowing this, producers will choose to use the "bad" technology when k is low and the more productive technology when $k < M$. In other words, the "effective" production technology is the outer envelope of the two production functions combined.

The fundamental growth equation of Solow–Swan, which describes the growth rate of capital for economies with constant savings rates, is

$$\gamma = sf(k)/k - (\partial + n), \tag{6}$$

where s is the savings rate, n is the population growth rate, and δ is the depreciation rate.[18,19] The second term in equation (6) is not a function of k so it can be depicted as a horizontal line in figure 4.2, given that both the depreciation rate and the rate of population growth are assumed to be constant. The first term is the constant savings rate times the average product of capital. If the effective production function is the outer envelope of the two production functions, then the average product of capital diminishes for low levels of capital, it increases for intermediate levels, and it stays constant for high capital-labor ratios. Thus, the savings line, (which is the constant savings rate times the average product of capital) is depicted in figure 4.2 as a curve that first declines, then increases, and finally becomes horizontal.

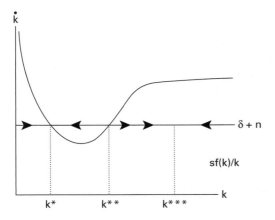

Figure 4.2
A poverty trap.

According to equation (6) the Solow–Swan theory of growth suggests that the growth rate of the economy is the vertical distance between the two lines. Growth is positive for all economies with a level of capital below k^*. The growth rate is negative for economies located between k^* and k^{**}, and it is positive for all economies above k^{**}. The implication is that *all* economies to the left of k^{**} will end up with a capital stock equal k^*, stagnated forever with zero growth. In other words, economies will end up being "sucked" into this low level of capital and that is why it is called a poverty trap. Economies to the right of k^{**} will end up with perpetual growth. The reason why the poverty trap exists is that poor countries who do not have enough initial wealth prefer to use "bad technology" because they cannot afford to pay the fixed cost. This leaves them with small productivity, small output, and small ability to grow. They end up not generating enough saving and investment to escape the trap, so they remain poor forever (that is, they fall into the poverty trap). This fall is caused by the fact that citizens react to the existence of malaria by using a more inefficient technology.

Institutions   This model shows that health problems leading to the choice of a nonproductive production function can end up condemning the country to a poverty trap. In a recent paper, Acemoglu, Johnson, and Robinson (2001, 2002) argue that poor health not only leads to a bad choice of production functions but that it can even lead to the wrong choice of institutions.[20] Indeed, they argue that the colonial powers of the sixteenth through nineteenth centuries chose which institutions to be implemented in the colonies based on its disease environment. The argument is that, when they found the land to be inhospitable, they chose to set up extractive institutions. That is, institutions that were right for "stealing" resources from the colony. These institutions may not have been right for the maintenance of property rights and economic prosperity, but they cared little because they did not plan to send many of their citizens and their families to colonize territories that were inhospitable from a public health point of view. Extractive institutions were enough for those colonies. Those institutions were, of course, later inherited by the independent countries once the colonial powers left. And it is precisely those institutions that today prevent these countries from achieving economic development.

At the other end, they chose to set up wealth-inducing institutions (with rule of law, property rights, etc.) wherever they found the land to be hospitable enough so that they were willing to send their own citizens and their families. Those "good" institutions were inherited by the newly independent nations and this explains why these countries have grown much faster on average than their "extractive" counterparts. Thus, the disease environment of the past had important effects on current institutions and, as a result, important consequences on current growth potential.

Finally, another effect of health on efficiency can appear through social unrest. Empirical evidence suggests that health inequality leads to less social cohesion and a larger probability of revolution, the collapse of the state, and widespread poverty. Social unrest, violence, and fractionalization have been shown to be important determinants of economic growth.[21]

3   What to Do

In section 1 we showed how poverty tends to affect health. In section 2 we argued that bad health tends to cause poverty and to slow down the process of economic growth and development. This two-way causation suggests that there is what could be called a health-poverty trap in the sense that one problem cannot be solved without simultaneously solving the other. If the mutual causality between health and education incentives is true, providing a good education system will not have the desired positive effects on growth unless we increase health and life expectancy. The reason is that children will have little incentive to attend school. And the reverse is also true: solving a particular health problem may not help much if the people who receive the intervention remain poor. Hence, action needs to be taken to solve simultaneously the problems of poor health and poor economic conditions. This section provides some guidelines on what might be done.

Promoting health   To promote health, we need to work on two main fronts: micro actions and macro actions. At the microeconomic level, we need widespread vaccination programs. Humanity has eradicated smallpox, nearly eradicated polio, and is making progress in measles. We need to continue to provide the vaccines that now exist. We also need to invest in hospitals, doctors, and general care. We need to keep making progress in making sanitation and clean water more widely available.

At the macroeconomic front, we need to provide the incentives to invest in pharmaceutical research and development. In this, we need to confront the usual time-inconsistency dilemma. Our patent system has worked well and we need to maintain it. The main engine of the patent system is the potential profits to be made by the inventor if he or she succeeds in creating a new vaccine or medicine. We need to realize that, at the end of the day, the new product will have to be invented by firms. If the intellectual property rights of those firms have to be protected, the desired vaccines will never be invented.

The problem is that, once the vaccine or the pills have been invented, we will want to supply them to the poorest citizens of the planet at affordable prices. Notice that this second objective contradicts the first one: if we want to induce the inventor to invest in R&D, we have to promise him that he will have the monopoly (the patent) in the supply of his invention, and he will charge high prices for the vaccine. If, on the other hand, we want the vaccine to be affordable to the poor, we need it to have a low price. These two objectives seem to be mutually self-destructive. How can we induce inventors to invest in R&D and, at the same time, guarantee affordable prices for the poor once the vaccine is invented?

The expropriation policy that seems to be favored by some third-world countries, by some policy advocates, and by some nongovernmental organizations (NGOs) associated with the antiglobalization movement does not seem to get the correct solution. When President Mbeki of South Africa celebrated his victory over the pharmaceutical industry regarding his right to purchase antiretroviral pills from India and Brazil, it was not realized at the time that such a victory would end up having adverse effects on the poor.[22] The reason is that the antiretroviral pills that were "expropriated" are not the final cure for AIDS. In fact, it is possible that their effectiveness is limited in time because the virus mutates so fast. The problem with having expropriated medication from the pharmaceutical firms is that they now have little incentive to invest in R&D to find a vaccine, given they correctly anticipate that, when the vaccine is invented, it will also be expropriated.

The true solution to the problem needs to both guarantee property rights (and, thus, the profits for researchers) as well as low prices for poor consumers. One proposal on the table involves dual pricing. That is, selling the vaccines at marginal cost in poor countries and at monopoly-patent prices in rich countries. In general, dual pricing is very dangerous because it may induce a widespread black market.

A clever solution that might work is Michael Kremer's proposal of an R&D fund financed by rich countries.[23] The idea is that rich countries should donate money to a fund that guarantees that the money received will be used to purchase vaccines at patent prices. These vaccines will then either be donated to poor countries or sold at marginal cost. Since the inventor will receive the monopolistic price, he has a large incentive to perform R&D and come up with a vaccine that prevents AIDS or malaria. Thus, we satisfy the first objective by solving the incentive problem and inducing the desired effort to invest in R&D. On the other hand, since the price at which the vaccines arrive in poor countries is either zero or marginal cost, the drugs are affordable to the poor, which is the second objective. Thus, Kremer's vaccine fund solves the two seemingly incompatible problems at once. Effort needs to be made by the governments of the rich countries to supply the necessary funds to implement this clever idea.

Promoting growth and poverty reduction   Many things need to be done in this area. It is important that poor countries set up institutions that promote a business environment that brings economic prosperity. These institutions should guarantee property rights, justice, and peace. Their governments need to be less corrupt, more transparent, and more accountable. We need to invest in education and create the environment where individuals have the incentives to become educated (that is, where they get a good return for their schooling). We need to promote markets: no economy has become rich and no country has ever been free and democratic without markets.

But free markets need to be promoted also in Europe, Japan, and the United States. In these countries, agricultural protectionism (and agricultural subsidies) induces poverty in the third world. We need to keep promoting foreign direct investment, which is the ultimate source of technological diffusion. And all of this needs to be done by keeping in mind that poverty reduction is crucial: if the poor do not actively participate in the process of welfare improvement, all programs are likely to collapse.

Obviously, some of this process will require international aid. Aid from the rich countries needs to include the reduction of their protectionist policies. It also needs to include additional money. Rather than burying resources in old projects that never worked, most of the aid should go to solve the one problem that poor countries cannot solve on their own: R&D. Thus, aid money should be redirected from current (inefficient) projects to the Kremer vaccine funds.

Although rich country and multilateral institutions can and should play a role in the process of growth and development of poor countries, most of the effort will have to be undertaken by their political and economic leaders. A lot of the problems they suffer from are self-inflicted and they will not get out of the hole until they deal with those (the devastating wars of Africa are a case in point). In fact, blaming the agricultural policies of the rich has now become the norm among African politicians and are often used as an excuse not to introduce the necessary reforms or implement the necessary policies.

In this regard, I have some doubts about the real desire of the political and economic elites of those countries to reform their institutions and adopt the correct policies. The reason is that they tend to do very well under the status quo. If we look at the evolution of the distribution of income of African countries we will see something very surprising: whereas the poor are becoming poorer, the rich are becoming richer. Figure 4.3, for example, shows the evolution of the distribution of income in Nigeria between 1970 and 1998.

We see that the income of the majority of Nigerian citizens falls over time. In other words, the distribution of 1998 lies to the left of that of 1970. But notice that this is not true for *all* citizens. In fact, the top 20 percent of the distribution shifts to the right, which suggests that the

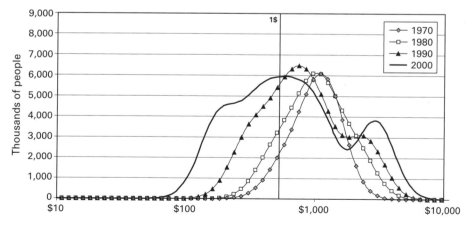

Figure 4.3
The distribution of income in Nigeria between 1970–1998.

richest Nigerians have been getting richer over the last 30 years. The problem is that the decisions need to be made by the political and economic elites, and those are the people at the top 20 percent. And if the leaders of poor countries do not want to introduce reforms, reforms will never be introduced.

4 Conclusions

This chapter discusses the mechanisms through which health affects poverty and poverty affects health. This two-way causation generates what can be called a health-poverty trap, a trap from which it may be very hard for poor countries to escape.

We argued that the citizens of poor countries have little resources and incentives to improve the state of their health. We also argued that poor health has adverse effects on the growth potential of a country. These effects occur through the process of education and training, through the effects on other diseases, through the accumulation of physical capital, and through the efficiency of the economy.

In order for a country to escape the health-poverty trap, health and poverty problems need to be solved simultaneously. Rich countries and donors can help by opening up their economies and by redirecting their aid to R&D funds. Poor countries also need to change their policies and introduce market-friendly institutions.

Acknowledgments

I thank the Centre de Recerca en Economia de la Salut at Universitat Pompeu Fabra, the "unrestricted educational grant from the Merck Foundation Company," Spain's Ministerio de Ciencia y Tecnología through grant SEC2001-0674 and the Pan American Health Organization for financial support.

Notes

1. See Sachs 2001.

2. This formula is exact if the patent is perpetual and the flow of profits is constant. If, more realistically, the patent has a finite lifetime, then the rate of return is slightly more complicated, although it still relates positively to the expected flow of future profits and negatively to the interest rate.

3. The recent literature on economic growth (sometimes called endogenous growth literature or new growth literature) emphasizes endogenous R&D as the main engine of economic growth. See Romer 1990, Aghion and Howitt 1992, or Grossman and Helpman
1991. For a technical and long survey of this literature, see Aghion and Howitt 1998 or
Barro and Sala-i-Martín 2003.

4. See Sachs 2001.

5. See, for example, Kiros and Hogan 2001 for empirical evidence on this for Africa.

6. See Dow, Phillipson, and Sala-i-Martín 1999.

7. In many African regions, people believe that AIDS and other sexually transmitted
diseases can be cured by having sex with virgin girls. Thus, girls are forced to have
sex with infected males, a phenomenon that tends to reinforce the spread of the
disease.

8. AIDS is now spreading rapidly through various regions of Asia, including India,
China, and some of the republics of the former Soviet Union.

9. Doppelhofer, Miller, and Sala-i-Martín 2004.

10. See Schultz 1962 and Becker 1993.

11. Artadi and Sala-i-Martín 2003.

12. Kremer and Miguel 2001.

13. Becker and Lewis 1973.

14. Dow, Phillipson, and Sala-i-Martín 1999.

15. This comes purely from the transversality condition of a life-cycle model with no
altruism: a person with a final horizon optimally chooses to leave no assets at time of
death. If wages increase with age, the optimal pattern of savings over the life cycle is to
borrow when young and to spend savings when older, leaving exactly zero assets at
death. See Modigliani and Ando 1963.

16. As mentioned earlier, Engel 2003 shows that another response to this problem is to
train older workers who are less likely to become infected.

17. See Barro and Sala-i-Martín 2003 for a more detailed description of this model.

18. See Solow 1956 and Swan 1956.

19. See Barro and Sala-i-Martín 2003 for a derivation of this result.

20. See also Easterly and Levine 2002.

21. See Doppelhofer et al. 2004.

22. The World Trade Organization allows third-world nations to produce their own
generics in case of an emergency. It does not allow them to import generics from other
countries. Of course, many of them do not have a pharmaceutical industry capable of
producing them. Thus, the debate is whether these countries can, in case of a crisis, purchase generic drugs from other poor countries.

23. See Kremer 2001.

References

Acemoglu, D., S. Johnson, and J. Robinson. 2001. The Colonial Origins of Comparative Development: An Empirical Investigation. *American Economic Review* 91: 1369–1401.

———. 2002. Reversal of Fortune: Geography and Institutions in the Making of the Modern World Distribution of Income. *Quarterly Journal of Economics* 117 (4): 1231–1294.

Aghion, P., and P. Howitt. 1992. A Model of Growth through Creative Destruction. *Econometrica* 60: 323–351.

———. 1998. *Endogenous Growth Theory*. Cambridge, Mass.: The MIT Press.

Artadi, E. V., and X. Sala-i-Martín. 2003. The Economic Tragedy of the Twentieth Century: Growth in Africa. Working paper no. 9865 (July), National Bureau of Economic Research, Cambridge, Mass.

Barro, R. J., and X. Sala-i-Martín. 2003. *Economic Growth*, second edition. Cambridge, Mass.: The MIT Press.

Becker, G. S. 1993. *Human Capital*. Chicago: University of Chicago Press.

Becker, G. S., and Lewis. 1973. On the Interaction between Quantity and Quality of Children. *Journal of Political Economy* 81 (part II): 279–288.

Doppelhofer, G., R. Miller, and X. Sala-i-Martín. 2004. Determinants of Long-Term Growth: A Bayesian Averaging of Classical Estimates (BACE) Approach. *American Economic Review* 94 (4): 813–835.

Dow, W., T. Phillipson, and X. Sala-i-Martín. 1999. Health Investment Complementarities under Competing Risks. *American Economic Review* 89 (5): 1358–1371.

Easterly, W., and R. Levine. 2002. Tropics, Germs, and Crops: How Endowments Influence Economic Development. Working paper no. 9106 (August), National Bureau of Economic Research, Cambridge, Mass.

Engel, R. C. 2003. Life, Death, and Human Capital: Essays on How African Firms and Workers Are Responding to the HIV/AIDS Crisis. Ph.D. dissertation, Columbia University, New York.

Grossman, G., and E. Helpman. 1991. *Innovation and Growth in the Open Economy*. Cambridge, Mass.: The MIT Press.

Kiros, G.-E., and D. P. Hogan. 2001. War, Famine, and Excess Child Mortality in Africa: The Role of Parental Education. *International Journal of Epidemiology* 30: 447–455.

Kremer, M. 2001. Creating Markets for New Vaccines. Part I: Rationale. In *Innovation Policy and the Economy*, vol. 1, ed. Adam B. Jaffe, Josh Lerner, and Scott Stern. Cambridge, Mass.: The MIT Press, pp. 35–72.

Kremer, M., and E. Miguel. 2001. Worms: Education and Health Externalities in Kenya. Working paper no. 8481, National Bureau of Economic Research, Cambridge, Mass.

Modigliani, F., and A. Ando. 1963. The Life Cycle Hypothesis of Saving. *American Economic Review* 53 (1): 55–84.

Romer, P. 1990. Endogenous Technological Change. *Journal of Political Economy*, part II, 98 (5): S71–102.

Sachs, J. 2001. Macroeconomics and Health: Investing in Health for Economic Development. Report of the Commission on Macroeconomics and Health. Geneva, World Health Organization, pp. 1–213.

Schultz, W. T. 1962. *Investment in Human Beings.* Chicago: University of Chicago Press.

Solow, R. 1956. A Contribution to the Theory of Economic Growth. *Quarterly Journal of Economics* 70 (February): 65–94.

Swan, T. W. 1956. Economic Growth and Capital Accumulation. *Economic Record* 32: 334–361.

5   Human Development Traps and Economic Growth

David Mayer-Foulkes

Modern economic history is characterized by a tremendous development in human capabilities that plays an important part in long-term economic growth. The extent of this improvement in human well-being has been ascertained only recently. Population-wide improvements in health status over the last 200 years amount to qualitative improvements beyond what was thought possible contemporaneously or even recently. Life expectancy in developed countries has risen from 40 to 80 years, stature has risen between 12 and 17 centimeters, and weight has almost doubled.[1] Even today we find it hard to believe that our children could expect to live to 100.[2] Together with these achievements, there have been tremendous rises in human capabilities associated with education and probably cognitive development. At the economywide level, increased health and life expectancy raise the returns for all types of investment. This leads to faster capital accumulation and triggers the tremendous explosion in knowledge and technology.

These discoveries lead to a more dynamic conception of human development than was current just one or two decades ago. Human capabilities increase with the income, technology, and social organization of the society of one's birth. The intergenerational nature of human development, and the slow rate of transition that market failures in human capital investment impose, take on an important role. Indeed, the first question in a dynamic conception of human development is: what happened in human history that led from a millenary period of stagnation to these achievements linked to modern economic growth?

To answer this question, it is necessary to think of thresholds, multiple steady states, and prolonged transitions. For example, Galor and Weil (2000), accounting also for the demographic transition, describe

stagnation as a Malthusian steady state with low incentives for human capital accumulation, in which slow technological change leads to
population growth without an attendant equilibrium in per-capita income. A slow increase in the rate of technological change eventually
makes this steady state unstable. The economy transits through a post-
Malthusian period to one of modern economic growth, a steady state
with high human capital and low population growth. More recent
explanations argue instead that slow technological change eventually
triggers a transition from an equilibrium with low life expectancy to
one with higher life expectancy in which the skills and knowledge that
make economic growth possible accumulate (Cervellati and Sunde
2002; Mayer-Foulkes 2003a). Another explanation invokes the search
for appropriate institutions, with success leading to a transition from
stagnation to growth (Kremer, Onatski, and Stock 2001). Lucas (2000)
argues that the exit from stagnation and subsequent convergence to
modern economic growth will account for much of what will be observed in the twenty-first century.

Since some countries developed before others, a second question
posed by a dynamic conception of human development is, what happened in stagnant countries once the leading countries developed?
Has the multiple steady-state structure persisted? Has a new one
appeared? How does human development interact with economic
growth?

This chapter begins by reviewing historical and macroeconomic evidence on the magnitude of the role of nutrition and health in long-term
economic growth. Then, it makes use of the research results from several papers by the author to address these questions, in two parts. The
first part gives macroeconomic evidence that prolonged transitions
involving, first, human development barriers in nutrition and health,
and second, barriers to productivity growth, continue to occur in the
present day. The second part discusses theoretical models for these
human development barriers and turns to microeconomic evidence
for the role of health in human development, including evidence for
present-day low human accumulation traps.

The theoretical finding shows that human development can be
thought to be subject to a sequence of market failures. These give rise
to dynamic poverty traps under which long-term cross-country growth
is characterized by stratification and transition. The microeconomic
finding supports the presence of human capital accumulation barriers
or traps involving 90 percent of the Mexican population, consistent

with the theoretical model. The intergenerational impact of early child development on adult education, and therefore on adult income, has a magnitude commensurate with the one found for the long-term historic and macroeconomic impact of nutrition and health on economic growth.

1 The Role of Health in Long-Term and Cross-Country Growth

It was Fogel's Nobel Prize–winning work that first brought out the extent of long-term changes in nutrition and health and their importance for long-term economic growth. Using nineteenth-century data on weight, stature, and mortality, Fogel (1991, 1994a, 1994b, 2002), and Fogel and Wimmer (1992) were able to establish that weight and stature have undergone secular increases of such a degree that they bring into question current standard tables of normalcy in height and weight. By setting up caloric national accounts (which include data on caloric and protein availability per capita), Fogel estimated that one-third of economic growth in Great Britain over two centuries was due to an increase in the work delivered by the human machine. These findings constituted a challenge: if nutrition, or alternatively a broad conception of health including nutrition, plays such an important long-term role, what is the role of health in economic growth today? Through what mechanisms? Further historical evidence of the importance of health for economic growth was provided by Arora (2001). Using sixty-two health-related time-series studies for nine advanced economies over the last 100–125 years, Arora finds that in the cointegrated relation between health and income, innovations in health lead to economic growth, and not vice versa. These variables account for between 26 and 40 percent of total income growth.

A series of macroeconomic cross-country studies also mostly found evidence for a significant impact of life expectancy on economic growth (Barro 1991; Barro and Lee 1994; Barro and Sala-i-Martín 1995; Barro 1996; Bhargava et al. 2000; Easterly and Levine 1997; Gallup and Sachs 2000; Sachs and Warner 1995, 1997; Caselli, Esquivel, and Lefort 1996 are notable exceptions). The impact of health on income is an important policy issue that has motivated research at the World Health (1999a, 2001) and Pan American (Mayer-Foulkes et al. 2001) Organizations. The first set of studies finds that the burden of disease has a very substantial impact on poverty, strongly affecting development and economic growth through a diverse set of channels. In the second set of studies, significant long-term (25- to 30-year) impacts of life expectancy on economic growth are found, using data panels on the Mexican states (Mayer-Foulkes 2001a) and Latin American countries (2001b). Their cumulative impact also adds up to about one third of economic growth. By studying the productivity gains associated with stature rises in Korea and Norway, Weil (2001) arrives at similar magnitudes for the contribution of health to economic growth.

None of these studies, however, is designed to distinguish whether there are qualitative differences in how health affects growth across countries. In a careful panel study of growth effects taking account of heterogeneity, endogenity, and reverse causality, Bhargava (2001) finds that adult survival rates lead to growth in low-income countries. This is consistent with a recent study by Arcand (2001) on the role of nutrition in growth. That study finds evidence for a low-nutrition trap by comparing a group of low-income countries not experiencing convergence, for whom nutrition is important for growth, with a high-income group experiencing convergence, for whom nutrition is not important for growth. Both studies are consistent with the global divergence found in Mayer-Foulkes (2002c), in which countries with low life expectancy also experience low rates of growth and are only just beginning to emerge from stagnation.

Turning to the dynamics of life expectancy instead of income, for which many more countries have data, leads to a remarkable finding (Mayer-Foulkes 2002b).[3] The cross-country distribution of life expectancy is clearly twin peaked in both 1962 and 1997 (figures 5.1.1, 5.1.2). But half of the countries in the lower peak shifted to the upper peak within this period of time. Thus three groups of countries can be defined; those remaining in the lower peak, those changing to the higher peak, and those in the higher peak throughout. The lower group has semistagnant life expectancy. The higher group has high and improving life expectancy, and the middle group can be thought to be in a rapid transition from semistagnant, low life expectancy to high life expectancy. Each of these groups can be shown to be β-conditionally convergent. The phase diagram for life-expectancy dynamics between 1962 and 1997 (figure 5.2.1 without the shading) forms an inverted "U" pattern corresponding perfectly with transition dynamics from a low to a high equilibrium with a high transition rate in between. At low levels of life expectancy, growth can be either high or low; at medium levels of life expectancy, improvement follows a high transition

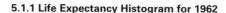

5.1.1 Life Expectancy Histogram for 1962

5.1.2 Life Expectancy Histogram for 1997

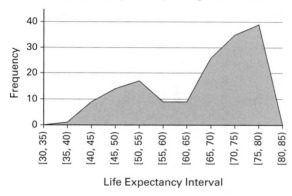

Figure 5.1.1, 5.1.2
Cross-country life expectancy (159 countries). Source: Mayer-Foulkes 2002b.

rate; and at high levels, the negative gradient of convergence to a high-equilibrium level becomes apparent. Thus the dynamics of stagnation to growth continued to be present in human development during the latter part of the twentieth century.

What about income per capita? When we examine the cross-country phase diagram of economic growth, is convergence apparent? Or, is there evidence for emergence from stagnation to growth? Is there additional stratification? It will become apparent that an answer to these questions is established more clearly by using the cross-country information contained in both income and life expectancy.

In asking whether there are complex dynamics in cross-country income (or income and life expectancy), what we are asking is if a characteristic shape or functional relation can be detected in the phase diagram (or diagrams). Thus an appropriate method is to cluster the data points in the phase diagrams in order to detect any shape that may be present.

This is done in Mayer-Foulkes 2005a,b in two different ways. The first uses an algorithm for fuzzy clustering (Bezdeck, Ehrlich, and Full 1984; Zimmermann 1996). This has the advantage, compared to hard clustering, of producing unique results. A parameter yielding a low level of fuzziness is used since countries are usually thought of as belonging wholly to a single dynamict of economic growth. The second uses a hard clustering technique.[4]

The fuzzy clustering is performed separately into two up to nine clusters, and is performed using life expectancy and income data both separately and jointly.[5] In every case, the cluster centers lie on an inverted U shape (figure 5.2.1). As noted above, this shape describes the emergence in life expectancy from a low to a high equilibrium. In the case of income, however, the expected shape for the emergence from stagnation to growth, as described in general terms for example by Lucas (2002), is an inverted U with a somewhat higher right leg representing a positive steady-state rate of growth. We find that the income cluster centers lie on the first half of such an inverted U, representing a transition for income in which the initial divergence has not been mitigated by convergence. When five or more clusters are used, though, an additional group of countries undergoing an especially fast transition is detected, which does converge to higher-income countries. Further subdivision does not uncover additional features in the phase diagram (figure 5.2.2).

The second clustering approach separates the phase diagram into five groups, but uses a hard-regression-clustering technique taking advantage of a wider set of countries for which either the income or the life expectancy data are complete.[6] The choice of five groups is used because it is the smallest number of clusters for which the main features of the phase diagram appear, as we just saw, and because it allows the subdivision of the higher life expectancy group mentioned above (Mayer-Foulkes 2002b) into developed, fast-growing, and undeveloped countries. The resulting phase diagrams are shown in figures 5.3.1 and 5.3.2, and the corresponding trajectory diagrams are shown in figures 5.4.1 and 5.4.2.

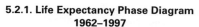

5.2.1. Life Expectancy Phase Diagram
1962–1997

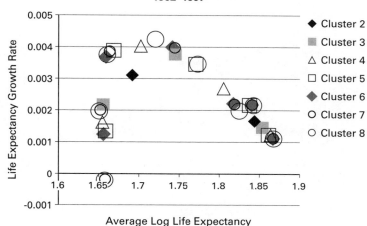

5.2.2. Income per Capita Phase Diagram
1960–1995

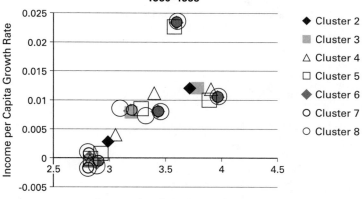

Figure 5.2
Cluster centers of joint income per capita and life expectancy fuzzy clusterings (into 2 to 8 clusters). Source: Mayer-Foulkes 2005a.

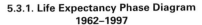

5.3.1. Life Expectancy Phase Diagram
1962–1997

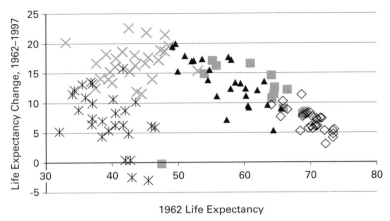

◇ Group 1   ■ Group 2   ▲ Group 3   ✕ Group 4   ✻ Group 5

5.3.2. Income per Capita Phase Diagram
1960–1995

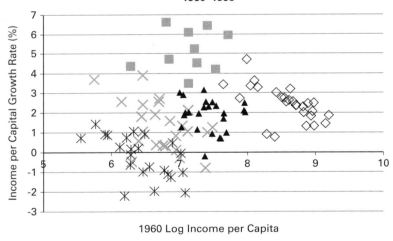

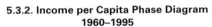

◇ Group 1   ■ Group 2   ▲ Group 3   ✕ Group 4   ✻ Group 5

Figure 5.3
Hard joint regression clustering of income per capita and life expectancy trajectories.
Source: Mayer-Foulkes 2005a.

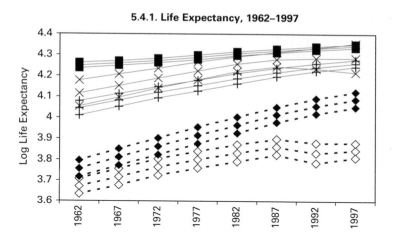

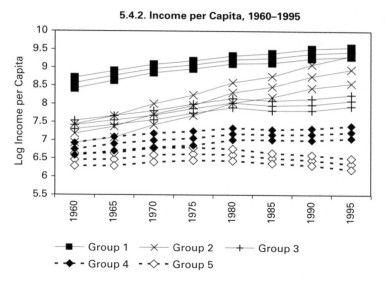

Figure 5.4
Average income per capita and life expectancy trajectories for the 5 groups in the hard joint regression clustering (3 standard deviation corridors). Source: Mayer-Foulkes 2005a.

Again, figure 5.3.1 shows the emergence from stagnant life expectancy. In the case of income, a portion of the initial, increasing branch of an inverted U representing the emergence from stagnation to growth is visible in figure 5.3b, consisting of groups 1, 3, 4, and 5. This phase diagram has as an additional feature the exceptionally fast transition of group 2. Looking at figure 5.4.2, although it is apparent that group 3 is growing slower than group 1, group 2 is bridging the gap between groups 3 and 1. Thus we have evidence for three steady states: development (group 1), semidevelopment (group 3), and semistagnation (group 5), with groups 2 and 4 following transitional paths between them. We can conclude descriptively that: (1) In the present day, group 5, the bottom tier of countries, is semistagnant rather than stagnant, presenting improvements in life expectancy. Average income has decreased, however, probably due to catastrophes involving war and AIDS. (2) Countries that recently emerged from semistagnation appear to have overcome a barrier, and fairly rapidly achieved substantial levels of life expectancy and medium levels of income, reaching a state of semidevelopment. (3) Countries that reached full development during the period, such as some of the Asian tigers, Spain and Portugal, achieved this through a further fast transition, appearing to overcome a high productivity barrier.

This evidence supports the view that the process of emergence from stagnation to modern growth, which lies at the origin of the great divergence, continues to this day. However, further stratification has emerged. The observed large-scale steady states do not only correspond to stagnation (or semistagnation) and sustained modern growth (or development). A further steady state, semidevelopment, has appeared in between.

The following three recent models give a technological explanation for such a stratification. Howitt and Mayer-Foulkes (2005) show that if R&D is distinguished from implementation, three convergence clubs can arise, corresponding to R&D, implementation, and semistagnation (a steady state growing at a lower rate than the leading edge technology). Acemoglu, Aghion, and Zilibotti (2002) show that institutional problems can keep a group of countries away from the frontier, thus explaining the stratification of the growing economies. Aghion, Howitt, and Mayer-Foulkes (2005) construct another three-club model in which credit constraints cause a lower group of countries to stagnate and a middle group of countries to grow with constrained innovation and lower income. Meanwhile, the higher group is not credit constrained and leads technological growth. The paper presents empirical evidence on the impact of financial development on convergence and nonconvergence.

Other explanations for varying long-term growth performances across countries are based on institutional differences between countries that lead to different incentives for human capital accumulation and technological change. For example, Engerman and Sokoloff (2002) argue that initial inequality due to different historical, geographical, and cultural conditions put Latin America on a path with less equality in income and worse institutions than the United States, and has therefore followed a lower development trajectory. As mentioned before, Kremer, Onatski, and Stock (2001) measure the emergence from stagnation in terms of success in the form of appropriate institutions.

In summary, this section presents evidence showing that nutrition and health improvements contribute both to levels of economic growth and, at lower incomes, to rates of economic growth. At lower levels of income, lack of nutrition and health thus prevent the emergence from stagnation or semistagnation to modern economic growth. Econometric techniques that can distinguish qualitatively between different patterns of growth show that the emergence from stagnation to modern growth continues today in both human development and income. Once a critical level of health has been reached, further progress takes place rather rapidly toward a state of semidevelopment characterized by a higher life expectancy but only medium income and education. Thus there is evidence of barriers to human development (e.g., market failures in human capital investment, low availability of employment, inadequate public institutions, and low levels and quality of urbanization), whose possible reasons will be explored below. Similarly, countries that have achieved full economic development have tended to do so in rapid transitions, appearing to overcome barriers to high productivity. These surely involve human capital accumulation in the form of skills and knowledge and institutional change fostering efficient economics and equality.

2 Some Theory and Microeconomics of Human Development Barriers

Over the last two centuries, the great leaps in human development have occurred selectively across countries. Although some countries have accumulated human and physical capital as well as knowledge, others have remained nearly stagnant or experienced only a medium level of growth. The convergence predicted by models with perfect markets has not occurred. The question therefore arises: what has prevented economic growth? Why have some countries remained stagnant? Why have others achieved only a medium level of growth? Why are some countries so poor while others are so rich?

Explanations of growth based on perfect market models are left with no alternative but to appeal to the institutional and cultural differences between countries—the model parameters—to fit the data. However, the social infrastructures these allude to are also endogenous. It is hard to believe that institutional, cultural, and social barriers would be able to successfully resist market and social pressures for human well-being and economic productivity, unless they were buttressed by strong economic forces, such as market failures, holding back convergence and creating deficient equilibria.[7]

The main explanations that have been proposed for slow human development involve market failures in human capital investment. Other kinds of human development barriers that might occur may involve problems in other aspects of the economy, such as the availability of employment ensuring the widespread availability of food (Sen 1999), adequate institutions ensuring the sufficient supply of public health goods, and sufficient levels and quality of urbanization to lower the costs of sanitation and health, a process that may have significant fixed costs and requires sufficiently equitable institutions.

In the previous section, macroeconomic evidence was presented for the presence of human development barriers to growth. Also, historical and macroeconomic evidence was given for the important role of nutrition and health in long-term economic growth. In this section I focus on theoretical explanations for these barriers based on market failures. These models are intergenerational by nature and account for failures in human capital accumulation including nutrition and health. I propose a model showing a dynamic, low human-capital trap that slows growth and induces stratification and transition. I then give microeconomic evidence for economywide failures in health and education investment in Mexico that are consistent with this model, and whose magnitude is commensurate with the long-term effects of health on economic growth.

2.1 Theoretical Models of Human Development Barriers

Several kinds of barriers to human capital accumulation have been modeled theoretically. At low levels of income, the efficiency theory of wages addresses the possibility of a low labor productivity trap due to low nutrition (e.g., Leibenstein 1957; Mazumdar 1959; Mirrlees 1975; Stiglitz 1976; Bliss and Stern (1978a,b); Dasgupta and Ray 1984, 1986; Dasgupta 1991). Econometric evidence for this theory has documented the substantial effects of nutrition on labor productivity (for surveys see Barlow 1979; Martorell and Arroyave 1988; Strauss 1985; Srinivasan 1992; Behrman and Deolalikar 1988). For later stages where education becomes increasingly important, Galor and Zeira (1993) have modeled low-schooling traps. They show that increasing returns in skill acquisition may lead to multiple equilibria in the presence of credit constraints to human capital accumulation. Under these conditions the distribution of human capital is an important determinant of the pattern of economic development (Galor and Tsiddon 1997). In relation to education, Azariadis and Drazen (1990) show that increasing social returns to scale in the accumulation of human capital may also lead to multiple equilibria. Educational market failures are also present in developed countries. Durlauf (1996) and Benabou (1996) show that in the United States, choice of neighborhood according to the availability of quality education may lead to persistent income inequality. Recent models include the relationship between education and health. Galor and Mayer-Foulkes (2002) show that the threshold requirements in nutrition and health for the acquisition of education may lead to persistent educational inequality at both low and high levels of education. Unequal distribution of social capital and early child nurture and stimulation may also be involved in low human-capital accumulation traps. These are noticeably prominent in families with low levels of income and education and are not significantly improved through the school system (Van Der Gaag 2002).

These and other theoretical models, and the empirical work surrounding them, lead to the proposition that *human development is subject to a sequence of market failures as the development process proceeds*. As each new generation is born, society's wealth, technology, and institutional endowment allow the children of well-to-do families to achieve higher levels of human capability and knowledge. Children of poorer families will achieve only what is allowed by a lower level of nutrition, health, and education, because of the presence, for example, of a credit constraint. One generation later, greater wealth, technology, and institutional capacity may be achieved, based on the new generation's human capital. However, unequal human capital investment will occur again, at a somewhat higher level and for perhaps somewhat different reasons. The distribution of nutrition, health, education, and income will be characterized by a *dynamic trap* in which poorer families cannot catch up with richer families, even though their income rises with time. This model, characterizing the relation between human development and economic growth, is proposed in Mayer-Foulkes 2003a. During the period through which human development occurs, stratification and transition characterize cross-country economic growth. When some further market failure is introduced, growth dynamics are further stratified. Credit constraints or knowledge barriers to technological change, as well as multiple institutional steady states (in which the low equilibrium is characterized by an unequal distribution in which the rich hold power and do not invest in public programs for the human development of the poor) are examples of such barriers. In these models, three steady states with two transitional trajectories can arise, consistent with the empirical findings in figures 5.4.1 and 5.4.2.[8]

2.2 Nutrition, Health, and Economic Growth: Microeconomic Evidence

The inclusion of nutrition and health investment in an integral conception of human capital has led to a body of empirical research documenting their role. Research has included the study of such indicators as height, weight, and body mass index, and their relation to nutrition, morbidity, and mortality.

Schultz (1997) and others have developed the econometric tools necessary to deal with the problems of endogeneity and heterogeneity that abound in this area of study. It is now well established that nutrition and health contribute to labor productivity (e.g., Schultz 1992, 1997, 1999; Thomas, Schoeni, and Strauss 1996; Strauss and Thomas 1998; Savedoff and Schultz 2000). Knaul (2000) obtains similar results using the age of menarche as a health indicator. However, the magnitudes found for the effects of health on productivity in these studies are smaller than those found in historical and macroeconomic studies.

The effects of health and nutrition on education have been documented in some detail in an attempt to detect specific links that may be addressed cost effectively (World Bank 1993). Temporary hunger, malnutrition, parasite load, micronutrient deficiencies, infections, and untreated sensory impairment are significantly related to worsened general conceptual and cognitive performance indicators, including problem solving, mental agility and capacity, absenteeism, underenrollment, and attrition. According to Levinger (1994), 42.8 percent of the children under 5 in twenty-one Latin American countries show moderate and severe stunting, a clear sign of malnutrition that is likely to be associated with poorer educational performance.

Stature is known to be determined early in life and is a predictor of lifelong health and longevity (Schürch and Scrimshaw 1987; Steckel 1995). This has led to a focus on early childhood development, particularly the combination of physical, mental, and social development in the early years of life. The biological mechanisms through which these interconnections occur, and their impact on school performance, IQ, improvements in practical reasoning, eye and hand coordination, hearing and speech, reading readiness, and the crucial rapid development of the brain have been documented in detail (Van Der Gaag 2002). Early childhood development is also considered worthy of major attention by developed countries such as Canada.[9]

A related line of inquiry is the investigation of the *gradient* of adult health with respect to income. Disentangling the underlying causal channels has presented a major challenge to microeconomic research. Recent work by Case, Lubotsky, and Paxson (2002) finds that important causal mechanisms may occur through the impact of household wealth on childhood health, which in turn affects adult income and health.[10] This result is strengthened and corroborated in a later, long-term study on a cohort of British children born in 1958 (Case, Fertig, and Paxson 2003). It is found that "controlling for parents' incomes, educations and social status, ... children who experience poor health have significantly lower educational attainment, and significantly poorer health and lower earnings on average as adults."

These findings emphasize the importance of child nutrition and health as a focal point for the intergenerational transmission of wealth. Parental health, education, and income all impinge on the realization of their children's capabilities, and these in turn determine their future, health, education, and therefore income. One of the main channels through which parental endowments affect their children's future performance is through their cumulative and successive impact on the children's nutrition, health, cognitive development, and motor skills, and hence on their scholastic performance (and other learning) and young adult health. This mechanism matches the poverty trap modeled by Galor and Mayer-Foulkes (2002).[11] Is it possible to find evidence for an actual poverty trap?

In a recent paper, Mayer-Foulkes (2003b) uses data from a Mexican health survey, ENSA 2000, including educational and income indicators to find evidence for just such a trap.[12] First, Mincerian econometric estimates including health as indicated by stature, schooling, and experience, show that adult human capital has increasing returns in Mexico.[13] Some of the literature on the subject argues that these may result from recent promarket reforms such as NAFTA (De Ferranti et al. 2003, chap. 3; Hanson and Harrison 1995; Revenga 1995; Tan and Batra 1997; Cragg and Epelbaum 1996; Robertson 2000; Scott 2003). Second, probit estimates show that childhood nutrition and health (also indicated by stature), as well as parental education, have substantial and possibly increasing returns in the acquisition of education, as measured by school permanence. This finding parallels the one mentioned above for the role of childhood health as a determinant of the adult health gradient along income (Case, Lubotsky, and Paxson 2002; Case, Fertig, and Paxson 2003).

Together, these results establish the presence of the following ingredients for a dynamic or static poverty trap: increasing returns to education in adult income (see figure 5.5); substantial and possibly increasing returns to children's health in the acquisition of education (see tables 5.1 and 5.2); increasing returns to parental education in the acquisition of education; and finally, transmission from parental wealth, health, and education to the health and education of their young. These increasing returns hold at educational levels above those achieved by most of the population.

By appealing to theory it is not hard to argue, in the presence of unrealized investment opportunities, that some or all of the following market failures must be present: imperfect parenting, such as parents unavailable, malnourished, unhealthy, or unknowledgeable; credit constraints, or the impossibility to acquire nutrition, health, education, and complementary inputs to education such as capital, social capital, or early childhood development; uncertainty or lack of information on the benefits of early childhood development with respect to nutrition, health, and education; excessive impatience due to poverty; and finally, unavailability of the necessary public goods of health or education.

Thus, 90 percent of the population in Mexico is unable to invest optimally in human capital. The presence of market failures slows the intergenerational dynamics of human capital accumulation, causing at minimum a prolonged transition. If the failures are strong enough, then multiple steady states, and therefore a static or dynamic poverty trap, may arise. To test for this possibility, Mayer-Foulkes (2003b) also conducts a transition matrix analysis for the intergenerational dynam-

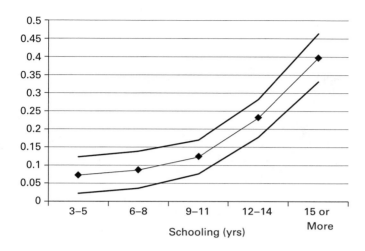

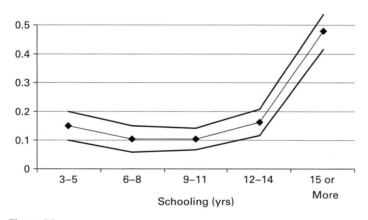

Figure 5.5
Human capital marginal returns for adult income by educational level (2 standard deviation corridors for OLS coefficients). Source: Mayer-Foulkes 2003b.

Marginal human capital returns associated with three-year periods of schooling.
Source: Mayer-Foulkes 2003b.

Table 5.1
Mean marginal probabilities associated with 1 cm stature increase in probit estimates for school permanence.

Estimate:	Lower to Higher Primary	Primary to Lower Secondary	Lower to Higher Secondary	Higher Secondary to Tertiary
Male	*0.042*	**0.042**	**0.039**	0
Female	0.039	*0.038*	**0.073**	0
Joint	**0.00019**	**0.05485**	**0.12043**	0.055015

(1% confidence in bold, 10% confidence in italics.)
Note: In joint regression for deciding to go beyond 15 yrs. of schooling, stature above 154.86 predicts decision perfectly.
Source: Mayer-Foulkes, D. (2003b).

Table 5.2
Increase in probit estimates for school permanence by gender and household head schooling.

Household Head Schooling	Female			Male		
	Lower to Higher Primary	Primary to Lower Secondary	Lower to Higher Secondary	Lower to Higher Primary	Primary to Lower Secondary	Lower to Higher Secondary
1–3	0.026	0.029	0.056	0.032	0.035	0.026
4–6	0.025	0.028	0.055	0.030	0.033	0.031
7–9	0.017	0.023	0.057	0.020	0.027	0.032
10–12	0.011	0.019	0.055	0.013	0.013	0.030
>12	0.004	0.010	0.031	0.005	0.008	0.016

Source: Mayer-Foulkes 2003b.

ics of schooling. The results support the presence of a barrier to education at 9 years of schooling (see figures 5.6.1 and 5.6.3). Further, a numerical policy experiment shows that a 5 centimeter average increase in stature (which South Korea achieved in one generation) would overcome this barrier and lead to higher levels of education (see figures 5.6.2 and 5.6.4).[14] This shows that the early childhood development deficit measured by low statures has substantial effects that are commensurate with the long-term effects of nutrition and health on economic growth found in historical and macroeconomic studies.

Further evidence for the presence of a human capital accumulation trap in Mexico is provided by Mayer-Foulkes (2004), who shows that the distribution of households according to spouses' education is twin

Women

5.6.1. Extrapolating From Current Transition.

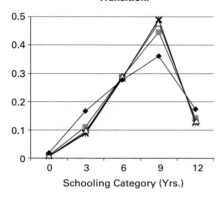

5.6.2. Increasing Education Probability According to 5 cm Increase in Stature.

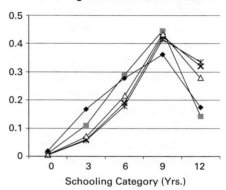

Men

5.6.3. Extrapolating From Current Transition.

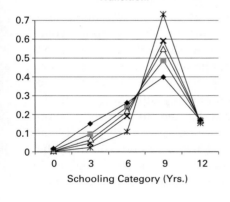

5.6.4. Increasing Education Probability According to 5 cm Increase in Stature.

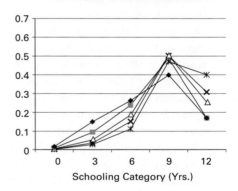

—◆— Grandparents   —■— Adults
—△— Children   —✕— Future Grandchildren
—✳— Ergodic

Figure 5.6
Distribution of educational levels according to transition matrix analysis. Source: Mayer-Foulkes 2003b.

peaked, according to data in ENSA 2000 and in the ENIGH surveys for 1984, 1989, 1992, 1994, 1996, 1998, and 2000. In effect, the population classifies itself through marriage into two social classes, those with a complete lower secondary education or less, and those with 15 or more years of education; 75 percent of the population is situated in the lower class.

In summary, this section has described the presence of a sequence of market failures in the process of human development and has outlined a model in which these market failures make economic growth slower, stratified, and transitional. Then, microeconomic evidence supporting the model has been presented for the case of Mexico. Early childhood development has been found to be an important channel through which nutrition and health affect economic growth.

3   Conclusions

Human capabilities have increased substantially in the last two centuries, thanks mainly to improved nutrition and health. These play an important part in the emergence from stagnation to modern economic growth. Contemporary macroeconomic studies find that health indicators have substantial effects on levels of income and, for poorer countries, on their rates of growth. Moreover, we show that the emergence from stagnation to modern growth continues to occur by examining the cross-country dynamics of life expectancy. When the dynamics of income and life expectancy are examined jointly, further stratification is found. First, where the basic barriers to human development have been overcome, life expectancy has risen fairly rapidly and a state of semidevelopment has been achieved. Second, countries that have achieved full economic development have done so through rapid transitions from semidevelopment, apparently overcoming barriers to high productivity.

Theoretical explanations for barriers to human development involve market failures due to increasing returns to nutrition, to education, credit constraints, threshold nutrition requirements for achieving higher levels of education, and other mechanisms involving societal provision of basic goods and services. Because of its intergenerational nature, the process of human development is characterized by a sequence of market failures at different stages of development. In turn, human development depends on and facilitates economic growth, technological change, and institutional development. Thus, the presence of a dynamic human development trap slows down economic growth. Consequently, economic growth across countries is characterized by stratification and transition.

Microeconomic evidence for the effects of health on labor productivity has been weak. Instead, it has been found (in developed countries) that an important component of the correlation between adult income and health is explained by an intergenerational mechanism: the impact of child health, itself determined by family endowments, on future adult health, education, and income.

In a study on Mexico, microeconomic evidence is found for an economywide intergenerational human capital accumulation trap: 90 percent of the population is unable to invest optimally in education, which presents increasing returns. Moreover, early childhood development, as measured by stature, is found to have an important impact on school permanence. An intergenerational transition analysis for education gives evidence for a barrier at 9 years of education, which would be overcome given a 5-centimeter rise in stature, an increase that was achieved in a generation in Korea. In addition, the distribution of households according to spouses' education is twin peaked. The population classifies itself through marriage into two social classes, those with a complete lower secondary education or less, and those with 15 or more years of education.

The intergenerational nature of human capital accumulation lies at the core of the process of human development. Policies aimed at diminishing market failure and achieving long-term growth must include a focus on the intergenerational dynamics of human capital accumulation.

Acknowledgments

The author acknowledges the leadership of Sir George Alleyne and the enthusiasm and support of the Pan American Health Organization, for conducting research on the impact of health on economic growth, and on the possible existence of health-related poverty traps.

Notes

1. Specifically, average stature rose from 164 to 181 cm. in Holland between 1860 and 2002 and from 161 to 173 cm. in France and Norway between 1705 and 1975. Weight rose from 46 to 73 kg. in Norway and France between 1705 and 1975. Life expectancy rose from 41 to 78 years in England between 1841 and 1998 and from 29 to 60 years in

India between 1930 and 1990. Schooling rose from 2.3 to more than 11 years in England between 1800 and the 1980s. (Fogel 2002; Cervellati and Sunde 2002).

2. Life expectancy for older people has continued to increase in recent years without any apparent signs of slowing down.

3. We use the World Bank database. The balanced 5-yearly life expectancy panel for 1962–1997 contains 159 countries.

4. "Global Divergence," silver medal in the Growth, Inequality, and Poverty category of the Global Development Awards at the Fourth Global Development Conference, Cairo, 2003.

5. The sample used for fuzzy clustering consists of 104 non-exsocialist non-petroleum-dependent countries for which a balanced sample in both income and life expectancy data is available. The data used for the clustering algorithm is the average log level and average period growth for income and life expectancy. The fuzziness parameter m is set at 1.5.

6. The sample used for the hard-regression-clustering algorithm consists of 126 non-exsocialist non-petroleum-dependent countries for which either a balanced sample for income (108 countries) or life expectancy (121 countries) is available.

7. Of course, an economic trap may have institutional ingredients.

8. The model can also explain Lynn and Vanhanen's (2002) findings on the cross-country correlation between wealth and IQ.

9. The government of Canada has been providing CAN$2.2 billion over five years, beginning in 2001–2002, to help provincial and territorial governments improve and expand early childhood development programs and services (see http://socialunion.gc.ca/ecd_e.html).

10. This article was awarded the Eleventh Annual Kenneth J. Arrow Award for Best Paper in Health Economics.

11. This can also be thought of as a dynamic trap at a certain stage of human development.

12. Gold medal for Research on Development in Pro-Market Reform and the Poor category at the Fifth Global Development Network Conference, New Delhi, 2004.

13. See Zamudio 1999 and Mayer-Foulkes and Stabridis 2003 for similar findings.

14. The numerical experiment uses the coefficients in table 5.2.

References

Acemoglu, D., P. Aghion, and F. Zilibotti. 2002. Distance to Frontier, Selection, and Economic Growth. Working paper no. 9066, National Bureau of Economic Research, Cambridge, Mass.

Aghion, P., P. Howitt, and D. Mayer-Foulkes. 2005. The Effect of Financial Development on Convergence: Theory and Evidence. *Quarterly Journal of Economics* 120 (1).

Arcand, J.-L. 2001. Undernourishment and Economic Growth. In *The State of Food and Agriculture 2001*. Rome: Food and Agriculture Organization of The United Nations.

Arora, S. 2001. Health Human Productivity and Long-Term Economic Growth. *Journal of Economic History* 61 (3): 699–749.

Azariadis, C., and A. Drazen. 1990. Threshold Externalities in Economic Development. *Quarterly Journal of Economics* 5 (105): 501–526.

Barlow, R. 1979. Health and Economic Development: A Theoretical and Empirical Review. *Human Capital and Development* 1: 45–75.

Barro, R. 1991. Economic Growth in a Cross Section of Countries. *Quarterly Journal of Economics* 106 (2): 407–443.

———. 1996. Health and Economic Growth. Unpublished paper.

Barro, R., and G. Becker. 1989. Fertility Choice in a Model of Economic Growth. *Econometrica* 57 (2): 481–501.

Barro, R., and J. Lee. 1994. Losers and Winners in Economic Growth. In *Proceedings of the World Bank Annual Conference on Development Economics, 1993: Supplement to The World Bank Economic Review and The World Bank Research Observer*, edited by Michael Bruno and Boris Pleskovic. Washington, D.C.: The World Bank, pp. 267–297.

Barro, R., and X. Sala-i-Martín, 1995. *Economic Growth*. New York: McGraw-Hill.

Becker, G. S., and M. Murphy. 1990. Human Capital, Fertility, and Economic Growth. *Journal of Political Economy* 98 (5), part 2: S12–S37.

Behrman, J., and A. Deolalikar. 1988. Health and Nutrition. In *Handbook of Development Economics*, vol. 1, ed. H. Chenery and T. N. Srinivasan. Amsterdam: North Holland.

Benabou, R. 1996. Equity and Efficiency in Human Capital Investment: The Local Connection. *Review of Economic Studies* 63 (2): 237–264.

Bezdek, J. C., R. Ehrlich, and W. Full. 1984. FCM: The Fuzzy C-Means Algorithm. *Computers and Geoscience* 10 (2): 191–203.

Bhargava, A., D. T. Jamison, L. J. Lau, and C. J. L. Murray. 2000. Modeling the Effects of Health on Economic Growth. Unpublished paper.

Bhargava, A., D. T. Jamison, L. J. Lau, and C. J. L. Murray. 2001. Modeling the Effects of Health on Economic Growth. *Journal of Health Economics* 20 (3): 423–440.

Bliss, C., and N. Stern. 1978a. Productivity, Wages, and Nutrition. Part I: The Theory. *Journal of Development Economics* 5 (4): 331–362.

———. 1978b. Productivity, Wages, and Nutrition. Part II: Some Observations. *Journal of Development Economics* 5 (4): 363–398.

Case, A., A. Fertig, and C. Paxson. 2003. From Cradle to Grave? The Lasting Impact of Childhood Health and Circumstance. Working paper no. w9788, National Bureau of Economic Research, Cambridge, Mass.

Case, A., D. Lubotsky, and C. Paxson. 2002. Economic Status and Health in Childhood: The Origins of Gradient. *American Economic Review* 92 (5): 1308–1334.

Caselli, F., G. Esquivel, and F. Lefort. 1996. Reopening the Convergence Debate: A New Look at the Cross-Country Growth Empirics. *Journal of Economic Growth* 1: 363–389.

Cervellati, M., and U. Sunde. 2002. Human Capital Formation, Lifetime Expectancy, and the Process of Economic Development. IZA Discussion Paper Series no. 585, Institute for the Study of Labor, Bonn.

Cragg, M. I., and M. Epelbaum. 1996. Why Has Wage Dispersion Grown in Mexico? Is It the Incidence of Reforms or the Growing Demand for Skills? *Journal of Development Economics* 51: 99–116.

Dasgupta, P. 1991. Nutrition, Non-Convexities, and Redistributive Policies. *Economic Journal* 101–404 (January): 22–26.

Dasgupta, P., and D. Ray. 1984. Inequality, Malnutrition, and Unemployment: A Critique of the Market Mechanism. Stanford IMSS Technical Report (December).

———. 1986. Inequality as a Determinant of Malnutrition and Unemployment: Theory. *Economic Journal* 96-384 (December): 1011–1034.

De Ferranti, D., G. Perry, I. Gill, J. Guasch, W. Maloney, C. Sánchez-Páramo, and N. Schady. 2003. *Closing the Gap in Education and Technology.* World Bank Latin American and Caribbean Studies. Washington, D.C.: The World Bank.

Durlauf, S. 1996. A Theory of Persistent Income Inequality. *Journal of Economic Growth* 1: 75–94.

Easterly, W., and R. Levine. 1997. Africa's Growth Tragedy: Policies and Ethnic Divisions. *Quarterly Journal of Economics* 112 (4): 1203–1250.

Engerman, S., and K. Sokoloff. 2002. Factor Endowment, Inequality, and Paths of Development among New World Economies. Working paper no. 9259, National Bureau of Economic Research, Cambridge, Mass.

Fogel, R. W. 1991. New Sources and New Techniques for the Study of Secular Trends in Nutritional Status, Health, Mortality, and the Process of Aging. Working Paper Series on Historical Factors in Long Run Growth no. 26 (May), National Bureau of Economic Research, Cambridge, Mass.

———. 1994a. Economic Growth, Population Theory, and Physiology: The Bearing of Long-Term Processes on the Making of Economic Policy. *American Economic Review* 84 (3): 369–395.

———. 1994b. The Relevance of Malthus for the Study of Mortality Today: Long Run Influences on Health, Morality, Labour Force Participation, and Population Growth. In *Population, Economic Development, and the Environment*, edited by L. K. Kerstin and L. Hans. Oxford and New York: Oxford University Press, pp. 231–284.

———. 2002. *Nutrition, Physiological Capital, and Economic Growth.* Washington, D.C.: Pan American Health Organization and Inter-American Development Bank. Available at http://www.paho.org/English/HDP/HDD/fogel.pdf.

Fogel, R. W., and L. T. Wimmer. 1992. Early Indicators of Later Work Levels, Disease, and Death. Working Paper Series on Historical Factors in Long Run Growth no. 38 (June), National Bureau of Economic Research, Cambridge, Mass.

Gallup, J., and J. Sachs. 2000. The Economic Burden of Malaria. Working paper no. 52, Center for International Development, Harvard University, Cambridge, Mass.

Galor, O., and D. Mayer-Foulkes. 2002. Food for Thought: Basic Needs and Persistent Educational Inequality. Unpublished paper.

Galor, O., and D. Tsiddon. 1997. The Distribution of Human Capital and Economic Growth. *Journal of Economic Growth* 2 (1): 93–124.

Galor, O., and D. Weil. 2000. Population, Technology, and Growth: From Malthusian Stagnation to the Demographic Transition and Beyond. *American Economic Review* 90: 806–828.

Galor, O., and J. Zeira. 1993. Income Distribution and Macroeconomics. *Review of Economic Studies* 60 (1): 35–52.

Hanson, G. H., and A. Harrison. 1995. Trade, Technology and Wage Inequality in Mexico. Working paper no. 5110, National Bureau of Economic Research, Cambridge, Mass.

Howitt, P., and D. Mayer-Foulkes. 2005. R&D, Implementation, and Stagnation: A Schumpeterian Theory of Convergence Clubs. Forthcoming in *Journal of Money, Credit, and Banking.*

Knaul, F. 2000. Health, Nutrition, and Wages: Age at Menarche and Earnings in Mexico. In *Wealth from Health: Linking Social Investments to Earnings in Latin America*, edited by W. Savedoff and T. P. Schultz. Washington, D.C.: Inter-American Development Bank.

Kremer, M., A. Onatski, and J. Stock. 2001. Searching for Prosperity. Working paper no. 8250 (April), National Bureau of Economic Research, Cambridge, Mass.

Leibenstein, H. 1957. *Economic Backwardness and Economic Growth.* New York: Wiley.

Levinger, B. 1994. *Nutrition, Health, and Education for All.* New York: Education Development Center, United Nations Development Programme (UNDP). Available at http://www.edc.org/INT/NHEA/index.html.

Lucas, R. 2002. *Lectures on Economic Growth.* Cambridge, Mass.: Harvard University Press.

Lucas, R. E., Jr. 2000. Some Macroeconomics for the 21st Century. *Journal of Economic Perspectives* 14 (1): 159–168.

Lynn, R., and T. Vanhanen. 2002. *IQ and the Wealth of Nations.* Westport, Conn.: Praeger.

Martorell, R., and G. Arroyave. 1988. Malnutrition, Work Output, and Energy Needs. In *Capacity for Work in the Tropics*, ed. K. J. Collins and D. B. Roberts. Cambridge: Cambridge University Press, pp. 57–75.

Mayer-Foulkes, D. 2001a. The Long-Term Impact of Health on Economic Growth in Mexico, 1950–1995. *Journal of International Development* 13 (1): 123–126.

———. 2001b. The Long-Term Impact of Health on Economic Growth in Latin America. *World Development* 29 (6): 1025–1033.

———. 2002a. El Efecto Recíproco a Largo Plazo entre Salud e Ingreso: México, 1950–1995. *El Trimestre Económico* 69 (2): 251–278.

———. 2002b. Convergence Clubs in Cross-Country Life Expectancy Dynamics. In *Perspectives on Growth and Poverty*, edited by Rolph van der Hoeven and Antony Shorrocks. New York: United Nations University Press, pp. 144–171.

———. 2003a. Human Development and Economic Growth: From Stagnation to Stratified and Transitional Growth. Unpublished paper.

————. 2003b. Market Failures in Health and Education Investment for the Young, Mexico 2000. Available at http://www.gdnet.org/pdf2/gdn_library/awards_medals/2003/r_m/reforms_poor/mayerfoulkes.pdf.

————. 2004. The Human Development Trap in Mexico. Unpublished paper. Available at http://papers.ssrn.com/abstract=539082. SSRN's top ten download list for "Latin American Economic Recent Hits" (5/21/04) and "Economic Growth Recent Hits" (6/6/04).

————. 2005a. Global Divergence. Forthcoming in *Focus on Global Economics*, Nova Science.

————. 2005b. From Stagnation to Modern Growth—and Underdevelopment. Unpublished paper.

Mayer-Foulkes, D., and O. Stabridis. 2003. Estimaciones de los Rendimientos Privados a la Escolaridad y Cálculo del PIB Educativo para México. Unpublished paper.

Mayer-Foulkes, D., H. Mora, R. Cermeño, A. B. Barona, and S. Duryea. 2001. Health, Growth, and Income Distribution in Latin America and the Caribbean: A Study of Determinants and Regional and Local Behavior, in Investment in Health, Social, and Economic Returns. Pan American Health Organization Scientific and Technical Publication no. 582. Washington, D.C.

Mazumdar, D. 1959. The Marginal Productivity Theory of Wages and Disguised Unemployment. *Review of Economic Studies* 26: 190–197.

Mirrlees, J. 1975. A Pure Theory of Underdeveloped Economies. In *Agriculture in Development Theory*, edited by L. Reynolds. New Haven: Yale University Press.

Revenga, A. 1995. Employment and Wage Effects of Trade Liberalization: The Case of Mexican Manufacturing. Working paper no. 1524, Latin America and the Caribbean Region Policy Research, The World Bank, Washington, D.C.

Robertson, R. 2000. *Trade Liberalization and Wage Inequality: Lessons from the Mexican Experience*. St. Paul, Minn.: Macalester College.

Sachs, J., and A. Warner. 1995. Economic Reform and the Process of Global Integration. *Brookings Papers on Economic Activity* 1: 1–118.

————. 1997. Sources of Slow Growth in African Economies. *Journal of African Economies* 6 (3): 335–376.

Savedoff, W. D., and T. P. Schultz. 2000. *Wealth from Health: Linking Social Investments to Earnings in Latin America*. Washington, D.C.: Inter-American Development Bank.

Schultz, T. P. 1992. The Role of Education and Human Capital in Economic Development: An Empirical Assessment. Discussion paper no. 670, Economic Growth Center, Yale University.

————. 1997. Assessing the Productive Benefits of Nutrition and Health: An Integrated Human Capital Approach. *Journal of Econometrics* 77 (1): 141–158.

————. 1999. Health and Schooling Investments in Africa. *Journal of Economic Perspectives* 13 (3): 67–88.

Schürch, B., and N. S. Scrimshaw. 1987. *Effects of Chronic Energy Deficiency on Stature, Work Capacity, and Productivity*. Lausanne: International Dietary Energy Consultancy Group.

Scott, J. 2003. Poverty and Inequality. In *Strengthening the North American Community: NAFTA at Ten*, ed. S. Weintraub. Washington, D.C.: Center for Strategic and International Studies.

Sen, A. 1999. *Development as Freedom*. New York: Alfred A. Knopf.

Srinivasan, T. N. 1992. Undernutrition: Concepts, Measurement, and Policy Implications. In *Nutrition and Poverty*, edited by S. Osmani. Oxford: Clarendon Press, pp. 103–109.

Steckel, R. 1995. Stature and the Standard of Living. *Journal of Economic Literature* 33 (4): 1903–1940.

Stiglitz, J. E. 1976. The Efficiency Wage Hypothesis, Surplus Labor, and the Distribution of Income in LDCs. *Oxford Economic Papers (New Series)* 28: 185–207.

Strauss, J. 1985. The Impact of Improved Nutrition in Labor Productivity and Human Resource Development: An Economic Perspective. Discussion paper no. 494, Economic Growth Center, Yale University.

Strauss, J., and D. Thomas. 1998. Health, Nutrition, and Economic Development. *Journal of Economic Literature* 36 (2): 766–817.

Tan, H., and G. Batra. 1997. Technology and Firm Size–Wage Differentials in Colombia, Mexico, and Taiwan (China). *World Bank Economic Review* 11 (1): 59–83.

Thomas, D., R. F. Schoeni, and J. Strauss. 1996. Parental Investments in Schooling: The Roles of Gender and Resources in Urban Brazil. Working paper no. DRU-1303-NICHD. RAND Labor and Population Program, New York.

Van Der Gaag, J. 2002. From Child Development to Human Development. In *From Early Child Development to Human Development: Investing in Our Children's Future*, edited by M. E. Young, Washington, D.C.: Education Sector, Human Development Network, The World Bank. Available at http://www-wds.worldbank.org/servlet/WDSContentServer/WDSP/IB/2002/04/26/000094946_02041304004942/Rendered/PDF/multi0page.pdf.

Weil, D. N. 2001. Accounting for the Effect of Health on Economic Growth. Unpublished paper.

World Bank. 1993. *World Development Report 1993: Investing in Health*. Washington, D.C.: The World Bank.

World Health Organization (WHO). 1999. WHO on Health and Economic Productivity. *Population and Development Review* 25 (2): 396–401.

———. 2001. Macroeconomics and Health: Investing in Health for Economic Development. Report of the Commission on Macroeconomics and Health. Geneva: World Health Organization, pp. 1–213.

Zamudio, A. 1999. Educación y distribución condicional del ingreso: una aplicación de regresión cuantil. Working paper no. DE 163, Centro de Investigación y Docencia Económicas (CIDE).

Zimmermann, H. J. 1996. *Fuzzy Set Theory—And Its Applications*. Norwell, Mass.: Kluwer Academic.

6

Health, Education, and Economic Development

Edward Miguel

The current volume is evidence of the growing awareness within economics of the important connections between health and poverty in less developed countries. The aim of this chapter is to review recent evidence on one potential channel through which health may affect income: education.

Establishing evidence for a causal link of health on education may help to reconcile the seeming contradiction in existing empirical research that although the cross-country correlation between various measures of health status and income is extremely strong (Bloom and Sachs 1998), the microevidence on the impact of poor health on individual labor productivity (as measured by wages) conditional on education is often weak (Strauss and Thomas 1998). However, this does not mean that poor health status through life does not affect wages. Poor health could have a profound impact on lifetime earnings to the extent it affects educational attainment and skills acquisition, in light of the evidence linking education to wages in less developed countries (for recent evidence, see Duflo 2001). These links are likely to be particularly salient in sub-Saharan Africa, the poorest region and the one with the highest tropical disease burden.

Both child and parental health problems potentially affect schooling. Child health-education linkages are the first focus of this survey (section 1). To illustrate, children suffering from acute malaria, say, may be unable (or unwilling) to attend school, and even if they do attend, may have limited ability to focus on learning their lessons.

The second focus is the parental health channel, and in particular the impact of parent death—the most extreme parental health shock—on the schooling of their children (section 2). If parent mortality or morbidity reduces household income, it could affect the ability to invest in child education. This issue is of growing academic and public policy interest given the rapid rise in the number of orphans during the HIV/AIDS epidemic, especially in Africa.[1]

A brief overview of the main themes of this chapter is in order. A key point about existing work is that research progress in disentangling the causal relationships between health, education, and income has been slowed by econometric difficulties, primarily due to both endogeneity and omitted-variable biases (see Behrman 1996 and Strauss and Thomas 1998 for more comprehensive discussions). To illustrate, consider the case in which children with poor health and nutrition status also tend to have below-average school performance (in terms of school attendance, say) in a given sample.

One possible interpretation of this observed pattern is that poor health is the cause of higher absenteeism for these children. But a second plausible explanation is that these children come from households with unobservably lower socioeconomic status, and that this fact leads both to worse health and educational outcomes, or similarly, the children have parents with unobservably less interest in both their child's health and education, leading to a correlation between child health and education that is not causal. In many existing studies, it is difficult—or impossible—to distinguish between these two explanations, especially when the data used in the analysis consists of a single cross-section of observations.

One goal of this chapter is to focus on recent studies that have made credible attempts to resolve these central identification concerns, through the use of either innovative research designs—including social experiments and randomized evaluations—or rich datasets, especially panel (longitudinal) microdata. There is a growing body of such work, and increasingly solid evidence that both child health status and parent death can have a large impact on education—in particular, on school attendance and enrollment—across a range of less developed country settings. We begin with a discussion of child health and schooling.

1   Child Health and Schooling

1.1   Evidence from Less Developed Countries

There is growing evidence that poor health reduces hours worked, but the evidence on the relationship between current health and wages—and by extension, productivity—conditional on education is largely inconclusive (Strauss and Thomas 1998). The existing research is often difficult to interpret since most studies examine the cross-sectional correlation between current health status and labor market outcomes, and as such are subject to well-known omitted-variable (confounding) and endogeneity (reverse causality) biases.

The parallel nonexperimental research on the impact of child health on education (as surveyed in Behrman 1996) reaches similarly ambiguous conclusions.[2] To illustrate in nonexperimental empirical research without panel data, Glewwe and Jacoby (1995) present cross-sectional evidence that delayed school enrollment in Ghana is related to child growth stunting. However, despite their creative efforts to address omitted-variable bias—using household-fixed effects (in which siblings are compared), and mother's height as an instrumental variable—the identification strategy Glewwe and Jacoby employ is still subject to many of the same biases discussed above, and as such, their results are difficult to interpret. The use of longitudinal data can alleviate many of these estimation concerns by allowing researchers to control for unobserved time-invariant household characteristics—for instance, parent tastes regarding child health and education—although such studies are still prone to bias from unobserved time-varying characteristics.

Several studies use a longitudinal dataset from Cebu, Philippines and provide evidence that improved early childhood nutrition may translate into better educational and cognitive performance. For instance, Mendez and Adair (1999) examine the impact of stunting in the first two years of life on cognitive ability test scores and school enrollment at ages 8–11, and find strong evidence consistent with a large impact of improved nutrition on subsequent performance in Cebu. Glewwe, Jacoby, and King (2001) examine children from the same dataset and use a structural econometric framework that they argue partially addresses omitted-variable concerns using older sibling height at age 2 as an instrumental variable for the nutritional status of younger siblings when they reach primary school age. Glewwe et al. find that better nourished children enroll in school earlier, and learn more per unit of time in school. However, once again the possibility of omitted variables (confounders) that change over time—for instance, a common shock that affects both child health and schooling—may lead to bias and somewhat complicates interpretation of the results.

Alderman et al. (2001) also utilize a panel dataset, this time for rural Pakistan, and once again find that early childhood health and nutrition have large consequences for school enrollment. Their structural modeling approach uses price shocks (from when the children were of preschool age) as instruments, and they conclude that the effects of child health using this estimation approach are three times as large as one would find relying only on naïve observational estimates.

Of course, the ideal economics study should allow researchers to credibly estimate the impact of child health on both education and later life outcomes such as income. However, the literature on links between child health, nutrition, and long-run life outcomes is even less conclusive, mainly because of the almost complete lack of panel datasets that track individuals from childhood into adulthood in less developed countries. Yet the childhood years are often considered the most important for determining life outcomes, and thus bear most directly on the feasibility of using public policy—including child nutrition and health programs—to break the cycle of poverty.

We are aware of only one existing study that both (1) was conducted with an experimental design, and (2) has a long-run panel dataset that allows the authors to estimate the impact of child health on nutrition and long-run life outcomes: the Institute for Nutrition in Central America and Panama (INCAP) nutritional project in Guatemala (Martorell, Habricht, and Rivera 1995). The project randomly divided four study villages into two groups; two villages where children (and expecting mothers) received a high-energy, high-protein drink (called "Atole") and two villages where children received a low-energy, no-protein drink ("Fresco"). In follow-up studies conducted at least a decade after the end of the intervention, the research team found that treatment children in the Atole villages showed height and weight gains (Rivera et al. 1995), greater work capacity, especially among boys (Haas et al. 1995), and gains in certain cognitive measures that are likely to be linked to school performance (Pollitt et al. 1993).

This project is arguably the most convincing existing research to show that childhood nutrition and health affects subsequent life outcomes. However, despite its obvious strengths, this project also has several important methodological shortcomings. The most obvious weakness is the small sample size of only four villages and less than two thousand individuals. Moreover, several of the INCAP studies (including Haas et al. 1995, and Khan et al. 1995) apparently fail to account for the intracluster correlation of respondent outcomes within villages in their statistical analyses, probably leading them to overstate statistical significance. Another major concern is sample attrition. Attrition in the 1988 follow-up sample was 27 percent of the original sample, and there was sometimes limited success in obtaining survey consent even from the 73 percent of respondents who had not attrited (especially when blood draws were sought). Clearly, more research is needed to definitively document the impact of child health and nutrition gains on education and, ultimately, on adult living standards.

1.2 Worms and Schooling in Rural Kenya

In a recent paper, Miguel and Kremer (2004) focus on the educational impacts of treatment for intestinal helminth (worm) infection in Kenyan primary schools using a randomized evaluation methodology. The paper's experimental design, large sample size, and extensive outcome measures make it a particularly useful setting to explore links between health and schooling.

Worm infections—including hookworm, roundworm, whipworm, and schistosomiasis—are among the most widespread diseases in less developed countries: recent studies estimate that 1.3 billion people worldwide are infected with roundworm, 1.3 billion with hookworm, 900 million with whipworm, and 200 million with schistosomiasis. Infection rates are particularly high in sub-Saharan Africa (Bundy et al. 1998; World Health Organization 1993). The geohelminths—hookworm, roundworm, and whipworm—are transmitted through poor sanitation and hygiene, and schistosomiasis is acquired by bathing in infected freshwater. School-aged children typically exhibit the greatest prevalence of infection and the highest infection intensity, as well as the highest disease burden (since morbidity is related to infection intensity), due to a combination of high exposure and immunological factors (Bundy 1988).

The adverse short-run health and nutritional impact of worm infections on children are reasonably well understood: intestinal helminth infections often lead to iron-deficiency anemia, protein-energy malnutrition, stunting (a measure of chronic undernutrition), wasting (a measure of acute undernutrition), listlessness, and abdominal pain (Pollitt 1990), and may also make individuals more prone to other infections by weakening the immune system. If untreated, the infections may have more serious consequences in some cases, especially for schistosomiasis (Bundy 1994).

Intestinal helminths are treated using low-cost single-dose oral therapies appropriate for delivery at infrequent intervals of six months to a year (Bundy and Guyatt 1996). The broad-spectrum antihelminthic albendazole is used for the geohelminths and praziquantel for schistosomiasis. These drugs have only minor side effects (World Health Organization 1992). Medical treatment with albendazole and praziquantel is also inexpensive: a single yearly treatment of albendazole costs less than 50 cents per person per year and praziquantel costs roughly one dollar for a primary school pupil of average weight (Partnership for Child Development 1999). School-based deworming programs that use the existing school infrastructure to deliver anthelminthics have been identified as especially cost-effective in high-prevalence areas, as mass treatment eliminates the need for costly individual screening.

The educational impacts of deworming are considered a key issue in assessing whether the poorest countries should accord priority to deworming, but existing research on these impacts is inconclusive (see Dickson et al. 2000 for a recent survey). Yet the existing randomized evaluations on worms and education suffer from several important methodological shortcomings that may partially explain their weak results. First, existing studies randomize the provision of deworming treatment *within* schools to treatment and placebo groups, and then examine the impact of deworming on cognitive outcomes. However, the difference in educational outcomes between the treatment and placebo groups understates the actual impact of deworming if placebo-group pupils also experience health gains due to local treatment externalities (due to breaking the disease transmission cycle). Second, although existing studies report the impact of deworming on tests of cognitive performance (such as tests of recall), they typically do not examine other outcomes of interest to policymakers, including school attendance, enrollment, academic tests, or ultimately, labor market outcomes. Finally, none of the existing studies adequately addresses sample attrition, an important issue to the extent that deworming improves school enrollment.

The Primary School Deworming Project (PSDP) in Busia, Kenya offers an opportunity to evaluate the impact of a school-based health program on education (as well as later labor market, health, cognitive, and demographic outcomes in planned follow-up studies) within the context of a prospective study. The Kenyan nongovernmental organization (NGO) International Christelijk Steunfonds Africa (ICS) began carrying out the project in Kenya's Busia district—a densely settled farming region in western Kenya adjacent to Lake Victoria—in late 1997. The 75 schools participating in the program consist of nearly all the rural primary schools in the Budalangi and Funyula divisions in the southern Busia district, and contained 32,565 pupils at the start of the study. Baseline parasitological surveys conducted by the Kenyan Ministry of Health indicate that these two divisions had high rates of helminth infection, at over 90 percent. Using modified World Health Organization (WHO) infection thresholds (described in Brooker et al. 2000), over one-third of children in the sample had a "moderate to heavy" infection with at least one helminth at baseline. Primary-school pupils in Kenya range roughly from 7–17 years old.

In January 1998, the 75 schools were randomly divided into three groups (groups 1, 2, 3) of 25 schools each: the schools were first stratified by administrative subunit (zone) and by their involvement in other NGO assistance programs, and were then listed alphabetically and every third school assigned to a given project group. Due to the NGO's administrative and financial constraints, the schools were phased into the deworming program over the course of 1998–2001, and the order of phase-in was randomly determined, creating treatment and comparison groups (table 6.1). Group 1 schools began receiving free deworming treatment in 1998, group 2 schools in 1999, while group 3 schools began receiving treatment in 2001.[3] To illustrate, the project design implies that in 1998, group 1 schools were treatment schools while group 2 and 3 schools were the comparison schools, and in 1999 and 2000, group 1 and 2 schools were the treatment schools and group 3 schools were comparison schools. Group 1, 2, and 3 schools were in fact similar along nearly all baseline characteristics, indicating that the randomization was successful at creating comparable groups of schools.

The program led to immediate health gains: treatment schools showed significant reductions in the prevalence of moderate-to-heavy helminth infections (25 percentage points); a significant reduction in the proportion of children reporting being sick (in answer to the

Table 6.1
Busia, Kenya Primary School Deworming Project (PSDP) treatment schedule.

Year	Group 1 (25 Schools)	Group 2 (25 Schools)	Group 3 (25 Schools)
1998	Treatment	Comparison	Comparison
1999	Treatment	Treatment	Comparison
2000	Treatment	Treatment	Comparison
2001	Treatment	Treatment	Treatment

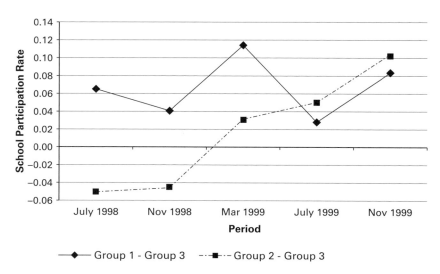

Figure 6.1
School participation rate (May 1998 to November 1999) in Busia, Kenya for girls under 13 years old and for all boys (Difference between group 1 and group 3 [solid line, diamonds], and difference between group 2 and group 3 [dashed line, squares]). Note: Group 1 began receiving treatment through the program in February 1998. Group 2 began receiving treatment through the program in February 1998.

question, "Were you sick during the past week?," from 45% to 41%); marginally significant gains in height-for-age Z-scores; and the proportion of children with severe anemia (Hb < 100 g/L) fell by half, from 4 percent to 2 percent.

In the paper's main finding, the intervention also reduced total school absenteeism by at least 7 percentage points—or one-quarter— in the first two years of the project (1998–1999), with particularly large school participation gains among the youngest primary school children. The school participation data were collected during unannounced school visits conducted by NGO enumerators, conducted approximately 4–5 times per year in each school. Figure 6.1 presents the time pattern of school participation in 1998 and 1999.

Younger children (grade 4 and below at baseline) had larger average school participation gains in the second year of the study (1999) than older children. These larger gains for the younger children are consistent with the fact that younger children typically have more intense worm infections than older children, and thus might be expected to show larger gains. There were similar school participation gains in

1998 among girls and boys, but girls showed considerably larger gains than boys in 1999. The school participation results are robust to the inclusion of individual and school controls, as expected when treatment is randomly assigned. In an instrumental variable specification—which implicitly assumes that all school participation effects work through the channel of reduced worm infection rates—we estimate that eliminating one moderate-to-heavy infection for one year boosts school participation by a fraction of 0.2 of a year.

In another important result, Miguel and Kremer (2004) find that deworming significantly reduces worm burdens and increases school participation among untreated children in treatment schools—including the older girls excluded from treatment—and among children in neighboring primary schools. Econometric identification of the cross-school treatment spillovers relies on the randomized design of the PSDP: conditional on the total local density of primary school pupils, there is random exogenous variation in the number of pupils assigned to deworming treatment through the program.

Identification of within-school externalities is not based on randomization, since pupils are selected into treatment, with 70–80 percent of eligible pupils receiving some treatment in a given year; however, the fact that new groups of schools are phased into deworming treatment in successive years allowed us to compare the 1998 outcomes of group 1 pupils who elected not to receive deworming treatment in 1998 to the outcomes of group 2 pupils who elected not to receive treatment in 1999 in order to estimate within-school externalities, partially addressing omitted-variable bias problems by comparing pupils who made the same treatment decision. The within-school externality in treatment schools (in the terms of the reduction of serious worm infections among untreated pupils) is over 70 percent as large as the overall effect of the program on treated pupils in the treatment schools—a large effect.

Failure to take these externalities (or spillovers) into account would lead one to substantially underestimate the cost effectiveness of deworming treatment: including the externality benefits of treatment, the cost per additional year of school participation is just $3.50, considerably less than the cost of any alternative method of increasing school participation of which we are aware (cf. Kremer 2003). Moreover, we find that internalizing these externalities would likely require not only fully subsidizing deworming, but actually paying people to receive treatment.

Yet we do not find any evidence that deworming increased either academic or cognitive test scores in Kenya. Deworming-treatment-effect point estimates are consistently near zero and statistically insignificant in the first three years of the program (1998–2000). This is consistent with other studies that concluded deworming has an immediate cognitive effect only for those with the heaviest worm burdens, or with other problems, such as severe undernutrition (Dickson et al. 2000).

However, this is not consistent with the Glewwe et al. (2001) study from the Philippines, which found that child health gains led to more learning per time spent in school. It is unclear exactly what the cause of this discrepancy is, although there are at least three possibilities. First, the deworming program in Kenya led to more crowded classrooms, and thus to potentially negative congestion effects for learning along the lines of Angrist and Lavy (1999); these may partially obscure the positive effects of deworming on learning in the treatment schools. Second, nonexperimental studies like Glewwe et al. and others may be suffering from omitted-variable bias (due to unobserved time-varying characteristics) that leads them to overstate the effect of health on learning. Third, the effects of health and nutrition gains on learning (as captured by tests) may differ between the Kenya and Philippines settings due to other factors, such as the quality of primary school instruction (for instance, the training of teachers or characteristics of the school curriculum), which could be complements to child health in the production of learning. Further empirical work is required to determine which of these explanations is correct.

Data from subsequent years of the Kenya project (2000–2002) have not been fully analyzed, but the preliminary results suggest that there were statistically significant educational attainment gains among girls in early treatment schools. To illustrate, girls initially in grades 5–7 in early treatment schools (groups 1 and 2) had attained nearly 0.2 more years of schooling through mid-2002 compared to girls in the late treatment (group 3) schools—a large impact—and this effect is statistically significant at over 90 percent confidence; by contrast, the gain for early treatment boys in the same grades is smaller and statistically insignificant.

Our results suggest that the impact of poor child health on educational attainment could account for part of the negative cross-country correlation between disease and income documented by Bloom and

Sachs (1998), among others. The finding that deworming treatment externalities are large also suggests an important role for public policy, especially given that nearly half of Africa's disease burden is due to infectious and parasitic diseases (World Health Organization 1999).

Yet the case for public subsidies would be considerably strengthened by further evidence on the long-run effects of deworming spillovers on adult labor market outcomes. The author and collaborators are currently collecting a new dataset, the Kenya Life Panel Survey (KLPS), in order to document the long-run impacts of the deworming program. The goal of that study is to resurvey a representative sample of 7,500 individuals from the baseline Kenya deworming (PSDP) sample many years after the start of the program as individuals enter adulthood, and assess the impact of the program on their labor market outcomes, fertility, marital choices, health (including mental health), cognitive skills, physical strength, and personal happiness, tracing out each step in the chain of causality—from child public health investments, to educational gains, to income and wellbeing later in life.

1.3   Anemia, Worms, and Preschool Participation in Delhi, India

A second project examines closely related issues in a different geographic setting (Bobonis, Miguel, and Sharma 2003). This study evaluates the impact of an NGO (Pratham, Delhi) preschool nutrition and health project in poor communities in eastern Delhi, India, which delivers a cheap package consisting of iron supplementation and deworming drugs to 2–6-year-old children through their existing preschool network. Approximately 68 percent of sample children were anemic (Hb < 11 g/dL) and 24 percent suffered from intestinal helminth (worm) infections at baseline in mid-2001. Anemia is among the world's most widespread nutritional problems, especially for children (Hall et al. 2001).

The 200 preschools in the study were randomly divided into three groups, and the schools were gradually phased into the program as it expanded over the course of two years. In the first year of the program, the group 1 preschools received the assistance package of iron supplementation (delivered to the schools by NGO field workers, and given to the children by teachers), deworming drugs (400 mg albendazole), and vitamin A, while the group 2 and 3 preschools received only vitamin A and served as comparison schools. In the second school year (2002–2003), group 1 and 2 preschools received the full package, while the group 3 schools served as the comparison group. This experimental design is thus very similar to the Kenya deworming project described above, and allows us to attribute differences between treatment and comparison schools to the health program rather than to omitted variables.

Existing results are described in an unpublished working paper. During the first year of the project, we find large gains in child weight—over 0.5 kg on average—in the treatment schools relative to comparison schools; estimated weight gains remain positive, although smaller and statistically insignificant, in the second year of the project. Most significantly for this chapter, average preschool participation rates increased sharply by 6.3 percentage points among assisted children over the two years, reducing preschool absenteeism by roughly one-fifth. (Unfortunately, we cannot decisively rule out that some of this effect is due to children attending school in the hopes of getting the iron pills, which were distributed daily at preschools in the weeks following health camps.)

Figure 6.2 presents the time pattern of program impacts, comparing group 1 to group 3 schools (diamonds) and group 2 to group 3 schools

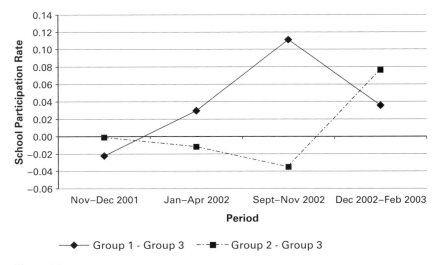

Figure 6.2
Pre-school participation rate (November 2001 to February 2003) in Delhi, India (Difference between group 1 and group 3 [solid line, diamonds], and difference between group 2 and group 3 [dashed line, squares]). Note: Group 1 began receiving treatment through the program in December 2001. Group 2 began receiving treatment through the program in November 2002.

(squares). Just as in Kenya, school participation rates increased sub-stantially in the months after schools were phased into the program: group 1 began receiving treatment in December 2001, and group 2 in November 2002.

Given the low cost of the intervention—less than $2 (USD) per child per year, on average—these results suggest that the package of iron supplementation and deworming is a highly cost-effective means of improving child school participation in a poor urban setting where anemia and worm infections are widespread. The results of Bobonis, Miguel, and Sharma (2003) thus largely confirm the earlier Kenya find-ings that child health gains translate into higher school participation. The demonstration that a nearly identical relationship holds in another geographic setting (urban India), with a younger age group and a dif-ferent health intervention, provides additional confidence that there exists a robust relationship between child health, nutrition, and school participation in poor countries.

However, note that the claim that improved health and nutri-tion boosts learning (as captured in academic test scores) is, at pre-sent, based solely on the results of nonexperimental studies, as in Glewwe et al. (2001). Due to the young age of the children in the urban India sample, it was not possible to estimate the effect of the program on academic performance. And unfortunately, unlike the rural Kenya study site, high rates of mobility in the dense urban com-munities of Delhi has made successful tracking of the study sample for follow-up tests logistically impossible given the project's financial resources.[4]

Randomized evaluations like those in Kenya and India provide particularly transparent and credible evidence to policymakers on pro-gram impacts, and have the potential to exert considerable influence on actual policy choices, as argued recently by Kremer (2003) and others. For instance, given the results presented in Bobonis et al. (2003), the Indian NGO that conducted this project is currently plan-ning to expand the preschool health model examined in Delhi to several other Indian cities. The school health program evaluated in Miguel and Kremer (2004) has recently been named a Kenya Ministry of Education "pilot site" for a future national program, and the NGO that conducted the Kenya project has included school health compo-nents in its projects elsewhere in Africa, including a districtwide school health project in Meatu, Tanzania.

2   Parent Death and Schooling

2.1   Evidence from Less Developed Countries

Understanding the impact of parent death on children has taken on a new urgency with the emergence of the global HIV/AIDS pandemic, especially for Africa, the poorest region and the region most affected by the disease. According to UNAIDS (2002), by 2001 12 percent of all children under the age of 15 years in sub-Saharan Africa had lost at least one parent, and the rate is forecast to continue rising rapidly. For instance, in the rural Kenyan setting in which the deworming study took place, and among the children who had been enrolled in primary school in 1998, by 2002 nearly 20 percent were orphans (either maternal or paternal), and a large proportion of them are likely to be AIDS orphans, given the estimated local adult HIV prevalence of 20–30 percent.

Several studies have examined the issue of parent death and child schooling in recent years, using a variety of empirical methods and data sources, and they yield divergent results. In what follows, in addition to summarizing the existing results, we focus on the methodological differences across studies that could be driving these different estimates. Then, in subsection 2.2, we present unpublished results from Evans and Miguel (2003), a study from rural Kenya that uses longitudinal data in an attempt to address some of the methodological weaknesses of existing work.

In particular, note that many existing studies consist of cross-sectional estimates of the observed differences between orphans and nonorphans at a single point in time, controlling for a limited set of currently observable child characteristics. The results of such studies may be misleading due to both omitted variables and endogeneity; in the absence of longitudinal data, it is impossible to know whether orphans and nonorphans were truly comparable before the parent death, and most significantly, current child and household characteristics used as regression controls may have themselves been affected by the death. Moreover, since parent death is relatively rare in most populations, few studies have sufficient statistical precision to reliably estimate moderate impacts.

The first two studies we focus on find that parent death does substantially reduce child school enrollment. Case, Paxson, and Ableidinger (2002) employed demographic and health surveys (DHSs) collected across 10 sub-Saharan African countries between 1992 and

2000 to estimate the impact of parent death on school enrollment. The large number of survey rounds (19 in all), combined with the relatively high incidence of parent death in their African sample, allowed them to precisely estimate its impact. Their main finding is that orphans are significantly less likely to be enrolled in school than nonorphans, and the result holds up even when including household-fixed effects: orphans are less likely to be enrolled in school than the nonorphans in their household. Part of this estimated effect is accounted for by the fact that orphans are more likely to stay with distant relatives than nonorphans, and they point to provocative theories suggesting that more distant relatives have fewer genetic "incentives" to care for these children. Case, Paxson, and Ableidinger (2002) find no significant difference in parent death effects between boys and girls.

Despite its many strengths, particularly its impressive data effort, the study has a number of limitations that complicate the interpretation of its findings. Foremost, because the data set consists of repeated cross-sections rather than a true panel, the study is unable to address obvious omitted-variable bias problems. Namely, it is unclear whether the estimates are capturing the impact of parent death, or rather the impact of being from the type of family where parents tend to die, perhaps because of particular health behaviors, or other unobserved characteristics (e.g., high discount factors). Although the DHS surveys do contain some household asset controls, this data is collected contemporaneously with the measurement of child orphan status and for that reason is potentially endogenous: households fostering orphans may choose to sell off some assets thus becoming poorer. It would be econometrically preferable to measure socioeconomic characteristics prior to the parent death. Finally, the DHS data gives no indication of how long a child has been an orphan.

Gertler, Levine, and Ames (2004) overcome some of the identification problems in Case, Paxson, and Ableidinger 2002 using panel data from Indonesia, and estimate similar parent death impacts. They use data from 600,000 households in Indonesia's National Socioeconomic Survey (SUSENAS) during the mid-1990s. This survey contains information on the occurrence of a first parent death within the twelve months previous to the survey. Thus they have individual-level panel data based on a recall of recent parent deaths, an improvement over several other studies. They are limited, however, by their inability to estimate the impacts of parent death over periods of time longer than one year.

Gertler, Levine, and Ames (2004) find striking effects in Indonesia: a parent death during the past twelve months leads to a doubling of the probability of a child dropping out of school that year. Recognizing the challenge that omitted-variable bias may pose, the authors use matching methods to create a comparison group of children from the same geographic area. One drawback to this technique is that current characteristics are again used to perform the matching, rather than characteristics previous to parent death, which would be ideal. Another limitation is the Indonesian setting, in which parent death is relatively rare, which makes it problematic to generalize findings to African settings, where parent death rates are much higher. Like Case, Paxson, and Ableidinger (2002), they find no robust differences in the impact of parent death by orphan or parent gender.

A number of earlier studies, however, do not find any evidence of large parent death impacts. Ainsworth, Beegle, and Koda (2002) analyze a true panel dataset of 1,213 children in northwestern Tanzania—an important methodological improvement over most other studies in this literature—and find much weaker impacts of parent death on schooling than either Case, Paxson, and Ableidinger (2002) or Gertler, Levine, and Ames (2004) did. In particular, child school enrollment is unaffected by parent death for nonpoor households, whereas for poor households they find that enrollment is merely delayed for younger children and basically unaffected for older children. Note that although Ainsworth, Beegle, and Koda (2002) control for baseline household characteristics, they do not use fixed effects to capture unobserved differences between households that experience parent death and those that do not.

Several other studies echo Ainsworth, Beegle, and Koda (2002) in finding little or no difference between orphans and nonorphans in terms of school enrollment (see Kamali et al. 1996; Ryder et al. 1994; Lloyd and Blanc 1996), although all of these studies rely on cross-sectional datasets for their analysis, and thus may be less persuasive than the panel studies. Ainsworth and Filmer (2002) employ data from 28 countries across the developing world and show diverse impacts of parent death on school enrollment, providing a possible explanation for the heterogeneity of findings across different settings in the existing studies. A number of reports have claimed that there are gender differences in parent death impacts, with girls suffering more than boys in terms of schooling (World Bank 2002; UNAIDS 2002).

The absence of consistent estimated impacts of parent death on children in sub-Saharan Africa has sometimes been attributed to the strength of extended family (or community) networks that care for orphans (Foster and Williamson 2000; Gregson et al. 2002). One explanation for differences across settings, then, is the possibility that these insurance networks weaken or break down when local orphan rates surpass a certain critical level—although the large estimated effects in Indonesia shown in Gertler, Levine, and Ames (2004) and the small effects in Tanzania (Ainsworth, Beegle, and Koda 2002) do not seem to fit this interpretation given the much higher rate of orphanhood in Tanzania.

An alternative explanation for the weak orphan effects in Africa is the possibility that HIV/AIDS victims are somewhat better-off than nonvictims in certain settings, at least at the start of the epidemic (perhaps since some occupations whose practitioners are vulnerable to infection—including truckers, soldiers, teachers, and prostitutes—tend to be relatively affluent). To the extent that this household socioeconomic variation is at least partially unobserved by the econometrician, this will lead to an upward bias in the estimated impact of being an orphan on life outcomes in studies relying on cross-sectional analysis. Hence it may partially obscure the true negative impacts of parent death.

2.2 Parent Death and Schooling in Rural Kenya

Evans and Miguel (2003) use the Busia, Kenya deworming study (PSDP) data set, and restrict attention to 13,748 individuals whose parents were all alive at baseline in January 1998 in grades 1 to 8. For fully 7,790 of these individuals (those in grades 3 to 8 present in school on the day of survey administration) we also have baseline 1998 survey information on socioeconomic status and other characteristics. This is a large longitudinal data set, spanning nearly five years, from January 1998 to October 2002, in an African area with high HIV/AIDS prevalence. In this sense, Evans and Miguel 2003 is methodologically closest to Ainsworth, Beegle, and Koda 2002.

Ainsworth et al.'s use of longitudinal data and rich set of baseline educational, household, and health information allow them to avoid some of the methodological shortcomings in existing research. In Evans and Miguel 2003, the identification strategy is simple: we compare those children whose parents died during the period 1998–2002 to those whose parent did not die, and make the case that that these two groups of individuals—the "became orphan" and "never orphan" groups—are remarkably similar along a range of observable characteristics at baseline. Note that of 11 baseline observables—including measures of child nutrition and health, household socioeconomic status, and school participation—there is a statistically significant difference across the two groups at 90 percent confidence in just one case (observed child cleanliness). Baseline 1998 school participation is nearly identical in the two groups. We also have information on 1997 school participation for a subset of 27 sample schools (that were participating in a previous NGO assistance project), and find that the "became orphan" and "never orphan" groups have nearly identical participation levels in that year, further evidence that the two groups were not experiencing differential levels or time trends with respect to school participation in the years before parent death.

These findings cannot completely eliminate concerns about the suitability of our comparison group—and in the absence of a clean natural experiment, it may be impossible to—yet we feel that we are able to allay most potential concerns about the comparability of the two groups. If "became orphan" and "never orphan" households indeed differed sharply on unobservable dimensions—for instance, parents' commitment to their children—it is likely that these differences would also be reflected along some observable dimension given the rich set of characteristics we employ; however, we do not find any such pattern of observed differences.

The information on child orphan status was collected in late 2002 during a follow-up survey of the 75 deworming program schools. For those pupils who were no longer attending the school, or were not present on the day of the survey, other students in the school were asked about their orphan status and year of parent death. In all, orphan status was unknown, or deemed insufficiently reliable by enumerators, for 23 percent of the original 1998 sample—predominantly those initially in the upper grades, who had been out of school longer than younger pupils (and thus were not as well known in the school); these missing cases are dropped from the analysis. The individuals without reliable orphan data tend to have worse school participation outcomes than other pupils, so note that to the extent that orphan status data are more likely to be missing for orphans (who are fostered in distant geographic districts, say) than for nonorphans, our estimates may understate true parent death effects due to attrition bias.

Table 6.2
Baseline (January 1998) differences between those who became orphans during 1998–2002, and those who were never orphans in the Busia, Kenya deworming (PSDP) dataset.

	Became Orphans	Never Orphans	Became Orphans– Never Orphans (s.e.)
1997 School participation rate	0.83	0.81	0.02 (0.03)
1998 School participation rate	0.92	0.92	0.00 (0.01)
Child weight-for-age (Z-score)	−1.40	−1.45	0.05 (0.03)
Child had malaria in past month	0.40	0.39	0.01 (0.02)
Child wears shoes to school	0.13	0.14	−0.01 (0.01)
Child wears school uniform to school	0.85	0.87	−0.02 (0.01)
Child appears "clean"	0.58	0.62	−0.04** (0.02)
Household has latrine	0.81	0.82	−0.02 (0.02)
Household owns cattle	0.49	0.49	−0.00 (0.02)
Household owns goats	0.38	0.41	−0.03 (0.02)
Household owns chickens	0.93	0.93	0.00 (0.01)

Notes: ** = Significant at 95 percent confidence, * = Significant at 90 percent confidence.

Moreover, to the extent that information on the exact year of parent death is captured with some error using this indirect survey method, this should lead us to further underestimate parent death impacts under plausible assumptions on measurement error (Aigner 1973). Finally, a third reason to think our results are likely to underestimate the true effects on children is the possibility that the health of parents who die begins to decline in the year (or years) before their death; in this case, the difference between child school enrollment immediately before and after the parent death understates the total effect of parent illness and death taken together.

Now to the findings themselves. Parent death has a large negative impact on the child school participation rate, defined as the total proportion of unannounced school attendance verifications that the child attended school: on average, school participation falls by 0.039 (standard error 0.013) in a specification including extensive individual baseline heath and socioeconomic controls, and 0.028 (standard error 0.014) when individual fixed effects are included. All specifications include birth year cohort-gender indicator variables and polynomial time trends to capture different enrollment patterns by different demographic groups. Effects are robust to the use of an alternative measure of school participation, an indicator variable for enrollment in school

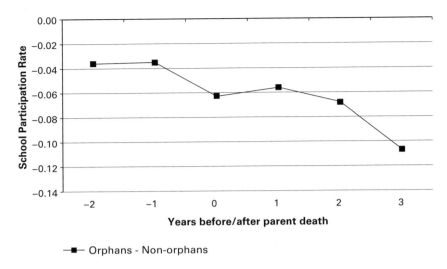

Figure 6.3
Impact of parent death on child school participation in Busia, Kenya during 1998–2002 (conditional on individual characteristics).

yielding estimated magnitudes similar to Gertler et al.'s (2004) findings in Indonesia, more than a doubling of the drop-out rate. The impacts of maternal and paternal death are nearly identical, and there are no significantly different impacts by child age or gender; the lack of difference in orphan impacts by child gender appears to be one of the most robust results of the recent literature (Case, Paxson, and Ableidinger 2002; Gertler, Levine, and Ames 2004).

Figure 6.3 presents the time patterns of the main effects, and indicates that although school participation rates were similar in the years before parent death, they drop sharply in the year of the death and then continue to fall for up to three years afterward. In other words, there is no evidence of orphan recovery after parent death as households adapt to their new circumstances.

In terms of the magnitude of effects, note that the estimated effect of a parent death in reducing school participation (0.03–0.04), although not trivial, is far smaller than the effect of eliminating one moderate-to-heavy worm infection for a year (approximately 0.2, see section 2)—although it remains likely that our parent death estimates are lower bounds on true effects, as discussed above. For another comparison, the effect of parent death is similar to the estimated impact of several measures of poverty. For example, households without latrines or toilets at their home compound (about 20% of the sample) have school participation rates during 1998–2002 that are about 0.03 less than households with latrines, conditional on the other household controls. Thus, the findings are broadly consistent with much of the existing literature. We find that the impact of parent death is indeed negative in terms of school participation, but that the average effect is relatively small, even in an area of Kenya with high HIV/AIDS prevalence—a finding that echoes work by Ainsworth, Beegle, and Koda (2002).

Also note that, again like Ainsworth, Beegle, and Koda (2002), we find that parent death impacts differ across socioeconomic groups, with children from the poorest households experiencing the greatest reductions in school participation: children from households without latrines or toilets experience a drop in school participation after parent death of 0.096 (significant at 99% confidence), whereas the effect for children from households with latrines is −0.012 (though not statistically significant). Similarly the likelihood that a child drops out of school (through 2002) after a parent death is 0.061 for children from households without cattle (about half of the sample does not have cattle), but near zero for households with cattle. This finding suggests that household wealth buffers children from the shock of parent death, or perhaps that households with greater wealth can call on relatives with more resources to foster the orphans, or at least assist in the payment of school expenses.

In contrast, community level characteristics do not lead to differential effects of parent death. Most significantly, there is no evidence that orphans fare any worse in primary school communities with higher rates of orphanhood. Nor is there significantly lower average school participation in communities with high rates of orphanhood, suggesting that nonorphans are not suffering from being in communities with more orphans. The large variation in orphan rates across communities in the Kenyan study area in Evans and Miguel 2003 makes it particularly well suited to explore this issue—there is considerable variation in local orphan rates within our study area, from 10 percent in the northern Funyula division (a subset of our study area) up to nearly 40 percent in southern Budalangi. These findings argue against the claim that social networks in rural western Kenya are largely breaking down under the strain of HIV/AIDS deaths, and that the growing number of orphans cannot be effectively taken care of by surviving relatives and other community members. Of course, further research is needed to understand how general these initial findings are beyond rural western Kenya.

3 Conclusions

Taken together, we conclude that there is increasingly strong evidence that both child health shocks and parent death have substantial effects on school participation rates, and thus presumably human capital accumulation, across a range of African, Asian, and Latin American settings. The evidence on how child health affects school learning (as measured by test scores) is, however, less conclusive than the now considerable evidence on school attendance and enrollment. Existing work also suggests that child health and nutritional status have a much larger impact on education than parent health, even in the extreme case of parent death.

Further long-term longitudinal studies are needed in less developed countries to definitively make the claim that health shocks affect income later in life, and to thus make the link with economic growth and development. The recent Indonesia Family Life Survey (IFLS) is the type of high-quality household panel that is needed for this endeavor, and presumably in future survey rounds it will allow investigators to approach these issues. Another ongoing data collection effort that may shed light on these issues is the Kenya Life Panel Survey (KLPS), which is discussed in section 1 above.

How large could the long-run effects of poor health on economic growth and development really be? Unfortunately, the answer to this question remains elusive, despite recent research progress in economics (much of which is surveyed in this volume). But there is suggestive evidence from at least one once-developing country—the United States—that the long-run effects of public deworming investments could be very large indeed. Recent economic history research finds that the Rockefeller Sanitary Commission's deworming campaigns in the U.S. South in the 1910s had major impacts on educational attainment and income (Bleakley 2002) and on agricultural productivity (Brinkley 1994). In fact, Bleakley estimates that each case of hookworm reduced school attendance by 0.2—which is nearly identical to the Kenya estimates presented in Miguel and Kremer 2004. This historical evidence provides hope that current public health investments in children in less developed countries might hold the seeds of their future prosperity.

Acknowledgments

I thank Gustavo Bobonis for his insightful comments. All errors remain my own. I also thank the Economics and Health Research Center at Universitat Pompeu Fabra for their unrestricted financial support via the Merck Foundation Company.

Notes

1. Another possible channel is through teacher health. To the extent that ill teachers miss class or teach poorly, this could also negatively affect child learning. Unfortunately, there has been limited empirical work—to my knowledge—on this issue and so it is not a focus of this survey.

2. One notable exception to this generalization is the literature on the impact of iron supplementation. Several studies on iron supplementation employing randomized evaluation methodologies find subsequent test score gains (see Nokes, van den Bosch, and Bundy 1998 for a survey).

3. In 2001, parents in half of the group 1 and group 2 schools were also required to pay a small amount of money for the deworming drugs in an NGO cost-recovery program.

4. In fact, by the end of the second year of the study, sample attrition rates were already high, owing mainly to the closure of numerous preschools between the first and second academic year (although fortunately for the econometric analysis, attrition rates are nearly identical between the treatment and comparison preschools).

References

Aigner, D. J. 1973. Regression with a Binary Independent Variable Subject to Errors of Observation. *Journal of Econometrics* 1 (1): 49–50.

Ainsworth, M., and D. Filmer. 2002. Poverty, AIDS, and Children's Schooling: A Targeting Dilemma. Working paper no. 2885, Policy Research, The World Bank.

Ainsworth, M., K. Beegle, and G. Koda. 2000. The Impact of Adult Mortality on Primary School Enrollment in Northwestern Tanzania. UNAIDS Africa Development Forum paper. Washington, D.C.: The World Bank.

Alderman, H., J. R. Behrman, V. Lavy, and R. Menon. 2001. Child Health and School Enrollment: A Longitudinal Analysis. *Journal of Human Resources* 36 (1): 185–205.

Angrist, J. D., and V. Lavy. 1999. Using Maimonides' Rule to Estimate the Effect of Class Size on Scholastic Achievement. *Quarterly Journal of Economics* 114 (2): 533–575.

Behrman, J. 1996. The Impact of Health and Nutrition on Education. *World Bank Research Observer* 11 (1): 23–37.

Bleakley, H. 2002. Disease and Development: Evidence from Hookworm Eradication in the American South. Massachusetts Institute of Technology. Unpublished paper.

Bloom, D., and J. Sachs. 1998. Geography, Demography, and Economic Growth in Africa. *Brookings Papers on Economic Activity* 2: 207–295.

Bobonis, G., E. Miguel, and C. Sharma. 2003. Child Nutrition and Education: A Randomized Evaluation in India. Unpublished working paper, University of California, Berkeley.

Brinkley, G. 1994. The Economic Impact of Disease in the American South, 1860–1940. Ph.D. dissertation, University of California, Davis.

Brooker, S., E. A. Miguel, S. Moulin, A. I. Luoba, D. A. P. Bundy, and M. Kremer. 2000. Epidemiology of Single and Multiple Species Helminth Infections among Schoolchildren in Busia District, Kenya. *East African Medical Journal* 77: 157–161.

Bundy, D. A. P. 1988. Population Ecology of Intestinal Helminth Infections in Human Communities. *Philosophical Transactions of the Royal Society of London, Series B* 321 (1207): 405–420.

———. 1994. The Global Burden of Intestinal Nematode Disease. *Transactions of the Royal Society of Tropical Medicine and Hygiene* 88: 259–261.

Bundy, D. A. P., and H. L. Guyatt. 1996. Schools for Health: Focus on Health, Education, and the School-Age Child. *Parasitology Today* 12 (8): 1–16.

Bundy, D. A. P., M.-S. Chan, G. F. Medley, D. Jamison, and L. Savioli. 1998. Intestinal Nematode Infections. In *Health Priorities and Burden of Disease Analysis: Methods and Applications from Global, National and Sub-National Studies*. Cambridge, Mass.: Harvard University Press for the World Health Organization and The World Bank.

Case, A., C. Paxson, and J. Ableidinger. 2002. Orphans in Africa. Working paper no. 9213, National Bureau of Economic Research, Cambridge, Mass.

Dickson, R., S. Awasthi, P. Williamson, C. Demellweek, and P. Garner. 2000. Effect of Treatment for Intestinal Helminth Infection on Growth and Cognitive Performance in Children: Systematic Review of Randomized Trials. *British Medical Journal* 320 (June 24): 1697–1701.

Duflo, E. 2001. Schooling and Labor Market Consequences of School Construction in Indonesia: Evidence from an Unusual Policy Experiment. *American Economic Review* 91 (4): 795–813.

Evans, D., and E. Miguel. 2003. Will the Sun Come Out Tomorrow? Orphans and Schooling. Unpublished working paper, University of California, Berkeley.

Foster, G., and J. Williamson. 2000. A Review of Current Literature on the Impact of HIV/AIDS on Children in Sub-Saharan Africa. *AIDS* 14 (suppl. 3): 275S–284S.

Gertler, P., D. Levine, and M. Ames. 2004. Schooling and Parental Death. *Review of Economics and Statistics* 86 (1): 211–225.

Glewwe, P., and H. Jacoby. 1995. An Economic Analysis of Delayed Primary School Enrollment in a Low Income Country: The Role of Early Childhood Nutrition. *Review of Economics and Statistics* 77 (1): 156–169.

Glewwe, P., H. Jacoby, and E. M. King. 2001. Early Childhood Nutrition and Academic Achievement: A Longitudinal Analysis. *Journal of Public Economics* 81 (3): 345–368.

Gregson, S., C. Nyamukapa, M. Mlilo, K. Tripp, L. Drake, and S. Chandiwana. 2002. Growing-Up in an AIDS-Afflicted Population: The Nature, Adequacy, and Sustainability of Family and Community Coping Mechanisms in Rural Zimbabwe. Medical Research Council of Zimbabwe. Unpublished paper.

Haas, J. D., E. J. Martinez, S. Murdoch, E. Conlisk, J. A. Rivera, and R. Martorell. 1995. Nutritional Supplementation during the Preschool Years and Physical Work Capacity in Adolescent and Young Adult Guatemalans. *Journal of Nutrition* 125 (4): 1078S–1089S.

Hall, A., E. Miguel, et al. 2001. Anaemia in Schoolchildren in Eight Countries in Africa and Asia. *Public Health Nutrition* 4: 749–756.

Kamali, A., J. A. Seeley, A. J. Nunn, J. F. Kengeya-Kayondo, A. Ruberantwari, and D. W. Mulder. 1996. *AIDS Care* 8 (5): 509–515.

Khan, A. D., D. G. Schroeder, R. Martorell, and J. A. Rivera. 1995. Age at Menarche and Nutritional Supplementation. *Journal of Nutrition* 125 (4): 1090S–1096S.

Kremer, M. 2003. Randomized Evaluations of Educational Programs in Developing Countries: Some Lessons. *American Economic Review (Papers and Proceedings)* 93 (2): 102–106.

Lloyd, C., and A. Blanc. 1996. Children's Schooling in Sub-Saharan Africa: The Role of Fathers, Mothers, and Others. *Population and Development Review* 22 (2): 265–298.

Martorell, R., J.-P. Habicht, and J. A. Rivera. 1995. History and Design of the INCAP Longitudinal Study (1969–77) and Its Follow-Up (1988–89). *Journal of Nutrition* 125: 1027S–1041S.

Mendez, M. A., and L. S. Adair. 1999. Severity and Timing of Stunting in the First Two Years of Life Affect Performance on Cognitive Tests in Late Childhood. *Journal of Nutrition* 129 (8): 1555–1562.

Miguel, E., and M. Kremer. 2004. Worms: Identifying Impacts on Education and Health in the Presence of Treatment Externalities. *Econometrica* 72 (1): 159–217.

Nokes, C., C. van den Bosch, and D. A. P. Bundy. 1998. The Effects of Iron Deficiency and Anemia on Mental and Motor Performance, Educational Achievement, and Behavior in Children: A Report of the International Nutritional Anemia Consultative Group. Washington, D.C.: USAID.

Partnership for Child Development. 1999. The Cost of Large-Scale School Health Programmes which Deliver Anthelmintics to Children in Ghana and Tanzania. *Acta Tropica* 73: 183–204.

Pollitt, E. 1990. *Infection: Schistosomiasis, Malnutrition, and Infection in the Classroom.* Paris: UNESCO.

Pollitt, E., K. S. Gorman, P. Engle, R. Martorell, and J. A. Rivera. 1993. Early Supplementary Feeding and Cognition: Effects Over Two Decades. *Society for Research in Child Development* 58 (7): 1–99.

Rivera, J. A., R. Martorell, M. Ruel, J.-P. Habicht, and J. Haas. 1995. Nutritional Supplementation during Preschool Years Influences Body Size and Composition of Guatemalan Adolescents. *Journal of Nutrition* 125: 1078S–1089S.

Ryder, R., M. Kamenga, M. Nkusu, V. Batter, and W. Heyward. 1994. AIDS Orphans in Kinshasa, Zaire: Incidence and Socioeconomic Consequences. *AIDS* 8: 673–679.

Strauss, J., and D. Thomas. 1998. Health, Nutrition, and Economic Development. *Journal of Economic Literature* 36 (2): 766–817.

UNAIDS. 2002. *Report on the Global HIV/AIDS Epidemic*. Geneva: UNAIDS. Available at http://www.unaids.org.

World Bank. 2002. *Education and HIV/AIDS: A Window of Hope*. Washington, D.C.: The World Bank.

World Health Organization (WHO). 1992. *Model Describing Information: Drugs Used in Parasitic Diseases*. Geneva: World Health Organization.

World Health Organization (WHO). 1993. The Control of Schistosomiasis. Second Report of the WHO Expert Committee. Technical report series no. 830. Geneva: World Health Organization.

World Health Organization (WHO). 1999. *The World Health Report 1999*. Geneva: World Health Organization.

7 Nutrition, Malnutrition, and Economic Growth

Harold Alderman, Jere R.
Behrman, and John Hoddinott

Malnutrition is widespread in many developing countries. It is estimated that at least 12 million low-birth-weight (LBW) births occur per year and that around 180 million preschool children are malnourished. Redressing this serious health problem has long been justified on intrinsic grounds; better nutrition has been widely seen as being of value in its own right. Others have also emphasized the importance of health and nutrition for productivity and economic growth. That is, the emphasis is on the instrumental, rather than the intrinsic, value of good health and nutrition. This chapter adopts such an approach, but differs from many of the other contributions to this book in three ways. First, our focus is on the microeconomic rather than the macroeconomic evidence of the links between nutritional status and representations of productivity. We perceive that the microeconomic analysis is likely to be more informative about the possible causal effects of nutrition on productivity because of enhanced opportunities to address estimation problems such as endogeneity at the microlevel and because aggregation problems may obscure nonlinear relationships. Second, we emphasize that these links are multiple and heterogeneous. In particular, there are important links between health/nutrition and cognitive development and between health/nutrition and schooling so that in adulthood, health and nutritional status may have direct links to productivity as well as indirect links through their effects on education. Third, we emphasize that many outcomes that reflect nutritional status are cumulative and this has implications for the design of policies and interventions designed to ameliorate malnutrition.

This chapter begins with a brief explanation of the causes and measurement of malnutrition as well as estimates of the extent of malnutrition across developing countries. It then surveys microevidence about the productivity impact of improved nutrition in developing countries—from conception through infancy and childhood on into adolescence and adulthood. These gains may operate through many channels—increasing cognitive development, physical stature, and strength, inducing earlier school enrollment and more regular school attendance, greater schooling and learning, and greater adult productivity—as well as saving resources that otherwise would go toward dealing with diseases and other problems related to malnutrition. Finally, the possible gains from different nutritional policy strategies and the policy bases for adopting such strategies are examined. Given the indirect links between improved nutrition and greater schooling, as well as the direct ones between nutrition and higher levels of productivity and incomes, such investments are crucial to achieving the outcomes valued both by society and its individuals.

1 Understanding Malnutrition

Indicators of nutritional status are measurements of body size, body composition, or body function that reflect single or multiple nutrient deficiencies.[1] They can be divided into three broad groups depending on the type of information. The first group is anthropometry, the measurement of body size and gross body composition. The second group uses clinical examinations to detect signs and symptoms of advanced nutritional depletion. Examples are assessments of iodine deficiency by inspection and palpation of enlarged thyroid glands. The third group uses laboratory methods to detect decreased levels of nutrients in body tissues or fluids, or decreased activity of an enzyme that is nutrient dependent.[2] While malnutrition is often seen as a manifestation of some form of deprivation, it also refers to circumstances of excess such as obesity. Table 7.1, adapted from Morris 2001, describes the most common measures.

Nutritional status is an outcome, reflecting the purposive actions of individuals given preferences and constraints. In behavioral models, an individual's nutritional status often is treated as an argument in the welfare function of individuals or the households in which they reside (Behrman and Deolalikar 1988; Strauss and Thomas 1995). It is assumed that welfare increases as nutritional status improves, but possibly at a diminishing rate and, as suggested above, increases in certain measures of nutritional status, such as body mass, may be associated with reductions in welfare beyond a certain point.

Table 7.1
Measures of nutritional status and their prevalence.

Indicator	Interpretation	Most common means of reporting
Group I: Anthropometric Indicators		
Prevalence of low birthweight	An indicator of intrauterine growth retardation resulting from short maternal stature, poor maternal nutrition before or during pregnancy, infection and smoking.	Percentage of children with birthweights below 2500 grams.
Prevalence of low height-for-age (stunting) in preschool or school-age children	Children's skeletal (linear) growth compromised due to constraints to one or more of nutrition, health, or mother–infant interactions. This is an indicator of chronic nutritional deprivation.	Expressed as a z score or as the percentage of children stunted. Z scores are calculated by standardizing a child's height given age and sex against an international standard of well nourished children. A z score of -1 indicates that given age and sex, the child's height is one standard deviation below the median child in that age/sex group. Children with z scores below -2 are classified as stunted; with z scores below -3 are classified as severely stunted.
Prevalence of low weight-for-height (wasting) in preschool or school-age children	Children suffer thinness resulting from energy deficit and/or disease-induced poor appetite, malabsorption, or loss of nutrients. This is an indicator of transitory nutritional deprivation.	Expressed as a z score or as the percentage of children wasted. Z scores are calculated by standardizing a child's weight given height and sex against an international standard of well nourished children. Children with z scores below -2 are classified as wasted; with z scores below -3 are classified as severely wasted.

Table 7.1
(continued)

Indicator	Interpretation	Most common means of reporting
Prevalence of low weight-for-age (underweight) in preschool or school-age children	This is a composite measure of child nutritional status, reflecting both chronic and transitory nutritional deprivation. This is a Millennium Development Goal indicator.	Expressed as a z score or as the percentage of children underweight. Z scores are calculated by standardizing a child's weight given age and sex against an international standard of well nourished children. Children with z scores below −2 are classified as underweight; with z scores below −3 are classified as severely underweight.
Prevalence of low body mass index in adults or adolescents	Adults suffer thinness as a result of inadequate energy intake, an uncompensated increase in physical activity, or (severe) illness.	Expressed as Body Mass Index (BMI). BMI is calculated by dividing weight in kilograms by the square of height in meters. Individuals are considered to be chronically energy deficient if they have a BMI below 18.5, overweight if they have a BMI greater than 25, and obese if they have a BMI greater than 30.

Group 2 Clinical Examinations or Group 3 Laboratory Methods

Prevalence of iodine deficiency	Iodine deficiency results from low intake of iodine in the diet.	Expressed by clinical inspection of enlarged thyroids or in terms of iodine concentrations in urine ($\mu g/L$). The benchmark for the elimination of iodine deficiency is to have less than 20 percent of the population with levels below 50 $\mu g/L$.

Table 7.1
(continued)

Indicator	Interpretation	Most common means of reporting
Group 3 Laboratory Methods		
Prevalence of low hemoglobin (anemia) in preschool or school-age children	Children suffer from anemia, either as a result of low iron intakes or poor absorption, or as a result of illness. Severe protein-energy malnutrition and vitamin B12/folate deficiency can also lead to anemia.	Expressed as grams of hemoglobin per liter of blood. Cutoffs to define anemia are 110 g/L for children 6–59 months, 115 g/L for children 5–11 years and 120 g/L for children 12–14 years.
Prevalence of low hemoglobin (anemia) in nonlactating, nonpregnant women	Women suffer from anemia as a result of low iron intakes, poor absorption, illness, or excessive losses of blood. Severe protein-energy malnutrition and vitamin B12/folate deficiency can also lead to anemia. Anemia is rare in adult men except in conditions of extreme iron-deficient diets.	Expressed as grams of hemoglobin per liter of blood. Cutoffs to define anemia are 120 g/L for nonpregnant women, 110 for pregnant women and 130 for adult men.

Source: ACC/SCN 2000 and Morris 2001.

In allocating resources, household decision makers take into account the extent to which these investments will make both their children and themselves better-off in the future as well as currently.[3] These allocations are constrained in several ways. There are resource constraints reflecting income (itself an outcome) and time available as well as prices faced by households. There is also a constraint arising from the production process for health outcomes, including nutritional status. This constraint links nutrient intakes—the physical consumption of macronutrients (calories and protein) and micronutrients (minerals and vitamins)—as well as time devoted to the production of health and nutrition, the individual's genetic make-up, and knowledge and skill regarding the combination of these inputs to produce nutritional status. Additionally, there are interdependencies in the production of nutritional status and other dimensions of health; for example, malaria limits hemoglobin formation.

It is important to recognize that many nutritional outcomes are the consequence of cumulative processes that begin *in utero*. A number of maternal factors have been shown to be significant determinants of intrauterine growth retardation (IUGR), the characterization of a newborn who does not attain his or her growth potential. Most important are mother's stature (reflecting her own poor nutritional status during childhood), her nutritional status prior to conception as measured by her weight and micronutrient status, and her weight gain during pregnancy. Diarrheal disease, intestinal parasites, and respiratory infections may also lead to IUGR and where endemic (such as sub-Saharan Africa), malaria is a major determinant. In developed countries, smoking is also a significant contributor to IUGR. IUGR is measured as the prevalence of newborns below the tenth percentile for weight given gestational age (ACC/SCN 2000). Because gestational age is rarely known, IUGR is often proxied by low birth weight. As of 2000, it is estimated that 11 percent of newborns, or 11.7 million children have low birth weight (ibid.).[4]

In preschool- and school-age children, nutritional status is often assessed in terms of anthropometry: "The basic principle of anthropometry is that prolonged or severe nutrient depletion eventually leads to retardation of linear (skeletal) growth in children and to loss of, or failure to accumulate, muscle mass and fat in both children and adults" (Morris 2001, p. 12). A particularly useful measure is height given age, as this reflects the cumulative impact of events affecting nutritional status that result in stunting. As of 2000, it is estimated that one child in three under the age of 5—182 million children in all—is stunted (ACC/SCN 2000).

A number of factors contribute to poor anthropometric status in children. One is low birth weight; a number of studies show a correlation between low birth weight and subsequent stature although, in the absence of any subsequent intervention, not between low birth weight and growth (Ashworth, Morris, and Lira 1997; Hoddinott and Kinsey 2001; Li et al. 2003; Ruel 2001). In addition, the first two years of life pose numerous nutritional challenges to newborns. Growth rates are highest in infancy, thus adverse factors have a greater potential for causing retardation at this time. Younger children have higher nutritional requirements per kilogram of body weight and are also more susceptible to infections. They are also less able to make their needs known and are more vulnerable to the effects of poor care practices such as the failure to introduce safe weaning foods in adequate quantities. Evidence from numerous studies clearly indicates that the immediate causes of growth faltering are poor diets and infection (primarily gastrointestinal) and that these are interactive. For these reasons almost all the growth retardation observed in developing countries has its origins in the first two to three years of life (Martorell 1995).

A growing body of evidence indicates that growth lost in early years is, at best, regained only partially during childhood and adolescence, particularly when children remain in poor environments (Martorell, Khan, and Schroeder 1994). For example, Martorell (1995, 1999), Martorell, Khan, and Schroeder (1994), and Simondon et al. (1998) all find that stature at age 3 is strongly correlated with the body size attained at adulthood in Guatemala and Senegal. Hoddinott and Kinsey (2001) find that children who were aged 12–24 months in the aftermath of a drought in rural Zimbabwe in 1994–1995 had z scores for height-for-age that are about six-tenths of a standard deviation below that of comparable children not exposed to this drought when measured at ages 60–72 months. However, older children did not suffer such permanent consequences; this is consistent with the evidence that child development has sensitive periods where development is more receptive to influence and that during such periods, some shocks may be reversible whereas others are not (Yaqub 2002). Alderman, Hoddinott, and Kinsey (2003) find that in rural Zimbabwe, children exposed to the civil war or to the 1982–1984 droughts were found to have lower stature compared to siblings not affected by these shocks when remeasured in 2000. The magnitudes of these shocks are large; exposure to the 1982–1984 drought reduced stature in late adolescence by 2.3 centimeters.

It is also important to recognize that "severe malnutrition in early childhood leads to deficits in cognitive development ... if the children return to poor environments" (Grantham-McGregor, Fernald, and Sethuraman 1999a, p. 66; see also Pollitt 1990). Although many studies from developed countries fail to show a difference in development levels for children with low birth weight, there are few longitudinal studies from developing counties from which to generalize (Hack 1998). More recent studies that test the impact of low birth weight indicate that the relationship between birth weight and cognitive function carries into the range of normal weights even in developed countries (Richards et al. 2001; Matte et al. 2001). Even if, as

Richards et al. observe, this association between birth weight and cognitive ability attenuates partially over time—they followed a cohort for 43 years—the significant difference in function at age 8 affects educational attainment.

Malnourished children are found to score poorly on tests of cognitive function and have poorer psychomotor development and fine motor skills. They tend to have lower activity levels, interact less frequently in their environments, and fail to acquire skills at normal rates (Grantham-McGregor et al. 1997; Grantham-McGregor, Fernald, and Sethuraman 1999b; Johnston et al. 1987; Lasky et al. 1981). Controlled experiments with animals suggest that this may occur because malnutrition results in irreversible damage to brain development such as that associated with the insulation of neural fibers (Yaqub 2002).

One such deficiency that has been studied both in laboratory and in epidemiological studies is iodine deficiency, which adversely affects the development of the central nervous system. A meta-analysis indicates that individuals with an iodine deficiency had, on average, 13.5 points lower IQ than comparison groups. Although interventions have shown that providing iodine to pregnant women can reduce this gap, the provision of iodine to school-aged children does not appear to reverse earlier damage (Grantham-McGregor, Fernald, and Sethuraman 1999b). Prevalences of iodine deficiency are not available by age; it is estimated that globally, more than 700 million people are affected.

Adequate iron intake is also necessary for brain development. The studies reviewed by Grantham-McGregor, Fernald, and Sethuraman (1999b) do not indicate that subsequent interventions to rectify these deficiencies reverse this damage. Given that more than 40 percent of children aged 0–4 in developing countries suffer from anemia (ACC/ SCN 2000) this could be a major global contributor to poor schooling outcomes. Anemia in school-aged children may also affect schooling whether or not there had been earlier impaired brain development. Supplementation trials for school-age children consistently indicate improved cognition, although this is less regularly observed with interventions aimed at deficient younger children.

Reduced breastfeeding—an effect of low birth weight as well as a common cause of childhood malnutrition—is also a well-documented influence on cognitive development, even in developed countries (Grantham-McGregor, Fernald, and Sethuraman 1999a). This is in keeping with the prevailing view that very young children are those most vulnerable to impaired cognitive development.[5]

2 The Links between Malnutrition and Economic Productivity

We now turn to the microevidence about the productivity impact of improved nutrition in developing countries—from conception through infancy and childhood into adolescence and adulthood. The many channels through which these gains may operate are grouped in the following way: the saving of resources that otherwise would go toward dealing with diseases and other problems related to malnutrition; the direct gains arising from improvements in physical stature and strength as well as improved micronutrient status; and the indirect gains arising from the links between nutritional status and schooling, nutritional status and cognitive development, and the subsequent links between schooling, cognitive ability, and adult productivity.

2.1 The Costs of Poor Nutrition
One significant cost of malnutrition is higher mortality. The probability of infant mortality is estimated to be significantly higher for LBW than for non-LBW infants. Conley, Strully, and Bennett (2003) conclude that intrauterine resources competition—and, by inference, nutrition—explains a substantial portion of excess mortality of LBW children in the United States. In their study, an additional pound at birth led to a 14 percent decrease in mortality in the period between 28 days and 1 year for both fraternal and identical twins. In contrast, the risk of death in the first 28 days was elevated 27 percent for each pound difference in weight for fraternal twins compared to only 11 percent for identical twins, implying a large role for genetic factors. Ashworth (1998) reviews twelve data sets including two from India and one from Guatemala, and concludes that the risk of neonatal death for term infants weighing 2,000–2,499 grams at birth is four times that for infants 2,500–2,999 grams and ten times that of infants 3,000–3,499 grams. Relative risks of post-neonatal mortality for LBW infants compared to the two respective groups were two and four times as large. These risk ratios translate into fairly large differences in mortality rates given the relatively high mortality rates in many developing countries. Using the data she reports for the Indian and Guatemalan samples, Alderman and Behrman (2004) estimate that the probability of an infant death (either neonatal or post-neonatal) drops by about 0.078 for each birth in the 2,500–2,999 gram range compared to the 2,000–2,499 gram range.

When the impacts of poor nutrition are added to the effects of low birth weight, Pelletier et al. (1995) venture the widely cited estimate that 56 percent of child deaths in developing countries are attributable to the potentiating effects of malnutrition (with 83% of this due to the more prevalent mild to moderate malnutrition rather then the severe cases most commonly monitored). More recently, the World Health Organization (WHO) (2002) has claimed that malnutrition contributed to 3.4 million child deaths in 2000 (60% of child deaths). Pelletier and Frongillo (2003) have recently employed data on changes in national malnutrition rates and mortality to get a different perspective on this association, yet one that supports the earlier evidence on the association of mortality and malnutrition.[6]

The availability of experimental evidence on the use of micronutrient supplements provides unambiguous evidence on the relationship of mortality and vitamin intakes in many environments including ones that show few clinical symptoms of deficiencies. The potential to reduce child deaths by distributing vitamin A on a 6-month basis is particularly dramatic; meta-analysis of field trials indicate that such a provision of vitamin A can reduce overall child mortality by 25–35 percent (Beaton et al. 1993). Among adults, anemia is a particular concern for the health of women of childbearing age not only because of the elevated risk of adverse birth outcomes but also because the risk of maternal death is substantially elevated for anemic women; over a fifth of maternal deaths are associated with anemia (Ross and Thomas 1996; Brabin, Hakimi, and Pelletier 2001).[7]

Beyond the issue of increased mortality, malnutrition increases the risk of illnesses that impair the welfare of survivors. This relationship between nutrition and both infection and chronic diseases can be traced through different parts of the life cycle. Children with low birth weight (reflecting a range of causes, not all of which are due to dietary deficiencies) have longer hospital stays in circumstances where births occur in such settings and have a higher risk of subsequent hospitalization (Vitora et al. 1999). In addition, they use outpatient services more frequently than do other children. For young children, in general, malnutrition leads to a vicious cycle with impaired immunity leading to infection along with the attendant loss of appetite and catabolism and, hence, an increased likelihood of additional malnutrition.

Increased morbidity has direct resource costs in terms of health care services as well as lost employment or schooling for the caregivers. The magnitudes of these costs differ according to the medical system, markets, and policies of a country. In developed countries the *additional* costs for the survivors can be substantial. Lightwood, Phibbs, and Glanz (1999) calculate the excess direct medical costs due to low birth weight in the United States attributable to one cause, maternal smoking, to be $263 million in 1995. For example, 75 percent of the $5.5–6 billion of excess costs due to LBW in the United States estimated by Lewit et al. (1995) is due to the costs of health care in infancy. A further 10 percent of these costs are attributed to higher requirements for special education as well as increased grade repetition. Such requirements for special education or social services are substantial in developed countries (Petrou, Sach, and Davidson 2001). Although these costs may be far less in low-income countries where, for example, the majority of births occur outside a clinical setting, these lower medical costs associated with LBW come at the expense of higher mortality. In the absence of an educational system that can recognize and accommodate the individual needs of students, however, these costs are not incurred during childhood but rather in the form of reduced productivity in adulthood.

Undernutrition, particularly fetal undernutrition at critical periods, may result in permanent changes in body structure and metabolism. Even if there are not subsequent nutritional insults, these changes can lead to increased probabilities of chronic noninfectious diseases later in life. The hypothesis that fetal malnutrition has far-ranging consequences for adult health is bolstered by studies that track low-birth-weight infants into their adult years and document increased susceptibility to coronary heart disease, non-insulin-dependent diabetes, high blood pressure, obstructive lung disease, high blood cholesterol, and renal damage (Barker 1998). For example, although the various studies on the impact of the Dutch famine indicate few long-term consequences on young adults, more recent evidence shows that children whose mothers were starved in early pregnancy have higher rates of obesity and heart disease as adults (Roseboom et al. 2001). In contrast, children of mothers deprived in later pregnancy—the group most likely to be of low birth weight—had a greater risk of diabetes (Ravelli et al. 1998).

The evidence for the fetal origins hypothesis is still being assessed. The fact that some consequences may not be observed until the affected individuals reached middle age is an important consideration for interpreting the range of evidence being assembled. There are few panels that follow cohorts this far, and extrapolation from shorter panels or from less affluent cohorts with different life histories is currently necessary, albeit uncertain. In addition, there are at least two other explanations for the association between low birth weight (LBW) and adult diseases. LBW may be an indicator of poor socioeconomic status. Low socioeconomic status (SES) may have a causal impact on adult disease probabilities via other variables such as poor nutrition later in life or higher rates of smoking. If so, LBW may only be a correlate and not a causal variable. A different possibility is that LBW may be due to a genetic predisposition to insulin resistance. This would tend to account for a higher predisposition to adult diabetes and coronary heart disease that reflects genetics rather than the aspects of the uterine environment that may be influenced by medical and nutritional interventions.[8] Finally, even if there are the effects proposed in the fetal orgins hypothesis, due to their long lag the present discounted value of improvements due to prenatal interventions to offset them is not likely to be very large (Alderman and Behrman 2004; also see the end of section 2).

In addition to the consequences of undernutrition, it is well known that poor diets can contribute to heart disease, stroke, and diabetes. Evidence that obesity as well as diseases commonly associated with overconsumption are occurring among a low-income population, often side by side with undernutrition, has added to the challenge of addressing nutritional deficiencies (Doak et al. 2000).

Lastly, malnutrition may have long-term consequences through the intergenerational transmission of poor nutrition and anthropometric status. Recall that there is considerable epidemiological evidence that stature by age 3 is strongly correlated with body size at adulthood. Taller women experience fewer complications during childbirth, typically have children with higher birth weights, and experience lower risks of child and maternal mortality (Ramakrishnan et al. 1999; World Bank 1993). However, Behrman and Rosenzweig (2004) find that intergenerational birth-weight effects are primarily genetic and not due to better nutrition in the womb.

2.2   Direct Links between Nutrition and Productivity

There is considerable evidence of a direct link between nutrition and productivity. Behrman (1993), Behrman and Deolalikar (1989), Deolalikar (1988), Foster and Rosenzweig (1993), Glick and Sahn (1997), Haddad and Bouis (1991), Schultz (1996), Strauss and Thomas (1998), and Thomas and Strauss (1997) all find that after controlling for a variety of characteristics, that lower adult height—a consequence, in part, of poor nutrition in childhood—is associated with reduced earnings as an adult. For example, Thomas and Strauss (1997) estimated the direct impact of adult height on wages for urban Brazil. Although the elasticity varies somewhat according to gender and specification, for both men and women who work in the market sector a 1 percent increase in height leads to a 2–2.4 percent increase in wages or earnings.[9] Although their study is particularly sophisticated in the methodology used to account for labor selectivity and joint determination of health, this result is similar to others reported in the literature. Indeed, height is even a significant explanatory variable for wages in the United States (Strauss and Thomas 1998). Nevertheless, the direct impact of height on wages is likely less than the impact of schooling on wages over plausible ranges for each, even if the indirect effect of height on wages mediated by the relationship between height and schooling is included.[10]

Micronutrient status also has important productivity effects. In particular, anemia is associated with reduced productivity both in cross-sectional data and in randomized interventions (Li et al. 1994; Basta, Karyadi, and Scrimshaw 1979). The magnitude of the effect may depend on the nature of the task. For example, piece work may have greater incentives for effort but heavy physical labor may show greater increases in productivity, although anemia is nevertheless a factor for productivity in relatively light work (Horton and Ross 2003).

2.3   Indirect Links: Nutrition, Cognitive Development, Schooling, and Productivity

Poorly nourished children, as evidenced for example by low height-for-age, tend to start school later, progress through school less rapidly, have lower scholastic attainment, and perform less well on cognitive achievement tests when older. These associations appear to reflect significant and substantial effects in poor populations even when statistical methods such as instrumental variables are used to control for the behavioral determinants of preschool malnutrition.

There are three broad pathways by which nutrition can affect schooling. In the first, malnourished children may receive less schooling because their caregivers seek to invest less in their education, because schools use physical size as a rough indicator of school readiness, or because malnourished children may have higher rates of morbidity and thus greater rates of absenteeism. Although delayed entry, the second way by which nutrition may influence schooling, does not necessarily lead to less completed education—although under a prevailing model of the returns to education this would be an expected consequence of delayed enrollment if the opportunity cost of a year of schooling increases with age—late enrollment leads to lower expected lifetime earnings. In order to maintain the total years of schooling with delayed entry, an individual would have to enter the work force later. As Glewwe and Jacoby (1995) illustrate, for each year of delayed entry to primary school in Ghana, a child loses 3 percent of his or her lifetime wealth. The third pathway from malnutrition to educational outcomes is via the capacity to learn, a direct consequence of the consequences of poor nutrition for cognitive development described in section 1. Additionally, a hungry child may be less likely to pay attention in school and, thus, learn less even if he or she has no long-term impairment of intellectual ability.[11] These three pathways clearly interact; a child with reduced ability to learn will likely spend less time in school as well as learn less while in class.

Though intuitively plausible, it is difficult to ascertain or quantify the causal pathway between nutrition and learning. Many of the observable factors that affect nutrition, such as family assets and parental education, are also ones that affect education. Similarly, unobservable attitudes about investment in children and in intrafamily equity influence heath provision and schooling decisions in a complex manner. Thus, although there are many studies that document associations between nutrition and schooling (see Pollitt 1990 and Behrman 1996 for reviews), there are far fewer studies that accurately portray the causal impact of child health and nutrition on school performance.

Four recent studies represent the most complete effort toward distinguishing the distinct causal role of nutrition on education. Glewwe and Jacoby (1995) found delayed enrollments among the malnourished in their cross-sectional study, but no difference in the total years of school completed. By contrast, Alderman, Hoddinott, and Kinsey (2003) track a cohort of Zimbabweans over two decades finding both delayed school initiations and fewer grades completed for those children malnourished as children. Extrapolating beyond the drought shocks used for identification, the study concludes that had the median preschool child in the sample achieved the stature of a median child in a developed country, by adolescence she would be 4.6 centimeters taller, would have completed an additional 0.7 grades of schooling, and would have started school seven months earlier.

Glewwe, Jacoby, and King (2001) track children from birth through primary school and find that better nourished children both start school earlier and repeat fewer grades. A 0.6 standard deviation increase in the stature of malnourished children would increase completed schooling by nearly 12 months. The Filipino setting of this study is one in which most children initiate school. Using longitudinal data from rural Pakistan where school initiation is much lower, Alderman et al. (2001) find that malnutrition decreases the probability of ever attending school, particularly for girls. An improvement of 0.5 standard deviations in nutrition would increase school initiation by only 4 percent for boys, but by 19 percent for girls. For the average girl (boy) completing 6.3 (7.6) years of schooling in villages studied, improvements in nutrition show a significant effect on that schooling's attainment.

Using the substantial literature on wages and schooling, it is relatively straightforward to draw inferences from the impact of nutrition on years of schooling to future productivity loss. There are hundreds of studies on the impact of completed grades of schooling on wages— many of which are surveyed in Psacharopoulos 1994 and Rosenzweig 1995. Wages, however, are also directly influenced by cognitive ability, as well as by the appreciable influence of cognitive ability on schooling achieved. Poor cognitive function as a child is associated with poorer cognitive achievement as an adult (see Martorell 1995; Martorell, Rivera, and Kaplowitz 1989; Haas et al. 1996; Martorell 1999; and Martorell, Khan, and Schroeder 1994). A series of studies show that reduced cognitive skills as an adult (conditional on grades of schooling completed) directly affect earnings. These include Alderman et al. 1996, Altonji and Dunn 1996, Boissiere, Knight, and Sabot 1985, Cawley, Heckman, and Vytlacil 2001, Glewwe 1996, Lavy, Spratt, and Leboucher 1997, and Psacharopoulos and Velez 1992.[12]

It is possible to use these studies to estimate the magnitude of the productivity costs of poor nutrition. For example, Alderman, Hoddinott, and Kinsey (2003) use the values for the returns to education and age or job experience in the Zimbabwean manufacturing sector provided by Bigsten et al. (2000, table 5) to infer the costs associated with poor nutrition in Zimbabwe. The loss of 0.7 grades of schooling and the 7-month delay in starting school there translates into a 12 percent reduction in lifetime earnings. Such estimates are likely to be lower bounds given Fogel's (1994) evidence that links short stature among males to the early onset of chronic diseases and to premature mortality.

Behrman and Rosenzweig (2004) take a more direct approach. They study a sample of adult monozygotic (identical) twins in the United States and determine that with controls for genetic and other endowments shared by such twins (which would not be affected by programs to increase birth weight), the impact of low birth weight on schooling or wages is far larger than it appeared without such controls (e.g., the impact on scholastic attainment is estimated to be twice as large, with a pound increase in birth weight increasing scholastic attainment by about a third of a year). This may reflect postnatal choices on investments (with fewer investments for children with greater birth weight) or a negative correlation between health and ability endowments.[13]

Alderman and Behrman (2004) associate the net present value of *all* benefits with reducing a particular dimension of malnutrition. They consider seven benefits (reduced infant mortality, reduced neonatal care, reduced childhood morbidity, lost productivity due to reduced cognitive ability and learning, lost productivity due to smaller stature, reduction of the costs of chronic illness, and intergenerational benefits due to better birth outcomes) associated with reducing low birth weights. Given the net present value approach, the absolute and relative benefits of these seven categories are affected by the discount rate. Lower discount rates allow benefits that occur later in life to add more to the total. Conversely, when discount rates are high, benefits that occur in infancy contribute a greater share to the total than they do under lower discount rates. Nevertheless, over a wide range of assumptions about both discount rates and the nominal value of benefits, the productivity gains from cognitive ability and schooling contribute most to the total, despite the fact that these are assumed not to begin to accrue until age 15. For example, at a discount rate of 5 percent and using the core assumption in this study, the productivity gains from increased cognitive ability represent 41 percent of the total gains ($580) per low birth weight prevented. The reduction in chronic disease was only 4 percent. At a 1 percent discount rate these two categories contribute 42 and 12 percent respectively.

Horton and Ross (2003) use a different approach to construct illustrative estimates of the costs of iron deficiency for 10 countries. Rather than reporting in terms of the benefits per case of anemia prevented they report the per-capita costs of anemia. Their estimate of the physical loss of productivity comes to 0.57 percent of the GNP. Considering the impact of anemia on schooling and cognitive development, they estimated the median for the total costs to these economies at 4 percent of the GNP or $16.78 per capita.

3   Potential Policy Interventions

On a very general level, policy interventions are warranted that increase social welfare. Often it is convenient to consider instead two related basic policy motives—increasing efficiency and improving distribution. The distributional goal that is most emphasized is reducing poverty.

Poverty and malnutrition are strongly linked empirically. Based on the available aggregate data, Behrman and Rosenzweig (2004) report that cross-country variation in GDP per capita in purchasing power partity (PPP) terms is inversely related to the percentage of low birth weights among all births and is consistent with almost half of the variation in the percentage of births that are low birth weight (below 2,500 grams) across countries.[14] Haddad et al. (2003) estimate that the cross-country elasticity of child underweight rates (for children under 5 years of age) with respect to per-capita income for 1980–1996 is −0.5. This is virtually the same as the mean for the elasticity from 12 household data sets (although estimates in both approaches decline somewhat in absolute value with the inclusion of fixed effects). Therefore, successful efforts to reduce most forms of malnutrition are likely to have incidences of benefits concentrated relatively among the poor. Thus policies that are focused on alleviating malnutrition are likely to be propoor, although explicit efforts at targeting such policies toward the poor are likely to make them more effectively attain the poverty-alleviation form of the distributional policy motive.

There may also be important efficiency reasons for policies pertaining to relieving malnutrition. From a social perspective the private incentives to invest in nutrition may be inadequate because there may be positive spillovers from better nutrition (e.g., better nourished individuals may be less susceptible to contagious diseases and therefore less likely to spread them to others), because of imperfect information about the benefits of better nutrition, and because of capital and insurance market imperfections that lead to less than socially desired levels of investment in nutrition and other forms of human capital. Therefore, there are likely to be efficiency reasons—that is, differentials between private and social rates of return—for using public resources to alleviate malnutrition. Moreover generally, these efficiency reasons are stronger for poorer than for better-off members of society—the poorer are more likely to be in environments in which disease contagion is greater, have more imperfect information, and have less access to capital and insurance markets and less possibility of self-financing and self-insuring investments. Thus there may be a number of "win–win" policy options that are both propoor and proefficiency.

To what extent there are actual, possible, propoor distributional gains and efficiency gains from policies that reduce malnutrition is, of course, an empirical question. The review of studies in section 2, together with the higher prevalence of malnutrition among poorer members of society noted above, suggests that there are a number of policies to alleviate malnutrition that might be warranted as part of antipoverty efforts. Malnutrition alleviation policies that improve education and improve economic productivity are likely to have positive long-run benefits for individuals from poor families.

The review of studies in section 2, however, does not suggest much that is very concrete about the efficiency policy motive. Although there are a priori reasons, as noted, to think that nutrition may be inadequate from a social perspective due to inefficiencies, the available literature provides virtually no empirical evidence on the extent of such inefficiencies or on whether nutritional programs are likely to be very high in policy hierarchies to address existing inefficiencies. Much of the empirical evidence focuses on what arguably are private impacts of improved nutrition and does not address the possibilities of differentials between the private and the social rates of returns to investing in nutrition. However, this distinction between public and private returns is a bit blurred in "second best" situations in which there exist a number of departures from allocative efficiency. In such situations, efficiency gains may come from reducing preexisting inefficiencies. For example, even if improved health is mainly a private benefit (and this is arguable, as discussed above), if the state already invests in curative health care, investments in nutrition that reduce these health expenditures are second-best efficiency gains. Similarly, given the resources most governments devote to the provision of education, there is a public finance argument for investments in nutrition that improve the efficiency of these schooling investments.

4 Conclusions

Malnutrition is widespread in many developing countries, with close to a billion people estimated to be malnourished. Recent work has emphasized the importance of health and nutrition for productivity and economic growth. This chapter adopts such an approach, with focus on the microeconomic evidence of the direct and indirect links between nutritional status and representations of productivity as they accumulate over the life cycle.

We present a brief explanation of the causes and measurement of malnutrition and of estimates of the extent of malnutrition across developing countries as preludes to our survey of microevidence about the productivity impact in developing countries of improved nutrition on individuals throughout their life cycles—from conception through infancy and childhood on into adolescence and adulthood. The available studies suggest that some of these gains may be considerable and may operate through many channels—increasing cognitive development, physical stature, and strength, inducing earlier school enrollment and more regular school attendance, greater schooling and learning, and greater adult productivity—as well as saving resources that otherwise would go toward dealing with diseases and other problems related to malnutrition over the life cycle.

We then examine the possible gains from different nutritional policy strategies and the policy bases for adopting such strategies. The empirical evidence supports the possible use of nutritional policy to attain better propoor distributional goals by helping to make individuals from poor families more productive over their life cycles. The available empirical evidence, however, is not very informative about the efficiency motive for nutritional policies. There are a priori reasons to suspect that there are possible efficiency gains from nutritional policies due to health spillovers and failures in information, capital, and insurance markets. But the available empirical evidence is almost silent on the existence of such possibilities, whether there are important differences between private and social rates of returns to investment in nutrition, whether nutritional policies would be effective means of addressing any related efficiencies, and to what extent some types of nutritional policies are likely to be "win–win": both propoor and proefficiency. There is thus an important research gap considering possible efficiency reasons for particular nutritional policies.

Notes

1. These are outcome indicators. In addition, measures of nutrient intake or access track some of the inputs that condition nutritional status.

2. This section draws heavily on ACC/SCN 2000, Gibson 1990, and Morris 2001, which provide very helpful introductions to these measures.

3. Implicit in this framework is the assumption that parents or other decision makers are in agreement regarding investments in nutrition and that they are willing to pool their resources in order to undertake these investments. Where there is disagreement on the nature and the allocation of these investments, the ability of individual parents to impose their preferences—their bargaining power—also plays a role (Alderman et al. 1995; Behrman 1997; Haddad, Hoddinott, and Alderman 1997).

4. Other estimates are higher. For instance. Ceesay et al. (1997) claim that there are over 22 million LBW children per year. Blanc and Wardlaw (2002) discuss aspects of estimates from microdata.

5. One exception is provided by Glewwe and King (2001), who find that malnutrition in the second year of life had a larger impact on the IQs of Filipino schoolchildren than that found in earlier periods.

6. These associations do not, however, control for changes in infrastructure or income that may both affect mortality directly as well as influence nutrition, nor can they indicate a counterfactual of the impact of improved nutrition on expected mortality. Guilkey and Riphahn (1998) use longitudinal data of Filipino children with controls for the endogeneity of nutrition and other health care choices. Their simulations indicate that children going two months without weight gain in the first year of life (about 10% of their sample) would have the risk of mortality elevated by 50 percent. Similarly, the scenarios show that if a mother is unable or unwilling to adopt standard recommendations on breast-feeding, the hazard of child mortality increases markedly. Care has to be taken, however, in interpreting the last association as causal because mothers may be less able to breast-feed infants who are at high risk.

7. As with associations of child mortality and nutrition, it is difficult to prove causality with these associations. Randomized controlled trials to substantiate the observational data would need to be large given the risk of maternal mortality and are generally considered unethical.

8. There is an additional aspect of the hypothesis of subsequent costs stemming from biological adaptation to deprivation *in utero* that has a bearing on the estimation of the consequences of LBW. The implications of the hypothesis will be different if the consequences are a direct result of the deprivation compared to the possibility that they only manifest themselves if the deprivation is followed by relative abundance (Lucas, Fewtrell, and Cole 1999; Cameron 2001). High rates of diabetes among Native Americans or Ethiopian immigrants to Israel, for example, seem to be an indirect effect of removal from an environment for which certain genes may once have been adaptive.

9. In related, rather grim work, Margo and Steckel (1982) found that the value of an American slave fell by roughly 1.5 percent for every reduction in height of one inch.

10. Strauss and Thomas (1998) point out that an illiterate man would need to be 30 cm. taller than his literate coworker to have the same expected wage.

11. A few studies have attempted to investigate the tie between hunger and classroom performance using experimental designs. Available results, however, are not conclusive regarding long-term consequences, perhaps, in part, because controlled studies are hampered by difficulties in running experiments for an appreciable duration as well as the difficulty of encouraging parents to conform to the protocols of research design and the inability to use a placebo. Moreover, as shown in Grantham-McGregor et al. 1997, although feeding children may improve attention, its impact on learning depends on classroom organization. On this point, see also Powell et al. 1998.

12. In addition, studies such as Behrman and Rosenzweig 2004 and Strauss 2000 that show the net impact of LBW on earnings capture both the indirect schooling effect and the direct impact of ability as well as any influence of stature.

13. In a similar vein, Conley and Bennett (2000) find that family fixed-effects models using siblings (not necessarily twins) indicate a much larger negative relation between LBW and the probability of completing high school than found in cross-sectional estimates.

14. Their estimates suggest, however, that only a small part of this association between LBW and GDP per capita is due to the causal effects of LBW on productivity.

References

ACC/SCN. 2000. *4th Report on the World Nutrition Situation*. Geneva: United Nations Administrative Committee on Coordination/Sub-Committee on Nutrition (ACC/SCN), in collaboration with the International Food Policy Research Institute (IFPRI).

Alderman, H., and J. R. Behrman. 2004. Estimated Economic Benefits of Reducing LBW in Low-Income Countries. Health Nutrition and Population (HNP) Discussion Paper Series, April 2004. Washington, D.C.: The World Bank.

Alderman, H., J. Hoddinott, and B. Kinsey. 2003. Long-Term Consequences of Early Childhood Malnutrition. Food Consumption and Nutrition Division (FCND) Discussion Paper no. 168. Washington, D.C.: International Food Policy Research Institute (IFPRI).

Alderman, H., J. Behrman, V. Lavy, and R. Menon. 2001. Child Health and School Enrollment: A Longitudinal Analysis. *Journal of Human Resources* 36 (1): 185–205.

Alderman, H., J. R. Behrman, D. Ross, and R. Sabot. 1996. The Returns to Endogenous Human Capital in Pakistan's Rural Wage Labor Market. *Oxford Bulletin of Economics and Statistics* 58 (1): 29–55.

Alderman, H., P.-A. Chiappori, L. Haddad, J. Hoddinott, and R. Kanbur. 1995. Unitary versus Collective Household Models: Is It Time to Shift the Burden of Proof? *World Bank Research Observer* 10 (1): 1–19.

Altonji, J., and T. Dunn. 1996. The Effects of Family Characteristics on the Returns to Education. *Review of Economics and Statistics* 78 (4): 692–704.

Ashworth, A. 1998. Effects of Intrauterine Growth Retardation on Mortality and Morbidity in Infants in Young Children. *European Journal of Clinical Nutrition* 52: 34–42.

Ashworth, A., S. Morris, and P. Lira. 1997. Postnatal Growth Patterns of Full-Term Low Birth Weight Infants in Northeast Brazil Are Related to Socioeconomic Status. *Journal of Nutrition* 127: 1950–1956.

Barker, D. J. P. 1998. *Mothers, Babies, and Health in Later Life*, second edition. Edinburgh, London, New York, Philadelphia, San Francisco, Sydney, and Toronto: Churchill Livingstone.

Basta, S., D. Karyadi, and N. Scrimshaw. 1979. Iron Deficiency, Anemia, and the Productivity of Adult Males in Indonesia. *American Journal of Clinical Nutrition* 32: 916–925.

Beaton, G. H., R. Martorell, L'Abbé, et al. 1993. Effectiveness of Vitamin A Supplementation in the Control of Young Child Morbidity and Mortality in Developing

Countries. Nutrition policy discussion paper no. 13, ACC/SCN State-of-the-art Nutrition Policy Discussion Paper no. 13. Geneva: United Nations Administrative Committee on Coordination/Sub-Committee on Nutrition (ACC/SCN).

Behrman, J. R. 1993. The Economic Rationale for Investing in Nutrition in Developing Countries. *World Development* 21 (11): 1749–1772.

———. 1996. Impact of Health and Nutrition on Education. *World Bank Research Observer* 11 (1): 23–37.

———. 1997. Intrahousehold Distribution and the Family. In *Handbook of Population and Family Economics*, edited by Mark R. Rosenzweig and Oded Stark. Amsterdam: North Holland, pp. 125–168.

Behrman, J. R., and A. B. Deolalikar. 1988. Health and Nutrition. In *Handbook on Economic Development*, vol. 1, edited by Hollis B. Chenery and T. N. Srinivasan. Amsterdam: North Holland, pp. 631–711.

———. 1989. Wages and Labor Supply in Rural India: The Role of Health, Nutrition, and Seasonality. In *Causes and Implications of Seasonal Variability in Household Food Security*, ed. D. Sahn. Baltimore: Johns Hopkins University Press, pp. 107–118.

Behrman, J. R., and M. R. Rosenzweig. 2004. Returns to Birthweight. *Review of Economics and Statistics* 86 (2): 586–601.

Bigsten, A., P. Collier, S. Dercon, M. Fafchamps, B. Gauthier, J. W. Gunning, A. Isaksson, A. Oduro, R. Oostendorp, C. Pattillo, M. Söderbom, F. Teal, A. Zeufack, and S. Appleton. 2000. Rates of Return on Physical and Human Capital in Africa's Manufacturing Sector. *Economic Development and Cultural Change* 48: 801–828.

Blanc, A. K., and T. Wardlaw. 2002. *Survey Data on Low Birth Weight: An Evaluation of Recent International Estimates and Estimation Procedures.* Columbia: Blancroft Research International.

Boissiere, M., J. B. Knight, and R. H. Sabot. 1985. Earnings, Schooling, Ability, and Cognitive Skills. *American Economic Review* 75: 1016–1030.

Brabin, B., M. Hakimi, and D. Pelletier. 2001. An Analysis of Anemia- and Pregnancy-Related Maternal Mortality. *Journal of Nutrition* 131: 604–615.

Cameron, N. 2001. Catch-Up Growth Increases Risk Factors for Obesity in Urban Children in South Africa. *International Journal of Obesity* 25: S48.

Cawley, J., J. Heckman, and E. Vytlacil. 2001. Three Observations on Wages and Measured Cognitive Ability. *Labor Economics* 8: 419–442.

Ceesay, S. M., A. M. Prentice, T. J. Cole, R. Ford, E. Poskitt, L. T. Weaver, and R. G. Whitehead. 1997. Effects on Birth Weight and Perinatal Mortality of Maternal Dietary Supplements in Rural Gambia: 5-Year Randomised Controlled Trial. *British Medical Journal* 315 (September): 786–790.

Conley, D., and N. G. Bennett. 2000. Is Biology Destiny? Birth Weight and Life Chances. *American Sociological Review* 65 (June): 458–467.

Conley, D., K. Strully, and N. Bennett. 2003. A Pound of Flesh or Just Proxy? Using Twins Differences to Estimate the Effects of Birth Weight on Life Chances. Working paper no. W9901, National Bureau of Economic Research, Cambridge, Mass.

Deolalikar, A. 1988. Nutrition and Labor Productivity in Agriculture: Estimates for Rural South India. *Review of Economics and Statistics* 70 (3): 406–413.

Doak, C., L. Adair, C. Monteiro, and B. M. Popkin. 2000. Overweight and Underweight Co-Exists in Brazil, China, and Russia. *Journal of Nutrition* 130: 2965–2980.

Fogel, R. 1994. Economic Growth, Population Theory, and Physiology: The Bearing of Long-Term Processes on the Making of Economic Policy. *American Economic Review* 84 (3): 369–395.

Foster, A., and M. Rosenzweig. 1993. Information, Learning, and Wage Rates in Low Income Rural Areas. *Journal of Human Resources* 28 (4): 759–779.

Gibson, R. 2000. *Principles of Nutritional Assessment*. Oxford: Oxford University Press.

Glewwe, P. 1996. The Relevance of Standard Estimates of Rates of Return to Schooling for Education Policy: A Critical Assessment. *Journal of Development Economics* 51 (2): 267–290.

Glewwe, P., and H. Jacoby. 1995. An Economic Analysis of Delayed Primary School Enrollment and Childhood Malnutrition in a Low-Income Country. *Review of Economics and Statistics* 77 (1): 156–169.

Glewwe, P., H. Jacoby, and E. King. 2001. Early Childhood Nutrition and Academic Achievement: A Longitudinal Analysis. *Journal of Public Economics* 81 (3): 345–368.

Glewwe, P., and E. King. 2001. The Impact of Early Childhood Nutrition Status on Cognitive Achievement: Does the Timing of Malnutrition Matter? *World Bank Economic Review* 15 (1): 81–114.

Glick, P., and D. Sahn. 1998. Health and Productivity in a Heterogeneous Urban Labor Market. *Applied Economics* 30 (2): 203–216.

Grantham-McGregor, S., L. Fernald, and K. Sethuraman. 1999a. Effects of Health and Nutrition on Cognitive and Behavioural Development in Children in the First Three Years of Life: Part 1: Low Birthweight, Breastfeeding, and Protein-Energy Malnutrition. *Food and Nutrition Bulletin* 20 (1): 53–75.

———. 1999b. Effects of Health and Nutrition on Cognitive and Behavioural Development in Children in the First Three Years of Life: Part 2: Infections and Micronutrient Deficiencies: Iodine, Iron, and Zinc. *Food and Nutrition Bulletin* 20 (1): 76–99.

Grantham-McGregor, S., C. Walker, S. Chang, and C. Powell. 1997. Effects of Early Childhood Supplementation with and without Stimulation on Later Development in Stunted Jamaican Children. *American Journal of Clinical Nutrition* 66: 247–253.

Guilkey, D., and R. Riphahn. 1998. The Determinants of Child Mortality in the Philippines: Estimation of a Structural Model. *Journal of Development Economics* 56: 281–305.

Haas, J., S. Murdoch, J. Rivera, and R. Martorell. 1996. Early Nutrition and Later Physical Work Capacity. *Nutrition Reviews* 54: S41–S48.

Hack, M. 1998. Effects of Intrauterine Growth Retardation on Mental Performance and Behavior: Outcomes during Adolescence and Adulthood. *European Journal of Clinical Nutrition* 52: 65–71.

Haddad, L., H. Alderman, S. Appleton, L. Song, and Y. Yohannes. 2003. Reducing Child Malnutrition: How Far Does Income Growth Take Us? *World Bank Economic Review* 17 (1): 107–131.

Haddad, L., and H. Bouis. 1991. The Impact of Nutritional Status on Agricultural Productivity: Wage Evidence from the Philippines. *Oxford Bulletin of Economics and Statistics* 53 (1): 45–68.

Haddad, L., J. Hoddinott, and H. Alderman. 1997. *Intrahousehold Resource Allocation in Developing Countries: Models, Methods, and Policy.* Baltimore: Johns Hopkins University Press.

Hoddinott, J., and B. Kinsey. 2001. Child Growth in the Time of Drought. *Oxford Bulletin of Economics and Statistics* 63 (4): 409–436.

Horton, S., and J. Ross. 2003. The Economics of Iron Deficiency. *Food Policy* 28 (1): 51–75.

Johnston, F., S. Low, Y. de Baessa, and R. MacVean. 1987. Interaction of Nutritional and Socioeconomic Status as Determinants of Cognitive Achievement in Disadvantaged Urban Guatemalan Children. *American Journal of Physical Anthropology* 73: 501–506.

Lasky, R., R. Klein, C. Yarborough, P. Engle, A. Lechtig, and R. Martorell. 1981. The Relationship between Physical Growth and Infant Development in Rural Guatemala. *Child Development* 52: 219–226.

Lavy, V., J. Spratt, and N. Leboucher. 1997. Patterns of Incidence and Change in Moroccan Literacy. *Comparative Education Review* 41 (2): 120–141.

Lewit, E., L. Baker, H. Corman, and P. Shiono. 1995. The Direct Costs of Low Birth Weight. *The Future of Children* 5 (1): 35–56.

Li, H., A. S. Stein, H. Barnhart, U. Ramakrishnan, and R. Martorell. 2003. Associations between Prenatal and Postnatal Growth and Adult Body Size and Composition. *American Journal of Clinical Nutrition* 77: 1498–1505.

Li, R., X. Chen, H. Yan, P. Deurenberg, L. Garby, and J. Hautvast. 1994. Functional Consequences of Iron Supplementation in Iron-Deficient Female Cottonmill Workers in Beijing. *American Journal of Clinical Nutrition* 59: 908–913.

Lightwood, J., C. Phibbs, and S. Glanz. 1999. Short-Term Health and Economic Benefits of Smoking Cessation: Low Birth Weight. *Pediatrics* 104 (6): 1312–1320.

Lucas, A., M. S. Fewtrell, and T. J. Cole. 1999. Fetal Origins of Adult Disease—The Hypothesis Revisited. *British Medical Journal* 319: 245–249.

Margo, R., and R. Steckel. 1982. The Heights of American Slaves: New Evidence on Slave Nutrition and Health. *Social Science History* 6 (4): 516–538.

Martorell, R. 1995. Results and Implications of the INCAP Follow-Up Study. *Journal of Nutrition* 125 (suppl.): 1127–1138.

———. 1997. Undernutrition during Pregnancy and Early Childhood and Its Consequences for Cognitive and Behavioural Development. In *Early Childhood Development: Investing In Our Children's Future,* edited by M. E. Young. Amsterdam: Elsevier.

———. 1999. The Nature of Child Malnutrition and Its Long-Term Implications. *Food and Nutrition Bulletin* 19: 288–292.

Martorell, R., K. L. Khan, and D. Schroeder. 1994. Reversibility of Stunting: Epidemiological Findings in Children from Developing Countries. *European Journal of Clinical Nutrition* 48 (suppl.): 45–57.

Martorell, R., J. Rivera, and H. Kaplowitz. 1989. Consequences of Stunting in Early Childhood for Adult Body Size in Rural Guatemala. Unpublished paper. Stanford: Stanford University, Food Research Institute.

Matte, T., M. Bresnahan, M. Begg, and E. Susser. 2001. Influence of Variation in Birthweight within Normal Range and within Sibships on IQ at Age 7 Years: Cohort Study. *British Medical Journal* 323: 310–314.

Morris, S. 2001. Measuring Nutritional Dimensions of Household Food Security. In *Methods for Rural Development Projects*, edited by John Hoddinott. Washington, D.C.: International Food Policy Research Institute.

Pelletier, D. L., and E. Frongillo. 2003. Changes in Child Survival Are Strongly Associated with Changes in Malnutrition in Developing Countries. *Journal of Nutrition* 133 (1): 107–119.

Pelletier, D. L., E. Frongillo, D. Schroeder, and J.-P. Habicht. 1995. The Effects of Malnutrition on Child Mortality in Developing Countries. *Bulletin of the World Health Organization* 73: 443–448.

Petrou, S., T. Sach, and L. Davidson. 2001. The Long-Term Costs of Preterm Birth and Low Birth Weight: Results of a Systematic Review. *Child: Care, Health, and Development* 27 (2): 97–115.

Pollitt, E. 1990. *Malnutrition and Infection in the Classroom. Infection: Schistosomiasis.* Paris: UNESCO.

Powell, C. A., S. M. Grantham-McGregor, S. P. Walker, and S. M. Chang. 1998. School Breakfast Benefits Children's Nutritional Status and School Performance. *American Journal of Clinical Nutrition* 69: 873–879.

Psacharopoulos, G. 1994. Returns to Investment in Education: A Global Update. *World Development* 22 (9): 1325–1344.

Psacharopoulos, G., and E. Velez. 1992. Schooling, Ability, and Earnings in Colombia, 1988. *Economic Development and Cultural Change* 40: 629–643.

Ramakrishnan, U., R. Martorell, D. Schroeder, and R. Flores. 1999. Intergenerational Effects on Linear Growth. *Journal of Nutrition* 129 (2): 544–549.

Ravelli, A. C., J. H. van der Meulen, R. P. Michels, C. Osmond, D. J. Barker, C. N. Hales, and O. P. Bleker. 1998. Glucose Tolerance in Adults after Prenatal Exposure to Famine. *Lancet* 351 (9097): 173–177.

Richards, M., R. Hardy, D. Ruth, and M. Wadsworth. 2001. Birth Weight and Cognitive Function in the British 1946 Birth Cohort: Longitudinal Population-Based Study. *British Medical Journal* 322: 199–203.

Roseboom, T., H. P. van der Meulen, A. Ravelli, C. Osmond, D. Barker, and O. Bleker. 2001. Effects of Prenatal Exposure to the Dutch Famine on Adult Disease in Later Life: An Overview. *Molecular and Cellular Endocrinology* 185: 93–98.

Rosenzweig, M. 1995. Why Are There Returns in Schooling? *American Economic Review* 85 (2): 153–158.

Ross, J. S., and E. L. Thomas. 1996. Iron Deficiency, Anemia, and Maternal Mortality. Profiles 3 Working Notes Series no. 3. Washington, D.C.: Academy for Education Development.

Ruel, M. 2001. Can Food-Based Strategies Help Reduce Vitamin A and Iron Deficiencies? A Review of Recent Evidence. Food Policy Review 5. Washington, D.C.: International Food Policy Research Institute, pp. 1–54.

Schultz, T. P. 1996. Wage Rentals for Reproducible Human Capital: Evidence from Two West African Countries. Unpublished paper. Yale University, Department of Economics.

Simondon, K., F. Simondon, I. Simon, A. Diallo, E. Benefice, P. Traissac, and B. Maire. 1998. Preschool Stunting, Age at Menarche, and Adolescent Height: A Longitudinal Study in Rural Senegal. European Journal of Clinical Nutrition 52: 412–418.

Strauss, J., and D. Thomas. 1995. Human Resources: Empirical Modeling of Household and Family Decisions. In Handbook of Development Economics, vol. 3A, ed. J. R. Behrman and T. N. Srinivasan. Amsterdam: North-Holland, pp. 1883–2024.

Strauss, J., and D. Thomas. 1998. Health, Nutrition, and Economic Development. Journal of Economic Literature 36 (2): 766–817.

Strauss, R. S. 2000. Adult Functional Outcome of Those Born Small for Gestational Age. Journal of the American Medical Association 283 (5): 625–632.

Thomas, D., and J. Strauss. 1997. Health and Wages: Evidence on Men and Women in Urban Brazil. Journal of Econometrics 77 (1): 159–187.

Victora, C., B. Kirkwood, A. Ashworth, R. Black, S. Rogers, S. Sazawal, H. Campbell, and S. Gore. 1999. Potential Interventions for the Prevention of Childhood Pneumonia in Developing Countries: Improving Nutrition. American Journal of Clinical Nutrition 70: 309–320.

World Bank. 1993. World Development Report 1993: Investing in Health. New York: Oxford University Press.

World Health Organization. 2002. The World Health Report: Reducing Risks, Promoting Healthy Lives. Geneva: World Health Organization.

Yaqub, S. 2002. Poor Children Grow into Poor Adults: Harmful Mechanisms or Over-Deterministic Theory. Journal of International Development 14: 1081–1093.

III

Human Capital, Health, and Demography

8 On Epidemiologic and Economic Transitions: A Historical View

Suchit Arora

A recent set of growth theories says that human capital's rise helped steer a transition out of the Malthusian regime by speeding up economic growth since the nineteenth century (Lucas 2002; Galor and Weil 1999). In models of economic transitions, however, human capital in the form of schooling has been given a central place while the role of health has remained peripheral. Health may have been left in the periphery because neither health-related data covering a long horizon nor the historical framework to study them is within the purview of mainstream macroeconomics. This chapter tries to narrow the gap by exploring nearly two centuries of a phenomenon known as the epidemiologic transition.

The transition refers to the progress of life expectancy as diminishing infectious diseases gives way to noninfectious diseases as the main causes of sickness and death in a population. It might appear that research on the transition and on growth theory could have little in common, but they are surprisingly similar enough to connect in a useful way.

Both areas assign a pivotal role to human capital even as they emphasize different aspects of it. Growth theory lays emphasis on skills, whereas the transition emphasizes health. Although skills and health may be studied as distinct facets of human ability, they are essentially inseparable and are likely shaped by a common set of underlying factors, especially over the long term. Another similarity is in their central themes: escape from the Malthusian regime. Schooling and skills invigorate an economic transition from the Malthusian regime to modern economic growth. Improving health leads to an epidemiologic transition from the Malthusian regime to the modern era of longer life spans. The unity of theme and the emphasis on what is essentially human capital then shows up in the similarity of their historical under-pinnings: onset of both epidemiologic and economic transitions in industrialized countries can be traced at least to the nineteenth century.

Salience of the nineteenth century to both transitions, however, poses a problem for studying their interplay. Data for only a few countries extend sufficiently into the past to allow reasonable inferences about health-related change since the Malthusian times. The countries selected are Australia, France, the Netherlands and the United Kingdom. However, owing to limited space this chapter uses only the United Kingdom's data to illustrate the main features of the transition.

The data for the United Kingdom show that health-related stimuli that appeared during the nineteenth century enabled households to curtail deaths from hundreds of diseases. This may have allowed human capital to surface as a productive force perhaps for the first time in centuries. Uncovering the nature of those stimuli, however, requires tracing the paths of infectious and non-infectious diseases since then. Doing so also helps find out whether the epidemiologic transition occurred the way it has been described in the literature.

The literature broadly says that decreasing death rates from infectious diseases, which used to dominate the Malthusian regime of short life spans, coincided with increasing death rates from noninfectious maladies, which now dominate the modern era of longer life spans. However, the paths of infectious and noninfectious diseases only partially agree with that description. Significantly, death rates from noninfectious maladies were at least as large as death rates from infectious diseases even during the Malthusian regime of short life spans and that that most noninfectious diseases diminished during the transition to the modern era of longer life spans. The inconsistencies call for a restatement of the main propositions of the epidemiologic transition.

The restated propositions then open a potentially fertile prospect: the tools that economists use for examining the role of human capital in economic growth may prove useful in studying the influence of epidemiologic change on economic growth as well. By assembling relevant insights from epidemiology and from health-related research in economic history, this chapter takes a preliminary step in that direction.

The first issues one faces in this direction is whether per capita GDP or its growth rate might have directly ushered-in epidemiologic change. After all, even as the jury is still out, scholars continue to view health-related improvements as by-products of economic growth. But an empirical assessment of the matter suggests that per capita income is a weak explanatory variable. This could either mean that per capita GDP is too blunt an instrument for studying subtle ways in which epidemiologic phenomena shape human affairs or that behavioral and institutional factors immediately relevant to epidemiologic change may appear exogenously (to incomes). At yet another level, it is also relieving to find weak explanatory power in per-capita GDP. If it were a substantively potent explanatory variable, then assigning it a causal role would have logically implied immortality within finite time.

On finding insufficient explanatory power in per-capita GDP or its growth rate, the discussion turns toward intergenerational human capital-based models that could potentially explain the way key features of the epidemiologic transition have turned out. After highlighting their relevance, this chapter evaluates whether diminishing disease-caused fatality, a potent sign of improving human durability, influenced the slope of the growth path permanently—human-capital-based growth theory's central prediction. Although the results indicate that health-related changes have a long reach, forging a consensus on their role in economic progress may require further interdisciplinary research.

It helps first to briefly review why health may be essential to the human-capital-based case for economic growth.

1 Does Health Qualify as Human "Capital"?

Although health and conventional forms of human capital are inseparable, health by itself does not measure up to the term "capital." To qualify as capital, economic theory requires a factor to have three attributes. Health has only two of them, but it is indispensable to conventional human capital with respect to all three.

The first attribute of capital is that it should be reasonably durable; durability allows it to function as a medium of storage so that its owner can benefit from it over time. It is self-evident that well-functioning organs allow people to work effectively; few skills would be useful without them. Durability of organs, which is essential to health, must be essential to conventional human capital.

Second, the factor should be alienable: like private property, the returns from ownership accrue solely to the owner (or to the owner's

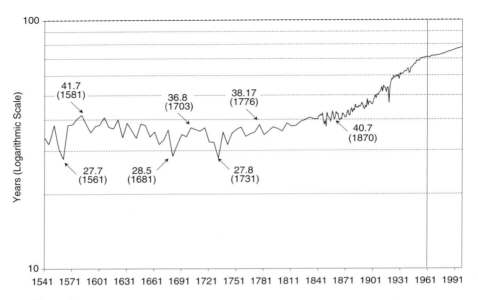

Figure 8.1a
Period life expectancy at birth, England and Wales, 1541–1998.

immediate family). Besides being self-evident, labor market returns to good or poor health have been documented in several empirical studies (Grossman 1972; Bartel and Taubman 1979; Schultz 1997; Schultz and Tansel 1996, among others).

The third property of capital is that its accumulation must entail some form of sacrifice that yields benefits in the future. Except for when the prospect of illness requires changing one's diet or habits away from unsalutary things, or when resources need to be set aside or borrowed for treating illness, the sacrifice involved in improving health is unclear. However, on this count health turns out to be historically crucial to human capital's conventional forms.[1]

Accumulating human capital through schooling, work experience, and on-the-job training requires sacrificing *time*, usually years. If it takes several years to school and accumulate skill and experience, then it is informative to find out how the years available to an average person have evolved.

Figure 8.1 shows that the period life expectancy at birth fluctuated between 27 and 41 years for three centuries. Despite the faster pace of economic progress since the second half of the eighteenth century, life expectancy had remained in the narrow range, breaching it perma-

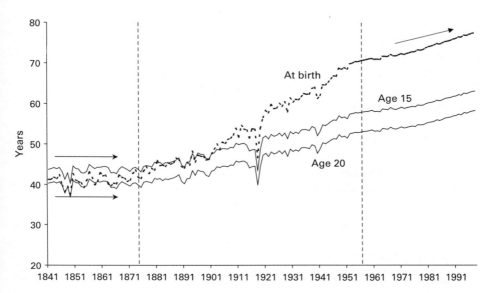

Figure 8.1b
Period life expectancy at birth, age 15 and age 20.

nently only toward the end of the nineteenth century. Its rise suggests
that the health-related stimuli that appeared during this time were
historically unique; they were also likely broad-based, involving the
masses, because life expectancy at chronologically older ages started
increasing as well (figure 8.1b).

   Why might life expectancy start increasing permanently? Calculation of life expectancy is based largely on disease-caused deaths. Instead of gauging the extent of sickness and deaths from hundreds of
diseases annually, life expectancy merely summarizes the consequence
in units of years. It follows that lasting reductions in disease-caused
deaths added years to people's lives. Disease by disease, these reductions must have involved deliberated household and social choices
that foster human durability. And since the durability of humans is
what produces more *time*, accumulating human capital without it is
inconceivable.

   If so, it seems reasonable to conjecture that more people may have
been able to school since the nineteenth century because life spans for
doing so had begun to grow, increasing schooling's present value, and
generating what Robert Lucas Jr. (2002) has called "opportunities for
human capital investment that face the mass of households in a

society." Consequently, health improvements may have been essential to human capital's ascent and thus essential to any theory that ties it to economic progress.

As a summary variable, however, life expectancy goes only so far. To find out why it changes, we need to look at disease-related shifts that happen beneath the surface: the epidemiologic transition.

2   The Epidemiologic Transition

Ever since Omran (1971), the literature has described the core structure of the transition in terms of disease-caused deaths during three stages: a Malthusian regime ("age of pestilence and famine"), which is followed by a transitional period ("age of receding pandemics") that culminates in a post-transitional regime ("age of degenerative and man-made disease").

Three central features characterize the Malthusian stage:

1. Sicknesses and deaths from infectious diseases persist at high rates; they dominate disease-caused deaths and their outbreaks recur frequently.

2. In contrast, the rate of noninfectious maladies is subdued; they form a smaller proportion of all deaths.

3. With rates of overall disease-caused deaths high, life spans are short and life expectancy low.

Then, for various reasons, there begins a transitional phase in which:

1. Infectious diseases start reducing and their share of all disease-caused deaths starts shrinking.

2. Lasting improvements in life expectancy appear.

3. However, along with rising life expectancy, rates of noninfectious diseases start increasing as well. Noninfectious diseases surface as leading causes, eventually accounting for the bulk of all deaths in the post-transitional regime.

Omran (1982) later amended the core structure by including another stage in which onset of and deaths from noninfectious maladies are deferred to older chronological ages than before.[2] However, it is unclear whether that stage should be considered as new, for it might have been an extension of things that had been underway for decades. For the time being, therefore, it might be better to withhold judgment on this issue and focus on the core.

To evaluate whether the transition happened the way it is sketched above, annual age-specific deaths from each disease in England and Wales were assimilated into the variable "all diseases." Based on the nosological guidelines outlined in the International Classification of Diseases (ICD-9) (WHO 1977), "all disease" was then partitioned into two main components dubbed as "infectious diseases" and "noninfectious diseases." Noninfectious diseases were then segmented further into their main components such as cancers, and maladies of the circulatory system, digestive system, nervous system, musculoskeletal system, genitourinary system, and so on. External causes (accidents, injuries, homicides, etc.) were excluded. For an extensive discussion on the proper disease compositions of each variable, the interested reader is referred to Preston, Keyfitz, and Schoen 1972, Preston 1976, D'Espaignet et al. 1991, Vallin and Mesle 1987, and Arora 1999, 2003 for details.

2.1 Infectious Diseases

Marked by several significant outbreaks, the contour of infectious diseases shown in figure 8.2 indicates roughly three regimes: (1) pre-1870 dubbed as the "Malthusian" regime, (2) a transitional phase, 1870–1940/1950, and (3) post-transitional regime after World War II.

Although the data for gauging rates of death from all infectious diseases are unavailable for the period before 1850, figure 8.3 gives the impression that rates of infectious diseases might have been larger then. Advances in transportation technology during the seventeenth, eighteenth, and nineteenth centuries had enabled mass migration of peoples, within countries and internationally. That may have led to a more frequent spread of contagious diseases, especially among populations that were previously unexposed to some types of germs (Crosby 1986; McNeil 1998). The escalation in frequency of outbreaks, lasting through three-quarters of the nineteenth century, included smallpox, influenza, typhus, typhoid fever, cholera, and diarrhea, among others.

Spanning as many as thirty years during the first half of the nineteenth century, epidemics unsurprisingly featured in Malthus's theory of population in which per-capita output tended to return to a roughly constant level over time. Flourishing in unsanitary conditions, preying on frail health and the public's ignorance about them, recurring outbreaks may have interrupted, possibly derailed, economic activity

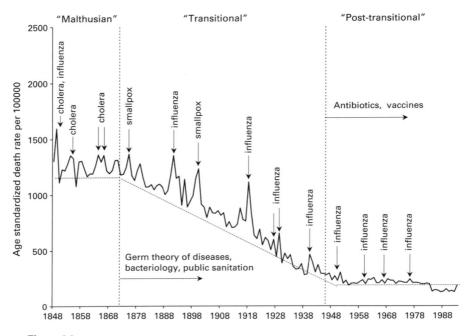

Figure 8.2
Infectious diseases in England and Wales, 1848–1994.

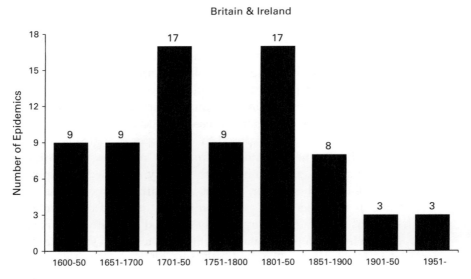

Figure 8.3
Frequency of epidemics since the 17th century.

often, returning per-capita incomes to roughly similar levels. That returning, however, may not necessarily have involved an increase in population because migration—a redistribution of population—could trigger outbreaks that undermine economic activity.

By most historical accounts, during the last quarter of the nineteenth century, ascendancy of the germ theory—the unique, knowledge-based stimulus—had renewed human understanding of disease etiology, stimulated public sanitation, and spurred further advances in bacteriology. Progressively, people learned how to check disease through effective arterial sewage and water supply systems; through pasteurization, sterilization, and antiseptic procedures; through behavioral change brought about by education; through legislation; and through the formation of institutions to administer public sanitation and contain potentially deadly outbreaks (Chadwick 1842; Bairoch 1988; Fraser 1950; Szreter 1988, 1997; Easterlin 1999; Mokyr 2000; Tomes 1990).[3]

The germ theory delivered perhaps a major blow to the Malthusian view. During the transitional stage, even as mass migration and urban crowding continued, infectious diseases and frequency of outbreaks began diminishing. Consequently, life expectancy started rising permanently for the first time in centuries, maybe altering people's worldview of the opportunities they and their children could avail themselves of. Finally, in the post–World War II period, advances in antibiotics and vaccines may have helped contain infectious diseases, cementing the new worldview as the standard.

That standard, however, appears to have been an exception in history. Economic theory tells us that low life spans of the Malthusian era would have discouraged investments. High death rates from infectious disease and the uncertainty caused by frequent outbreaks may have perpetuated the view that there is little point in investing as you may not be around to reap the benefits.

Human-capital-based growth theory says that households enrich society's stock of human capital by having fewer children but by nurturing each child well. Why is it that during the Malthusian regime households were unable to do so adequately? There could be at least two reasons why restricting the number of children might have been seen as a perilous option. First, households may have sought replacement on the death of a child, which happened all too frequently. Second, fear of juvenile death might have led to a heightened precautionary demand for children—having more of them increased the chances that some would survive. Fearing such loss, they may also have been reluctant to school each child until it was reasonably certain the child would live long enough for such an investment to be worthwhile (Sah 1991; Kalemli-Ozcan 2003; Kalemli-Ozcan, Ryder, and Weil 2000).

The germ theory likely shifted the production function of human capital substantially. Joel Mokyr has called it a "quantum leap" in humanity's grasp of disease causation (Mokyr 2000). Equipped with this new knowledge, households may have been able to check disease more effectively. This may have activated salutary dynamics in which they had fewer children and nurtured each child better than was previously possible. Elevated average productivity then may have invigorated economic activity permanently, bringing about a transition—epidemiologic and economic—from the Malthusian era. Without this knowledge, the dynamic might have reversed, perhaps vindicating the Malthusian worldview again.

The relevance of infectious diseases to conventional forms of human capital formation is illustrated in figure 8.4. Circa 1850, children (0–14 years) and the age group 15–64 years accounted for about three-quarters of all infectious disease-caused deaths. They accounted for 95

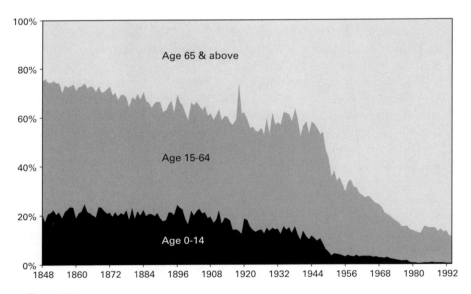

Figure 8.4
Age distribution of deaths from infectious diseases, 1848–1994.

percent of the total reduction in infectious diseases, about two-thirds of it occurring in 15- to 64-year-olds. The sharp fall in their share immediately after World War II suggests that the use of antibiotics and vaccines may have resulted in considerable social returns.[4]

Besides affecting largely younger sections of the population in the past, a noteworthy feature about the path of infectious diseases is that about 97 percent of their total decline had been attained through 1950–1960 (figure 8.2). In the post-transitional regime, infectious diseases were restrained largely to ages 65 and above (mostly influenza and pneumonia).

2.2   The Transition and Noninfectious Diseases

As infectious diseases started diminishing, an epidemiologic shift began. Figure 8.5 shows the fraction of all disease-caused deaths attributable to infectious and noninfectious diseases. In line with the received view of the transition, the share of all disease-caused deaths attributable to noninfectious diseases started increasing.

However, noninfectious diseases were a significant proportion even during the Malthusian stage. This is slightly different from the received

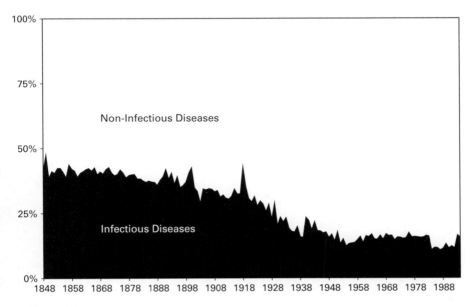

Figure 8.5
Infectious and noninfectious diseases as proportions of all-disease-caused deaths.

view, which says that infectious diseases were the larger component then.[5] Consequently, until about 1870–1875, we have a regime in which life expectancy was low and not so different from prior centuries (figure 8.1), the rate of deaths from infectious diseases was high (figure 8.2), and major outbreaks recurred frequently (figure 8.3)— distinct Malthusian features all. Yet, noninfectious maladies were a substantial fraction of all disease-caused deaths as well. The core structure of the transition outlined by Omran (1971), however, has the "age of pestilence and famine" distinctly preceding the "age of degenerative and man-made diseases." Figure 8.5 appears to suggest that the basis for that distinction might be tenuous. Thus,

Proposition 1   During the Malthusian regime, both infectious diseases and noninfectious diseases coexisted as significant proportions of all disease-caused deaths.

Figure 8.6 shows the contour of noninfectious maladies along with that of infectious diseases (the broken line, reproduced from figure 8.2). Since at least the mid-nineteenth century, the rate of noninfec-

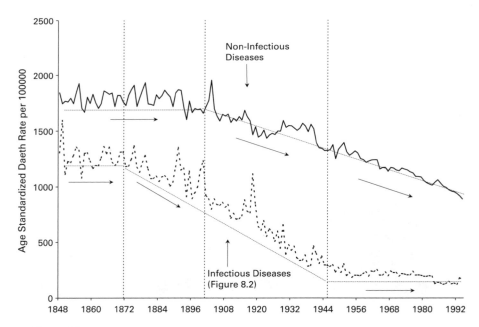

Figure 8.6
Noninfectious diseases and infectious diseases, England and Wales, 1848–1994.

tious maladies has been larger than infectious diseases. However, the received view says that infectious disease was the dominant feature. On the contrary,

Proposition 2 During the Malthusian regime, the rate of noninfectious-disease-caused fatality was larger than that of infectious-disease-caused fatality.

Given that life expectancy during the Malthusian stage persisted between 27 and 41 years, it is reasonable to infer that average life spans would have been short. And shorter average life spans coincided with a much higher rate of noninfectious maladies than today. It follows that

Proposition 3 During the Malthusian stage, noninfectious maladies likely surfaced or turned fatal, or both, at younger ages than during the post-transitional stage.

Therefore, besides infectious diseases, noninfectious diseases likely constrained human capital too. Furthermore, like infectious diseases, conditions that generate most noninfectious maladies were also much worse during the Malthusian era than during the post-transitional period.

It is also clear from figure 8.6 that as infectious diseases started declining, noninfectious diseases started diminishing shortly afterward. However, the received view of the transition is that death rates from noninfectious diseases increased during the transitional and post-transitional stages. Thus,

Proposition 4 During the transitional stage, the rate of noninfectious diseases decreased. Their decrease lagged briefly the onset of reduction in infectious diseases. Although infectious diseases diminished more rapidly, the fall of both categories around the same time suggests an underlying synergy between them.

This synergy seems inescapable: both categories of disease caused high rates of death during the Malthusian regime; both started diminishing within a short interval. It were as if underlying factors that curtailed one disease category likely hastened the decline of the other as well (although not necessarily at the same time). The following sections will explore that vein of thought in some detail.

Meanwhile, it is noteworthy that the downward trend in noninfectious diseases is not a recent phenomenon; it had occurred throughout the twentieth century. Further, that trend has coincided with increasing average life spans. Here, the converse of proposition 3 seems applicable: fatality from noninfectious diseases was being deferred to older chronological ages throughout the twentieth century.

However, the overall decrease of noninfectious diseases needs to be qualified. Unlike infectious diseases, not all noninfectious diseases diminished through the twentieth century.

A reasonable way to assess disparate trends among disease categories is to calculate their contribution to the reduction of *all* diseases. This would highlight two features simultaneously. First, it clarifies the direction of change in each disease category. A disease that had increased would have *added* to the aggregate death rate even as that aggregate figure diminished under the weight of diseases that fell. Second, it would ascertain the size of each disease category's contribution to the total reduction in deaths from all causes.

Table 8.1 shows the results of the accounting, for both the aggregate population and for various age groups. Columns 2 through 5 show an accounting through 1955–1960, which is chosen as a reference point because through 1955–1960 the transitional stage had ended, achieving along with it about 85 percent of the total increase in life expectancy (figure 8.1). It is informative to know which disease categories contributed to the bulk of improvement during the transitional stage. Columns 6 through 9 then provide an accounting over an extended period. Expressed as percentages, a negative sign denotes that the disease category helped *reduce* the all-disease-caused death rate.

Consider the main italicized categories. Through 1960, reductions in infectious diseases contributed about two-thirds of the total decline in the all-disease-caused death rate for the aggregate population (column 5), for ages 0–14 (column 2), and for ages 15–64 (column 3). For ages 65 and above (column 4), the contribution is substantial as well.

Over the entire period (columns 6 through 9), the contribution of infectious diseases is reduced because since 1960 much of the decrease in all-disease-caused fatality has come from noninfectious maladies, particularly for age groups 15–64 and 65 and above. Therefore,

Proposition 5 During the transitional stage, reduction in infectious diseases accounted for the bulk of decrease in all-disease-caused fatality for the aggregate population and for the broader age groups.

The decrease of infectious diseases, therefore, was broad based. It affected all age groups perhaps because their containment involved a scale effect (e.g., containing cholera for one means doing so for all).

Table 8.1
Percentage contribution of principal disease groups to reduction in all-disease-caused death rate.

Disease category	1871/75–1956/60				1871/75–1990/94			
	Age groups				Age groups			
	0–14	15–64	65 & +	Aggregate	0–14	15–64	65 & +	Aggregate
	(2)	(3)	(4)	(5)	(6)	(7)	(8)	(9)
Infectious diseases	−69.2	−68.4	−57.2	−65.5	−67.0	−64.3	−38.8	−55.2
Noninfectious diseases	−30.8	−29.9	−42.8	−34.5	−33.1	−35.8	−61.2	−44.8
Circulatory system	−1.6	−6.6	+116.2	+34.1	−1.5	−14.7	+29.3	+5.4
Neoplasms (Cancers)	+0.1	+5.9	+23.6	+9.8	−0.1	+3.4	+20.5	+8.9
Nervous system	−0.4	−6.7	−22.7	−10.1	−0.5	−6.1	−15.0	−8.1
Digestive system	−0.7	−7.0	−5.4	−4.8	−0.8	−6.4	−3.9	−4.1
Nutritional and metabolic disorders	−0.4	−2.3	−1.1	−1.3	−0.4	−2.1	−1.1	−1.1
Genitourinary system	−0.3	−3.4	−2.6	−3.4	−0.4	−3.7	−3.2	−2.7
Musculoskeletal system	−0.3	−0.1	−0.33	−0.6	−0.3	−0.9	0.0	−0.4
Ill-defined causes	−2.4	−4.0	−116.6	−39.2	−2.1	−4.0	−81.6	−33.2
Perinatal causes	−25.5	—	—	−7.3	−28.2	—	—	−6.7
Others	−0.7	−5.7	−8.9	−15.4	0.0	−1.3	−6.2	−2.8

Notes: Time series for each cause was considered separately for each age group and for the aggregate population. "Others" includes congenital anomalies, causes pertaining to pregnancy and childbirth, maladies of the skin and subcutaneous tissue, and of blood and blood-forming organs. Over 1870–1960, All-disease-caused deaths reduced by 93% for ages 0–14, by 73.5% for ages 15–64, by 32.5% for age 65 and above, and by 54.4% for the aggregate population; over 1870–1994, the percentage reductions are, 98.1%, 82.8%, 47.4%, and 66.4%, respectively.

Since information on all disease-caused deaths is the basis for life expectancy calculations, it follows that

Proposition 6 During the transitional phase, reduction in infectious diseases likely accounted for the bulk of increase in life expectancy at various ages. However, during the post-transitional regime, infectious diseases have been restrained, while noninfectious diseases have continued to diminish, adding further to life expectancy.

Moreover, excepting cancers, the decline of all noninfectious disease categories for ages 15–64 seems to be in line with proposition 3—the death rates from noninfectious diseases in this age group were much higher in the past. The data show that noninfectious diseases first began reducing among the chronologically younger age groups.

The deferment of death that began among the chronologically younger sections of the population was likely to surface sometime among the chronologically old as well. That is, 25-year-olds who do not die may not do so ten years later when they are 35, or two decades later when they are 45, and so on. However, the time when it becomes visible in a particular age group depends on the age limit to the human life span. If that limit had been 65 or 75, the deferment might have ended by now. However, it has continued, becoming visible among the oldest of the old only recently because it would have taken 70 to 80 years or more, for that to happen. The delayed deaths from noinfections diseases, therefore, are not new to the transition. It has been the central feature throughout. "Aging" today—the increase in the proportion of people 75 or 85 years of age or older—is perhaps a consequence of the process that began among the chronologically young more than a century ago.

However, through 1960, for the aggregate population (column 5), cancers and maladies of the circulatory system increased. For maladies of the circulatory system, all of that increase came from age group 65 and above.[6] Only cancers have increased in all age groups (though trends of different types of cancers have varied). It follows that these two disease categories impeded the progress of life expectancy.

The negative contribution of both circulatory maladies and cancers shrinks when it is calculated over the entire period (columns 6 through 9) because their rates have reduced substantially since 1960 (even for ages 65 and above). Better medical technology may have contributed to that improvement.

3 The Relevance of Human Capital Frameworks to the Transition

The way some key aspects of the transition have turned out suggests that transgenerational apparatus of human capital theory could be applied to the study epidemiologic change and its influence on economic growth. Envisioned in an overlapping-generations setting, their central element—nurture of offspring and the long reach of that nurture into adulthood—has the potential to generate key outcomes of the epidemiologic transition. Here, nurture is construed broadly to include deliberated private and social choices that influence offspring health from infancy through adolescence.

A growing body of biomedical knowledge indicates that early-age infection and other forms of deficiency in nurture result in poorer cellular development of organs. Unsalutary diets and frequent infections from infancy through adolescence impede cellular development because infections break down metabolic tissue, exacerbate nutrient deficiency, and deprive the human body of the elements necessary for proper development of the vital organs. During infection, the biological system diverts its resources from cellular growth toward the synthesis of antibodies and repairing damaged tissue. That repair draws from existing stores of protein (tissue), depleting them, and hence retarding cellular growth. If infections and unsalutary diets persist, cellular development of organs is impaired, often irreversibly (Tanner 1990; Martorell et al. 1975).

The long reach of early-age damage extends to several organ systems of the human anatomy: the lungs, circulatory system, gastrointestinal tract, endocrine system, central nervous system, and musculoskeletal system.

For example, Barker (1992, 1994) finds that bronchitis, pneumonia, and whooping cough before age 5 are linked to diminished respiratory function at ages 59 to 70. Abnormalities of lungs persist years after contraction of pneumonia (Wesley 1991); measles has been implicated in acute lower respiratory infection (Markowitz and Neiberg 1991).

The link between infectious disease and rheumatic heart disease is well established; acute rheumatic fever is known to damage heart valves. Late-stage syphilis (aortic syphilis), measles, and malaria have all been known to affect the functioning of the circulatory system. Khosla (1981) reports that electrocardiogram readings of about 12 percent of typhoid patients show cardiac involvement; Charles and Bertrand

(1982) report that malarial chronic anemia can result in changes either in the myocardium or myocardiopathy; Olowu and Taiwo (1990) report that 35 percent of the children with measles in their study show abnormal activity in electrocardiogram assessments.

Atherosclerosis is another example of the link between infectious agents and a degenerative malady. Buck and Simpson (1982) conjectured that infection early in life produces fatty streaks (as early as age 10) that are precursors to atherosclerotic lesions. Several studies have detected the bacterium chlamydia pneumoniae, the cause of acute respiratory infections, in atherosclerotic lesions (Lindholt et al. 1999; Valtonen 1991; Wong, Gallagher, and Ward 1999).

Impaired functioning of the central nervous system because of early-age deficiencies has been documented in Idaquez 1988. Cognitive disorders with links to infections of bacterial meningitis (Bohr et al. 1983) and to Lyme disease (Logigian, Kaplan, and Steere 1990), among others, are known.

Furthermore, Barker (1991, 1992, 1998) has reported that conditions such as coronary heart disease, hypertension, non-insulin-dependent diabetes, autoimmune thyroiditis, and stroke that do not become apparent until mid-adult or later stages, begin early in life, often in utero, making infectious diseases during pregnancy a key risk factor.

Infectious etiologies of several noninfectious maladies such as cervical cancer, liver cancer, liver cirrhosis, multiple sclerosis, epilepsy, type I diabetes mellitus, cardiovascular disease, and schizophrenia are too detailed to discuss here, and have been explored in Knobler et al. 2004.

The role of infections in curtailing cellular growth and cognition among children has long been well-known to nutritionists and auxologists. Studies such as Scrimshaw, Taylor, and Gordon 1968, Scrimshaw 1970, Martorell et al. 1975, and Tanner 1990, among others, have long established that by impeding the nutritional process—digestion, metabolism, absorption, and storage—infections tend to hinder human physiologic development. Infections, particularly ones that disrupt absorption, deprive the human body of the nutrients necessary for optimal cellular growth (Chen and Scrimshaw 1983). The relation of diarrheal infections, for example, to children's growth is a widely observed phenomenon in less developed countries (Martorell 1980; Martorell and Habicht 1986; Mata 1978).[7]

Deficiency in cellular development, in turn, increases the susceptibility of organs to malfunction during adulthood, the time when the biological system is unable to generate new cells to replace damaged cells in vital organs. It follows, the greater the damage inflicted during developmental stages, the lesser the chances of successful repair during adulthood. Although the exact biochemical mechanisms that turn early-age deficiencies to organ dysfunction later in life are not yet fully understood, it is reasonable to infer that, all else held constant, poorly developed organs would tend to break down sooner than well-developed ones and that early-age infections would thus tell on vitality further on in life.

Suppose that infections and deficient (or contaminated) diets are closely linked to cellular growth. Suppose too that households are unable to check infections and contagious diseases because either effective knowledge for doing so is undiscovered or the proper information is unavailable for various reasons. That inability would show up concurrently in sickness and deaths from infectious diseases across age groups. But it may then have an intertemporal effect too. Vital organs of children who suffered but survived infections may have incurred irreversible cellular damage, which could show up later in life as frailer organs. That frailty, in turn, would lead to a faster rate of organ degeneration and perhaps eventually to high rates of fatality from various noninfectious diseases; insult accumulation throughout life may worsen things further. Thus, the persistence of infections and insalubrity of diets may result in high death rates from both infectious and noninfectious diseases: the Malthusian epidemiologic regime (proposition 1).

Now suppose effective knowledge arrives; households use it to prevent infections and improve diets, especially those of children. As infectious diseases diminish, cellular development of successive birth cohorts may improve. When these cohorts reach adulthood, the intertemporal effect comes into play: their better cellular development might diminish incidence, fatality, or both, from chronic and degenerative conditions; deaths from noninfectious diseases may start receding. Improving human durability in this way would then show up in the form of diminishing fatality from both infectious and noninfectious maladies. As that happens, people's life spans increase, and as a result period life expectancy increases.

Even as life spans increase, however, the reduction of aggregate noninfectious diseases would become visible after a lag. Since several birth cohorts coexist—some brought up under the older regime and others who grew up under a regime of fewer infections—the downward trend of the aggregate would become clear only when the recent birth cohorts begin dominating an evolving distribution of cohorts in the population. As the younger cohorts grow, they may suffer fewer chronic ailments; may suffer them much later in life than preceding cohorts; may recuperate sooner; or may respond more positively to medical treatment.

Therefore, all else held constant, as younger cohorts with better cellular development live, noninfectious maladies may begin to turn fatal at older chronological ages progressively (the converse of proposition 3).

Accordingly, the transition would involve diminishing fatality from both infectious and noninfectious diseases (proposition 4). However, infectious diseases may diminish more rapidly because their containment likely involves a scale effect that does not necessarily, and immediately, apply to noninfectious diseases. Consequently, the *share* of infectious diseases would diminish rapidly, leaving behind noninfectious maladies to dominate the epidemiologic picture even as the latter continue to decrease. This mechanism does not necessarily rule out the role of genes in the incidence of and deaths from noninfectious diseases. Genes, as endowments of potential human capital could be bequeathed stochastically to subsequent generations, predisposing them to various types of noninfectious maladies. The central issue is not genetic causation but whether genetic evolution has occurred in the population over the last two centuries.

The change over the last two centuries may have been driven substantially by socioeconomic changes, rather than genetic evolution, for two reasons. First, the decline in noninfectious diseases was rapid, perhaps too rapid for radical genetic change in the population to have been the underlying cause. Genetic change in humans is understood to have occurred over a much longer horizon, usually millennia. For example, studies of senescence and mutation even in fruit flies, short-lived organisms compared to humans, use populations that have been sustained under controlled settings of the laboratory for more than a hundred generations (Rose et al. 2002). If each decade of births since the late nineteenth century were one generation, then the rapid change has occurred within about ten.

Second, as the evidence indicated, noninfectious diseases have decreased substantially among the chronologically younger sections of the population. If genes had preset the age of death from various noninfectious maladies, then the deferment in the age of death from such maladies since the Malthusian era may not have happened at all. That is, if genes that predispose people to various noninfectious maladies lead to death later in life (ages 70, 80, 90, as they do today), then could the early-age deaths (at ages 40, 50, 60) from the same maladies during the nineteenth century have occurred solely for genetic reasons? If not, then the deferment of the age of death from such maladies in the nineteenth century to the twentieth could have happened without a radical genetic change in the population.

Once the younger sections of the population survive, chronological aging ensures that survival rates may improve among older age groups down the line as well. However, that manner of survival is likely to end sometime because life spans are finite. But when that is likely to happen has proven difficult to ascertain. The potential limit to human life spans has been an elusive target (Vaupel 1997) as people in industrialized countries have ended up living longer than the limit experts had previously predicted (Fries 1980, 1989).

Nevertheless, encouraged by prospects of new medical technologies, but despite the inaccuracy of prior predictions, scientists continue to conjecture what the new limit to human life spans might be. The way key features of the transition have turned out suggests that without studying cohort-level developments, estimates of that elusive limit are likely to be off the mark. The 70-, 80-, and 90-year-olds who suffer and die from noninfectious maladies today were born and brought up during much worse epidemiologic conditions of the early twentieth century. If diminishing death rates from infectious diseases since then have coincided with reduced incidence rates, cohorts born during the post-transitional regime (after World War II) may have grown up under significantly more salutary conditions than cohorts brought up during the transitional stage or before. All else held constant, as they reach the ranks of the chronologically old in the future, intertemporal effects of their improved nurture might surface in the form of further reductions in noninfectious diseases. Thus the century-long decline of noninfectious diseases, aided by potential advances in medical technologies, may have yet to run its course. Consequently, life spans and life expectancy may increase further (proposition 6).

Anthropometric indicators of health since the nineteenth century also indicate that change in cellular development may have been the underlying mechanism for the transition. Figure 8.7 shows the adult stature of successive cohorts of Britons born since the early nineteenth

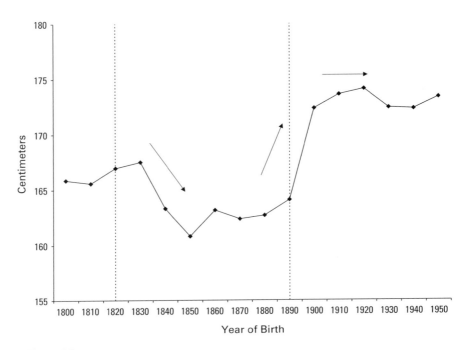

Figure 8.7
Stature of 18-year-old males in the U.K., 1800–1950.

century. Adult stature indicates the cumulative cellular development of a human being from infancy through adolescence. It is known to be impeded by persistent infections during childhood. The prolonged downturn in stature appears to have coincided with the escalation of outbreaks of contagious diseases during at least the first half of the nineteenth century (figure 8.3). Despite rising incomes brought about by the industrial revolution since the late eighteenth century, disorderly urbanization and urban crowding before the ascendancy of the germ theory was likely detrimental to human development. Once the public health infrastructure and institutional arrangements for the containment of contagious diseases were in place, adult stature began increasing, first gradually and then rapidly (Steckel and Floud 1997).

The rising stature of successive cohorts since then has coincided with decreases in noninfectious diseases, first among the chronologically younger sections of the population and then, as those cohorts aged, among the chronologically older sections (Fogel 1994; Fogel and Costa

1997; Steckel and Costa 1997). The onset of decline in noninfectious diseases lagged that of infectious diseases because the contour of non-infectious diseases was initially encumbered by cohorts born and brought up during the shocking health conditions of Malthusian regime. The long reach of cellular development may have helped maintain the descent of noninfectious diseases during the twentieth century, even through stressful economic times such as the depression of the 1930s when incomes had dropped sharply.

Thus, health-related change may operate subtly through intergenerational or intertemporal biological pathways. These hidden pathways are likely to confound studies, particularly aggregate-level studies that examine the influence of current economic conditions on current health-related change. To understand this further we need to assess whether an increase in the level of GDP per capita or its growth rate, by itself, may have diminished disease-caused fatality over time.

4   The Transition and Per-Capita GDP

Health improvements at the aggregate level are widely considered a result of economic growth. It is therefore prudent to ascertain whether the level of current per-capita GDP or its growth rate might have directly reduced disease-caused deaths since the nineteenth century.

Consider the growth rate of per-capita GDP. The results in table 8.2 indicate that the growth rate of per-capita output relates tenuously to the reduction of all-disease-caused deaths, infectious diseases, and noninfectious diseases. Furthermore, some positive coefficients, albeit with large standard errors, suggest the opposite: disease-caused fatality increases as per-capita output grows more rapidly, and faster growth would eventually lead us back into the Malthusian epidemiologic regime. The results indicate that the pace of growth is perhaps an inappropriate explanatory variable for epidemiological change.

Now consider the level of per-capita GDP. Table 8.3 shows that irrespective of disease category, the level of per-capita GDP has scant explanatory power as well, although the sign on some coefficients is more in line with what would be expected.

Why is it that per-capita GDP has little explanatory power?

Consider the case for the United Kingdom. Historically, per-capita GDP levels had been rising gradually since late eighteenth century (Crafts 1985; Clark 2001). However, this had not coincided with any substantial life expectancy improvement for almost a century (figure

Table 8.2
Explanatory power of growth rate of GDP per capita.

	$\hat{\theta}$	Standard error	t-statistic
All Diseases			
Australia	0.129	0.225	0.576
France	−0.026	0.246	−0.105
Netherlands	−0.070	0.157	−0.045
United Kingdom	−0.050	0.334	0.151
Infectious diseases			
Australia	0.184	0.530	0.347
France	−0.113	0.374	−0.302
Netherlands	0.070	0.372	0.189
United Kingdom	0.539	0.832	0.648
Noninfectious diseases			
Australia	0.116	0.164	0.707
France	0.032	0.324	0.099
Netherlands	−0.030	0.114	−0.265
United Kingdom	0.075	0.158	0.476

Notes: This table presents estimates of θ obtained from implementing the following equation:

$$\Delta \ln d_t = \alpha + \theta g_t + \sum_{i=-m}^{m} \varphi_i \Delta g_{t-i} + \varepsilon_t$$

where, the left-hand-side variable is the first difference of the natural log of the disease variable, and g is the first difference of the natural log of per-capita GDP.

8.1). It seems reasonable to suspect that the direct effect of rising per-capita income levels during that time may have been weak. By most historical accounts, lack of knowledge for checking disease, rather than income levels themselves, may have been the main reason for poorer health.

Per-capita GDP might also be too blunt an instrument for the matter at hand. Current changes in disease-caused fatality include people from several birth-cohorts. Each cohort may have been subject to varying health-related circumstances in their pasts. And those circumstances, rather than current per-capita GDP, may have been of direct relevance.

Arguably, one would try to relate each cohort to their past health-related choices and perhaps to past GDP levels. But that is an

Table 8.3
Explanatory power of current level of GDP per capita.

	$\hat{\theta}$	Standard error	t-statistic
	All Diseases		
Australia	−0.0072	0.0087	−0.8331
France	−0.0003	0.0101	−0.0339
Netherlands	−0.0002	0.0084	−0.0277
United Kingdom	−0.0019	0.0099	−0.1930
	Infectious diseases		
Australia	0.0120	0.0278	0.4327
France	0.0146	0.0203	0.7315
Netherlands	0.0700	0.0262	2.6679**
United Kingdom	−0.0128	0.0187	−0.6830
	Noninfectious diseases		
Australia	−0.0170	0.0062	−2.8335**
France	−0.0034	0.0097	−0.3525
Netherlands	−0.0051	0.0070	−0.7273
United Kingdom	−0.0048	0.0078	−0.6230

Notes: This table presents estimates of θ obtained from implementing the following equation:

$$\Delta \ln d_t = \alpha + \theta \ln y_t + \sum_{i=-m}^{m} \varphi_i \Delta \ln y_{t-i} + \varepsilon_t$$

where, $\ln y_t$ is the natural log of the level per-capita GDP.

impractical proposition at the aggregate level because current fatalities include infants to 80-year-olds or older. Moreover, trying to relate each age group to past levels of per-capita GDP itself is an acknowledgment that the explanatory power of the current level of per-capita output is inadequate and that we need to look elsewhere for coherent explanations.

Furthermore, the transition in industrialized countries began at per-capita income levels that were substantially less than today. It suggests that income levels may not necessarily be a constraining factor for health improvements. Triggered at least partly by the germ theory, lasting health improvements since the nineteenth century have involved behavioral change and newer forms of civil engineering to check disease, particularly in urban areas that became centers of economic activity during industrialization. The lagged effects of public

health sanitation projects may be another reason for the weak explanatory power of current per-capita income levels. The fixed costs of sanitation infrastructure may have featured prominently in GDP accounts
for a short period but not afterward. However, if benefits of these
investments had continued, then it might result in a tenuous relationship between diseased-caused deaths and current GDP levels during
the transitional and post-transitional stages.

Moreover, at the aggregate level, the notion that rising income by
itself would reduce disease-caused deaths leads to untenable implications about human affairs. It implies immortality in finite time because
income levels, which have been growing for almost two centuries,
show no signs of abating anytime soon. One might say that the income elasticity of deaths from various diseases might be so small that
immortality cannot be even a remote possibility. In that case, the relationship between income levels and disease-caused deaths would be
substantively insignificant anyway.

If current incomes may not always matter, it is possible there
may have been a structural break in the relationship between income
levels and disease-caused deaths. A type of structural break is an
income threshold. It is plausible that the level of per-capita income
matters up to a particular point; but after that threshold, factors other
than income largely govern population health and disease-caused
fatalities.

However, identifying such thresholds at the aggregate level is difficult. Consider the case for the United Kingdom shown in table 8.4.
Suppose we consider income level during 1870 as one such threshold
before which incomes mattered but not afterward. However, much of
the evidence indicates there was little if any improvement in health
before 1870. If we consider 1960 as another arbitrary threshold, then
per-capita income level should relate strongly before 1960 but not afterward; this result does not obtain either. If we admit the possibility
that a threshold in income levels may not have yet been reached, then
the two variables would correlate closely over the entire period; the
results, however, indicate otherwise.

Although thresholds may be relevant to extreme microlevel situations, identifying them at the aggregate level is difficult because a large
number of diseases afflict people at any point in time. Mechanisms
that trigger disease may be too idiosyncratic to correlate meaningfully
with particular income levels. Furthermore, the notion of income
thresholds raises uncomfortable questions: what minimal income level,

Table 8.4
In search of income thresholds, United Kingdom.

Disease category	$\hat{\theta}$	Standard error	t-statistic
	1870–1994		
All diseases	−0.0019	0.0099	−0.193
Infectious diseases	−0.0128	0.0187	−0.683
Noninfectious diseases	−0.0048	0.0078	−0.623
	1870–1912		
All diseases	−0.0010	0.0626	−0.156
Infectious diseases	−0.0176	0.1591	−0.111
Noninfectious diseases	−0.0101	0.0608	−0.166
	1870–1960		
All diseases	−0.0172	0.0252	−0.682
Infectious diseases	−0.0292	0.0539	−0.587
Noninfectious diseases	−0.0009	0.0199	−0.045
	1960–1994		
All diseases	−0.0001	0.0258	−0.004
Infectious diseases	−0.0167	0.1222	−0.137
Noninfectious diseases	−0.0036	0.0238	−0.155

Notes: This table presents estimates of θ obtained from implementing the following equation:

$$\Delta \ln d_t = \alpha + \theta \ln y_t + \sum_{i=-m}^{m} \varphi_i \Delta \ln y_{t-i} + \varepsilon_t$$

where, $\ln y_t$ is the natural log of the level per-capita GDP.

by itself, might contain maladies such as smallpox, influenza, and cancer, among hundreds of others? Is there a minimum per-capita GDP level that would reduce cancer, high blood pressure, and obesity? Such questions likely lack coherent answers because new biomedical knowledge or technologies may arrive stochastically at any income level. For example, would we say that 1955's per-capita GDP is a pivotal income threshold for polio, or would we say that the fortuitous discovery of Salk's vaccine was the catalytic event for polio containment?

Therefore, epidemiologic change may occur for reasons other than income levels; both types of diseases may occur at low incomes or high incomes (Preston 1975; Caldwell 1986; Easterlin 1999; Kunitz and Engerman 1992). It then seems reasonable to say that income thresholds may not be a useful device for organizing thought about the epidemiologic transition. Thus,

Proposition 7   The explanatory power of both the growth rate and the level of per-capita GDP appears to be weak. The hypothesis that rising income levels caused disease-caused fatality to diminish is unsound because it implies immortality within finite time; income thresholds do not seem to be a reliable guide as well.

This does not imply, however, that economic progress has no bearing on epidemiologic change. It says only that there is little confidence in current income level or its growth rate as primary explanatory variables. If so, examining factors more closely associated with disease-related phenomena might provide us with a better understanding of the transition. Intergenerational or intertemporal connections (as were discussed in the previous section) may operate in ways that current per-capita GDP or its growth rate may not adequately explain or capture. Moreover, even if the "living standard" correlates with current per-capita GDP, this correlation might come from diverse components of the standard that are not included in GDP accounts. And if they are not, then it is desirable to identify them and explore their significance instead. Doing so, however, may require examining the institutional and technological requirements of each country according to its epidemiologic regime. Inference from cross-country frameworks that use GDP to explain disparate health-related outcomes across countries may be fragile and perhaps unreliable, particularly if their sample periods are short.

Meanwhile, it is clear that the transition led to substantial improvements in human durability, a potent signal of improving human capital. Did that improvement invigorate an economic transition from the Malthusian regime?

5   "Engine" of Growth: Temporary versus Permanent Influence

In human-capital-based theories, an economic transition from the Malthusian regime involves a permanent increase in the pace of growth. Acting as an engine, human capital helps sustain that faster pace. On the other hand, in models of growth à la Solow (1956), physical capital did not provide such an engine. Diminishing returns to its accumulation prevented an economy from maintaining a permanently faster pace, a prediction corroborated in numerous empirical studies.

Figure 8.8 stylizes temporary versus permanent effects. Consider a growing economy. Suppose there occurs a stimulus to human capital, say, eradication of a hundred diseases that afflicted people before time T_0 (panels A.1 and B.1). If that economy were to behave in accordance with the Solow model, the stimulus would increase the growth rate of per-capita output to g_1 (panel A.1). However, after the transitional period, the growth rate reverts to its prior pace g_0— a temporary influence. Consequently, the slope of the long-term growth path remains unchanged (panel A.3). After the transitional period, only the level of per-capita output rises permanently: the level effect.

On the other hand, in an economy that behaves according to human-capital-based theory, disease eradication stimulates a permanently faster growth rate (panel B.2). Its influence on the pace of growth lasts. Consequently, the level of per-capita output (in panel B.3) increases (the level effect). However, it does so more rapidly than before; the slope of the growth path becomes permanently steeper (the growth rate effect).

Under both scenarios, the level of per-capita output increases. However, only under the human-capital-based framework the pace of growth increases permanently. Consequently, it is necessary and sufficient to find out whether the stimulus influenced the growth rate. If it influenced the growth rate permanently, it follows that it influenced the final level as well. The converse is not necessarily true. The left-hand-side variable, therefore, must be the growth rate of per-capita output. And a factor (like physical capital) known to generate only level effects, as such, does not belong to the right-hand-side. That suggests the following econometric framework:

$$\Delta \ln y_t = \alpha + \xi \ln d_t + e_t \quad t = 1, 2, 3, \ldots, T \tag{1}$$

where, α and ξ are parameters, $\Delta \ln y_t$ is the first difference of the natural log of per-capita output, $\ln d_t$ is the natural log of disease-caused fatality, and e_t is an error term.

The method of "cointegration" devised by Engle and Granger (1987) may estimate equation (1). However, as it stands, estimating it would produce inconsistent estimates of standard errors and t-ratios. The method of dynamic-ordinary-least-squares (Stock and Watson 1988) addresses the problem by accounting for the correlation of the disease variable and the error term. Furthermore, a procedure outlined by Newey and West (1987) corrects the standard errors and t-ratios for

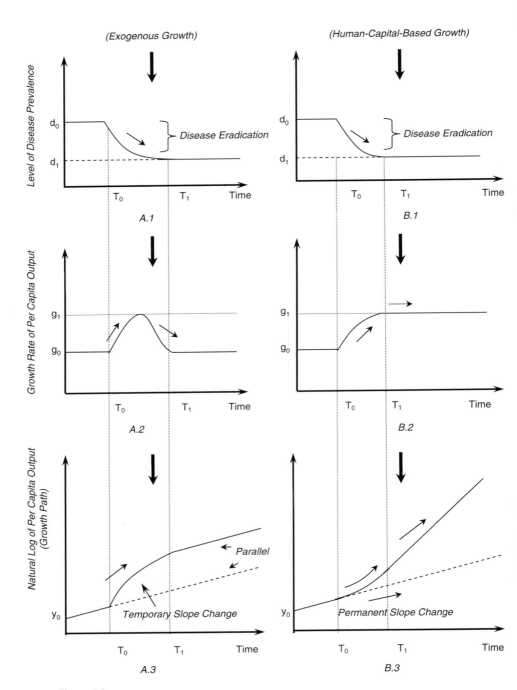

Figure 8.8
Stylized temporary versus permanent growth-rate effects.

serial correlation and heteroscedasticity of the error term. Dynamic-ordinary-least-squares entails estimating

$$\Delta \ln y_t = \alpha + \beta \ln d_t + \sum_{i=-m}^{m} \phi_i \ln d_{t+i} + \varepsilon_t \quad t = 1, 2, 3, \ldots, T \tag{2}$$

where m is a parameter. The hypothesis test

$$H_0 : \beta = 0$$
$$H_1 : \beta < 0$$

$$\tag{3}$$

evaluates the influence. Under the null, the level of disease-caused fatality does not cointegrate with the long-term growth rate of per-capita output (panels A.1 and A.2), whereas under the alternative, the two cointegrate (panels B.1 and B.2). (For life expectancy variables and stature at adulthood, the alternative hypothesis is $\beta > 0$.)

This framework is useful only if data over a long horizon are available. Short-spanned data are unsuitable because the transitional stages, economic and epidemiologic, tend to be prolonged. Transitional periods of growth have been known to last two-to-three decades (Young 1994, 1995). A short sample period is unlikely to discern a temporary effect from a permanent one because after the transitional stage growth may return to its prior pace (as in panel A.2) or to a pace less than the transitional.

Similarly, as figures 8.2 and 8.6 show, 97 percent of the total decrease in infectious diseases and 65 percent of the total decrease in noninfectious diseases had already occurred through 1960. A post-1960 sample period would overlook much of that improvement. It would be unable to assess the central tenet of human-capital-based theory: distinct levels of human capital would be associated with distinct steady-state growth rates. Only a longer sample period—one that includes the time when disease-caused fatality was high (the Malthusian or early transitional stage) and the time when it was restrained (the post-transitional regime)—may reasonably assess the change.

Proposition 8   To ascertain temporary versus permanent influence on growth, the sample period must encompass as much of the transition as is possible. Shorter sample periods would likely conflate temporary and permanent effects because both economic and epidemiologic transitional stages tend to be prolonged.

Therefore, for countries that have only recently begun their epidemiologic transitions this method would likely lead to unreliable results.

For the countries under consideration, even if much of the disease-caused fatality had been reduced before 1950–1960, it does not imply that health became irrelevant to their growth afterward. Their economies may have been able to sustain a faster pace of growth *because* diseases that had constrained people in the past ceased to do so. The influence would endure after 1960 (panel B.2 of figure 8.8). A post-1960 study of growth that does not consider this important historical feature might erroneously credit something else for the growth since the 1960s. Thus,

Proposition 9 Once a set of diseases is restrained or eradicated, its economic consequences endure because the population becomes permanently more able than in the past and may sustain a faster pace of economic activity than was possible before.

This proposition is particularly relevant to infectious diseases because they had been restrained substantially *before* 1955–1960. Any growth accounting of health done after that time is likely to capture only the incremental effects, which are likely to be minimal. However, that does not diminish the total effects that can be assessed only through a much longer sample period. Only maladies that persist at high rates may offer tangible incremental gains. Consequently, results from short-spanned cross-country studies are likely to be unreliable guides because the post-1960 data would be unable to properly assess the importance of health-related changes to growth *within* industrialized countries.

Table 8.5 shows the estimated effects of disease variables along with results obtained from other health-related variables from Arora 2001. The robustness of results across countries and variables suggests that the emergence of human capital during the transition influenced the pace of growth permanently, a finding that supports the human-capital-based case for economic growth. The results suggest that had the Malthusian epidemiologic regime persisted—high rates of disease-caused fatality, frequent recurrence of epidemics, low and volatile life expectancy—it would have taken about 172 years to reach 1994's level of per-capita output, about 50 years longer than what actually occured.

The estimates also imply that the pace of economic growth before the transitional stage began would have been much slower. Assuming that there was no health-related improvement before about 1870, the

Table 8.5
Estimated long-term effects (Fraction of total growth).

	e_0	e_{15} or e_{20}	Stature	All diseases	Infectious	Non-infectious
Australia	0.43	0.49	—	0.35	0.20	0.48
France	0.42	0.62	0.56	0.20	0.39	0.15
Netherlands	0.62	0.47	0.40	0.28	0.47	0.18
United Kingdom	0.35	0.35	0.31	0.27	0.30	0.25

Notes: e_0 is life expectancy at birth and e_{15} is life expectancy at age 15. The results for life expectancy and stature come from Arora 2001. Excepting the United Kingdom, sample periods for life-expectancy variables and disease variables vary.

long-term growth rate in the United Kingdom, for example, would have been about 0.8 to 0.9 percent per annum, a result roughly consistent with historical experience (Crafts 1985; Clark 2001). The pace of growth would have been slower if the contribution of any health improvement to growth during that period were subtracted and if poorer health had constrained conventional forms of human capital. Although economic growth may have begun for several reasons, epidemiologic shifts that began toward the end of the nineteenth century may have hastened the onset of a steeper growth path.

Looking ahead, the total influence of infectious diseases is unlikely to *recur* because their reductions that occurred in the past would have to repeat in the future. On the other hand, the ongoing decline of noninfectious diseases seems to suggest that there might be scope for further improvement in growth. But that too is less likely for industrialized countries because much of the progress is likely to occur among the chronologically older sections of the population. Any economic gains, if at all, are likely to take the form of a level effect rather than a growth rate effect. Nevertheless, that prospect does not diminish the contribution health may have made to economic progress over the last century or so.

If population health has been influential in stimulating economic progress, it is important to know the conditions that could dampen the potential gains. Although health appears to have been an indispensable asset to human capital, health improvements may not necessarily lead to sustained increases in skilled labor force essential for long-term economic growth. By increasing the present value of schooling, improving health and longevity are likely to increase the size of a labor force and could diminish labor market skill premiums. In turn, shrinking skill premiums may act as a disincentive to school and skill. Improving health may result in increases in skilled labor force and lasting economic progress *only* in the presence of skill-biased technological change. Newer occupations generated by technological change may prevent skill premiums from shrinking asymptotically to zero. For health-related policy to raise the level of long-term well-being, economic policies that engender technological change may be crucial.

Furthermore, over the very long term, progress in food production is perhaps the main source of health-related outcomes in a society. If health is vital to human capital formation, then advances in food production may be the principal ultimate cause for human capital's ascent since the nineteenth century. Besides enabling basic human function, food's synergistic role in curtailing the incidence of infectious diseases is well-known. Progress in food production in the past also may have tipped the balance in favor of humans (instead of pathogens). However, for the United Kingdom, for example, despite progress in agriculture since the eighteenth century, population health had either suffered or remained as poor as prior centuries. It suggests that food production, by itself, may not have been a panacea.

Institutions of public health that administered sanitation and helped contain outbreaks of contagious diseases since the end of the nineteenth century may have contributed significantly to health improvements since then. Recent research by Acemoglu, Johnson, and Robinson (2001, 2002) highlights the role of fundamental institutions in generating long-term economic growth. Institutions such as the protection of property rights and commitments to the rule of law and good governance, they argue, account for substantial differences in cross-country economic performance over time.

However, more than a century had elapsed between the inception of such institutions and sustained improvements in health in the United Kingdom (see figure 8.1). The assignment of property rights, for example, culminating in the enclosure movement, may have stimulated productivity in agriculture. But that had coincided with the migration of labor from rural to urban areas exacerbating problems of sanitation and pubic health there. Figures 8.2 and 8.3 indicate that this was also the time of severe death rates from infectious diseases and of escalating frequency of such outbreaks in England and Wales. Indeed, the contour denoting stature in figure 8.7 suggests that the cellular development of successive cohorts born since the early nineteenth century had suffered, leading perhaps to high death rates from noninfectious maladies as those cohorts aged. All told, for more than a century after forming the types of institutions the British considered crucial to long-term economic progress, population health had either suffered or had remained as poor as it was in prior centuries.

This evidence suggests that institutions of the kind they emphasized may not be sufficient for improved health-related outcomes. We know Britain was one of the major colonial powers. If institutional development did not necessarily generate better health within Britain, how could institutional transfer through colonization, by itself, have been the reason for better health in some former British colonies that are cited as examples of institutional success?

The missing link perhaps is in the knowledge that came from the germ theory more than a century after property rights were instituted in Britain. The germ theory, however, spurred formation of a different set of institutions in response to the shocking health conditions of the late nineteenth century. Before germ theory, the types of institutions emphasized by Acemoglu, Johnson, and Robinson (2001, 2002) were not necessarily configured to generate the rapid gains in life expectancy, cellular development, reductions in infectious diseases, and the subsequent fall of noninfectious diseases that the British population has experienced since the end of the nineteenth century. Thus, some caution needs to be exercised in painting a broad-brush-stroke view of institutions; functions of institutions may differ depending on the purpose and rationale for their creation.

6 Conclusions

The epidemiologic transition since the late nineteenth century may have been the pivotal force behind the emergence of human capital since then. By reassessing its salient features, this chapter has tried to reason that data over the last 150 years only partially agree with the received view of the transition. Significantly, Malthusian times were characterized by high rates of both infectious and noninfectious diseases (the received view has infectious diseases as the dominant category). Further, noninfectious maladies turned fatal at a much younger age during Malthusian times than they do today because high rates of noninfectious diseases coincided with much shorter life spans than

today. As infectious diseases receded, so did noninfectious diseases after a short interval (the received view has noninfectious diseases
increasing during the transitional and post-transitional stages). The deferment of the age of death is the central feature of the transition and
had been occurring since its inception (the literature has this deferment
as a special final stage). The deferment likely began among the chronologically younger sections of the population who were able to survive
both infectious and noninfectious maladies.

Occurring rapidly after the ascendancy of germ theory into social
consciousness, these developments accomplished substantial improvements in life expectancy, cellular development, and perhaps the durability of human capital within a century. Their effects might still be
rippling gradually through the population, contributing significantly
to what we today call "aging." However, neither the level of per-capita
GDP nor its growth rate appears to have played a causal role in bringing about epidemiological change. Whereas health-related changes
seem to have led to an economic transition, allowing populations to
sustain a faster pace of economic progress than was ever possible during Malthusian times.

Acknowledgments

I am grateful to my dissertation committee, Paul Evans (co-chair),
Richard Steckel (co-chair), and Peter Howitt, for their guidance on
the project (doctoral dissertation "Health and Long-Term Economic
Growth; A Multi-Country Study" submitted to the Ohio State University, June 1999). Geoffrey Bump (STRS) and participants of the Senior
Policy Seminar on Health, Human Capital, and Economic Growth at
the Pan American Health Organization, Washington, D.C., October
2002, provided useful suggestions. The views expressed here are not
those of the STRS.

Notes

1. See Grossman 1972 for an alternative view.

2. See also Olshansky and Ault 1986; Wilmoth and Lundström 1996; Kannisto et al. 1994;
Thatcher 1992; Vaupel and Lundström 1994.

3. The data used in this chapter is itself evidence that new institutions began collecting
and examining information on population health. These data are unavailable in such
detail before the 1840s.

4. Limited space prohibits discussing all infectious diseases separately for each age group. Suffice it to mention that age group 0–14 benefited from the reduction of all infectious maladies whether they were water-and-food- or air-borne (cholera, typhoid, diarrhea, dysentery, infective enteritis, smallpox, scarlet fever, diphtheria, whooping cough, and measles, among hundreds of others). The age group 15–64 benefited from a reduction in water-borne infections and respiratory infections (respiratory tuberculosis, influenza, and pneumonia); the same is true for the age group 65-and-above.

5. A reason for this difference could be that noninfectious diseases include a category called "ill-defined causes," which accounted for 20–25 percent of all disease-caused deaths until about 1870–1880. However, the bulk of the ill-defined causes were due to "old age (and senility)," a condition pertinent to ages 65 and above. I have included them in noninfectious diseases because they are likely to have been some unidentifiable chronic or degenerative condition in the elderly. Ill-defined causes diminished rapidly early in the twentieth century; perhaps what was previously considered ill defined became identifiable and was assigned presumably to various noninfectious disease categories.

6. And some of the increase in cardiovascular maladies may be attributable to a mere transfer from what was previously thought to be ill defined. Although there is no a priori reason to believe that cardiovascular maladies were the only beneficiary of that transfer, it is likely that this may have occurred because "old age and senility," which occurred in ages 65 and above, dominated the ill-defined causes. And it is in this age group and not in ages 15–64 that circulatory maladies have increased.

7. Many studies suggest that a closely paced series of common childhood infections is the most important cause of malnutrition, retarded growth, and child mortality. (See FAO World Food Survey 1987.)

References

Acemoglu, D., Simon Johnson, and James Robinson. 2001. The Colonial Origins of Comparative Development: An Empirical Investigation. *American Economic Review* 91: 1369–1401.

———. 2002. Reversal of Fortune: Geography and Institutions in the Making of the Modern World Income Distribution. *Quarterly Journal of Economics* 117: 1231–1294.

Arora, S. 2001. Health, Human Productivity, and Long-Term Economic Growth. *Journal of Economic History* 61 (3): 699–749.

———. 1999. Health and Long-Term Economic Growth: A Multi-Country Study. Ph.D. dissertation, The Ohio State University, Columbus, Ohio.

———. 2003. The British Epidemiologic Transition, 1850–1994. Working paper, The Ohio State University, Columbus, Ohio.

Bairoch, P. 1988. *Cities and Economic Development from the Dawn of History to the Present.* Translated by C. Brauder. Chicago: University of Chicago Press.

Barker, D. J. P. 1992. *Fetal and Infant Origins of Adult Disease.* London: British Medical Journal.

———. 1994. *Mothers, Babies, and Disease in Later Life.* London: British Medical Journal Publishing Group (BMJ).

————. 1998. *Mothers, Babies, and Health in Later Life*. Edinburgh: Churchill Livingstone.

Barker, D. J. P., K. M. Godfrey, C. Fall, C. Osmond, P. D. Winter, and S. O. Shaheen. 1991. Relation of Birth Weight and Childhood Respiratory Infection to Adult Lung Function and Death from Chronic Obstructive Airways Disease. *British Medical Journal* 303: 671–675.

Barker, D. J. P., and D. T. Lackland. 2003. Prenatal Influences on Stroke Mortality in England and Wales. *Stroke* 34 (7): 1598–1602.

Barker, D. J. P., and C. Osmond. 1986a. Infant Mortality, Childhood Nutrition, and Ischaemic Heart Disease in England and Wales. *Lancet* 10: 1077–1081.

————. 1986b. Childhood Respiratory Infection and Adult Chronic Bronchitis in England and Wales. *British Medical Journal* 15 (November): 1271–1275.

Bartel, Ann, and Paul Taubman. 1979. Health and Labor Market Success: The Role of Various Diseases. *Review of Economics and Statistics* 61 (1): 1–7.

Becker, Gary S. 1975. *Human Capital*, second edition. New York: Columbia University Press.

Bohr, V., B. Hansen, H. Kjersem, N. Rasmussen, N. Johnsen, H. S. Kristensen, and O. Jessen. 1983. Sequelae from Bacterial Meningitis and Their Relation to the Clinical Conditioning During Acute Illness, Based on 667 Questionnaire Returns. Part II of a Three Part Series. *Journal of Infection* 7 (2): 102–110.

Buck, C., and H. Simpson. 1982. Infant Diarrhoea and Subsequent Mortality from Heart Disease and Cancer. *Journal of Epidemiology and Community Health* 36 (1): 27–30.

Caldwell, J. C. 1986. Routes to Low Mortality in Low Income Countries. *Population and Development Review* 12: 171–220.

Chadwick, E. 1965 (1842). *Report of the Sanitary Condition of the Laboring Population of Great Britain*. Edited by M. W. Flinn. London: Reprinted by Edinburgh University Press.

Charles, D., and E. Bertrand. 1982. Coeur et Paludisme. *Medecine Tropicale: Revue Francaise de Pathologie et de Sante Publique Tropicales* 42 (4): 405–409.

Chen, L. C., and N. S. Scrimshaw. 1983. *Diarrhoea and Malnutrition: Interactions, Mechanisms, and Intervention*. New York: Plenum.

Clark, G. 2001. The Secret History of the Industrial Revolution. Unpublished paper. University of California, Davis.

Costa, Dora L. 2000. Understanding Mid-Life and Older Age Mortality Declines: Evidence from Union Army Veterans. NBER Working paper no. w8000 (November), National Bureau for Economic Research, Cambridge, Mass.

Crafts, N. F. R. 1985. *British Economic Growth during the Industrial Revolution*. New York: Oxford University Press.

Crosby, A. 1986. *Ecological Imperialism: The Biological Expansion of Europe, 900–1900*. Cambridge, Mass.: Cambridge University Press.

D'Espaignt, Edouard T., Marijke Van Ommeren, Fred Taylor, N. Briscoe, and P. Pentony. 1991. *Trends in Australian Mortality, 1921–1988*. Australian Institute of Health, Mortality Series no. 1, Canberra, Australia.

Easterlin, Richard A. 1999. How Beneficent Is the Market? A Look at the Modern History of Mortality. *European Review of Economic History* 3: 257–294.

Engle, R. F., and C. W. J. Granger. 1987. Co-Integration and Error-Correction: Representation, Estimation, and Testing. *Econometrica* 55: 251–276.

Floud, Roderick, Kenneth Wachter, and Annabel Gregory. 1990. *Height, Health, and History, Nutritional Status in the United Kingdom, 1750–1980.* Cambridge: Cambridge University Press.

Fogel, Robert W. 1994. Economic Growth, Population Theory, and Physiology: The Bearing of Long-Term Processes on the Making of Economic Policy. *American Economic Review* 84 (3): 369–395.

Fogel, Robert W., and Dora L. Costa. 1997. The Theory of Technophysio Evolution, with Some Implications for Forecasting Population, Health Care Costs, and Pension Costs. *Demography* 34 (1): 49–66.

Food and Agriculture Organization (FAO). 1987. *The Fifth World Food Survey.* Rome: FAO.

Fraser, W. M. 1950. *History of English Public Health 1834–1939.* London: Bailliere, Tindall, and Cox.

Fries, J. F. 1980. Aging, Natural Death, and Compression of Morbidity. *New England Journal of Medicine* 303 (3): 130–135.

———. 1989. The Compression of Morbidity: Near or Far? *Milbank Quarterly* 67: 208–232.

Galor, Oded, and David N. Weil. 1999. From Malthusian Stagnation to Modern Economic Growth. *American Economic Review* 89: 150–154.

Grossman, M. 1972. *The Demand for Health: A Theoretical and Empirical Investigation.* New York: Columbia University Press.

Idiaquez, J. 1988. Nutritional Status and Autonomic Nervous System Function. *Functional Neurology* 3 (2): 205–209.

Kalemli-Ozcan, Sebnem. 2003. A Stochastic Model of Mortality, Fertility, and Human Capital Investment. *Journal of Development Economics* 70: 103–118.

———, Harl E. Ryder, and David N. Weil. 2000. Mortality Decline, Human Capital Investment, and Economic Growth. *Journal of Development Economics* 62 (1): 1–23.

Kannisto, V., J. Lauristen, A. R. Thatcher, and J. W. Vaupel. 1994. Reductions in Mortality at Advanced Ages: Several Decades of Evidence from 27 Developed Countries. *Population and Development Review* 20: 793–810.

Knobler, Stacey L., Siobhan Ó Connor, Stanley M. Lemon, and Marjan Najafi, eds. 2004. *The Infectious Etiology of Chronic Diseases.* Washington, D.C.: Institute of Medicine of the National Academies, National Academic Press.

Kunitz, Stephen J., and Stanley L. Engerman. 1992. The Ranks of Death: Secular Trends in Income and Mortality. *Health Transition Review* 2 (suppl.): 29–45.

Khosla, S. N. 1981. The Heart in Enteric (Typhoid) Fever. *Journal of Tropical Medicine and Hygiene* 84 (3): 125–131.

Komlos, J. 1995. *Biological Standard of Living on Three Continents.* Boulder: Westview Press.

Lindholt, J. S., H. Fasting, E. W. Hennenberg, and L. Ostergaard. 1999. A Review of Chlamydia Pneumoniae and Atheroclerosis. *European Journal of Vascular and Endovascular Surgery* 17: 283–289.

Logigian, E. L., R. F. Kaplan, and A. C. Steere. 1990. Chronic Neurologic Manifestation of Lyme Disease. *New England Journal of Medicine* 323 (21): 1483–1544.

Lucas, Robert E., Jr. 2002. *Lectures on Economic Growth*. Cambridge, Mass.: Harvard University Press.

Markowitz, L. E., and P. Neiburg. 1991. The Burden of Acute Respiratory Infection Due to Measles in Developing Countries and the Potential Impact of Measles Vaccine. *Review of Infectious Diseases* 13 (suppl. 6): 555–561.

Martorell, R., and J. P. Habicht. 1986. Growth in Early Childhood in Developing Countries. In *Human Growth: A Comprehensive Treatise*, vol. 3, ed. F. Falkner and J. M. Tanner. New York and London: Plenum Press, pp. 241–263.

Martorell, R., J. P. Habicht, C. Yarborough, A. Lechtig, R. E. Klein, and D. Western. 1975. Acute Morbidity and Physical Growth in Rural Guatemalan Children. *American Journal of Diseases of Children* 129: 1296–1301.

———. 1980. Inter-relationships between Diet, Infectious Disease, and Nutritional Status. In L. S. Greene and F. E. Johnsston, eds., *Social and Biological Predictors of Nutritional Status, Physical Growth, and Neurological Development*. New York: Academic Press.

Mata, L. J. 1978. *The Children of Santa Maria Cauque: A Prospective Field Study of Health and Growth*. Cambridge, Mass.: The MIT Press.

McNeill, William H. 1998. *Plagues and Peoples*. New York: Anchor.

Mokyr, Joel. 2000. Why "More Work for Mother"? Knowledge and Household Behavior, 1870–1945. *Journal of Economic History* 60 (1): 1–41.

Murphy, Kevin M., and Robert Topel. 2003. The Economic Value of Medical Research. In Kevin M. Murphy and Robert H. Topel, eds., *Measuring the Gains of Medical Research*. Chicago: University of Chicago Press.

Newey, Whitney K., and Kenneth D. West. 1987. A Simple, Positive Semi-Definite, Heteroskedasticity and Autocorrelation Consistent Covariance Matrix. *Econometrica* 55 (May): 703–708.

Olowu, A. O., and O. Taiwo. 1990. Electrocardiographic Changes after Recovery from Measles. *Tropical Doctor* 20 (3): 123–126.

Olshansky, S. J., and A. B. Ault. 1986. The Fourth Stage of the Epidemiologic Transition: The Age of Delayed Degenerative Diseases. *Milbank Memorial Fund Quarterly* 64 (3): 355–391.

Omran, A. R. 1971. The Epidemiologic Transition: A Theory of the Epidemiology of Population Change. *Milbank Memorial Fund Quarterly* 49 (4): 509–538.

———. 1982. Epidemiologic Transition. In J. A. Ross, ed., *International Encyclopedia of Population*. London: The Free Press, pp. 172–183.

Paneth N., and M. Susser. 1995. Early Origins of Coronary Heart Disease (the "Barker Hypothesis") (editorial). *British Journal of Medicine* 310 (6977): 411–412.

Preston, Samuel H. 1975. The Changing Relation between Mortality and Economic Development. *Population Studies* 29: 213–248.

———. 1976. *Mortality Patterns in National Populations, with Special Reference to the Recorded Causes of Death*. New York: Academic Press.

———, Nathan Keyfitz, and Robert Schoen. 1972. *Causes of Death: Life Tables for National Populations*. New York: Academic Press.

Rose, Michael R., Mark D. Drapeau, Puya G. Yazdi, Kandarp H. Shah, Diana B. Moise, Rena R. Thakar, Cassandra L. Rauser, and Laurence D. Mueller. 2002. Evolution of Late-Life Mortality in Dorsophilia Melanogaster. *Evolution* 56 (10): 1982–1991.

Sah, R. K. 1991. The Effects of Child Mortality Changes on Fertility Choices and Parental Welfare. *Journal of Political Economy* 99 (3): 582–606.

Schultz, T. Paul. 1997. Assessing the Productive Benefits of Nutrition and Health: An Integrated Human Capital Approach. *Journal of Econometrics* 77 (1): 141–158.

———, and Aysit Tansel. 1996. Wage and Labor Supply Effects of Illness in Côte d'Ivoire and Ghana: Instrumental Varriable Estimates for Days Disabled. *Journal of Development Economics* 53 (2): 251–286.

Scrimshaw, N. S., and G. J. E. Gordon. 1970. Synergism of Malnutrition and Infection: Evidence from Field Studies in Guatemala. *Journal of American Medical Association* 212: 1685–1692.

Scrimshaw, N. S., C. E. Taylor, and J. E. Gordon. 1968. *Interactions of Nutrition and Infection*. Geneva: World Health Organization.

Solow, Robert M. 1956. A Contribution to the Theory of Economic Growth. *Quarterly Journal of Economics* 70 (1): 65–94.

Steckel, Richard H., and Dora L. Costa. 1997. Long-Term Trends in Health, Welfare, and Economic Growth in the United States. In Richard H. Steckel and Roderick Floud, eds., *Health, Welfare, and Industrialization*. Chicago: University of Chicago Press.

Steckel, Richard H., and Roderick Floud, eds. 1997. *Health, Welfare, and Industrialization*. Chicago: University of Chicago Press.

Stock, James H., and Mark W. Watson. 1988. Testing for Common Trends. *Journal of the American Statistical Association* 83: 1097–1107.

Szreter, S. 1988. The Importance of Social Intervention in Britain's Mortality Decline circa 1850–1914: A Re-interpretation of the Role of Public Health. *Social History of Medicine* 1: 1–37.

———. 1997. Economic Growth, Disruption, Deprivation, Disease, and Death: On the Importance of Politics of Public Health for Development. *Population and Development Review* 23 (4): 693–728.

Tanner, J. M. 1990. *Fetus into Man: Physical Growth from Conception to Maturity*. Cambridge, Mass.: Harvard University Press.

Thatcher, A. R. 1992. Trends in Numbers and Mortality at High Ages in England and Wales. *Population Studies* 46: 411–426.

Tomes, N. 1990. The Private Side of Public Health: Sanitary Science, Domestic Hygiene, and the Germ Theory, 1870–1900. *Bulletin of History of Medicine* 64: 509–539.

Vallin, Jacques, and France Mesle. 1987. *Les Causes de Deces en France de 1925–78*. Paris: Institut Nationale d'Etudes Demographiques, University of Paris.

Valtonen, V. V. 1991. Infection as a Risk Factor for Infarction and Atheroclerosis. *Annals of Medicine* 23: 539–543.

Vaupel, J. 1997. Trajectories of Mortality at Advanced Ages. In K. Wachter and Cleb Finch, eds., *Between Zeus and Salmon: The Biodemography of Longevity*. Washington, D.C.: National Academy Press.

Vaupel, J. W., and H. Lundström. 1994. Longer Life Expectancy? Evidence from Sweden of Reductions in Mortality Rates at Advanced Age. In *Studies in the Economics of Aging*, ed. D. A. Wise. Chicago: University of Chicago Press, pp. 79–104.

Wesley, A. G. 1991. Prolonged After-Effects of Pneumonia in Children. *South African Medical Journal* 79 (2): 73–76.

Wilmouth, J. R., and H. Lundström. 1996. Extreme Longevity in Five Countries: Presentation of Trends with Special Attention to Issues of Data Quality. *European Journal of Population* 12 (1): 63–93.

Wong, Y. K., P. J. Gallagher, and M. E. Ward. 1999. Chlamydia Pneumoniae and Atherosclerosis. *Heart* 81 (3): 232–238.

World Health Organization. 1977. *Manual of the International Statistical Classification of Diseases, Injuries, and Causes of Death*, 9th rev., vol. 1. Geneva: World Health Organization.

Wrigley, E. A., and R. S. Schofield. 1981. *The Population History of England, 1541–1871: A Reconstruction*. Cambridge, Mass.: Harvard University Press.

Young, A. 1994. Lessons from East Asian NICs: A Contrarian View. *European Economic Review* 38: 964–973.

———. 1995. The Tyranny of Numbers: Confronting the Statistical Realities of the East Asian Growth Experience. *Quarterly Journal of Economics* 110: 641–680.

9 Economic Growth, Health, and Longevity in the Very Long Term: Facts and Mechanisms

Olivier F. Morand

Empirical findings from a broad literature of various fields reveal some important facts concerning changes in health in the very long term. In particular, paleodemographers and historical demographers have been able to construct a clear picture of one proxy for health, longevity, or life expectancy, from prehistoric populations to the present. The picture that emerges, discussed in more detail in section 1, is as follows: first, life expectancy at birth is quasi-constant before the eighteenth century all the way back to prehistoric populations. Second, the gains in longevity in the nineteenth and twentieth century are dramatic. Third, the change from one regime to the other has specific characteristics in terms of mortality causes and patterns.

Much work has been done to identify the factor responsible for these changes in longevity and, more generally, to grasp the interaction between health and the level of economic development. The precise relationship between economic growth and the health of a population appears difficult to understand, and section 2 in this chapter will discuss various mechanisms linking health and economic growth, from the traditional role of economic growth in promoting better health to the less obvious connections between health and growth through changes in incentives to invest.

Since health is such an important component of well-being, it is important to be able to construct a model of long-term economic growth that is consistent with the stylized facts. Such a unified model of health and growth may help researchers to better understand the complex relationship between demographic and economic variables, and may also foster the generation of new hypotheses. In section 3 of this chapter a model will be constructed that introduces health capital in a setting of economic growth where physical and human capital accumulation are dual engines of growth. It will be shown that this model is consistent with the stylized facts revealed in the first part of the chapter and that it encompasses a number of the mechanisms previously discussed. The implications of the model will be discussed in the end.

1 Health and Longevity in the Very Long Term

1.1 The Path of Life Expectancy

Paleodemographic studies have established that life expectancy at birth hardly increased between the time of prehistoric hunter-gatherers and the beginning of the eighteenth century (Acsadi and Nemeskeri 1970; Hassan 1981), despite a change in the mode of production—the agricultural revolution—and a slow but irregular rise in income per-capita over time. The average age at death of 32 years for Paleolithic populations does not differ much from that of late Middle Ages populations, around 35 years (see Hassan 1981). Despite undeniable decreases in child mortality during that period, a similar picture holds for life expectancy at age 15 or 20.

Although the paleodemographic record indicates little, if any, long-term gains in adult life expectancy, there were important swings in mortality due to diseases, famines, and wars (Malthus's positive checks). Coleman (1986) also documents the rise of infectious diseases in relation to human population and shows that high demographic concentration can act as a reservoir for pathogens. Cohen (1989) argues that settlement patterns associated with large population density, as well as with the domestication of animals, produced large increases in mortality and sickness because they broadened the range of infections to which human beings were exposed and increased the reproductive success of various parasites. Increased population sedentarization after the agricultural revolution, followed by improvements in trade and communications, led the historian LeRoy-Ladurie (1984) to speak of "unification of the globe by diseases" during the Middle Ages.

1.2 The Recent Dramatic Gains in Longevity

Demographers and economists have documented the tremendous gains in many countries in life expectancy, characterizing the period from the nineteenth century to the present. Economic historians and demographers have long debated the causes of these changes, even if most agree that early gains were primarily due to increases in nutrient intake, were strengthened in the nineteenth century by improvements in sanitation and the water supply, and in the twentieth century by the application of specific knowledge and tools for improving health (immunization, medical technology, etc.). (See, for instance, McKeown 1976 and Fogel 1997.) Combined with a decline in fertility, these great gains in life expectancy have resulted in population aging in many developed economies, where epidemics of noncommunicable diseases and injuries now drive the demand for health.

1.3 The Theory of the Epidemiologic Transition

The clear differences in the main causes of mortality between these two periods, one of relatively constant life expectancy, the other of increasing longevity, has led epidemiologists to use the term of "epidemiologic transition" to refer to the dramatic changes between the two periods; it is a transition that seems to parallel the demographic and technological transition in the developed economies, and that occurred more recently in less developed economies (Omran 1971; 1982; Haines 1995).

The analysis and comparison of mortality patterns and causes of death between several economies has led Omran (1971, 1982) to formulate his theory of the epidemiologic transition. This theory starts with the premise that mortality is a fundamental factor in population dynamics (proposition 1) and with the observation that the epidemiological transition represents a long-term shift in mortality from a regime of mostly infectious diseases to a regime of mostly degenerative and man-made diseases (proposition 2). The epidemiologic transition is shown to favor the young over the old, and females over males (proposition 3), and to be closely associated with rising standards of living and improved nutrition in the nineteenth century, and improved medical and health practices in the twentieth century (proposition 4). The most interesting feature of the theory of the epidemiologic transition is that three basic patterns of the transition emerge (proposition 5): The classical or Western model, the accelerated model, and the delayed model.

The classical model of the epidemiologic transition   (England and most Western European countries). Here, the mortality pattern follows three stages. A preindustrial age of pestilence and famine generates a cyclical population growth with frequent peaks in mortality, followed by an intermediate stage of receding pandemics in the nineteenth century, giving way to a gradual mortality decline. A stage of degenerative and man-made diseases in the twentieth century corresponds to more precipitous declines. Economic factors (improvements in standards of living and nutrition in the nineteenth century) were the primary determinants of the classical transition, but were later augmented in the twentieth century by sanitary improvements, followed by medical and public health progress. The epidemiologic transition closely parallels the demographic transition and the industrial revolution, and is therefore followed by a population explosion and sustained economic growth. England and most Western European countries followed this classical epidemiologic transition.

The accelerated transition The transition follows a similar pattern to that of the classical model, but the changes in mortality were more rapid and occurred at a later stage of the country's economic development. Japan is a typical example of the accelerated transition.

The delayed epidemiologic transition The substantial decreases in mortality for these economies are very recent. Public health measures have been a major component of generally imported medical packages that pull mortality rates down while keeping fertility rates high, thus generating a population explosion. This pattern corresponds to a transition triggered by changes in the exogenous parameters characterizing health technology. This scenario applies to most countries in Africa, Latin America, and Asia.

2   The Complex Interaction between Health and Economic Growth

2.1   Growth and Health: The Traditional Channels

In the long run, it is to be expected that economic growth leads populations to live better and longer lives. First, economic growth means rising per-capita income, and part of this increased income is translated into the consumption of higher quantity and better quality nutrients (including water). Through nutrition, health (and therefore longevity) responds to increases in income, a key point made by Fogel (1994), who emphasizes the role of the economic growth process in explaining long-term increases in longevity. Second, economic growth is fueled by technological progress, and part of this progress is reflected in improvements in medicine and medical technology (Rosen 1993) that ought to contribute to increased longevity. However, most researchers recognize that the large-scale application of such medical improvements is relatively recent, and can hardly explain increases in longevity before the end of the nineteenth century. Progress in medicine and medical technology are relatively recent, and their large-scale application is even more recent, as discussed in McKeown 1979.

However, the interaction seems also to run from health to growth, since many studies show that life expectancy is a significant predictor of income levels and also of future economic growth. Barro and Sala-i-Martín (1995) estimate that a 13-year increase in life expectancy raises the annual growth rate by 1.4 percent. More recently, based on microeconomic estimates of the structural effect of health on income, Weil and Shastry (2002) establish that differences in adult survival explain 19 percent of the log variance of income per capita. There are a number of mechanisms through which health may have significant effects on economic growth.[1] For instance, healthier populations generally have higher labor productivity: more generally, there is a large literature on the implications of health for labor market outcomes, and microeconomic studies have measured precisely the cost to households of particular diseases, including the direct cost of prevention and the indirect cost of labor time lost because of illness.[2] Smith (1999) documents that a household's self-reported health status is an excellent predictor of its wealth, and it is no surprise that a cross-country study shows that 17 percent of the variance in output per worker is explained by variations in health (Weil 2002).

But the links between health and growth can also be indirect, emerging, for instance, through demographic or geographic variables. For example, health improvements influence economic growth through their impact on demography: improvements in health lead to a decline in infant and child mortality (and subsequently to a decline in fertility) which induces changes in the composition of the population and eventually causes an increase in the proportion of working-age adults. In Asia, such demographic changes may have contributed significantly to the "economic miracle" of the 1965–1990 period.[3] Improvements in adults' health reduce early retirements due to illness, but, overall, population aging requires transferring an increasing fraction of resources toward caring for dependent elderly. The implied effects on aggregate production, consumption, and labor supply are discussed in Weil 1997, who estimates a significant impact of population aging on the growth rate of output per capita in the near future. The evidence connecting growth to geographic variables is more controversial, even if there is no doubt that tropical locations are highly correlated with a disease burden, which may represent an obstacle to economic development.

Economic growth has an impact on health through the implied changes in the type of diseases affecting human populations. Numerous channels contribute to this impact, including changes in technologies (primarily the change from hunting-gathering to agriculture), increases in trade, and increases in population densities. How the spread of diseases in turn had dramatic effects on the shape of human history has been illustrated by many authors (see, e.g., Diamond 1997 or Zinsser 1935). Lagerlof (2002) introduces exogenous mortality shocks (epidemics) in a model of long-term economic growth and shows that a series of relatively mild epidemic shocks may enable an economy to escape from a Malthusian trap.

2.2 Health and Growth: The Investment Channel

In recent years, a growing literature has attempted to explain the complex relationship between economic growth and health through changes in households' incentives to invest. For instance, in van Zon and Muysken 2001, agents' preference for health entices them to allocate resources away from the production of consumption goods and toward the health sector to increase health and longevity. The authors show that there exists an optimum size for the health sector consistent with maximum growth, but also that increased demand for health from an aging population may adversely affect growth. The authors also emphasize how changes in the productivity of the health sector may have a large impact on the economic growth of a country.

Another class of models concentrates on one specific aspect of health, longevity. As discussed in Fuchs 1982, increased life spans make people more patient and therefore entice them to increase their investments, whether in physical capital (as in the literature on savings under uncertainty), or human capital. Consistent with Ram and Schultz's (1979) argument that increased life expectancy provides incentives to increase investment in education at any age, a finding documented by de la Croix and Licandro (1999) about postwar India is that an agent's decision concerning the time to spend in school is affected positively by life expectancy.[4] Longevity thus has an effect on growth through human capital accumulation, although the authors show that this positive effect could be offset by the increase of the average age of the working population when life expectancy is above a particular threshold. Chakraborty (2002) recognizes that high mortality adversely affects investment returns, and shows that societies may be trapped in poverty in which high mortality and low income reinforce each other.

Similarly, in Kalemli-Ozcan, Ryder, and Weil 2000, improvements in health increase the incentives to acquire education, and in Kalemli-Ozcan 2002 it is the changes in the life expectancy of children that alter the incentives of parents to invest in the quantity and quality (i.e., the number and human capital accumulation) of children. Longevity thus affects economic growth through the channels of fertility and education, and calibration exercises show that these effects can be significant.

3   A Unified Model of Health and Growth in the Long Term

In this section, a simple model of long-term economic growth is constructed using some features of the work by Galor and Weil (1999, 2000) and Galor and Moav (2000), with some microfoundations of health economics as developed in Grossman 1972; it adds some insights from the literature on savings and uncertainty (Mirman 1971) to build a unified model of longevity and growth consistent with the stylized facts of health and longevity in the very long term.

3.1   Economic Growth

Consider a simple model with overlapping generations of identical agents characterized by two distinct periods, one called young age and the other maturity, and suppose that cohorts are of a constant size. An agent born at t has preferences over the consumption of a single good at each of these periods of his life, denoted respectively by c_t^y and c_{t+1}^m, which are represented by the following utility function:

$$u(c_t^y, b_t^y) + u(c_{t+1}^m, b_{t+1}^y), \tag{1}$$

where

$$u(c, b) = \ln(c^\theta b^{1-\theta}) \quad \text{with } 0 < \theta < 1.$$

The superscript indicates which cohort the agent belongs to (young versus mature) and the subscript the particular period considered.

The unique consumption–investment good in each period is produced by a firm using a constant return-to-scale technology in aggregate physical capital K_t and human capital H_t according to the production function

$$Y_t = AK_t^\alpha H_t^{1-\alpha} = Ak_t^\alpha H_t \quad \text{with } k_t = K_t/H_t \quad \text{and} \quad 0 < a < 1. \tag{2}$$

The quantity k_t is thus the capital stock per unit of human capital during period t. The firm is perfectly competitive in the output and input markets, and capital fully depreciates after being used, so the interest rate and the wage rate per unit of labor are, respectively,

$$w_t = A(1 - \alpha)k_t^\alpha \quad \text{and} \quad r_t = A\alpha k_t^{\alpha-1}. \tag{3}$$

Young agents in period t are endowed with a basic human capital level denoted h_t^y. Human capital has two important characteristics. First, the young generation can increase its stock of human capital by making costly investments, as in the seminal work by Lucas (1988). Specifically, if e_t denotes the resources invested in human capital accumulation-production in period t by a young agent, then

$$h_{t+1}^m = h_t^y(1 + \gamma e_t) \quad \text{with } 0 < \gamma. \tag{4}$$

The second characteristic of human capital stems from the property that some of the existing body of knowledge and skills does not have to be entirely rediscovered by the new generation, but is communicated or transmitted from one generation to the next at no cost. As a consequence, we assume that if the mature generation has increased its stock of human capital, then the next cohort of young agents is endowed with a higher initial stock than the previous one. Of course, if there has been no learning, nothing can be transmitted. As a simplifying assumption, it is assumed that all the new knowledge and skills of the mature are entirely transmitted to the young, so that

$$h_{t+1}^y = h_{t+1}^m,$$

while each young agent of the first generation is endowed with one unit of human capital, that is, $h_0^y = 1$.

Assuming for now that the health capital of agents is constant (and, without loss of generality, equal to 1), the model is simply a standard endogenous growth model in the tradition of Galor and Moav (2000) and Galor and Weil (1999, 2000). The reader is reminded of its implications. Assuming a small capital stock per unit of capital in period t, agents make no investments in human capital and the equilibrium law of motion for k is given by

$$k_{t+1} = Bk_t^\alpha, \tag{5}$$

where $B = A[(1-a)/(3+1/a)]$. Along the path described by this law of motion, growth is fueled exclusively by physical capital accumulation, and capital stock per unit of human capital converges to a unique steady-state k^* satisfying

$$k^* = B^{1/(1-\alpha)},$$

while human capital levels are constant and equal to h_0^y: in this growth regime agents will make no investments in human capital as long as $k_{t+1} < \bar{k} = [\alpha/(1-\alpha)\gamma]$, that is, as long as

$$k_t < (\bar{k}/B)^{1/\alpha}.$$

Since aggregate human capital is therefore unchanged over time, this is called the "neoclassical growth regime."

Either the economy stays in this growth regime perpetually, or there exists a period in which, for the first time, the capital stock per unit of human capital k reaches the threshold $(\bar{k}/B)^{1/\alpha}$ above which agents start investing in human capital. Young agents then make strictly positive investments in human capital, and set their investments in physical capital so as to equate the return on physical capital investments to that of human capital investments. As a result, aggregate human capital grows over time and aggregate physical capital continues to grow as well, but k decreases (which implies that wages rise over time). This regime is identified as the "modern growth regime" since growth is fueled by the joint accumulation of both human and physical capital.

3.2   Investments in Health

We now introduce investments in health to this standard endogenous growth model. Recall from the formulation of the preferences above that better health is more enjoyable (utility is increasing in health capital), and that better health (which is assumed to be associated with higher life expectancy) increases the demand for the consumption good during maturity (health capital and consumption are weak complements). Suppose that young agents have the opportunity to raise their health stock by investing some of their first-period resources. Specifically, an agent's stock of health is assumed to evolve according to the following technology:

$$b_{t+1}^m = b_t^y (1 + \delta g_t)^\varepsilon,$$

where g_t are the resources invested in health accumulation during the first period of the agent's life, and (δ, ε) are productivity parameters of the technology transforming resources into health capital ($0 < \delta$ and $0 < \varepsilon < 1$). Without loss of generality b_t^y is normalized to 1.[5]

Because the rate of return to investments in health are finite, it can be shown that agents invest in health if and only if their first period consumption is above the threshold level $c_{\min} = \theta/[(1 - \theta)\varepsilon]$, in which case, agents invest the quantity:

$$g_t = [(1 - \theta)\varepsilon/\theta]c_t^y - 1/\delta,$$

in health. Note that the first period consumption threshold $c_{\min}$ depends negatively on $\delta\varepsilon$.

Recall that prior to agents starting to invest in health, an economy is either in one of the two regimes discussed in the previous section of the chapter. Under both regimes consumption rises monotonically over time, and the term "epidemiologic transition" denotes the first period during which consumption rises above the threshold level $c_{\min}$. Above this critical consumption level, agents begin investing in health and longevity increases.

It is important to note that the relationship between economic growth and health (longevity) runs both ways. Economic growth, and the associated rise in income and consumption levels, can affect the health status of a population by inducing an epidemiologic transition after which health and longevity increase monotonically over time. Reciprocally, investments in health can affect economic growth through the combination of the following two channels. First, investing in health requires foregoing some amount of consumption and physical and human capital expenditures: it is therefore analogous to a negative wealth effect and growth is affected negatively. Second, investing in health results in longer life expectancy, and thus leads to a shift of the demand for consumption in the second period, which in turn alters agents' incentives to substitute away from consumption in the first period and toward accumulating capital, thus affecting growth in a positive manner.

Transition during the neoclassical growth regime (the classical model) Suppose first that the transition takes place during the neoclassical growth regime, which happens if and only if consumption during that regime attains the threshold level $c_{\min}$ defined above. At this moment agents start investing in health and the law of motion for the per-capita capital stock thus changes. Under some restrictions on the parameters of the model, it can be shown that the economy converges to a new steady state, which can be shown to be higher than that of the neoclassical regime. It should also be noted that, because the epidemiologic transition generates an immediate jump in per-capita capital stock and puts the economy on a higher growth path, it may facilitate the transition from a neoclassical to a modern growth regime, because the threshold $\bar{k}$ may be more rapidly reached during the higher growth path. Further, the epidemiologic transition may help an economy reach a modern growth regime that it would not have entered otherwise. The model in this chapter thus leads to the important hypothesis that health is a very critical determinant of long-term economic growth because it can accelerate or even induce the switch from a neoclassical to a modern growth regime.[6]

Transition during the modern regime (the accelerated transition) Alternatively, suppose that the epidemiological transition takes place during the modern growth regime. The per-capita human capital level rises over time and the economy combines a modern growth regime with strictly positive investments in health-generating increases in agents' longevity.

Exogenous transition (the delayed transition) Finally, there is also the possibility that the economy does not reach the epidemiological transition endogenously through the growth process, but that this transition is initiated by external factors such as technological changes affecting the health parameters (i.e., exogenous improvements in medicine or medical technologies). This happens because an increase in either δ or ε makes investments in health more attractive for agents, leading to a lowering of the threshold consumption level c_{min} at which agents start investing in health. Longer life expectancies in turn entice agents to invest more in physical capital, which in turn affects economic growth positively. In a neoclassical growth regime, these changes in incentives may even induce agents to start investing in human capital and thus pull an economy out of a neoclassical growth regime and into a modern growth regime. Without the exogenous change in health technology, this switch may not have been possible and the economy would have been locked into a regime of low education, low health, and relatively low income.[7]

4   Conclusions

It is universally recognized that economic growth impacts the health and longevity of a population through increasing levels of income leading to greater consumption and investments in health. The evidence that income affects health and longevity has a direct policy implication; governments interested in improving the health status of their population should consider the provision of cash benefits as an important policy tool (Case 2001a,b). This is just one of many mechanisms connecting health and economic growth. Most economists now admit that improvements in health and economic growth are mutually reinforcing, and microeconomic studies have demonstrated that the relationship between health and income runs in both directions. This chapter reviewed some of the mechanisms connecting health and growth.

It is only recently that these mechanisms have become important as building blocks for models of long-term economic growth, as in the model presented in section 3 of this chapter. In this model, the health status of an agent, assumed to be perfectly correlated to his longevity or life expectancy, affects his consumption and investment decisions. That is, longer life expectancy raises the demand for consumption when old, and therefore increases the agent's incentive to invest in capital (human and physical) when young. A similar link is at the heart of the literature on savings under uncertainty.

The findings are as follows: first, at the macroeconomic level, if increased longevity induces agents to spend more on capital investments, then economic growth can be affected by changes in health, a hypothesis strongly supported by the findings that health indicators are significant predictors of future growth in the standard studies of Barro and Sala-i-Martín (1995) and Sala-i-Martín (1997), among others. Second, combining channels to and from growth, the implications of the model for the long-term interaction between economic growth and longevity are consistent with the stylized fact exposed in section 1 of this chapter. The model shows that health (longevity) increases with income, but only above a specific threshold level at which an economy undergoes a transition from a regime of high mortality and steady low life expectancies to a regime of increasing longevity and sustained economic growth. The three patterns of this transition predicted by the model correspond precisely to the empirical observations of Omran (1971, 1982) in his seminal work on the epidemiologic transition. Such work combines observations for developed countries in the nineteenth century, as well as for recent experiences of many developing countries.

Third, the model generates an important new hypothesis: a health transition can help a country switch from a neoclassical growth regime to a modern growth regime. For instance, an exogenous increase in the rate of return on health investments can prompt agents to also start investing in human capital, in addition to increasing their health investments. As a result, an economy under a neoclassical growth regime can be pulled into a modern regime of growth fueled by the combination of human and physical capital accumulation. This corroborates the findings of Kalemli-Ozcan (2002) that even small changes in the survival probability can cause large changes in agents' educational investment choices and lead an economy into a modern growth regime.[8] This hypothesis suggests that health policies in developing countries can have important consequences for long-term growth, and not only for the immediate well-being of the population. In addition, measuring the returns to health investments simply in terms of increases in life expectancy would underestimate the true returns to health expenditures because it ignores the induced effects on education. Also, inducing economic growth through policies aimed at increasing the rate of return on education may be best achieved in combination with health policies, since rising life expectancies lead to increases in investment in education, and longer length of education.

Although the model can be amended to allow for improvements in health to have a positive effect on agents' productivity without altering the qualitative implications of the model, it is clear that additional theoretical work is needed to incorporate other mechanisms into a unified model of the long-term interaction between economic growth, population health, and longevity, and that further empirical work is also needed to test the hypothesis generated by these models.

Acknowledgments

I thank the Center of Economics and Health at Pompeu Fabra University for the unrestricted financial support via the Merck Foundation Company.

Notes

1. See Bloom and Canning 2000 for a discussion.

2. Also relevant is the substantial literature on the nutrition-based efficient wage (see, e.g., Dasgupta 1993).

3. See Bloom and Williamson 1998.

4. See also Meltzer 1995 for Mexico and Chakraborty 2002 for sub-Saharan Africa.

5. Each generation thus starts with the same health capital, although the model can be amended to allow for some health spillover from one generation to the next.

6. Other researchers have also argued that a mortality decline can foster the transition to a modern growth regime, although other mechanisms were considered (see, e.g., Kalemli-Ozcan 2002).

7. A poverty trap similar to that found in Galor and Mayer-Foulkes 2002.

8. In Kalemli-Ozcan 2002 parents make human capital investments in their children, but the mechanism is similar to the one in this chapter.

References

Acsadi, G., and J. Nemeskeri. 1970. *History of Human Life Span and Mortality*. Budapest: Akademiai Kiado.

Barro, R., and X. Sala-i-Martín. 1995. *Economic Growth*. New York: McGraw-Hill.

Bloom, D. E., and D. Canning. 2000. The Health and Wealth of Nations. *Science* 287: 1207–1209.

Bloom, D. E., and J. G. Williamson. 1998. Demographic Transitions and Economic Miracles in Emerging Asia. *The World Bank Economic Review* 12 (3): 419–455.

Case, A. 2001a. *Does Money Protect Health? Evidence from South African Pensions*. Princeton: Princeton University Center for Health and Well-Being.

———. 2001b. Health, Income, and Economic Growth. Paper presented at ABCDE Conference, The World Bank (May). Washington, D.C.

Chakraborty, S. 2002. Endogenous Lifetime and Economic Growth. University of Oregon. Unpublished paper.

Cohen, M. N. 1989. *Health and the Rise of Civilization*. New Haven: Yale University Press.

Coleman, D. 1986. Population Regulation: A Long-Range View. In *The State of Population Theory: Forward from Malthus*, edited by D. Coleman and R. Schofield. Oxford: Basil Blackwell.

Dasgupta, P. 1993. *An Inquiry into Well-Being and Destitution*. Oxford: Clarendon.

De la Croix, D., and O. Licandro. 1999. Life Expectancy and Endogenous Growth. *Economic Letters* 65: 255–263.

Diamond, J. 1997. *Guns, Germs, and Steel: The Fates of Human Societies*. New York: W. W. Norton.

Fogel, R. W. 1994. Economic Growth, Population Theory, and Physiology: The Bearing of Long-Term Processes on the Making of Economic Policy. *American Economic Review* 84: 369–395.

Fogel, R. W. 1997. New Findings on Secular Trends in Nutrition and Mortality: Some Implications for Population Theory. In *The Handbook of Population and Family Economics*, vol. 1A, edited by M. Rosenzweig and O. Stark. Amsterdam: North Holland.

Fuchs, V. R. 1982. Time Preference and Health: An Exploratory Study. In *Economic Aspects of Health*, edited by V. R. Fuchs. Chicago: University of Chicago Press, pp. 93–120.

Galor, O., and D. Mayer-Foulkes. 2002. Food for Thought: Basic Needs and Persistent Educational Inequality. Brown University. Mimeograph.

Galor, O., and O. Moav. 2000. Das Human Kapital. Brown University. Unpublished paper.

Galor, O., and D. Weil. 1999. From Malthusian Stagnation to Modern Growth. *American Economic Review* 89: 150–154.

———. 2000. Population, Technology, and Growth: From the Malthusian Regime to the Demographic Transition. *American Economic Review* 90: 806–828.

Grossman, M. 1972. *The Demand for Health: A Theoretical and Empirical Investigation*. New York: Columbia University Press.

Haines, M. 1995. Disease and Health through the Ages. In *The State of Humanity*, edited by J. L. Simon. Oxford: Basil Blackwell, pp. 51–60.

Hassan, F. A. 1981. *Demographic Archaeology*. London: Academic Press.

Kalemli-Ozcan, S. 2002. Does the Mortality Decline Promote Economic Growth? *Journal of Economic Growth* 7 (4): 411–439.

Kalemli-Ozcan, S., H. E. Ryder, and D. Weil. 2000. Mortality Decline, Human Capital Investments, and Economic Growth. *Journal of Development Economics* 62 (1): 1–23.

Kremer, M. 1993. Population Growth and Technological Change: One Million B.C. to 1990. *Quarterly Journal of Economics* 108: 681–716.

Lagerlof, N. P. 2002. From Malthus to Modern Growth: Can Epidemics Explain the Three Regimes? Concordia University. Unpublished paper.

LeRoy-Ladurie, E. 1984. *The Mind and Method of the Historian*. Chicago: University of Chicago Press.

Lucas, R. 1988. On the Mechanics of Economic Development. *Journal of Monetary Economics* 22: 3–42.

McKeown, T. 1976. *The Modern Rise of Population*. London: Academic Press.

———. 1979. *The Role of Medicine: Dream, Mirage, or Nemesis?* Princeton: Princeton University Press.

Meltzer, D. 1995. Mortality Decline, the Demographic Transition, and Economic Growth. University of Chicago. Unpublished paper.

Mirman, L. J. 1971. Uncertainty and Optimal Consumption Decisions. *Econometrica* 39 (1): 140–146.

Omran, A. R. 1971. The Epidemiologic Transition. *Milbank Memorial Fund Quarterly* 49 (1): 509–538.

———. 1982. Epidemiologic Transition. In *International Encyclopedia of Population*, vol. 1, edited by J. A. Ross. New York: The Free Press.

Ram, R., and T. W. Schultz. 1979. Life Span, Health, Savings, and Productivity. *Economic Development and Cultural Changes* 13: 399–421.

Rosen, G. 1993. *A History of Public Health*. Baltimore: John Hopkins University Press.

Sala-i-Martín, X. 1997. I Just Ran Two Million Regressions. *American Economic Review* 87: 178–183.

Smith, J. P. 1999. Healthy Bodies and Thick Wallets: The Dual Relation between Health and Economic Status. *Journal of Economic Perspectives* 13 (2): 145–166.

Weil, D. 1997. The Economics of Population Aging. In *Handbook of Population and Family Economics*, vol. 1B, edited by M. Rosenzweig and O. Stark. Amsterdam: Elsevier.

———. 2002. Accounting for the Effects of Health on Economic Growth. Brown University. Unpublished paper.

Weil, D., and G. K. Shastry. 2002. How Much of Cross-Country Income Variation Is Explained by Health? Brown University. Unpublished paper.

Zinsser, H. 1935. *Rats, Lice, and History*. Boston: Little, Brown.

Zon, A. H. van, and J. Muysken. 2001. Health and Endogenous Growth. *Journal of Health Economics* 20: 169–185.

IV

Productivity, Labor
Markets, and Health

10 Productive Benefits of Health: Evidence from Low-Income Countries

T. Paul Schultz

The benefits due to improving health in the last century are obvious and far reaching. Yet there is little agreement on how to quantify these benefits and compare them to the costs of achieving such improvements. Four reasons for this gap in our knowledge seem relevant. First, there is no consensus among health specialists on how to conceptualize and measure health status at the individual level. Consequently, validating the survey instruments that approximate these measures of health status has progressed slowly. Second, there is a deep reluctance to summarize the benefits of health in terms of only their productive payoffs, or value as human capital, because this appears to deny the "consumption value" of health and the distinctive "capability" aspect of health. Third, self-reported health status involves errors in measurement, even when continuous health indicators of a relatively objective form are analyzed. Fourth, although healthier people may be more productive, more productive people may also allocate more resources toward creating and maintaining their good health. Because of this two-directional relationship, the association between individual health and personal productivity is not a satisfactory estimate of the true causal effect.

These four barriers to assessing the benefits of health may help account for our ignorance on these matters. But they hardly justify this state of affairs. Such a situation also contributes to the lack of consensus on how to analyze nonexperimental survey data on individuals and families, so as to evaluate the health consequences of health programs, policies, or developments. The overall priority assigned to health programs and the relative effectiveness of specific categories of health expenditures are therefore adjudicated by appeal to the "best judgments" of professional experts (Murray and Lopez 1994).

Similar arguments on the limitations of the human capital framework for guiding social policy have been raised with regard to education. The relationship between the schooling of workers and their wage rates (or hourly earnings, if self-employed) has been empirically replicated from scores of countries during the last 30 years, and has gradually attained the status of causal fact in the eyes of most social scientists, although not without long technical debate and extensive exploration of alternative frameworks and statistical methodologies (Griliches 1977; Card 1999, 2001). Research into the conceptual, statistical, and empirical methods designed to link health status and productivity of individuals might place health and education on a more comparable footing for the purposes of policy making, without claiming that either health or education fails to serve broader social objectives than economic growth. Areas of agreement on how to collect more suitable data and use them to describe this health-productivity relationship with less bias should clarify how private and social health inputs affect health status and influence labor productivity in different socioeconomic environments in developing countries.

Section 1 discusses these four barriers to progress and indicates which ones I focus on. Section 2 sketches a general schematic framework within which the determinants and consequences of health can be analyzed. Section 3 reviews accumulating empirical evidence on some of these critical links in Ghana, Côte d'Ivoire, and Brazil. Section 4 concludes with some ideas on how new data and analytical approaches could help us answer these questions more confidently.

1   Basic Limitations in Health Evaluation Methods

1.1   Multiple Indicators of Health

Health has many dimensions, and it may be optimal at this stage to consult a variety of indicators of health status rather than select one as preferred. The most commonly cited health indicator is life expectancy given a person's age and sex. It has the appeal of an intrinsic capability on which personal welfare depends (Sen 1998). But there is, as of yet, no agreement on how to forecast an individual's expected lifetime. Without a consensus on how to measure health status at the individual level, the impact of four different types of health indicators on wages may be useful: (1) self-assessments of health status; (2) morbidity rates; (3) physical functional limitations; and (4) nutritional and physical growth outcomes.

In the first type, self-reported general health status may range from health being "much better" to "much worse" than the benchmark group. Are individuals consulting an identical benchmark to measure health, and are they referencing, for example, the health status of other persons in their neighborhood or socioeconomic class, or age group? In addition, any self-reported health status might reflect the conditioning experiences and perceptions of the particular individual that are potentially related to her socioeconomic behavior and outcomes, rather than being an objective index of health status. Nonetheless, these general indicators of health status have been shown to be related significantly to the subsequent morbidity and mortality of the individual, and even social experiments that collect extensive clinical information continue to evaluate health outcomes by these self-assessed questions (Manning, Newhouse, and Ware 1982).

The second type of health indicator is based on morbidity, as reported by individuals or administrative units for a given reference period. Different socioeconomic groups have access to different medical care and possess a different knowledge of health needed to self-diagnose illness and seek out professional care. Morbidity rates derived from administrative records by individual, socioeconomic group, or region tend to be, therefore, less-than-reliable evidence of clinically confirmed incidences of illness across all individuals, groups, or regions of a low-income country, even when the specific class of morbidity, such as malaria, is reasonably well identified by the respondent and the law requires those afflicted to register.

Sample surveys also collect self-reported responses on illness or disability (from a 14-, 28-, or 180-day retrospective period), or the number of days ill, or days sufficiently ill to be disabled (i.e., unable to engage in her regular activity) during the reference period. Questions of this form are included in many labor force and household general surveys, and are not commonly subjected to multivariate analysis as an indicator of acute or chronic health status, perhaps because they are viewed as subjective and affected by culture (Johansson 1991).[1]

A third type of health indicator is based on the limitations individuals report in their physical capacity to perform activities of daily living (ADLs). Typically they are asked whether these tasks can be performed easily, with difficulty, or cannot be performed at all, such as, for example: is the respondent capable of walking 300 meters; of carrying a pail of water; of engaging in light domestic chores; and of bathing oneself? In contrast to self-reported general health status, or recent illnesses, or days disabled, the number of functional limitations currently experienced may be more concrete, and in some cases the interviewer can validate the response through observation. It is argued, therefore, that since ADLs appear to be less based on socioeconomic endowments, conditioning factors, and perceptions, they are less likely to be biased (Strauss et al. 1995). Functional limitations seem to approximate a continuum of health statuses among the elderly for whom these physical limitations on everyday activities are commonplace. Concurrent clinical examinations have also validated the reliability of ADL responses, at least for the elderly in high-income countries (Stewart and Ware 1992). How well indicators of functional limitations differentiate health status among younger persons or those living in poor rural societies is less well documented. Yet ADLs are a class of health-status indicators that promise to reduce reporting bias, but may be collected at a moderate cost without incurring the risks of infection associated with the collection of blood or biological samples.

The fourth type of health indicator measures the physical-growth outcomes that result from a lifetime accumulation of nutritional inputs, health care, diminished exposure to infectious diseases, and reduced work and strenuous activities that consume calories (Faulkner and Tanner 1986; Floud, Wachter, and Gregory 1990; Fogel 1994; Strauss and Thomas 1995, 1998; Steckel 1995). Both the health environment of and the nutritional inputs to the mother and child affect early childhood development including uterine growth (Barker 1992; Scrimshaw 1997), and factors during the adolescent growth spurt may modify adult physical stature and capabilities (Scrimshaw and Gordon 1968; Martorell and Habicht 1986). These indicators include a variety of anthropometric dimensions, the most common being adult height, which is thought to be particularly sensitive to early childhood nutritional-health status. Because adult height does not change substantially from about age 25 to 55, it provides a readily observed, relatively fixed, indicator of adult health potential and is thought to convey information about early nutritional and health conditions that may proxy more general living standards (Fogel 1986, 1994; Floud, Wachter, and Gregory 1990; Steckel 1995). Adult height thus conveniently bridges the widely separated moments in the life cycle: from when the critical health inputs of childhood appear to be most important to adulthood, where the stock of health human capital impacts on productivity, and finally, where those early inputs ultimately delay the onset and diminish the severity of chronic health conditions such as cardiovascular problems and diabetes (Costa 2002). To otherwise link panel data for the entire life cycle from childhood environments to adult functional capacity and productivity is complex and costly (Waterlow et al. 1977; Beaton et al. 1990; Fogel 1991; Scrimshaw 1997).

Weight-to-height squared, or body mass index (BMI), reflects a shorter-term nutritional-health status, which at low levels (less than about 21 in metric units) is referred to as "wasting" and is associated with elevated risks of mortality and morbidity. Conversely, at high levels of BMI (above about 28) obesity increases the risk of mortality and morbidity (Waaler 1984; Beaton et al. 1990; Fogel 1994). But in low-income countries the majority of the population is likely to have a BMI below 27, and the predominant empirical tendency is for BMI to be associated with better levels of health and productivity, although it tends to be subject to diminishing returns (Thomas and Strauss 1997; Schultz 2003). BMI is also approximately orthogonal to height, and consequently, both BMI and height may be included as determinants of productivity without introducing severe multicollinearity among regressors. Other anthropometric physical growth indicators have also been proposed, such as menarche or the age at first menstruation for women (Knaul 2000). The adolescent growth spurt and the timing of puberty has occurred earlier in high-income countries in the last century, presumably due to better nutrition and health conditions (Eveleth and Tanner 1976; Faulkner and Tanner 1986). A host of child physical development indicators, graduated by age and sex, have become standard tools for child health assessments and monitoring (Beaton et al. 1990).

But few studies have measured family endowments and local policy conditions that might be responsible for variation in a respondent's childhood health and potentially affect adult productivity. If these formative health conditions could be accurately measured and assumed predetermined for explaining adult acute and chronic health outcomes, these long-gestating health human capital investments might be fruitfully analyzed, allowing one to calculate the internal rates of return on the social resources needed to achieve these early improvements in health.[2] For example, Costa (1996, 2002) reports a similar relationship between labor force participation for older men and their nutritional health represented by BMI in the U.S., observed first in a sample of Civil War veterans in 1900 and then replicated across all males age 50–64 in 1985–91. During this period the fraction of the U.S. population reporting a low BMI below 23 decreased from half to a quarter, for whom mortality risks are relatively high, chronic morbidities relatively common, and labor force participation low. Strauss and Thomas

(1998) find a similar pattern between height and BMI and participation in the labor force for urban male adults in Brazil in 1975. I shall focus on the health effects on wage rates, or labor productivity per unit of time worked, and neglect the parallel effects of health on labor force participation, hours worked, and intensity of work. These labor supply effects of health could be due to the decreased disutility of working in better health, and the increased real reward from working (i.e., substitution effect), which may be offset by an income effect encouraging the consumption of more leisure. The potential market income of males has increased more rapidly in high-income countries during the last century than has the actual realized market income, because annual hours worked have declined due to shorter work hours during prime working ages, as well as later entry and earlier exit from the labor force. Reckoning the hours worked by women is more complex, because time-series data on women's work in the household are scarce, and tend to be excluded from both sides of national income accounts.

1.2 Health Human Capital

The objective here is to estimate how labor productivity is affected by different components of health status: that which is affected by the behavior of individuals, families, and society and can therefore be called reproducible health human capital, and that which is unaffected by social behavior and may be referred to as exogenous. Additional social benefits of health, especially for the young, old, and infirm dependents may require different methods to empirically assess.

1.3 Measurement Error in Health Human Capital

A standard problem in statistics is measurement error in explanatory variables. In estimating the effect of human capital, such as education, on wages, it is common to consider the education variable—years of education completed—as if it were measured with error. In a simple setting with random error, the resulting ordinary least squares (OLS) estimate of education's effect on the wage tends to be biased downward, or more precisely biased downward in proportion to the ratio of the variance of the measurement error in education to the total variance of education (Griliches 1977). Extending this approach to the estimation of the effect of health human capital on the individual's wage, it is expected that health status variables are also measured with error. The error in measured health might arise because of the subjective nature of health, but also because of the heterogeneous sources of variation in health. Measured health status may be thought of as being the sum of genetic endowments and the accumulation of behaviorally influenced health human capital. There is no reason to believe that the productive effects of genetic and human-capital health variations are identical. The productive benefits of the socially accumulated health component is, of course, the payoff that is relevant for most policy interventions that seek to improve health through changing private behavior and public expenditure programs.[3]

Although the reasons for measurement error in health are not precisely the same as in the case of education, the statistical methods required to correct for measurement error are analogous. If there are instrumental variables (IVs) that are correlated with the human capital component of health, yet they are uncorrelated with the wage or genetically dominated and fortuitous (non-human-capital) component, it may still be possible to predict the health human capital based on the variation in the instruments, and estimate in a second stage the unbiased impact on the wage of the human capital component. Combining these two stages corrects the downward bias due to measurement error in estimating health effects on productivity and is otherwise consistent.[4] If the return to human capital investments differs for different groups, this individual heterogeneity in response to a policy treatment suggests that IV estimates disproportionately weight the groups that are most affected in their health behavior by the instruments (Card 1999; Kling 1999). For example, if the demands of relatively rich households for health care or nutrition inputs for their children are price inelastic, whereas the demands of the relatively poor are price elastic. Then, if the price of these health inputs are treated as instruments to predict the use of health inputs, and thus identify the returns to these forms of child health inputs, the instrumental variable estimates will approximate the payoff to poor households of increasing their investment in their children's health and nutrition, and may overestimate in this case the effect of this health "treatment" on the average household. Consequently, the choice of an instrument on which to base an IV estimate of health human capital returns should be selected to mimic the policy options that are being evaluated for implementation.

1.4   Feedbacks from Productivity to Health Behavior

There are several overlapping relationships described in section 2 involving health that should be analyzed when designing an approach to identify the benefits of improving health. To identify the productive effect of health it is essential to understand how household and community factors produce good health. This is true if the productive effect of health status is heterogeneous, or if there is simultaneous feed-back from productivity to the demand for inputs that contribute to altering health. The standard example of this latter source of bias involves estimating the contribution of improved nutrition to worker productivity but recognizes the reverse causal effect of more produc-tive workers being able to purchase more nutrients (Strauss 1986). Al-though progress has been made at the individual level in separating out these two simultaneous causal relationships, it is doubtful that at the national level the relationship between the average health and pro-ductivity of workers has yet been satisfactorily identified (Pritchett and Summers 1996).

2   A General Framework for the Analysis of Health Human Capital

Two questions motivate this chapter. What is the effect of change in health status on the productive capabilities of an individual, and what are the malleable conditions of the individual, family, or com-munity that determine changes in health status? With answers to these questions, one can assess the resource costs of modifying those con-ditions that will improve health, and then calculate the internal rate of return on those outlays as a human capital investment. Several studies reviewed below have begun to answer the first question, but few studies have taken the next step to estimate the social costs of pro-grams that have produced improvements in health.

To evaluate the returns to health human capital involves many of the same problems that have occupied economists in estimating the returns to schooling, plus a few added complications specific to health. There is agreement that years of schooling completed by a worker is a reasonable first approximation of the physical units of education, although it may be further refined to include various dimensions of duration and quality associated with that education. But in the case of measuring the stock of health human capital there is no natural metric at the individual level. In sum, health presents greater problems for survey measurement, more leeway for measurement error, and a need to distinguish more carefully between at least two parts of health: a fixed genetic endowment and a socially acquired human capital component.

The literature on health economics has emphasized that individual health heterogeneity can bias direct estimation of health production functions, $h\,(.)$, that seeks to characterize the technological relationship between health inputs (I) and health outcomes (H), and residual variation in health (e_1) (Rosenzweig and Schultz 1983). Individuals, their families, and perhaps their medical advisors will know more about the severity of illness or the frailty of individuals (g) than does the statistician trying to account for health outcomes. The health production function can thus be described, where both g and e_1 are unobserved, as

$$H = h(I, g, e_1),\tag{1}$$

where subscripts for individuals have been suppressed for simplicity.

The demand for medical care and other health-related inputs, I, may be modified by g, private knowledge of the individual's health endowment in the family and medical system, as well as by other factors affecting health input demand, X, such as the market prices of health inputs, the value of the time of the individual that is expended to use medical inputs, individual and household other income sources, and another error, e_2, inclusive of differences in the preferences of individuals or families:

$$I = d(X, g, e_2).\tag{2}$$

For example, individuals who know they are particularly ill will be the first to seek out medical care, contributing to a negative correlation between the demand for curative health inputs and good health, rather than the anticipated positive technical relationship that is expected if beneficial health treatment were randomly allocated to equally sick patients. If the unobserved part of health heterogeneity is subsumed in the error in the health production function, e_1, this error is likely to be correlated with the unexplained use of health inputs, e_2, imparting an omitted-variable bias to the health-production function (1) when it is estimated by single-equation methods, such as ordinary least squares, in which health inputs are assumed exogenous.

The solution to this health heterogeneity problem is to treat the health inputs, I, as endogenous in health-production function (1), or as behaviorally controlled, and employ instrumental variables, such as the prices of, or access to, health inputs X as the basis for identifying the health input demands. Then, estimates of the health-production function by two-stage methods are free of the heterogeneity bias caused by the unobservable g (ibid.). Assuming that the input prices and access are not correlated with individual health heterogeneity, or that the covariance $(X, g) = 0$, and that the prices variables explain a statistically significant share of the variation in input demand, these IV estimates of the health-production technology are consistent and should have desirable properties.

In the case at hand of evaluating how health human capital affects wages, an analogous problem arises. Assume that health status can be decomposed into two components: Hb, which is explained by the technological effect of behaviorally controlled health inputs responding to exogenous price constraints, X, and a remainder, Hg, that subsumes genetic heterogeneity, differences in preferences, other unexplained factors, misspecifications, and stochastic errors from both the production and input demand equations (Schultz 2003):

$$H = Hb(X) + Hg(g, e_1, e_2). \tag{3}$$

Only the first component can be viewed as "man-made" or a form of reproducible human capital, derived from predicting the health outcome from the fitted reduced-form equation for health that embodies both the health-production function (1) and the health-input demand equations (2). Following the health-production literature, the instrument, X, that is suitable for predicting the human capital component, is an individual's local price of health inputs or community-level institutional investments that affect exposure to disease and efficacy of treatment when ill. Social scientists have perennially sought to distinguish between those factors associated with nature (genetics) and nurture (human capital), as they apply to individual achievement. There is, however, no entirely satisfactory method for separating the human capital component from other factors including genetic potential, and covariances between the two sets of factors cannot be allocated to one side or the other. In our case, some genetic variation in health will be correlated with household income, price, and community variables and thus may become embedded in the health outcome. Then, the instrumental variable estimate of the effect of health capital on wages will contain some of the genetic health effect, in addition to the behaviorally induced variation in health human capital.[5]

Labor productivity, approximated by the hourly wage rate, is then fitted to variation in individual human capital stocks, where health human capital (Hb) is only the variation in health status that is accounted for by the instrumental variable, and hence uncorrelated with e_1, e_2, or g, because these production and demand errors or genetic variations are likely to be correlated with e_3 in the wage function

$$W = w(Hb(X), E, Z, e_3), \tag{4}$$

where W is the logarithm of the hourly wage rate, E education, Z other observed factors affecting the wage that are not behaviorally determined, such as age, and e_3 the error in the wage function. As noted, these instrumental variable estimates of the effect of health human capital on the wage also correct for classical measurement error in the health indicators.

3   Empirical Evidence of the Productivity of Health Status in Low-Income Countries

In the last few years, the relationship between labor productivity and indicators of adult health and nutritional status has been analyzed for a growing number of low-income countries. Indicators of adult health that have a comparable meaning across age groups, such as height, can also clarify the changes underlying health that occurred over time. First, analysis has dealt with the increased intake of calories as an endogenous decision made by individuals and families in response to factors including the local prices of nutrients (Strauss 1986). This approach was then extended to other nutritional intakes such as proteins, and nutritional status as proxied by BMI, both of which are expected to increase the productivity of a laborer and help him resist the debilitating effects of infections and parasitic diseases (Scrimshaw, Taylor, and Gordon 1968). Although adult height may be largely determined during early childhood development (Martorell and Habicht 1986; Thomas and Strauss 1997), adult height appears to be both heterogeneous and measured with error, and consequently, instrumental variable methods are needed even to estimate the human capital effect of adult height on wages.

Strauss (1986) argued that the relationship between nutrition and agricultural labor productivity could be biased because productivity also stimulates the demand for increased nutrition and health inputs.[6] He estimated the marginal productivity of agricultural labor in Sierra Leone, where he hypothesized that labor might be more productive when family workers were supplied with more calories. Rather than estimate a wage function including calories as a human capital argument, as outlined in the previous section, he estimated the household agricultural production function, including an interaction between an endogenous supply of calories, and the labor input into farm production. He thereby allowed calories to raise labor productivity and be subject to diminishing returns as per-capita calories in the family approached healthy levels. Because higher family labor productivity could also contribute to increased food consumption, Strauss used community variation in the price of nutrients as an instrumental variable to predict the family's supply of calories. He found calories driven by food prices raised the marginal product of family labor, especially at low calorie levels.

Subsequent studies replicated and extended Strauss's findings, with Deolalikar (1988) analyzing data for wage earners in India, Sahn and Alderman (1988) in Sri Lanka, Haddad and Bouis (1991) in the Philippines, and Foster and Rosenzweig (1993) in India and the Philippines. In urban Brazil, Thomas and Strauss (1997) estimated the joint effects on hourly earning of calories, proteins, and BMI, all three of these endogenously instrumented on local relative food prices, while also controlling for education and height. They found strong effects for the various endogenous nutrition and health variables, with calories again subject to diminishing returns. They estimated the elasticity of earnings with respect to exogenous height for men and women and found it to be significant but small.

An important feature of adult height is its persistence, changing relatively little from about age 20–55. Consequently, height can be compared across birth cohorts for 30–40 years in a single cross-sectional survey, with periods of economic development marked by improvements in childhood nutrition and health conditions that are evidenced by increased height. Economic historians construct time-series data on the height of select populations, such as recruits into the military or criminals for whom height was recorded, and seek to correct for sources of sample selection bias (Floud, Wachter, and Gregory 1990). In France, where all young males at a certain age registered for military conscription, time-series data on male height by region closely parallel estimates of GNP per capita from twenty years earlier, when the registrants were infants (Weir 1993). Fogel (1994) consolidated figures for Western European countries in which adult height is estimated for periods of one to two centuries. For example, in the United Kingdom in the nineteenth and twentieth centuries, male health increased by 0.45 centimeters per decade on average. Japanese men reaching age 20 have been estimated by Shay (1994) to have added 0.88 centimeters per decade from 1892–1937. Economic historians have relied on national time-series data on height, BMI, and output per capita, to shed light on the likely impact of health status on productivity, but without focusing on the estimation problems raised in section 2.

3.1   Health and Wages in Côte d'Ivoire and Ghana

Living standards measurement surveys conducted by the World Bank from 1985–1989 in Côte d'Ivoire and Ghana allow for the joint estimation of the effects on wages of height, BMI, lifetime migration, and years of schooling for men and women (Schultz 1995, 2003). In addition to Strauss's instruments—local relative food prices—parent education and occupation and the distance to health and school facilities are added to account for these four human capital variables. If individuals reside in a different region from their birthplace, then these migrants are attributed the average local characteristics of their region of birth for the relevant community instruments that are expected to influence human capital investments. When Wu-Hausman specification tests are performed to judge whether the human capital variables are heterogeneous or measured with error, the IV estimates differ significantly from the OLS estimates, rejected exogeneity. Different combinations of these instrumental variables are considered and they suggest that the IV wage equations are robust, or pass overidentification tests (Schultz 2003).

The OLS coefficients of these four human capital variables in the wage functions for men and women in the two countries are summarized in table 10.1 in rows 1, 3, 5, and 7, whereas the IV coefficients are reported in rows 2, 4, 6, and 8. On the whole, the OLS and IV estimates for education and migration are roughly the same, whereas the wage effects of health (height) and nutrition (BMI) are sensitive to the choice of IV versus OLS estimates. As argued in the previous sections of this chapter, height and BMI are expected to be heterogeneous, and the IV estimates are designed to focus on the wage differences associated with the reproducible variation in height and BMI, rather than the genetic and random variation in these anthropometric indicators. In the country with the greater child malnutrition, Ghana, the IV coefficient on height is 3.8 times larger for males than the OLS coefficient in the wage function, whereas the IV coefficient on height for women is 5.8 times larger than the OLS coefficient.[7] An increment of one centimeter in height is associated with a 6 to 8 percent increase in wages in Ghana, according to the preferred IV estimates. In the smaller samples from Côte d'Ivoire, the IV estimates of height on wages are not statistically significantly different from zero at the 5 percent level.

The IV coefficients on BMI are significant in all four gender–country samples, increasing threefold from the OLS coefficients for males in Côte d'Ivoire and by one-half for females, whereas in Ghana the IV

Table 10.1
Alternative estimates of human capital wage returns for schooling, mobility, and nutrition-health: Côte d'Ivoire and Ghana, 1985–1989.[a]

	Sample Size	Years of Education	Migration from Brithplace (Migrant = 1)	Height in centimeters	Weight to Height Squared (BMI)
Côte d'Ivoire: LSMS: 1985–1987					
Males	1692				
1. OLS:		0.109	0.715	0.00862	0.0451
In wage effects		(16.4)	(8.73)	(2.00)	(4.55)
2. IV:		0.107	0.691	−0.0105	0.159**
In wage effects		(3.88)	(3.09)	(0.56)	(3.00)
Females	1180				
3. OLS:		0.0730	0.891	0.00416	0.0613
In wage effects		(7.18)	(8.26)	(0.62)	(6.88)
4. IV:		0.0731	0.961	−0.0435*	0.0950**
In wage effects		(3.58)	(4.80)	(1.78)	(2.50)
Ghana: LSMS: 1987–1989					
Males	3414				
5. OLS:		0.0437	0.348	0.0148	0.0530
In wage effects		(9.86)	(6.75)	(5.02)	(6.80)
6. IV:		0.0445	0.218	0.0569**	0.0793
In wage effects		(2.46)	(2.26)	(3.45)	(1.95)
Females	3400				
7. OLS:		0.0375	0.531	0.0129	0.0420
In wage effects		(7.26)	(8.46)	(3.63)	(7.63)
8. IV:		0.0356[c]	0.361	0.0748**	0.0981**
In wage effects		(2.69)	(2.98)	(3.44)	(4.11)

Notes:
[a] Coefficients estimated on four human capital variables in log hourly wage equation, including dummy variables for age, region of birth, ethnic/language group, and season. Hausman (1978) test of the exogeneity of this human capital input in the wage function is rejected at the 5 percent confidence level (**), and should therefore be estimated by IV methods (* is 10 percent level).
Source: Schultz 2003.

coefficient on BMI increases by half for males, and more than doubles for females. An increase in BMI of one unit is associated with a 9 percent increase in wages for men in both Ghana and Côte d'Ivoire, whereas for women an increase in BMI of one unit is associated with a 7 percent increase in wages in Ghana and a 15 percent increase in Côte d'Ivoire. As a whole, these estimates of wage functions for two West African countries imply that the productive wage benefits associated with the reproducible variation in health human capital (i.e., height and BMI) are substantially larger than the OLS productive wage benefits associated with all of the measured variation in height and BMI. These results are consistent with the hypothesized heterogeneity in measures of nutrition and health.[8]

The LSMS surveys document the different achievements of neighboring countries. The heights of adult females and males, respectively, from Ghana who were age 20–60 at the time of the survey, have been plotted as 5-year moving averages by date of birth (Schultz 2001). Height has increased until the cohorts born in 1960, but after independence the increase in height slows or is nonexistent.[9] Males in Ghana age 20–29 report an average height of 170 centimeters, an increase of 2 centimeters over Ghanaian men age 50–65, whereas in neighboring Côte d'Ivoire the height of males 20–29 years old is 171 meters, or an increase of 4 centimeters over men age 50–65 (ibid., figures 3, 4). The estimated GNP per capita has also increased more rapidly in Côte d'Ivoire than in Ghana during the three decades 1960–1990; 316 versus 70 percent, respectively (World Bank 1991). For these same age groups, women increased their height in Côte d'Ivoire by 3 centimeters and in Ghana by 1 centimeter. Little research has been conducted on how gender differences in height are affected by health or economic developments, perhaps because much of the historical evidence is derived from military records (Steckel 1995).

Instrumental variable predictions of the number of days disabled are used to account for variations in wages among adult workers in Ghana and Côte d'Ivoire (Schultz and Tansel 1997). The instruments employed to predict the self-assessed morbidity variables include local access to health services and facilities, development infrastructure that should improve access to health care, climate and local malaria problems, parent education and occupation, region of birth, and local relative food prices. Although reported days disabled is only weakly related to wages, based on OLS estimates of the wage function by sex, the instrumental variable coefficients on this measure of days disabled are larger and statistically significant for men and women in Ghana and Côte d'Ivoire (ibid.). According to the preferred IV estimates, an increase of one more day disabled within the last four weeks is associated with a reduction in hourly wages of 10 percent, and an additional 3 percent reduction in hours worked.

3.2 Height and Wages in Brazil

Based on the 1989 Health and Nutrition Survey (PNSN) of Brazil, the height of individuals born from 1929–1969 (age 20–60 at the time of the survey) has been plotted (Schultz 2001, figures 5, 6). Fitting a linear time trend of height for individuals implies that Brazilian women born a decade later were on average 1 centimeter taller, and men 0.96 centimeters taller. Among only wage earners in 1989, the linear estimate of the increase in height was 1.18 centimeters per decade for women and 0.98 centimeters for men. The first regression in table 10.2 estimates the determinants of height for the wage earners conditional on a quadratic in age, controls for three nonwhite racial categories, and seven characteristics of local communities (i.e., municipios) as measured in the 1990 Instituto Brasiliero de Geografia e Estatistica (IBGE) census that were expected to affect the local public health environment and exposure to disease. Communities in which a larger fraction of the households have safe running water, more hospital beds per capita, and higher family incomes per capita have taller residents, but increased access to household sanitation and higher average adult education in the community is not partially associated with greater height.

Table 10.2, column 2, reports OLS estimates of the log-hourly wage regressions for the same Brazilian samples of male and female wage earners, based on the assumption that height is homogeneous, measured without error, and exogenous. Since it is likely that part of the wage differences by race is due to other human capital or environmental factors and is not caused entirely by differences in healthiness proxied by height, the three race dummies are also included directly in the specification of the conventional Mincerian wage function. Table 10.2, column 3, reports the IV estimates of the wage equation, treating height as endogenous and measured with error. The IV estimates imply a 3.9 percent wage gain per centimeter in male height, and a 5.6 percent wage gain per centimeter for females. The IV estimates are three to four times the magnitude of the OLS estimates, and the Wu-Hausman (1978) specification tests confirm that the OLS and IV estimates are significantly different, strengthening the statistical argument

Table 10.2
Estimates of height and log hourly wage functions, Brazil 1989: Age 20–60, wage earners.[a]

	Males			Females		
	Height	Wage	Wage	Height	Wage	Wage
Dependent Variable	OLS	OLS	IV[b]	OLS	OLS	IV[b]
Estimation Method	(1)	(2)	(3)	(1)	(2)	(3)
Height in		0.0131	0.0394		0.0153	0.0564
Centimeters		(11.1)	(9.01)		(8.55)	(7.60)
Post School		0.0735	0.0744		0.0599	0.0630
Experience		(25.7)	(25.9)		(16.3)	(16.9)
Experience Squared		−0.101	−0.0976		0.0782	−0.0734
$(\times 10^{-2})$		(20.1)	(19.2)		(11.3)	(10.6)
Education Years		0.147	0.152		0.148	0.157
		(56.4)	(59.1)		(43.2)	(44.9)
Rural Resident		−0.458	−0.444		−0.416	−0.399
		(24.5)	(23.7)		(12.9)	(12.3)
Age Years	0.0187			−0.0406		
	(0.40)			(0.67)		
Age Squared	−0.156			−0.0985		
$(\times 10^{-2})$	(2.61)			(1.23)		
Race:						
Black	−0.455	−0.310	−0.279	0.346	−0.367	−0.356
	(1.33)	(7.77)	(6.97)	(0.80)	(6.66)	(6.45)
Yellow	−5.06	0.128	0.264	−3.99	0.299	0.452
	(4.37)	(0.95)	(1.94)	(2.85)	(1.67)	(2.50)
Brown	−2.29	−0.182	−0.0879	−1.42	−0.208	−0.102
	(14.0)	(10.5)	(3.91)	(6.81)	(8.59)	(3.43)
Density Population	−0.102			0.053		
	(2.24)			(1.05)		
Density Squared	0.0042			−0.0023		
	(2.07)			(1.02)		
Percent Household	0.0536			0.0597		
with Running	(9.15)			(7.59)		
Water						
Percent Household	−0.0025			−0.0054		
with Sanitation	(0.77)			(1.21)		
Hospital Beds per	99.1			103.8		
1000	(4.59)			(3.98)		
Family Income per	0.942			0.838		
Capita	(3.77)			(2.89)		
Years of Education	−0.079			−0.359		
Adults Age 15+	(0.82)			(2.98)		
Intercept	165.6	−3.99	−8.53	−8.53	−4.52	−11.1
	(177.0)	(19.5)	(11.4)	(11.4)	(15.7)	(9.36)

Table 10.2
(continued)

	Males			Females		
	Height OLS	Wage OLS	Wage IV[b]	Height OLS	Wage OLS	Wage IV[b]
Dependent Variable Estimation Method	(1)	(2)	(3)	(1)	(2)	(3)
R^2 Adj. (Prob > F)	0.103 (0.0001)	0.419 (0.0001)	0.417 (0.0001)	0.0894 (0.0001)	0.410 (0.0001)	0.408 (0.0001)
Hausman t test of exogeneity of height (Prob > t)	—	—	9.17 (0.0001)	—	—	6.97 (0.0001)
Mean Dependent Variable (standard deviation)	168.0 (7.29)	−0.297 (1.05)	−0.297 (1.05)	156.0 (6.69)	−0.557 (1.06)	−0.557 (1.06)

Notes:
[a] Beneath regression coefficients are the absolute value of t (OLS) and asymptotic t (IV) statistics.
[b] The instrumental variables identifying the effects of height in the wage equation (3) are the seven community characteristics for population density to adult years of education.

for accepting the asymptotically unbiased IV estimates. Interpreting these results with the model outlined in section 2 having two components of health, the coefficient on the human capital component is significantly larger than that on the socially unexplained residual health variation.

The specification appears to be relatively robust to changes in the subset of IV variables used to identify the effect of health human capital.[10] The magnitude of height's effect on wages estimated by instrumental variables appears to be substantial in Brazil, even though incomes levels are much higher than in Ghana and Côte d'Ivoire and that one might expect to find diminishing returns to this dimension of health status. Even in the United States in 1989–1993, IV estimates suggest that an additional centimeter in height is associated with men receiving 3 percent higher wages, and women 4.6 percent higher wages, where instruments include both regional health conditions and residence at age 14 (Schultz 2002).

3.3 Wage and Inequality Changes Associated with Height and Education

To illustrate the likely contribution of advances in height and education to the growth in Brazilian wages from 1950–1980, the 1989 wage regressions (Table 10.2, column 3) are used to weight the changes in height and schooling as reported in the third row of each panel of table 10.3, for adults born in 1930–1934 and 1960–1964, who might have entered the Brazilian labor force in approximately 1950 and 1980. The increase in height of 1.03 centimeters per decade between these birth cohorts (3.10/3 in table 10.3), separated by 30 years, could account for a rise per decade in male wages of 4.1 percent (0.0394 ∗ 1.03), and in female wages of 5.8 percent (0.0564 ∗ 1.03). In contrast, the increase in years of schooling completed was 1.05 years per decade for males, associated in 1989 with a rise in wages of 16 percent (0.152 ∗ 1.05) per decade for males, while the increase in schooling for females accounts for growth in wages of 22 percent. Thus, improvements in nutrition and health associated with birth cohort height accounted for somewhat less than a third of the wage growth associated with schooling (i.e., 5 percent versus 18 percent per decade).

Economic inequality in Brazil is among the highest in the world (Schultz 1998). Measuring inequality by the variance in the logarithms of wages, the variance in human capital endowments help to account for inequality in wages or its change over time, neglecting as second-order effects the covariances between age (experience), schooling, and height. According to table 10.3, the variance in height has remained relatively stable in Brazil across these thirty years of birth cohorts, decreasing for men by 5.3 percent while increasing slightly for women by 0.9 percent. The variance in years of schooling, however, increased by 78 percent for Brazilian males and by 127 percent for females. The growing variance in the receipt of schooling has contributed to increasing economic inequality in Brazil (holding the 1989 wage structure constant), whereas inequality in health status, represented by height, is not linked to changes in inequality between the older and younger birth cohorts (cf. Strauss and Thomas 1995, fig. 34.3).

3.4 Health and Wages: Latin America

The Inter-American Development Bank coordinated a series of health and productivity studies based on recent Latin American household surveys (Savedoff and Schultz 2000). These studies examined data from Peru collected in 1994 and 1995, Colombia from 1991 and 1993, and Mexico from two 1995 surveys. In each analysis of one or more health indicators—height, BMI, self-assessed health status, self-reported days disabled, ADLs, and age at menarche for women—were found to be weakly related to wages in a standard OLS specification,

Table 10.3
Means and standard deviations in parentheses of height and schooling by country, selected age groups, and sex.

Country Age	Height (cm.)		Schooling (yrs.)	
	Female	Male	Female	Male
Ghana: 1987–1989				
Age 25–29	158.53	169.46	5.29	8.29
	(6.25)	(6.63)	(4.97)	(5.09)
Age 55–59	156.93	169.00	2.12	5.68
	(5.96)	(6.51)	(4.29)	(5.97)
Change	+1.60	+0.46	+3.17	+2.61
	(+0.29)	(+0.12)	(+0.68)	(−0.88)
Côte d'Ivoire: 1985–1987				
Age 25–29	159.11	170.11	2.78	6.12
	(5.67)	(6.70)	(3.99)	(5.07)
Age 55–59	157.57	168.48	0.23	2.30
	(6.11)	(6.88)	(1.32)	(3.98)
Change	+1.54	+1.63	+2.55	+3.82
	(−0.44)	(−0.18)	(+2.67)	(+1.09)
Brazil: 1989				
Age 25–29	156.27	168.90	6.36	5.66
	(6.62)	(7.27)	(4.31)	(4.22)
Age 55–59	153.16	165.79	2.21	2.52
	(6.59)	(7.47)	(2.86)	(3.16)
Change	+3.10	+3.10	+4.15	+3.14
	(+0.03)	(−0.20)	(+1.45)	(+1.04)
Vietnam: 1992–1993				
Age 25–29	152.16	162.10	7.90	8.35
	(5.39)	(5.39)	(3.21)	(3.38)
Age 55–59	148.73	159.19	3.74	6.48
	(5.64)	(5.93)	(2.59)	(3.82)
Change	+3.43	+2.91	+4.16	+1.87
	(−0.25)	(−0.54)	(+0.62)	(−0.44)

Source: Author's tabulations.

but when the health status indicators were estimated by IV techniques, relying on local health infrastructure and socioeconomic characteristics, all of these health indicators were related to wages in the anticipated manner, although the results for males were frequently more significant than for the smaller samples of female wage earners and self-employed workers.[11]

4   Conclusions

A range of survey indicators of adult nutritional and health status have been reviewed as potential determinants of individual wages and labor productivity in low-income countries. Several investigations have analyzed adult height as a proxy for uterine and early childhood nutritional and health status, which are widely thought to be important determinants of adult chronic health problems, particularly cardiovascular, and a determinant of longevity among the elderly (Barker 1992; Fogel 1991). Estimates of wage functions at the individual level from representative household surveys that include adult height find that height is partially associated with modest increments to wages, confirming its association with health and productivity as emphasized by physical anthropologists and economic historians. When wage functions are estimated at the individual level, as outlined in section 2 of this chapter, identifying the endogenous and measured-with-error health indicators by instrumental variable methods, based on local food prices, community health services, and parental family resources, the estimated effect of these health human capital variables, such as height, are increased substantially and generally become more statistically significant. An additional centimeter in height is associated with a gain in wage rates of roughly 5–10 percent, and more rapidly growing countries, such as Brazil, have achieved increases in adult height of a centimeter per decade. These instrumental variable estimates of adult health status on labor productivity are larger than the OLS estimates, presumably because these health indicators are not homogeneous and are measured with error. The instruments for health status are local food prices, health infrastructure, and in some cases parental socioeconomic characteristics that are designed to explain the socially reproducible component of adult health status that is akin to the status of health human capital. The statistical interpretation is that the socially predictable component of the observed variation in height, BMI, days disabled, ADLs, and age at menarche exerts a stronger influence on wages, and presumably on adult health, than does the unexplained remainder of the variation in health indicators that are largely attributable to genetic diversity and measurement error.

Self-reported morbidity, such as days disabled, may exhibit no significant direct partial (OLS) relationship with wages, whereas community health instrumental variables suggest that these health indicators tend to be better in communities in which wages are higher. Functional limitations of daily living, disability days, height, and age at menarche are all found to be similarly powerful in IV estimates of wage functions for workers in Mexico, Colombia, Peru, Brazil, Côte d'Ivoire, and Ghana.

These studies of wages and health human capital are only beginning to propose suitable functional forms to approximate these relationships, which might be expected to exhibit some degree of biological generality across national populations. Diminishing returns to nutritional inputs are expected, and perhaps a similar pattern will emerge with respect to other physical growth indicators of health. Because of the discrete and unusual distributions of such health indicators, such as number of days disabled in a reference period or aggregated ADLs, the estimation of ordered probit models may provide a useful method to begin scaling and aggregating health indicators.

It should be emphasized that all of the IV studies referred to in this chapter have used concurrent community- and family-health-related conditions as instruments to predict health human capital. The health conditioning variables should be measured over the individual's entire lifetime, weighted for the sensitivity of adult health to inputs at each stage in the individual's prior lifetime. Current clinical and some panel studies conclude that the uterine and early childhood environments are the most important, suggesting that the community and family health conditions should be measured for the individual prenatally and in the first years of life. If individual migration histories were collected retrospectively by household surveys, the individual could then be matched to regional records for locality-specific health programs for when the adult respondent was a susceptible infant. Food prices and rainfall in rural residential regions have provided random shocks to identify an exogenous source of variations in child growth in the Cebu survey, which permitted the estimation of the effect of this child growth on later child achievement in school tests (Glewwe, Jacobi, and King 1999). The resulting IV estimates become a useful tool for evaluating community health policy, which seeks to achieve food security for the poor. The empirical problems in evaluating the consequences of new health programs and policies would be facilitated if community health interventions were implemented in a staggered and randomized manner, to assure that the local allocations of health program resources would be statistically independent of unobserved heterogeneity across localities.

The connection between the accumulation of health human capital and labor productivity is a starting point for appraising the priorities in many health programs and policies. The major complexity posed by health, which is less of a problem with education, is that the indicators that represent health are multifaceted and are not always adequately justified by their correspondence with mortality, morbidity, and the quality of life. Many of these health indicators may represent proxies for human capital, consuming current social resources and yielding increased production potential over the life cycle of cohorts. These indicators are a mixture of exogenous measurement error and genetic components, on the one hand, and an endogenous (or human capital) component. This distinction is perhaps most evident in the case of adult height, which has been emphasized here. In all of these studies of height, community health services and the socioeconomic characteristics of parents account for only 2–10 percent of the variation in the population, and much of the unexplained variation in height is undoubtedly due to genotypic variation across individuals and survey measurement errors.[12]

The weakest link in the conceptual and empirical methodology outlined in this chapter is in measuring satisfactory instrumental variables at the level of the formative family and childhood community. Certain instruments should be most relevant to different health indicators. The choice of these instruments should be informed by consulting the medical literature on what are likely to be effective interventions, since the choice of instrumental variables should mimic policy variations if the IV estimates are to be at their most useful in guiding policy choices.

Finally, heterogeneity in a population in its response to health treatments is to be expected, and this should lead to estimation of the impact of policy interventions on wages for different socioeconomic groups. Quantifying these distributional consequences of interventions is a critical ingredient in policy evaluation. The convenient simplifying assumption of homogeneity in treatment response that is implicit in many program evaluation studies needs to be reconsidered. With the analysis of individual data collected in matched household-community surveys, there is nothing to prevent such a reappraisal at several levels. First, interactions can be directly estimated between the treatment (price instruments, or random health inputs) and different exogenous socioeconomic groups in either the health reduced-form or wage equation (Schultz 1984). Second, the analysis should choose instrumental variables that capture distinctive program strategies that promise to yield special benefits for disadvantaged groups. The choice of these program characteristics may be informed by theories drawn from the biomedical sciences, sociology, anthropology, political science, or economics. Third, quantile wage regressions using instrument variable methods may be employed to clarify what health determinants have larger productive benefits for individuals who are the least productive.

Notes

1. It is worrisome that self-assessed morbidity rates are often higher in higher-income countries, where survival (the "gold" standard measure of health) is higher, or that morbidity is reported more frequently in the higher-income classes of a developing country. How then can the researcher explain these divergent trends in morbidity and mortality (Schultz and Tansel 1997; Foster 1994)? Labor contracts can affect how many working days people miss due to illness, as when workers are eligible for a certain number of paid sick-leave days per year. On the one hand, many wage workers in a low-income country are casual laborers and are penalized by the loss of their wages if they do not report for work during any given day. Alternatively, if they are caught "working" while ill and are thus presumably less productive, the employer may view the worker as shirking and not employ the individual in the future, damaging his reputation. However, if the reported number of days unable to work in the retrospective period is a more informative indicator of productive health status for wage earners than for other persons, some procedure is then needed to correct for sample selection bias, if the statistical relationship between health determinants and reported morbidity rates for wage earners is corrected to represent the relationship in the entire population (Schultz and Tansel 1997).

2. The analyst would still face the challenge of determining how much of the costs of changing the formative health conditions, e.g., of improving nutrition, is attributable to the health investment objective and how much is attributable to the satisfaction of immediate consumption preferences, i.e., reduced hunger.

3. Discredited eugenic approaches to improving the fitness of populations might have promoted selective reproduction and thereby sought to enhance genetic health potential. But modern biotechnology may be redrawing the limits of health human capital today.

4. For example, if the public-subsidized price of health services is the policy intervention that is expected to induce variation in the use of health services and to thereby affect the production of health human capital, the instrumental variable methodology requires only that the price of health services be significantly correlated with the indicator of health status in the first stages, and that the instrumental variable not be correlated with the residual variation in genetic health predisposition or measurement error. Income shocks due to weather deviations from long-term averages have also been used to infer the health ef-

fect of exogenous variations in household income, and linked to perturbations in health human capital. This approach can document how poorer families with less capacity to borrow to finance unusual consumption and investment needs may not be able to protect their children's physical development and growth (and schooling) from such weather-induced income shocks (Jacoby and Skoufias 1997). What has not yet been done is to use these weather-induced variations in human capital to explain adult wage productivity or performance.

5. Hausman (1978) specification tests could be performed to determine whether the health human capital variable appears to be exogenous (or endogenous) in the wage function. Endogeneity would be confirmed if the behavioral and genetic components of the health human capital variable received significantly different coefficients in the wage equation. In some health measures the genetic component appears to account for most of the variable's variation, such as height, whereas the categorical or disability measures of health are more readily explained by individual–family–community instrumental variables.

6. This possibility of a nutrition-based efficiency wage has led development economists to speculate that poor laborers have been unable to invest efficiently in their own nutrition. Moreover, employers may not have captured the full productive benefits of paying their workers a higher wage and having them consume a more adequate diet, whereas a slave owner might have had the incentives to feed their workers efficiently. Yet agricultural wages in India appeared sufficient in the 1960s to escape such a Malthusian trap, although some European populations may have had large shares of their population malnourished in the eighteenth century (Fogel 1986).

7. The World Bank estimated that 36 percent of the children under age 5 were malnourished in Ghana in 1990, whereas only 12 percent were in Côte d'Ivoire (World Bank 1991). It is also documented in a variety of sources that the rate of infant and child mortality has declined rapidly in Côte d'Ivoire since 1960, as incomes per capita have risen sharply. In Ghana, which started the postcolonial era as one of the richest countries in Africa and initially had relatively high schooling rates and low infant mortality rates, growth has been slow, with little if any improvements in under-5 mortality during the 1970s and early 1980s (Benefo and Schultz 1996).

8. In Côte d'Ivoire a subset of the survey sample is reinterviewed in the following year and can be matched, allowing one to assess the random measurement error by comparing the wage estimates for this smaller group based on the average height in the two years versus that based on the individual year observations that are expected to be more noisy. As anticipated, the wage effects associated with the two-year averaged health-human-capital indicators are larger than those estimated from the individual-year values. Classical measurement error may be important in these health status indicators, but is not likely to account fully for the increase in the magnitude of the IV over the OLS estimates. Additional heterogeneity or endogeneity is probable. Nonetheless, the panel averages illustrate that there can be serious problems in reliably measuring height and weight in a household survey (Schultz 2003).

9. The lack of growth in height may also be due to the selective outmigration from Ghana that is said to have led to the departure of half their professional medical staff in the 1960s and 1970s, and it might be expected that the outmigrants would have been taller on average than the nonmigrants.

10. Including 31 additional control instrumental variables for local climate and population density to improve the predictions for the regional variations in height does not

greatly affect the second stage IV estimates of the impact of height on wages. The wage gains for males are then estimated to be 4.0 percent per centimeter and for females 5.6 percent (not reported) (Schultz 2001).

11. For example, in 1995 a Mexican survey asked women ages 18–54 what age their first menstruation occurred, and the average was 13.1 years, with the linear time trend implying age at menarche decreased by 0.11 years per decade (t = 8.54) (Knaul 2000). Knaul interprets this variable as an indicator of the timing of the adolescent growth spurt in Mexican women that is expected to occur earlier when childhood nutrition and health status improves (Wyshak and Frisch 1982; Faulkner and Tanner 1986). Age at menarche occurred later for Mexican women residing in rural areas than in urban ones, and for women who had completed fewer years of schooling, controlling for age. When age at menarche is added to the wage equation for these women, and instrumented by local public health, education, and housing variables, a highly significant partial relationship is obtained, in which a one month decrease in age at menarche is associated with a 1.9 to 2.3 percent increase in female adult wage rates.

12. More explicit analysis of matched siblings, and the exploitation of fixed-effect estimation, might illuminate the relative importance of family and sibling fixed effects. It would not be clear, however, whether the sibling–family effects were only genetic in origin, even after many observed socioeconomic characteristics of the family had already been controlled. Nonetheless, such estimates should provide another way to identify how changes over time in the community public programs work their effect on height and correspondingly affect adult wages of persons who benefited from these local programs because they came into a specific family before or after the program started.

References

Barker, D. J. P. 1992. *Fetal and Infant Origins of Adult Disease.* London: British Medical Journal Publishing Group.

Beaton, G., A. Kelley, J. Kevany, R. Martorell, and J. Mason. 1990. Appropriate Uses of Anthropometric Indices with Children. Nutrition Policy Discussion Paper no. 7, ACCISCN, United Nations, Geneva.

Benefo, K., and T. P. Schultz. 1996. Fertility and Child Mortality in Côte d'Ivoire and Ghana. *World Bank Economic Review* 10 (1): 123–158.

Card, D. 1999. The Causal Effect of Education on Earnings. In *The Handbook of Labor Economics*, vol. 3A, edited by O. Ashenfelter and D. Card. Amsterdam: Elsevier.

———. 2001. Estimating the Returns to Schooling: Progress on Some Persistent Problems. *Econometrica* 69 (5): 1127–1160.

Costa, D. L. 1996. Health and Labor Force Participation of Older Men, 1900–1991. *Journal of Economic History* 56 (1): 62–89.

———. 2002. Changing Chronic Disease Rates and Long-Term Declines in Functional Limitations among Older Men. *Demography* 39 (1): 119–137.

Deolalikar, A. 1988. Nutrition and Labor Productivity in Agriculture. *Review of Economics and Statistics* 70 (3): 406–413.

Eveleth, P. B., and J. M. Tanner. 1976. *Worldwide Variation in Human Growth.* Cambridge: Cambridge University Press.

Faulkner, F., and J. M. Tanner. 1986. *Human Growth: A Comprehensive Treatise*, vol. 3, second edition. New York: Plenum Press.

Floud, R., K. W. Wachter, and A. Gregory. 1990. *Height, Health, and History: Nutritional Status in the United Kingdom, 1750–1980*. Cambridge: Cambridge University Press.

Fogel, R. 1986. Growth and Economic Well Being: 18th and 19th Centuries. In *Human Growth*, vol. 3, edited by F. Faulkner and J. M. Tanner. New York: Plenum Press.

———. 1991. Early Indicators of Later Work Levels, Disease, and Death. Project proposal first submitted to the National Institute of Health and National Science Foundation, through the National Bureau of Economic Research, Cambridge, Mass.

———. 1994. Economic Growth, Population Theory, and Physiology. *American Economic Review* 84 (3): 369–395.

Foster, A. D. 1994. Poverty and Illness in Low-Income Rural Areas. *American Economic Review* 84 (2): 216–220.

Foster, A. D., and M. Rosenzweig. 1993. Information, Learning, and Wage Rates in Low-Income Rural Areas. *Journal of Human Resources* 28 (4): 759–790.

Foster, A. D., and M. Rosenzweig. 1994. A Test for Moral Hazard in the Labor Market: Effort, Health, and Calorie Consumption. *Review of Economics and Statistics* 76 (2): 213–227.

Glewwe, P., H. Jacoby, and E. King. 1999. Childhood Nutrition and Academic Achievement: A Longitudinal Analysis. FCND Discussion Paper no. 68, International Food Policy Research Institute, Washington, D.C.

Griliches, Z. 1977. Estimating the Returns to Schooling. *Econometrica* 45 (13): 1–22.

Haddad, L. J., and H. E. Bouis. 1991. The Impact of Nutritional Status on Agricultural Productivity: Wage Evidence from the Philippines. *Oxford Bulletin of Economics and Statistics* 53 (1): 45–68.

Hausman, J. A. 1978. Specification Tests in Econometrics. *Econometrica* 46 (6): 1251–1272.

Jacoby, H., and E. Skoufias. 1997. Risk, Financial Markets, and Human Capital in a Developing Country. *Review of Economic Studies* 64: 311–335.

Johansson, S. R. 1991. The Health Transaction: The Cultural Inflation of Morbidity during the Decline of Mortality. *Health Transition Review* 1 (1): 39–68.

Kling, J. 1999. Interpreting Instrumental Variable Estimates of the Returns to Schooling. Working paper no. 415, Industrial Relations Section, Princeton University, Princeton.

Knaul, F. 2000. Linking Health, Nutrition, and Wages. In *Wealth from Health*, edited by W. Savedoff and T. P. Schultz. Washington, D.C.: Inter-American Development Bank.

Manning, W. G., J. P. Newhouse, and J. E. Ware. 1982. The Status of Health in Demand Estimation; or Beyond Excellent, Good, Fair, Poor. In *Economic Aspects of Health*, edited by V. R. Fuchs. Chicago: University of Chicago Press.

Martorell, R., and J. P. Habicht. 1986. Growth in Early Childhood in Developing Countries. In *Human Growth*, vol. 3F, edited by F. Faulkner and J. M. Tanner. New York: Plenum Press.

Murray, C. J. L., and A. D. Lopez. 1994. *Global Comparative Assessments in the Health Sector: Disease Burden, Expenditures, and Intervention Packages.* Geneva: World Health Organization.

Pritchett, L., and L. H. Summers. 1996. Wealthier is Healthier. *Journal of Human Resources* 31 (4): 841–868.

Rosenzweig, M., and T. P. Schultz. 1983. Estimating a Household Production Function. *Journal of Political Economy* 91 (5): 723–746.

Sahn, D. E., and H. Alderman. 1988. The Effect of Human Capital on Wages and the Determinants of Labor Supply in a Developing Country. *Journal of Development Economics* 29 (2): 157–183.

Savedoff, W., and T. P. Schultz. 2000. *Wealth from Health.* Washington, D.C.: Inter-American Development Bank.

Schultz, T. P. 1984. Studying the Impact of Household Economic and Community Variables on Child Mortality. *Population and Development Review* 10 (suppl.): 215–235.

———. 1993. Investments in the Schooling and Health of Women and Men: Quantities and Return. *Journal of Human Resources* 28 (4): 694–734.

———. 1995. Human Capital and Development. In *Agricultural Competitiveness: Market Forces and Policy Choice*, ed. G. H. Peters and D. D. Hedley. Aldershot: Dartmouth, pp. 523–539.

———. 1998. Inequality in the Distribution of Personal Income in the World. *Journal of Population Economics* 11 (3): 307–344.

———. 2001. *Productive Benefits of Improving Health.* Yale University, New Haven. Available at http://www.econ.yale.edu/~pschultz/productivebenefits.

———. 2002. Wage Gains Associated with Height from Health Human Capital. *American Economic Review* 92 (2): 349–353.

———. 2003. Wage Rentals for Reproducible Human Capital: Evidence from Ghana and Ivory Coast. *Economics of Human Biology* 1 (3): 331–366.

Schultz, T. P., and A. Tansel. 1997. Wage and Labor Supply Effects of Illness in Côte d'Ivoire and Ghana: Instrumental Variable Estimates for Days Disabled. *Journal of Development Economics* 53 (2): 251–286.

Scrimshaw, N. S. 1997. More Evidence That Foetal Nutrition Contributes to Chronic Disease in Later Life. *British Medical Journal* 315 (7112): 825–826.

Scrimshaw, N. S., and J. E. Gordon. 1968. *Malnutrition, Learning, and Behavior.* Cambridge, Mass.: The MIT Press.

Sen, A. 1981. *Poverty and Farmers: An Essay on Entitlement and Deprivation.* Oxford: Clarendon Press.

———. 1998. Mortality as an Indicator of Economic Success and Failure. *Economic Journal* 108 (446): 1–25.

Shay, T. 1994. The Level of Living in Japan, 1885–1938. New Evidence. In *Stature, Living Standards, and Economic Development: Essays in Anthropometric History*, ed. J. Komlos. Chicago: University of Chicago Press.

Steckel, R. H. 1995. Stature and the Standard of Living. *Journal of Economic Literature* 33 (4): 1903–1940.

Stewart, A. L., and J. E. Ware, Jr. 1992. *Measuring Functioning and Well Being*. Durham, N.C.: Duke University Press.

Strauss, J. 1986. Does Better Nutrition Raise Farm Productivity? *Journal of Political Economy* 94 (2): 297–320.

Strauss, J., and D. Thomas. 1995. Human Resources: Empirical Modeling of Household and Family Decisions. Chap. 34 in *Handbook of Development Economics*, vol. 3A, edited by J. R. Behrman and T. N. Srinivasan. Amsterdam: North Holland.

———. 1998. Health, Nutrition, and Economic Development. *Journal of Economic Literature* 36 (2): 766–817.

Strauss, J., P. J. Gertler, O. Rahman, and K. Fox. 1995. Gender and Life-Cycle Differentials in the Patterns and Determinants of Adult Health. In *Investment in Women's Human Capital*, edited by T. P. Schultz. Chicago: University of Chicago Press.

Thomas, D., and J. Strauss. 1997. Health, Wealth, and Wages of Men and Women in Urban Brazil. *Journal of Econometrics* 77: 159–185.

Waaler, H. T. 1984. Height, Weight, and Mortality: The Norwegian Experience. *Acta Medica Scandinavia* 77 (suppl. no. 679): 1–56.

Waterlow, J. C., R. Buzina, W. Keller, J. M. Lane, M. Z. Nichaman, and J. M. Tanner. 1977. The Presentation and Use of Height and Weight Data for Comparing the Nutritional Status of Groups of Children under the Age of 10 Years. *Bulletin of the World Health Organization* 55 (4): 489–498.

Weir, D. 1993. Parental Consumption Decisions and Child Health in France. *Journal of Economic History* 53 (2): 259–274.

World Bank. 1991. *Social Indicators of Development 1990*. Baltimore: Johns Hopkins University Press.

Wyshak, G., and R. Frisch. 1982. Evidence of a Secular Trend in Age of Menarche. *New England Journal of Medicine* 306 (17): 1033–1035.

11

Individual Returns to Health in Brazil: A Quantile Regression Analysis

Berta Rivera and Luis Currais

It is now generally accepted that improvements in a population's health come about as a consequence of economic development. As countries obtain higher levels of income, so are there greater resources available to be spent on health. Higher incomes favor better nutrition, improvements in hygiene and sanitation, better education, and healthier lifestyle habits, all of which lead to higher health levels.

However, when it comes to actually carrying out policies aimed at boosting economic growth, governments tend to prefer other kinds of investments such as those for infrastructure or education rather than health. Of course it remains true that infrastructures and education are important components of economic growth, but the good health of a population, as well as being a consequence of economic development, is also an important factor for development. Thus, investment directed at improvements in health should be envisaged not solely as a social or moral obligation, but also as an effective of means of stimulating economic growth within any given country.

The public sector plays a key role in the provision of health services. A large proportion of the population who are unwell and who seek medical advice are provided with health care by the public sector. The percentage of the population dependent on public health services increases as incomes diminish, that is, poorer households rely more heavily on public services. Within this context then, public investment in health is essential in order to improve a population's health status and to increase economic development.

Human capital, in its broadest sense, has become an important driving force behind economic development and income distribution. Recent studies, such as those of Schultz and Tansel (1997), and Thomas and Strauss (1997), confirm the idea that health is a form of human capital that influences individual wage levels, and thus, in their capacity to generate a sustained income that increases over time, and all of the positive consequences that this implies in terms of spending power and the standard of living for all of those in the household.

Health, as a form of human capital, should be envisaged as a property that may be improved on through investment in resources. It is within this framework that the mechanisms affecting the way in which health investment dictates the future incomes of individuals should be studied. From a microeconomic viewpoint, the idea that healthier individuals are more productive has been the recent object of various rigorous empirical analyses of Latin American countries and the Caribbean (Savedoff and Schultz 2000).

The first studies that linked health and productivity were carried out within the framework of the efficient wage hypothesis (Behrman 1993; Pit, Rosenzweig, and Hassan 1990; Behrman and Deolalikar 1988; Sahn and Alderman 1988). This research looks at developing countries and associates nutrition with productivity. Recently, economic literature has begun to place a heavier emphasis on measuring health conditions via the use of indicators obtained from household surveys and health surveys.

The main object of this chapter is to analyze the relationship between health and labor outcomes in Brazil, with the aim of exploring the impact of health on individual productivity. To this end we examine the relationship between wages and health variables at different levels of earnings distribution. We carry out quantile regressions in order to estimate the returns of health for different quantiles of the conditional distribution of wages. We are also interested in exploring the causal effects of health and whether there is evidence of individual heterogeneity in returns to health or conversely, if there are constant returns for all workers.

Section 1 of this chapter contains the basic model and the empirical framework used for carrying out the analyses. Section 2 provides a description of the data and section 3 presents the results of the estimations. The final section outlines the key empirical findings.

1   The Basic Model and Quantile Regressions

In this section we specify a simple structural model that aims to highlight the main aspects of the problem. We focus on the following questions: what constitutes a logical way of envisaging the link between health and productivity? Are returns to health homogenous across the population? If not, how can we model the source of this heterogeneity and how can it be explored? Why is quantile regression the right kind of tool for exploring these types of effects that involve unobservable factors? How does the availability of health data allows us to deal with measurement error and simultaneity bias in the quantile regression method?

1.1 The Basic Model

In order to analyze how health status may be determined we use the Becker model (1965) as our starting point. In the Becker model household decisions are taken in an attempt to maximize utility. The explanatory variables in the model are: consumer goods (C^i), consumer goods that improve health (Y^i), health status (H^i), and the level of leisure (l^i). Household decisions are unitary and are restricted in terms of time and income. Thus the model is in effect in the form of a household made up of n individuals, with a household head who aims to maximize the utility function.

$$U = U(C^i, Y^i, H^i, l^i) \quad i = 1, 2 \ldots \ldots, n. \tag{1}$$

If we take into account the restriction of the health production function (which depends on the level of consumption, items related to household health, leisure, and other individual characteristics) and on the income restriction (which indicates that all of the available household resources are spent on goods, services, and leisure) we obtain the reduced health demand function

$$H^i = h(P_c, P_y, S, F, Z^i, u^i), \tag{2}$$

where P_c and P_y are the prices of consumption relevant to health and the costs of health inputs respectively; S represents the income restriction, F the availability of welfare or health programs and of community infrastructure, and Z^i and u^i are the observable and non-observable characteristics of individuals.

1.2 The Empirical Framework

In order to assess the impact of health on wages we adopt the model first formulated by Mincer (1974) and obtain the wages equation. This model integrates an equation that explains the decision to participate in the labor market and also facilitates the correction of bias with respect to the choice of the wage function. When an earnings equation is estimated based on a sample of individuals who are market participants, the estimated returns may be biased. This potential selection bias is particularly important in the case of women.[1]

The wage function depends on the individual characteristics of age and sex, on the human capital variables of years of education and work experience, and the regional variables that describe the labor market, and may be expressed as:

$$\ln(w_i) = \alpha + \sum \alpha_j X_{ji} + \sum \alpha_k C_{ki} + \sum \alpha_h H_{hi} + \varepsilon_i, \tag{3}$$

where w_i is the measure of productivity (wages), X_{ji} are exogenous endowments that are not modified by the individual or family, C_{ki} are reproducible forms or human capital, and H_{hi} are the health status indicators.[2]

The wage distribution: Quantile regression   It is important to analyze the potential differences in returns to health across the wage distribution.[3] To this end, wage equations are estimated at different quantiles of the dependent variable distribution. This procedure is based on the quantile regression methodology developed by Koenker and Basset (1978) and applied to wage equations (Buchinsky 1994).

The quantile regression model can be written as

$$\ln w_i = x_i \beta_\theta + \mu_{\theta i} \quad \text{with Quant}_\theta(\ln w_i | x_i) = x_i \beta_\theta, \tag{4}$$

where x_i is the vector of the exogenous variables and β_θ is the vector of the parameters. $\text{Quant}_\theta(\ln w_i | x_i)$ denotes the θth conditional quantile of $\ln w$ given x. The θth regression quantile, $0 < \theta < 1$, is defined as a solution to the problem

$$\min_{\beta \in R^k} \left(\sum_{i: y_i \geq x_i \beta} \theta |\ln w_i - x_i \beta_\theta| + (1 - \theta)|\ln w_i - x_i \beta_\theta| \right).$$

This is normally written as

$$\min_{\beta \in R^k} \sum_i \rho_\theta(\ln w_i - x_i \beta_\theta), \tag{5}$$

where $\rho_\theta(\varepsilon)$ is the check function defined as $\rho_\theta(\varepsilon) = \theta \varepsilon$ if $\varepsilon \geq 0$ or $\rho_\theta(\varepsilon) = (\theta - 1)\varepsilon$ if $\varepsilon < 0$.

This problem can be solved by linear programming methods and standard errors are obtainable by bootstrap methods. The least absolute deviation (LAD) estimator of β is a particular case within this framework. The estimator is obtained by setting θ to 0.5, the median regression. The first quantile is obtained by setting θ to 0.25 and so on. As θ is increased from 0 to 1, the entire distribution of y conditional on x is traced.

Quantile regressions constitute a parsimonious way of describing the whole distribution and are especially useful if the relationship between the regressor and the dependent variable evolves across its conditional distribution. In this sense, we consider the possibility that the returns to health change at different points on the conditional distribution. With these assumptions the wage equations are estimated using the design matrix bootstrap method to obtain the covariance matrix vector of parameter estimates.[4]

Endogeneity and measurement error When compared to other forms of human capital, health is somewhat difficult to measure. Not all of the indicators are objective, some are linked to just one facet of health, and others fail to measure a complete range of conditions. Health status may be considered as a nonobservable variable that may be estimated only by recourse to imperfect indicators such as whether or not the individual suffers from a particular illness, the number of days that the illness or incapacity lasts or, the number of days during which the individual's main activity is impeded. These indicators, obtained via surveys, constitute data given voluntarily by the interviewee and as such are subject to measurement errors, and these errors might constitute a source of bias with respect to the effect of health on other variables.

Further, the self-perception of the individual's health status is correlated to certain personal characteristics. Therefore individuals with higher educational levels and better access to health services will be more likely to detect the symptoms of illness. This might potentially distort the effects of education or medical assistance on health. In this sense, these factors could give rise to heteroscedasticity in the health equation given that variability in the measurement error is also determined by some of the equation's explanatory variables. The choice of one given variable or another depends, to a large extent, on the options made available by different surveys.

In addition, the fact that the relationship between income and health may be two-way would make difficult the estimation of the impact of health on productivity. For instance, higher incomes mean that individuals are potentially more likely to consume goods and services that affect health positively such as the right kinds of foods or medicines.

There is also an indirect effect on health via improved lifestyle habits, greater participation in the workplace, and higher individual educational levels, all of which result in improvements in health status through increases in income.[5] Individuals also possess a set of personal characteristics that affect both health and productivity and these traits are not observable but rather random and exogenous such as physical build.

The correlation of health with unobserved factors that determine wages can produce inconsistent estimates and instrumental variables techniques need to be used in the estimation of the quantile regressions.[6] Instrumental variables techniques require the utilization of fitted values for health. These are derived from the least squares regression of the endogenous variables on the instruments and are used as regressors in the standard quantile regression. In this case the explanatory variables that reflect wages are included in the equation that is instrumented by the health indicator H:

$$H = \beta_0 + \beta_1 X_H + \beta_2 X_W + \varepsilon_H, \tag{6}$$

where the term ε_H takes in the measurement error.

It is, therefore, within the broad context of health as a form of human capital that it may be included within the explanatory variables of productivity. Thus the wage equation must be expressed as:

$$\ln(W) = a_0 + a_1 X_W + a_H H^* + \varepsilon_W, \tag{7}$$

where X_W represents a set of relevant variables, H^* the individual's corrected health status, and ε_W the term for random error.

2   The Database and Sample

The database utilized is the Living Standard Survey (Pesquisa sobre Padrões de Vida [PPV] 1996–1997). The survey was conducted by the Instituto Brasileiro de Geografía e Estadística (IBGE 2003), in accordance with the World Bank, over a period of one year (March 1996 to March 1997). The survey collected data from 19,409 individuals in 4,800 households that were representative of only the northeast and southeast regions of Brazil.[7] Each household completed the survey questionnaires on two separate occasions, there being a two-week gap between each of the visits in order to ensure a certain quality control.

The questionnaire for individuals provided data related to the personal characteristics of each respondent in the sample, as well as the respondent's labor and income data. The questionnaire for households provided data on housing conditions, water supply and sanitation, family income, and other areas. The values of the variables included were assigned equally to all the individuals within the household.

Of the 11,033 individuals of working age (18–65) who were surveyed in the sample, a total of 6,842 were excluded from this analysis for a number of reasons; either they did not work, did not report hourly wages, did not report their type of employment, or they were missing variables or responses that were outside a reasonable range of values. The final sample, therefore, was made up of 4,473 individuals, of whom 57.32 percent were men. The analysis used wage earners, defined as respondents who stated they were workmen, employees, or domestic servants.[8] The information on public services was obtained from the IBGE (2004) and is calculated according to the levels of resources in the given area and divided by population. A complete description of the variables used in the estimations can be seen in table 11.1.

2.1 Dependent Variables

The variables related to the labor market analyzed in this study include whether the individual was working at the time of the survey, and if so, a second variable measuring hourly earnings as a proxy of wage rates. The latter variable was constructed by dividing the wage income by the average number of hours worked per week multiplied by the number of weeks worked during the previous year.

Personal income data was obtained by asking interviewees how much they had received for the work they had carried out during the seven days immediately prior to the survey, together with payments "in kind," business meals, uniforms, housing, transport allowances, vouchers, and wage bonuses. The information obtained with respect to payment in kind was not included as one of the model's variables, and only monetary income was considered. All forms of monetary income were standardized by calculating an average monthly income and then calculating an implicit hourly wage.[9]

Table 11.1
Descriptive Statistics Living Standard Survey 96/97: wage earners (18–65 years old).

Variables		Women	Men	Total
Labor Market Outcomes				
Log Income per hour	Logarithm of individual hourly wage (in reales)	0.32 (1.49)	0.22 (1.54)	0.26 (1.52)
Health Status Indicator				
CHRONIC	1 = reported chronic illness, 0 = otherwise	13.43%	9.96%	11.38%
LIMIT	1 = reported limitation of activity in 30 days prior to the interview, 0 = otherwise	8.12%	6.70%	7.28%
BMI	Body mass index (calculated as weight in kilograms divided by height in meters squared)	22.1 (3.4)	23.2 (4.2)	22.6 (3.9)
Individual Characteristics				
Age	Age in years	31.39 (10.87)	33.47 (10.84)	33.30 (10.70)
Elementary education	1 = if the individual has not graduated studies, 0 = otherwise	67.23%	68.6%	68.07%
Secondary education	1 = if the individual has graduated studies from high school, 0 = otherwise	17.11%	10.4%	13.12%
Tertiary education	1 = if the individual has graduate and postgraduate studies, 0 = otherwise	15.65%	20.9%	18.80%
Experience	Age of the individual minus the age at which the individual began to work	18.22 (10.25)	17.50 (10.12)	18.15 (10.18)
Race black	1 = if the individual is black, 0 = otherwise	6.31%	7.18%	6.82%
Race white	1 = if the individual is white, 0 = otherwise	48.89%	47.10%	47.82%
Other race	1 = if the individual is neither black nor white, 0 = otherwise	44.80%	45.70%	45.36%
Housing Conditions				
Bath	1 = if the individual has a bath in his house, 0 = otherwise	93.87%	92.3%	92.94%

Table 11.1
(continued)

Variables		Women	Men	Total
Sidewalk	1 = if the individual has a sidewalk in front of his house, 0 = otherwise	69.57%	61.70%	64.85%
Favela	1 = if the individual lives in makeshift housing, 0 = otherwise	3.21%	3.75%	3.53%
Municipal Characteristics				
Hospitals	Number of hospitals in geographical area per 10,000 inhabitants	3.92 (0.86)	3.75 (0.75)	3.85 (0.79)
Doctors	Number of doctors in geographical area per 10,000 inhabitants	26.74 (9.24)	26.19 (9.18)	26.62 (9.57)
Unemployment rate	Unemployment rate in the geographical area of the individual's residence	9.12 (2.87)	6.52 (2.25)	7.55 (2.42)

2.2 Independent Variables: Health Status

The literature has extensively analyzed the kinds of indicators that are felt to be most adequate for measuring health status, particularly because different facets of health have different effects on health. Further, these studies reflect the divergence of opinion as to the weight of their impact on wages. We thus consider it to be important to examine different dimensions of health, since none of these used as health measures affect health outcomes in exactly the same way.

On the one hand, a distinction must be made between whether the illness is one that is likely to be long or short term. Most surveys utilize questionnaires that ask respondents if they have had an illness in the previous 7, 15, or 30 days depending on the survey. These short-term measurements might not necessarily be a good indicator of the general economic impact of illness on wage levels since they fail to take in the effects of illness over a period of one year or more and might be statistically insignificant in the long run. Thus it would seem logical to try and make a qualitative distinction between the effects of chronic and nonchronic illness.

It must also be remembered that the health status evaluation provided in these kinds of surveys is essentially subjective and this might give rise to both random and systematic reporting error. Anthropometric measurements, particularly height and weight, have been suggested as less subjective indicators of health status, although they measure different facets of health. There is a direct link between height and productivity, but height also reflects previous health investments, primarily early on in life, and it is possibly correlated with other kinds of human capital investment made during childhood. Weight is also potentially related to productivity, at least among those who are very light or very heavy, through such mechanisms as metabolic efficiency and maximum physical capacity.

A more complete measurement of health would be the weight–height ratio. Different ways of expressing this proportion are possible, but one that is often used is the body mass index, or BMI. This is defined as weight (in kilograms) divided by height (in meters) squared. Extreme values (below 20 and above 30 or so) are associated with a higher risk of adult mortality (Waaler 1984; Fogel 1994).

In addition to the BMI variable, the health indicators used in the analysis are provided by responses to the survey questionnaires. Individuals are asked if they have a chronic health problem (chronic variable) and if so, what the illness is.[10] Respondents are also asked whether they have had a health problem during the thirty days immediately prior to the interview, and whether this problem prevented them from carrying out one or more of their normal activities (limit variable).

2.3   Non-Health-Related Independent Variables

In addition to the health variables, the regressions control for other respondent characteristics that might influence outcomes in the labor market. Respondent characteristics included age and their quadratic term to observe possible nonlinear effects, education (represented by three levels: primary school, secondary school, and tertiary school); experience, formulated as the age of the individual minus the age at which the individual began to work; race (black, white, and other); housing conditions (represented by the variables bath, sidewalk, and "favela"—a shantytown or slum, especially in Brazil), the health infrastructure characteristics of the municipal district such as the numbers of hospitals and doctors, and a variable that represents the differences in labor market conditions, in particular, the unemployment rate.

To identify health in the wage equation, housing conditions and health infrastructures are used as instrumental variables (IVs). We assume that these variables are highly correlated with the individual's health status and uncorrelated with individual wages. We test these assumptions with appropriate specification tests.

3   Estimation Results

3.1   Health Equations

Table 11.2 presents the estimates for the health equation used to form the prediction to be included as a regressor in the wage equation in estimator IVs. Different health indicators are used in the estimations that include BMI, which is essentially an objective indicator, the limit variable, which indicates whether or not the individual's activity has been limited in the previous thirty days, and the chronic variable, which measures whether the individual was suffering from a chronic illness at the time when the survey was carried out and as such is a more long-term indicator than the limit variable.

In general, the results of the health equations are in accordance with expectations. In all of the estimations, with the exception of those that use the BMI as a health indicator, the age variable is linked to worse health status, and this effect is especially important after a certain age. This is reflected in the quadratic coefficient.

Education levels have a positive impact on health levels and this relationship is probably linked to a better use of available information and health care related inputs.[11] The effects that are compared are secondary and tertiary school levels versus primary levels. In all of the estimations carried out the coefficients obtained are significant, returns being positive with respect to health. Further, the relationship is always positive, in that health status always improves as the levels of educational attainment increase. By contrast, the effect of the experience does not have a significant effect on individual health status.

The variables related to the individual's ethnicity do not appear to be relevant when it comes to determining individual health status, contrary to housing conditions that are important determinants of individual health status. The negative coefficient indicates that those individuals that have higher quality housing also enjoy better health. This is particularly true when the variables used indicate that the dwelling has its own bathroom and that the individual does not live in a favela.

The variables that refer to the features of the municipal area are also-significant. The per-capita availability of health centers and doctors have a positive, significant impact on health status for all three indicators. The effects are greater however, when the dependent variables used are whether the individual suffers from a chronic illness or the number of days in which the individual's main activities are impeded. When the indicator used is the BMI, the coefficients and significance levels are lower.[12] In this sense, therefore, investment in a greater supply of professionals, better health services, and improvements in accessibility to these give positive returns with respect to improvements in individual health.[13] Finally, according to all of the estimations carried out, people living in areas with higher local unemployment tend to have lower health levels.

Tests of joint significance for the identifying variables show that they are jointly significant. We can reject the hypothesis that the coefficients of the identifying variables in each model are jointly equal to 0 at the 5 percent level.

The results provided in this section underline the importance of a group of individual factors in determining health status. In general, there is a strong positive link between age, education, housing variables and health services, and the resulting levels of health. Ethnicity and experience, on the other hand, have a negligible impact.

3.2 Wage Estimations

This section estimates the impact of health on wages. In tables 11.3 and 11.4 we present different specifications for the earnings equations separately for men and women. The dependent variable is the logarithm of earnings for wage earners. The tables present the estimated earnings equations, one of which excludes health, one that treats health exogenously, and a third in which health is instrumented (IV). Although the main aim of the paper is not to estimate effects at the mean, it proves useful to discuss these results since they provide a benchmark against which the quantile regression estimates can be compared. They are also useful for indicating the direction in which the bias induced by the endogeneity and measurement error of health operates. The residual from the health regressions is included in the wage equation in order to be able to perform an exogeneity test on health. A significant t-value was obtained confirming the endogeneity of health.

Based on the results obtained (tables 11.3 and 11.4), we find that health status has a significant positive effect on productivity. Thus, better health status increases wage levels in both groups. There were differences in the magnitude of the effects of health status on produc-

Table 11.2
Estimations for health determinants: first-stage regressions.

Variables	BMI Male	BMI Female	LIMIT Male	LIMIT Female	CHRONIC Male	CHRONIC Female
Individual Characteristics						
Age	0.13	0.16	˙ 0.47**	0.45**	0.42***	0.46***
	(1.16)	(1.41)	(2.21)	(2.35)	(5.20)	(4.23)
Age squared/100	−0.32*	−0.35	1.33**	1.32**	1.35**	1.51**
	(−1.40)	(−1.27)	(2.17)	(2.08)	(2.49)	(2.23)
Tertiary school	0.45**	0.40**	−0.78***	−0.71***	−0.76***	−0.77***
	(2.83)	(2.19)	(−3.01)	(−3.45)	(−3.37)	(−2.95)
Secondary school	0.94**	0.27**	−0.14**	−0.12**	−0.66**	−0.56**
	(2.25)	(2.12)	(−2.25)	(−2.14)	(−2.88)	(−2.35)
Experience	0.01	0.004	0.04	0.02	0.02	0.03
	(0.25)	(0.10)	(0.36)	(0.39)	(0.48)	(0.51)
Experience squared	0.001	0.001	0.01	0.01	0.002	0.004
	(0.32)	(0.41)	(0.16)	(0.18)	(0.09)	(0.12)
Race white	−0.03	−0.09	−0.09	−0.08	−0.05	−0.06
	(−1.30)	(−1.45)	(−0.56)	(−0.41)	(−0.33)	(−0.36)
Other race	−0.05	−0.04	0.10	0.19	−0.12	−0.28
	(−0.95)	(−0.46)	(1.30)	(0.98)	(−0.89)	(−1.61)
Housing Conditions						
Bath	0.13**	0.20**	−0.31**	−0.13**	−0.29**	−0.17**
	(2.29)	(1.98)	(−2.38)	(−2.17)	(−2.22)	(−1.98)
Sidewalk	0.09**	0.03**	−0.07	−0.08	−0.18**	−0.06**
	(2.84)	(1.97)	(−0.74)	(−0.54)	(−2.11)	(−2.05)
Favela	−0.20**	−0.24*	0.38**	0.29**	0.44*	0.48*
	(−2.27)	(−1.87)	(2.28)	(2.03)	(1.97)	(1.98)
Municipal Characteristics						
Hospitals	0.07*	0.05	−0.12**	−0.09**	−0.10**	−0.07*
	(1.75)	(1.63)	(−2.45)	(−2.12)	(−2.22)	(−1.85)
Doctors	0.12*	0.10*	−0.18**	−0.15**	−0.19**	−0.12**
	(1.89)	(1.78)	(−2.19)	(−2.12)	(−0.24)	(−2.03)
Unemployment rate	−0.02**	−0.03**	−0.12**	−0.15**	−0.16**	−0.17**
	(−2.29)	(−3.92)	(−2.27)	(−2.58)	(−2.24)	(−2.41)
Model Statistic	7.8***	2.59***	32.02***	29.19***	119.78***	76.82***
Adjusted R²	0.054	0.069				
Prob (H*) < 1			29%	31%	35%	34%
Number of observations	2,177	1,547	2,463	1,712	2,479	1,712

Note: The omitted education category is "elementary education." The omitted race category is "black." For the OLS regression, t-statistics are reported in parentheses. For the probit regressions, z-statistics are reported in parentheses.
*Statistically significant to 10% confidence level.
**Statistically significant to 5% confidence level.
***Statistically significant to 1% confidence level.

Table 11.3
Wage Determinants (Men)

Variables	Without Health	BMI Exogenous	BMI IV	LIMIT Exogenous	LIMIT IV	CHRONIC Exogenous	CHRONIC IV
Health indicator	—	0.10* (1.77)	0.18** (2.62)	−0.26** (−2.63)	−0.31** (−2.61)	−0.15** (−2.43)	−0.29** (−2.01)
Age	0.37** (2.12)	0.32* (1.79)	0.33** (2.88)	0.34** (2.13)	0.35** (2.82)	0.33** (2.11)	0.35** (2.15)
Age squared/100	−0.16* (−1.84)	−0.17 (−1.46)	−0.09 (−1.45)	−0.17* (−1.85)	−0.19* (−1.86)	−0.17* (−1.87)	−0.11* (−1.84)
Tertiary school	0.42*** (4.25)	0.39** (2.57)	0.37** (2.42)	0.45*** (4.22)	0.41*** (4.29)	0.44*** (4.26)	0.42*** (4.59)
Secondary school	0.21** (2.05)	0.19** (2.29)	0.18** (2.57)	0.15** (2.33)	0.11** (2.30)	0.18** (2.29)	0.11** (2.23)
Experience	0.02** (2.25)	0.02** (2.18)	0.02** (2.24)	0.03** (2.19)	0.03** (2.16)	0.03** (2.15)	0.04** (2.18)
Experience squared	−0.10** (−2.16)	−0.08* (−1.89)	−0.08* (−1.78)	−0.05** (−1.95)	−0.06** (−1.97)	−0.04* (−1.85)	−0.05* (−1.86)
Race white	0.13** (2.71)	0.11** (2.31)	0.15** (3.63)	0.13** (2.71)	0.15** (2.88)	0.13** (2.71)	0.14** (2.77)
Other race	0.08** (2.38)	0.06* (1.89)	0.08** (2.17)	0.09** (2.40)	0.06** (2.63)	0.08** (2.37)	0.06** (2.52)
Unemployment rate	−0.06*** (−4.23)	−0.07*** (−4.59)	−0.02*** (−2.43)	−0.05*** (−4.19)	−0.03*** (−2.64)	−0.06*** (−4.24)	−0.06*** (−4.25)
Selection term	−0.05 (−1.24)	−0.07 (−1.32)	−0.04 (−1.12)	−0.06 (−1.43)	−0.06 (−1.41)	−0.07 (−1.54)	−0.08 (−1.56)
Model Statistic	24.5***	19.24***	21.12***	32.02***	29.19***	19.78***	16.82***

Hausman Test				4.23**	6.79***		5.82***
R² adjusted	0.17	0.18	0.19	0.19	0.22	0.20	0.23
Number of observations	2,430	2,043	2,043	2,430	2,430	2,430	2,430

Note: The estimates are OLS corrected by the Heckman two-stage estimate for participation in the labor force. The dependent variable is the logarithm of the hourly wage. T-statistics are in parentheses. Hausman test is the value of t-statistics on coefficient of residual health status measure when actual value and residuals are included in the wage equation.

* Statistically significant to 10% confidence level.
** Statistically significant to 5% confidence level.
*** Statistically significant to 1% confidence level.

Table 11.4
Wage Determinants (Women)

Variables	Without Health	BMI		LIMIT		CHRONIC	
		Exogenous	IV	Exogenous	IV	Exogenous	IV
Health indicator	—	0.06*	0.08*	−0.18**	−0.27**	−0.12**	−0.24**
		(1.81)	(1.98)	(−2.68)	(−2.90)	(−2.41)	(−2.59)
Age	0.33**	0.39**	0.34**	0.43**	0.46**	0.44**	0.47**
	(2.17)	(2.50)	(2.04)	(2.13)	(2.27)	(2.19)	(2.42)
Age squared/100	−0.10*	−0.11*	−0.10*	−0.11*	−0.08*	−0.07*	−0.08*
	(−1.71)	(−1.77)	(−1.86)	(−1.87)	(−1.84)	(−1.91)	(−1.92)
Tertiary school	0.68***	0.64***	0.43***	0.58***	0.47***	0.58***	0.50***
	(5.59)	(5.73)	(3.63)	(5.60)	(6.13)	(5.56)	(5.68)
Secondary school	0.41***	0.30***	0.20**	0.30***	0.17**	0.30***	0.34***
	(3.45)	(3.05)	(2.20)	(3.43)	(2.63)	(3.39)	(3.59)
Experience	0.03	0.04	0.03	0.02	0.02	0.03	0.02
	(1.57)	(1.66)	(1.59)	(1.48)	(1.54)	(1.35)	(1.42)
Experience squared	−0.05	−0.04	−0.06	−0.04	−0.05	−0.03	−0.03
	(−1.34)	(−1.39)	(−1.55)	(−1.47)	(−1.62)	(−1.45)	(−1.52)
Race white	0.17**	0.10**	0.14**	0.17**	0.18**	0.17**	0.13**
	(2.56)	(1.97)	(1.81)	(2.56)	(2.61)	(2.55)	(2.28)
Other race	0.06**	0.05	0.09**	0.03**	0.06	0.09**	0.06
	(2.08)	(1.60)	(2.01)	(2.10)	(1.68)	(2.06)	(1.06)
Unemployment rate	−0.08***	−0.08***	−0.07***	−0.08***	−0.08***	−0.07***	−0.07***
	(−6.52)	(−6.71)	(−2.99)	(−6.52)	(−6.47)	(−6.53)	(−6.72)
Selection term	−0.12**	−0.14**	−0.12**	−0.12**	−0.13**	−0.13**	−0.14**
	(−2.54)	(−2.65)	(−2.62)	(−2.54)	(−2.56)	(−2.43)	(−2.41)
Model Statistic	23.2***	17.4***	20.3***	25.9***	26.7***	23.2***	19.9***

Hausman Test		4.16***		6.41***		5.43***
R² adjusted	0.11	0.12	0.14	0.14	0.16	0.15	0.17
Number of observations	1,702	1,539	1,702	1,702	1,702	1,702	1,702

Note: The estimates are OLS corrected by the Heckman two-stage estimate for participation in the labor force. The dependent variable is the logarithm of the hourly wage. T-statistics are in parentheses. Hausman test is the value of t-statistics on coefficient of residual health status measure when actual value and residuals are included in the wage equation.
*Statistically significant to 10% confidence level.
**Statistically significant to 5% confidence level.
***Statistically significant to 1% confidence level.

tivity with respect to sex however, good health having a greater positive impact on men than on women.

The results provided by the other variables were roughly as
expected. It is worthwhile stating though, that when the health variable was excluded the age and education coefficients were biased
slightly upward, probably because they were capturing part of the
impact of health on the dependent variable.

The effect of the local unemployment rate is negative for both samples. The variable reflects the differences in the working conditions
among geographical areas. Fairly predictably, in a normal labor market
model, higher unemployment is associated with lower wages for all of
the samples. These negative effects are also statistically significant.

The correction term of the selectivity bias is significant for women
and has a negative sign. This indicates that the unobservable characteristics that increase the probability of participation in the labor market
have a negative effect on market wage levels.

In general, the above results remain the same for all of the estimations carried out when the instrumented health variable is used. However, the coefficients and the significance level increase. The adjusted
health variable also has implications for educational returns. In general, the returns of education are slightly lower after including health,
especially in the case of men. These results may be due to the greater
effect of the different types of work that men and women carry out or
because of unobservable characteristics.

The problems of endogeneity and measurement error are confirmed
further by various diagnostic tests. The Hausman specification tests
suggest that the endogeneity of health status is relevant and that the
coefficient for the health indicator from the OLS estimates is significantly different from that of the IV estimates.

3.3 Quantiles of the Conditional Wage Distribution

Tables 11.5 and 11.6 present the estimates for the quantile functions.
We use the same specification as for that of the conditional mean and
carry out two regressions, one in which health is treated as an exogenous variable and a second in which it is endogenous. The covariance
matrix for the standard quantile regression estimates is based on the
Koenker and Basset (1982) method. The covariance matrix for the two-
stage quantile regression is obtained by bootstrapping the design
matrix with 100 replications. Given that there are no appreciable significant differences in the results when distinct health indicators are used,

Table 11.5
Wage Determinants. Quantile Regression Estimates

	10		25		50		75		90	
Variables	Male	Female	Male	Female	Male	Female	Male	Female	Male	Female
Health indicator	−0.43**	−0.25**	−0.36**	−0.22**	−0.25**	−0.20**	−0.20**	−0.18**	−0.15**	−0.13**
	(−2.51)	(−2.31)	(−2.48)	(−2.16)	(−2.39)	(−2.14)	(−2.35)	(−2.16)	(−2.37)	(−2.14)
Age	0.24*	0.21*	0.41**	0.38**	0.39**	0.34**	0.35**	0.28**	0.40**	0.35**
	(1.85)	(1.87)	(2.21)	(2.16)	(2.12)	(2.25)	(2.15)	(2.08)	(2.58)	(2.41)
Age squared/100	−0.19	−0.15	−0.16*	−0.14*	−0.14**	−0.10**	−0.13**	−0.9**	−0.11**	−0.9**
	(1.74)	(1.84)	(1.94)	(1.89)	(2.21)	(2.18)	(2.25)	(2.21)	(2.31)	(2.16)
Tertiary school	0.12***	0.25***	0.29***	0.36***	0.43***	0.58***	0.61***	0.75***	0.53***	0.62***
	(3.21)	(3.46)	(3.28)	(3.51)	(3.35)	(3.41)	(3.46)	(3.52)	(3.32)	(3.55)
Secondary school	0.28**	0.36**	0.25**	0.34**	0.22**	0.25**	0.15**	0.19**	0.10**	0.12**
	(2.54)	(2.57)	(2.32)	(2.41)	(2.12)	(2.19)	(2.09)	(2.11)	(2.05)	(2.10)
Experience	0.04*	0.02*	0.05*	0.04*	0.03	0.03	0.03	0.02	0.02	0.02
	(1.86)	(1.84)	(1.88)	(1.86)	(1.59)	(1.63)	(1.48)	(1.50)	(1.43)	(1.46)
Experience squared	−0.05	−0.02	−0.06	−0.04	−0.03	−0.04	−0.02	−0.03	−0.04	−0.03
	(−1.42)	(−1.24)	(−1.45)	(−1.36)	(−1.32)	(−1.28)	(−1.19)	(−1.17)	(−1.35)	(−1.26)
Race white	0.05**	0.07**	0.12**	0.14**	0.16**	0.18**	0.14**	0.12**	0.10**	0.12**
	(2.18)	(2.23)	(2.31)	(2.41)	(2.35)	(2.46)	(2.35)	(2.12)	(2.16)	(2.22)
Other race	0.02**	0.03**	0.02**	0.04**	0.04**	0.06**	0.06**	0.09**	0.04**	0.06**
	(2.02)	(2.11)	(2.04)	(2.14)	(2.10)	(2.16)	(2.12)	(2.14)	(2.11)	(2.17)
Unemployment rate	−0.08**	−0.10**	−0.09**	−0.13**	−0.07**	−0.08**	−0.03**	−0.04**	−0.03**	−0.03**
	(−2.15)	(−2.35)	(−2.29)	(−2.41)	(−2.36)	(−2.38)	(−2.25)	(−2.27)	(−2.41)	(−2.19)
Pseudo R-squared	0.19	0.25	0.20	0.26	0.22	0.23	0.21	0.22	0.18	0.20
N. observations	2,430	1,702	2,430	1,702	2,430	1,702	2,430	1,702	2,430	1,702

Note: The estimates have been corrected for selectivity. Value of t-statistics in parentheses.
*Statistically significant to 10% confidence level.
**Statistically significant to 5% confidence level.
***Statistically significant to 1% confidence level.

only the estimations that utilize the variable that reflects whether the individual's main activity has been limited in the 30 days prior to the survey are shown here.

Table 11.5 presents how variations in health affect productivity across different income levels. The results reflect that, in the case of men, as we move across the different levels of income distribution, health has a greater impact on those individuals in the first quintile of the distribution and this impact decreases as we move toward the top of the wage distribution. In the case of the male conditional wage distribution it may be observed that heath returns go from −0.43 percent at the very lowest decile to −0.15 percent in the ninth decile. This clearly shows that the negative effects derived from the limitation of the individual's main activity through adverse health, has a greater impact on those workers with low wages. In the case of women these changes vary from −0.25 in the tenth percentile to −0.13 in the third quartile. Improvements in health therefore contribute to a greater dispersion in male wage distribution patterns when compared to those of women.

The direction of the effects of the health variable on productivity in the quantile estimations remains the same as in the previous analysis at the conditional mean, both in the case of men and women (table 11.6). It is assumed that these estimations are unbiased by problems of simultaneity. According to the results, the coefficients for the health variable in the two-stage LAD estimates are higher than in the quantile regression estimates, and the coefficients that correspond to the male sample continue to be higher than those for the female sample. Further, the increase in the coefficients obtained for men is greater than that for women. That is, in the case of the corrected estimates, the influence of health on productivity accentuates the differences between the male and female samples.

In general these results would seem to suggest that the individual differences in health might be a source of wage dispersion in Brazil, fundamentally among male workers. These wage differences can be attributed to the variations in the returns of health status depending on where the individual is situated within the range of the wage scale.

Finally, after discussing health effects, the results obtained for education suggest that the returns from high levels of education, as opposed to either basic or primary levels, are greater in the case of the upper quartiles. The higher earnings derived from medium levels of education are to be found in the first quartiles of the wage distribution. In all

Table 11.6
Wage Determinants. Two-Stage Quantile Regressions

Variables	10		25		50		75		90	
	Male	Female	Male	Female	Male	Female	Male	Female	Male	Female
Health indicator	-0.45**	-0.23**	-0.38**	-0.19**	-0.26**	-0.20**	-0.22**	-0.18**	-0.18**	-0.14**
	(-2.62)	(-2.42)	(-2.56)	(-2.29)	(-2.41)	(-2.23)	(-2.38)	(-2.24)	(-2.47)	(-2.18)
Age	0.27**	0.24**	0.40**	0.38**	0.36**	0.32**	0.36**	0.26**	0.34**	0.30**
	(1.95)	(1.97)	(2.41)	(2.36)	(2.22)	(2.35)	(2.25)	(2.17)	(2.38)	(2.35)
Age squared/100	-0.22*	-0.17*	-0.18**	-0.16**	-0.17**	-0.13**	-0.13**	-0.11**	-0.10**	-0.10**
	(1.93)	(1.90)	(2.04)	(2.19)	(2.32)	(2.35)	(2.41)	(2.36)	(2.26)	(2.19)
Tertiary school	0.17***	0.28***	0.33**	0.37***	0.44**	0.62*	0.68	0.77**	0.58	0.64*
	(3.41)	(3.64)	(3.51)	(3.62)	(3.41)	(3.54)	(3.63)	(3.58)	(3.42)	(3.61)
Secondary school	0.34**	0.39**	0.27**	0.38**	0.25**	0.26**	0.18**	0.23**	0.09**	0.14**
	(2.62)	(2.71)	(2.41)	(2.41)	(2.23)	(2.21)	(2.21)	(2.30)	(2.19)	(2.35)
Experience	0.06**	0.04**	0.07**	0.04*	0.05*	0.04	0.04*	0.02	0.03*	0.02
	(2.05)	(1.98)	(2.12)	(2.08)	(1.89)	(1.73)	(1.95)	(1.87)	(1.89)	(1.68)
Experience squared	-0.05	-0.03	-0.08*	-0.06	-0.06	-0.05	-0.04	-0.02	-0.05	-0.03
	(-1.53)	(-1.42)	(-1.87)	(-1.45)	(-1.32)	(-1.29)	(-1.23)	(-1.26)	(-1.55)	(-1.56)
Race white	0.03**	0.05**	0.10**	0.14**	0.14**	0.16**	0.14**	0.14**	0.12**	0.11**
	(2.29)	(2.31)	(2.41)	(2.53)	(2.35)	(2.65)	(2.43)	(2.22)	(2.47)	(2.23)
Other race	0.02*	0.03**	0.02**	0.03**	0.05**	0.06**	0.05**	0.07**	0.02*	0.04**
	(1.85)	(2.26)	(2.16)	(2.23)	(2.23)	(2.43)	(2.41)	(2.32)	(1.87)	(2.11)
Unemployment rate	-0.10**	-0.13**	-0.10**	-0.14**	-0.06**	-0.11**	-0.06**	-0.08**	-0.04**	-0.06**
	(-2.26)	(-2.43)	(-2.39)	(-2.54)	(-2.24)	(-2.64)	(-2.19)	(-2.26)	(-2.29)	(-2.35)
Pseudo R-squared	0.21	0.26	0.22	0.28	0.23	0.23	0.20	0.24	0.19	0.22
N. observations	2,430	1,702	2,430	1,702	2,430	1,702	2,430	1,702	2,430	1,702

Note: The estimates have been corrected for selectivity. Value of t-statistics in parentheses.
*Statistically significant to 10% confidence level.
**Statistically significant to 5% confidence level.
***Statistically significant to 1% confidence level.

of the estimations carried out, the returns are greater for women than for men, although the pattern is the same right across the whole of the wage distribution.

4 Conclusions

The main objective of this study was to examine the effects of health on individual productivity in Brazil within the framework of the wage distribution. An attempt has been made to quantify that proportion of the difference in the wage distribution that is due to the different characteristics of the individuals specified, and that which is attributable to the variations in the returns for the same characteristics. Thus a sample of workers is used in order to estimate the conditional mean and the quantiles of the wage distribution but taking into account the problems of endogeneity and selectivity in the wage equations.

The results suggest that health has a significant impact on worker productivity when productivity is measured as a function of the salary they receive. This effect is present in all of the estimations carried out and is magnified when it is the corrected health variable that is utilized. This result is particularly significant in the case of the sample of men.

Health affects the distribution of wages in that its impact is greater at the lowest wage levels for both men and women and decreases as one moves up the wage distribution level. When the corrected health measure is used, the direction of the effects is the same but the difference between men and women becomes more accentuated.

According with these results, it would seem logical to treat health as one of the principal components of human capital rather like education, given that health affects individual wage levels. In this sense, public policy that attempts to improve individual health conditions also contributes to improving working conditions, and encourages higher salaries and an overall better standard of living for the population. This is particularly important if one takes into account the fact that health has a greater effect on productivity on the lowest wage earners within the population. Thus, these types of measures serve to reduce inequalities in income while exerting their effects more forcefully on the underprivileged.

Therefore, improved health may be considered as one of the causes and consequences of economic growth. The relationship, although complex, is important for establishing the priorities and adequate execution of appropriate policy. In this sense a deeper understanding of the different effects of health on income is essential if we are to carry out policy aimed at promoting the relationship between the health of a population and their economic development.

Acknowledgments

We are indebted to participants in the Health Economics Meeting (Madrid 2004) and Public Economics Meeting (Barcelona 2004) where earlier versions of this work were presented. Financial support for this research from the Ministerio de Ciencia y Tecnología is gratefully acknowledged.

Notes

1. For an application of quantile regressions that involves selectivity issues, see Buchinsky 1998.

2. In this equation health is assumed to be exogenous with respect to the dependent variable and not correlated with the errors.

3. This approach has been used recently for estimating returns to education (Garcia, Hernandez, and López-Nicolás 1997; Machado and Mata 1999; Buchinsky 1996; Ribeiro 1997; Blanco 2001. For an application using health see Murragarra and Valdivida 2000).

4. See Buchinsky 1998 for a detailed discussion of this methodology.

5. The opposite effect may also be considered whereby the impact of employment or increased productivity might favor an increase in the effort exerted in the workplace, hence increased occupational hazards and work-related pressure, and this would, in turn, have a negative effect on health (Waldron 1976).

6. See Amemiya 1982 and Powell 1983 for the corrections of the biases induced by the endogeneity of education in a quantile regression context.

7. The metropolitan region of Recife, metropolitan region of Salvador, the rest of the urban area of the northeast, the rest of the rural area of the northeast, metropolitan region of Belo Horizonte, metropolitan region of Rio de Janeiro, metropolitan region of Sao Paulo, the rest of the urban area of the southeast and the rest of the rural area of the southeast.

8. Of the total individuals in the sample 65 percent were wage earners.

9. In the case of Brazil, fringe benefits or bonuses are of particular importance and include transport vouchers and aid for the purchase of food or clothes and uniforms ("vale transporte," "auxilio alimentaçao," "auxilio moradia," "roupa-uniforme"), and in lower-income groups this aid may constitute up to 50 percent of total income.

10. It would have been useful to have had a variable that was capable of capturing the severity of the respondent's limitations; the number of health problems the individual had, for example. This was not possible, however, since the questionnaire utilized only asks individuals about the main cause of their health problem.

11. The education coefficients might be biased downward if there were a systematic correlation between education and reported health status, for example, if more highly educated individuals were more likely to report their illnesses more often than individuals with low educational levels.

12. Ribero and Nuñez (2000, 2001) obtain similar results with BMI although these results improve when height is used.

13. For an analysis of the effects of health spending on health status see Rivera 2004. In Rivera and Currais 2004, the effects of health spending on productivity are analyzed at an aggregate level.

References

Amemiya, T. 1982. Two-Stage Least Absolute Deviations Estimators. *Econometrica* 50: 689–711.

Becker, G. 1965. A Theory of the Allocation of Time. *Economic Journal* 75 (299): 493–517.

Behrman, J. 1993. The Economic Rationale for Investing in Nutrition in Developing Countries. *World Development* 21: 1749–1771.

Behrman, J., and A. Deolalikar. 1988. Health and Nutrition. In *Handbook of Development Economics*, vol. 1, edited by H. Chenery and T. N. Srinivasan. New York: North Holland, pp. 631–711.

Blanco, A. 2001. A Comparative Analysis of Wage Changes for Spanish Young and Older Workers during the 1980s: Differences within and between Groups at Different Quantiles. In *IV Jornadas de Economía Laboral*. Valencia: Departamento de Análisis Económico, Universidad de Valencia.

Buchinsky, M. 1994. Changes in the U.S. Wage Structure 1963–1987: Application of Quantile Regression. *Econometrica* 62: 405–458.

———. 1996. Women's Return to Education in the U.S. Exploration by Quantile Regression with Non-parametric Sample Selection Correction. Working Paper, Department of Economics, Brown University.

———. 1998. Recent Advances in Quantile Regression Models: A Practical Guideline for Empirical Research. *Journal of Human Resources* 33: 88–126.

Fogel, R. 1994. The Relevance of Malthus for the Study of Mortality Today: Long-Run Influences on Health, Mortality, Labor Force Participation and Population Growth. Historical Working Paper no. 54, National Bureau of Economic Research, Cambridge, Mass.

Garcia, J., P. J. Hernandez, and A. López-Nicolás. 1997. How Wide Is the Gap? An Investigation of Gender Wage Differences Using Quantile Regression. Working Paper no. 287, Department of Business and Economics, University Pompeu Fabra.

Instituto Brasileiro de Geografia e Estatística (IBGE). 2003. *Pesquisa sobre Padroes de Vida 1996–1997*. Rio de Janeiro: Departamento de Populaçao e Indicadores Sociales, IBGE.

———. 2004. *Estadísticas de Saúde: Asistência Médico-Sanitaria*. Rio de Janeiro: IBGE.

Koenker, R., and J. Basset. 1978. Regression Quantiles. *Econometrica* 46: 33–50.

———. 1982. Robust Tests for Heterscedasticity Based on Regression Quantiles. *Econometrica* 50: 43–61.

Machado, J., and J. Mata. 1999. Sources of Increased Wage Inequality. Unpublished paper.

Mincer, J. 1974. *Schooling, Experience, and Earnings*. New York: Columbia University Press.

Murragarra, E., and M. Valdivida. 2000. The Returns to Health for Peruvian Urban Adults by Gender, Age, and Across the Wage Distribution. In *Wealth from Health: Linking Social Investments to Earnings in Latin America*, edited by W. Savedoff and T. P. Schultz. Washington, D.C.: Inter-American Development Bank.

Pit, M., M. Rosenzweig, and M. Hassan. 1990. Productivity, Health, and Inequality in the Intrahousehold Distribution of Food in Low-Income Countries. *American Economic Review* 80 (5): 1139–1156.

Powell, J. 1983. The Asymptotic Normality of the Two Stage Least Absolute Deviations Estimator. *Econometrica* 51: 1569–1575.

Ribeiro, E. 1997. Conditional Labour Supply Quantile Estimates in Brazil. Texto de discussão no. 97/02, Universidade Federal do Rio Grande do Sul.

Ribero, R., and J. Nuñez. 2000. Adult Morbidity, Height, and Earnings in Colombia. In *Wealth from Health: Linking Social Investments to Earnings in Latin America*, ed. William D. Savidoff and T. P. Schultz. Washington, D.C.: Inter-American Development Bank, pp. 35–62.

———. 2001. Productivity of Household Investment in Health: The Case of Colombia. In *Investment in Health: Social and Economic Returns*. Washington, D.C.: Pan American Health Organization.

Rivera, B. 2004. Evidence on the Relationship between Public Medical Resources and Health Indicators. *Journal of Economic Studies* 31 (2): 98–111.

Rivera, B., and L. Currais. 2004. Public Health Capital and Productivity in the Spanish Regions: A Dynamic Panel Data Model. *World Development* 32 (5): 871–885.

Sahn, D. E., and H. Alderman. 1988. The Effects of Variables of Human Capital on Wages, and the Determinants of Labor Supply in a Developing Country. *Journal of Development Economics* 29 (2): 157–183.

Savedoff, W., and T. P. Schultz. 2000. Earnings and the Elusive Dividends of Health. In *Wealth from Health: Linking Social Investments to Earnings in Latin America*, edited by W. Savedoff and T. P. Schultz. Washington, D.C.: Inter-American Development Bank.

Schultz, T. P., and A. Tansel. 1997. Wage and Labor Supply Effects of Illness in Côte d'Ivoire and Ghana: Instrumental Variable Estimates for Days Disabled. *Journal of Development Economics* 53 (2): 251–286.

Thomas, D., and J. Strauss. 1997. Health, Wealth, and Wages: Evidence on Men and Women in Urban Brazil. *Journal of Econometrics* 77 (1): 159–185.

Waaler, H. T. 1984. Height, Weight, and Mortality: The Norwegian Experience. *Acta Medica Scandinavia* 77 (suppl. 679): 1–56.

Waldron, I. 1976. Why Do Women Live Longer Than Men? *Social Science and Medicine* 10: 240–262.

V

Quantity of Life and the Welfare Costs of AIDS

12

The Economic Cost of AIDS in Sub-Saharan Africa: A Reassessment

Tomas J. Philipson and
Rodrigo R. Soares

Perhaps one of the most significant changes in health across the world in the last few decades has been the emergence of HIV and AIDS. The pandemic has affected most economies, especially in developing nations where the disease is most prevalent. Any discussion of the recent impact of health on the world economy would therefore have to come to terms with how to assess the impact of AIDS.

Given the significance of AIDS, several studies have estimated its economic cost. For example, Bloom and Mahal (1995) find no effect of AIDS on long-term growth, and Dixon, McDonald, and Roberts (2001) find only modest effects. Similarly, a recent UNICEF report calculates the economic cost of the AIDS epidemic in Africa to be of the order of 5 percent of the continent's GDP (UNICEF 2000).

However, these studies assess only the direct impact of AIDS on the material well-being of the population, as represented by reduced GDP and, therefore, the reduced consumption of marketed goods. Although GDP per capita is usually used as a proxy for the quality of life in different countries, material gain is obviously only one of many aspects of life that enhance economic welfare. Overall economic welfare depends not only on the material well-being of a person but also on other aspects of life, such as the quantity (or length) of life over which this material well-being can be enjoyed and general health status. Therefore, the full economic impact of AIDS should include not only its impact on material well-being but also the reduction in welfare from lowered health and higher mortality.

To compare changes in health to changes in material welfare, there is a longstanding economic literature, initiated by Schelling (1968) and Thaler and Rosen (1975). This literature has produced behaviorally based estimates of the willingness to pay for mortality reductions, stemming from compensating differentials between occupations with different mortality risks. In this chapter, we review this "value-of-life" methodology and discuss how it can be used to assess the full economic cost of AIDS in sub-Saharan Africa.

More precisely, we first attempt to construct counterfactual mortality rates that would be observed if AIDS did not exist. We then use the marginal willingness-to-pay approach to estimate the welfare loss from the changes in mortality rates brought about by the AIDS epidemic. This number is an estimate of how much the population would be willing to pay in order to experience the counterfactual survival rates without AIDS rather than those observed with AIDS. Using this value-of-life approach, we show that the monetary value of the economic cost of AIDS in sub-Saharan Africa is extremely high. Our estimate of the reduction in welfare due to increased mortality swamps any estimates of the direct impact of AIDS on material well-being, as measured by the reduction in consumption of marketed goods alone (implicit in the calculations using GDP statistics done in previous studies).

Our calculations use data on AIDS deaths from the Joint United Nations Program on HIV/AIDS (UNAIDS), and life tables from the World Health Organization (WHO). Despite the extreme poverty in the area, we estimate the social cost of AIDS in sub-Saharan Africa to be of the order of $800 billion, which corresponds to virtually the whole production of the region during one year. This value is at least one order of magnitude larger than any available estimate of the partial economic cost of AIDS due to reduced consumption of marketed goods as measured by previous studies. The full economic cost of AIDS, taking into account nonmarketed goods, is overwhelmingly larger than the cost previously measured by considering the direct material costs alone.

This chapter relates to several previous studies that attempt to measure the social value of changes in population mortality. Cutler and Richardson (1997), Nordhaus (2003), Murphy and Topel (2001, 2003), and Garrett (2001) applied the value-of-life methodology to analyze different aspects of mortality and morbidity-related welfare gains in the United States. Philipson and Soares (2002) suggested an economically founded index of economic development including aggregate health not subject to the arbitrariness of measures such as the Human Development Index of the United Nations. Becker, Philipson, and Soares (2004) evaluated the evolution of welfare inequality across countries once improvements in life expectancy are accounted for. Finally,

Soares (2003) used the same methodology to evaluate the welfare cost of violence in different countries of the world.

The remainder of the chapter is structured as follows. Section 1 reviews the value-of-life methodology and discusses how it can be used to assess the economic value of health improvements across countries. Section 2 discusses the data and describes the construction of the counterfactual mortality rates that are used in the calculation of the welfare cost of AIDS. Section 3 presents and discusses the results. The final section concludes the chapter.

1   The Value of Changes in Mortality

This section builds on the methodology inaugurated by Usher (1973), and developed in further detail by Rosen (1988). Define $S(t,a)$ as the individual survival function, or the probability that an agent at age a will survive up to age t. Following Murphy and Topel (2003), assume that some exogenous factor θ affects the survival function, so that we can write $S(t,a;\theta)$. Exogenous changes in θ shift this function according to $\partial S(t,a;\theta)/\partial\theta$. To save on notation, we define $S_\theta(t,a) = \partial S(t,a;\theta)/\partial\theta$. Our goal is to give monetary values to the welfare gains induced by $S_\theta(t,a)$.

Changes in θ can be thought of, on the one hand, as technological developments and improvements in medical practices, and, on the other hand, as the emergence of new diseases and epidemics. In the empirical section, we think of the spread of AIDS as a change in θ that shifted the whole survival function downward, determining the welfare cost that we intend to measure.

1.1   Theory
Consider an individual at age a facing survival probabilities up to age t given by the survival function $S(t,a)$. Lifetime discounted utility at age a can be written as

$$V(a) = \int_a^\infty e^{-\rho(t-a)} S(t,a)u(c(t))\, dt, \tag{1}$$

where $c(t)$ is consumption at t, and ρ is the rate of time preference. This formulation implicitly assumes that utility on the "death state" is normalized to zero (for a detailed discussion, see Rosen 1988). Assume a complete contingent claims market, such that the budget constraint can be written as

$$\int_a^\infty e^{-r(t-a)} S(t,a) y(t) \, dt = \int_a^\infty e^{-r(t-a)} S(t,a) c(t) \, dt, \tag{2}$$

where $y(t)$ is income at age t, and r is the interest rate.

First-order conditions for the agent's optimum imply

$$e^{-\rho(t-a)} u'(c(t)) = \lambda_a e^{-r(t-a)}, \tag{3}$$

for every t, where λ_a is the Lagrangian multiplier on the constraint (for an individual at age a).

The marginal willingness to pay for changes in $S(t,a)$, brought about by changes in θ, is defined as

$$MWP_a = \frac{\partial V(a)}{\partial \theta} \frac{1}{\lambda_a}.$$

It can be interpreted as the income value of the marginal utility of θ, or, alternatively, as the marginal rate of substitution between income and θ. From the envelope theorem:

$$MWP_a = \frac{\partial V(a)}{\partial \theta} \frac{1}{\lambda_a} = \frac{\int_a^\infty e^{-\rho(t-a)} u(c(t)) S_\theta(t,a) \, dt}{\lambda_a}$$
$$+ \int_a^\infty e^{-r(t-a)} (y(t) - c(t)) S_\theta(t,a) \, dt.$$

Rearranging terms and using the first-order conditions:

$$MWP_a = \int_a^\infty e^{-r(t-a)} \left[\frac{u(c(t))}{u'(c(t))} + y(t) - c(t) \right] S_\theta(t,a) \, dt. \tag{4}$$

Defining $\varepsilon(c(t))$ as the elasticity of the instantaneous utility function $u(.)$ in relation to its argument (evaluated at $c(t)$), we can write equation (4) as:

$$MWP_a = \int_a^\infty e^{-r(t-a)} \left[\frac{c(t)}{\varepsilon(c(t))} + y(t) - c(t) \right] S_\theta(t,a) \, dt. \tag{5}$$

This expression summarizes the main determinants of the willingness to pay for changes in survival probabilities. Discounting of the future implies that individuals will be willing to pay more for given mortality reductions the closer they are to the moment where the largest changes in survival probabilities take place. From a social perspective, the population distribution will be important because it will determine the weight attributed to mortality reductions at each given age, according to the size of the population that is immediately affected by it.

In addition, income and consumption throughout life will also determine the value of changes in survival probabilities. The higher consumption is at a point in time, the higher the direct utility gain $(c(t)/\varepsilon(c(t)))$ from increasing the probability of survival up to that moment. Similarly, the higher the income surplus from a given period that can be used to "subsidize" consumption in other periods $(y(t) - c(t))$ is, the higher the value of increasing the probability of survival up to that moment. In short, the value of surviving up to a given moment is determined by the utility directly enjoyed in that moment and by the income surplus generated in that moment that can be used to increase utility in other periods. These are the two factors inside brackets in equation (5).

Equation (5) can be used to evaluate the welfare gains from given reductions in mortality rates for an individual at any age a. With this expression, the social value is obtained by integrating MWP_a through all ages, weighting the value at each age by the population in the respective age group.

If the population P of a country is distributed across ages according to the density function $f(.)$, the social value of changes in survival probabilities brought about by changes in θ is

$$Social\ MWP = P \int_0^\infty MWP_a f(a)\, da. \qquad (6)$$

This is the sum of the willingness to pay of every individual in society. Equation (6) is analogous to the one that characterizes the optimal provision of a continuous public good in the traditional public finance literature.

In this general formulation, the calculation of the marginal willingness to pay for changes in survival probabilities requires data on income and consumption at every point in time. In a cross-country context, these data are not available for the vast majority of countries. When the main goal is the comparison of lifetime welfare levels and changes, a feasible alternative is to abstract from life-cycle considerations by assuming that $r = \rho$ and $y(t)$ is constant $(y(t) = y)$. This allows for the calculation of values of changes in mortality rates using only national income figures that are widely available (GDP per capita as y). With these assumptions, first-order conditions imply that $c(t)$ is also constant, such that we can write $c(t) = c = y$, and that MWP_a can be expressed as

$$MWP_a = \frac{y}{\varepsilon(y)} \int_a^\infty e^{-r(t-a)} S_\theta(t,a)\, dt. \tag{7}$$

The interpretation of MWP_a in this context is straightforward. For a given country at a point in time, it tells us how much an individual at age a, earning the average income of the country in every period of life, would be willing to pay for the changes in survival probabilities summarized by $S_\theta(t,a)$. Our approach corresponds to assuming that all individuals within a country share the average material living standards of that country, and that individuals at age a face the cross-sectional mortality profile observed from age a onwards in that country.

Welfare discussions based on GDP per capita implicitly make similar assumptions in relation to income. We follow Becker, Philipson, and Soares (2004) and extend this notion to incorporate also survival probabilities. This is what allows us to evaluate the welfare gains from reductions in mortality rates for any country for which GDP and age-specific mortality data are available.

It is obviously true that mortality by different causes of death and income are unequally distributed across any given population, and that health inequalities are related to income inequalities. This is clearly true when we compare different genders, races, age groups, or socio-economic strata. These differences will generally bias the results obtained with the simplifying assumption outlined above, and it is important to keep in mind the limitations of the methodology proposed. As equation (5) makes apparent, whenever higher mortality reductions take place in periods—or among groups—where incomes are higher, the calculation assuming homogeneity will underestimate the value of mortality reductions, and vice versa. In the case of AIDS, where the most distinguishing feature of the disease is its high mortality at prime ages, it is very likely that our calculations will underestimate the true welfare costs of AIDS.

In the simple case where individuals live for a deterministic amount of time (τ), and all life expectancy gains are concentrated in the last period of life, equation (7) takes on a very simple form:

$$MWP_a = \frac{y}{\varepsilon(y)} e^{-r(\tau-a)}\, d\tau = \frac{u(y)}{u'(y)} e^{-r(\tau-a)}\, d\tau. \tag{7'}$$

This simple version of the model stresses the two main determinants of the value of reductions in mortality: the value of income (or consumption) throughout life (fraction term), and the size and moment of the reductions in mortality (term multiplying the fraction). Countries with higher income attach more value to given longevity gains, since marginal extensions in life expectancy are more valuable the higher the consumption in this extended lifetime, or, in other words, the higher the income. This is so because, with a time-separable utility function, longevity and income are complements in the indirect utility function (in terms of the cross-derivatives of the marginal utilities). Additionally, mortality reductions far off in the future are discounted at higher rates. So countries with higher life expectancy attach less value to given longevity gains. In the general case, the timing of mortality reductions is also important because of the competing risks nature of mortality rates (see Dow, Philipson, and Sala-i-Martín 1999).

1.2 Parameterization and Calibration
We need to parameterize the utility function $u(.)$ in order to be able to use this model to estimate the economic value of some hypothetical or real change in mortality rates. In this regard, we follow closely the discussion in Becker, Philipson, and Soares 2004.

There are two dimensions of the instantaneous utility function $u(.)$ that are relevant for the analysis of changes in survival probabilities: the substitutability of consumption in different periods of life (intertemporal elasticity of substitution), and the value of being alive relative to being dead. Rosen (1988, p. 287) stresses the importance of this last factor as a consequence of the normalization of utility in the death state to zero.

This means that the intertemporal elasticity of substitution cannot possibly contain enough information to calibrate all the relevant dimensions of choice involved in the problem. Therefore, we follow Becker, Philipson, and Soares (2004) and assume the following functional form for the instantaneous utility function:

$$u(c) = \frac{c^{1-1/\gamma}}{1-1/\gamma} + \alpha, \tag{8}$$

where α is the parameter that arises from the normalization of utility in the death state to zero, and γ is the intertemporal elasticity of substitution.

In a deterministic setting, with no choice involving the margin between life and death, the parameter α would be irrelevant. But when we are analyzing choices involving survival probabilities, and utility in the death state is normalized to zero, α affects the utility of being alive relative to being dead. The issue is one of state-dependent utilities, where utility in the death state is normalized to a fixed number independent of the level of consumption.[1]

Intuitively, the question can be understood as follows. If we could always ignore α and represent $u(.)$ with some constant elasticity function, it would mean that all the relevant parameters for value-of-life calculations could be estimated exclusively from intertemporal consumption decisions. This would seem rather puzzling, since this dimension of choice is not linked to decisions that entail trade-offs between mortality and consumption (or income). It would only be possible because the constant elasticity functional form would be artificially restrictive, bunching up different parameters together and assuming implicitly a certain trade-off between utilities in the death and life states.

Also note that, contrary to superficial intuition, it is not true that α is necessarily positive. Rigorously, α is the parameter determining the level of annual consumption at which the individual is indifferent between being alive and dead. If we think that there is such a level of consumption, γ larger than one necessarily means α smaller than zero.

Two pieces of information available in the literature are enough to fully calibrate this instantaneous utility function: the intertemporal elasticity of substitution, and the consumption elasticity of the instantaneous utility function. Define ε as the consumption elasticity of the utility function. We have

$$\varepsilon = \frac{u'(c)c}{u(c)} = \frac{c^{1-1/\gamma}}{\frac{c^{1-1/\gamma}}{1-1/\gamma} + \alpha}, \tag{9}$$

and, from this expression, $\alpha = c^{1-1/\gamma}\left(\frac{1}{\varepsilon} - \frac{1}{1-1/\gamma}\right)$.

The value of ε can be estimated from compensating differentials for occupational mortality risks. Murphy and Topel (2003), using numbers from the literature on occupational risks, estimate ε to be 0.346.

In relation to the intertemporal elasticity of substitution, a wide range of values is available in the empirical literature. Browning, Hansen, and Heckman (1999, p. 614), after exhaustively reviewing the estimates, suggest that the intertemporal elasticity of substitution for nondurables is probably slightly above 1.

We use $\gamma = 1.25$, $\varepsilon = 0.346$, and $c = \$26,365$ to calibrate the value of α. The value of consumption is the value of U.S. per-capita income in 1990, from Heston, Summers, and Aten (2002), Penn World Tables version 6.1 (PPP, in 1996 international prices). We use this value because Murphy and Topel (2003) estimate ε using U.S. data for 1990, and our income data comes from the PWT 6.1 data set. Our calculations give a value of α equal to -16.16. Together with the value of γ, this implies that an individual with annual income equal to $353 would be indifferent between being alive or dead.

The only country with GDP per capita below this threshold in our sample, and also in the entire PWT 6.1 dataset, is the Democratic Republic of the Congo, with $306. According to the model and the calibration, this means that the consumption level in the Democratic Republic of the Congo is so low that the marginal willingness to pay for extensions in life expectancy is actually negative. People would be willing to forgo life expectancy in order to increase consumption, and not the other way around. This issue will arise again in the empirical section, where the values for the Democratic Republic of the Congo, although small, will be negative.

The functional form adopted is flexible enough to accommodate an income elasticity of the marginal willingness to pay that actually changes with income. So, the calibration using U.S. data is not limiting in the sense of imposing an income elasticity that does not belong to the African countries we want to analyze. For average levels of income per capita, around $10,000, the parameters imply an income elasticity of the marginal willingness to pay around 1.2. This number is close to the income elasticity of the "value of life" found by Becker and Elias (2003), after correcting the estimates of Viscusi and Aldi (2003) to account for the presence of some critical outliers. But our specification allows this elasticity to vary with the income level, so that it reaches very high values for low income per capita. For example, it reaches 1.9 and 3.8 for, respectively, $1,000 and $500 of income per capita. Therefore, the functional form adopted is flexible enough to identify underlying preference parameters that can be used more generally, irrespective of the level of income.[2]

With the values of α and γ, we can use equation (7) to value any given mortality reductions. With the assumptions made, equation (7) can be rewritten as:

$$MWP_a = \left(\frac{y}{1 - 1/\gamma} + \alpha y^{1/\gamma}\right) \int_0^\infty e^{-r(t-a)} S_\theta(t, a) \, dt.^3 \tag{10}$$

Once equation (10) is used to calculate the marginal willingness to pay for individuals at each age a, we can use the age distribution of the population and equation (6) to calculate the social value of mortality reductions.

In this chapter, we consider changes in mortality rates that would be brought about if AIDS deaths were reduced to zero. Calculating the welfare gain from this AIDS eradication scenario is analogous to calculating the welfare cost of AIDS: it gives the monetary value of the welfare loss due to the existence of AIDS itself. Since we will be looking at some of the world's poorest nations, and in order to get a conservative estimate of the welfare cost of AIDS, we assume that interest rates and subjective discount rates are equal to 10 percent per year.

2 Data and Empirical Implementation

The age-specific population and number of deaths for 2000 are available from the World Health Organization estimated life tables.[4]

The number of AIDS deaths in 2001 for children and adults (0–49) is obtained from the Joint United Nations Program on HIV/AIDS (UNAIDS). There is no information on the age-specific number of AIDS deaths for African countries, so we use these data, together with other information and some simplifying assumptions, in order to estimate the age distribution of AIDS deaths.

UNAIDS also provides estimates of the number of children (0–14) and adults (15–49) infected by HIV. We assume that AIDS mortality is proportional to infection rates and use the numbers on HIV infection to assign the total number of deaths between children and adults. Following, we assume that the age distribution of AIDS deaths within each of these groups is proportional to the age distribution of the total number of deaths within the group. With these assumptions, we are able to assign the total number of children and adults' AIDS deaths estimated by UNAIDS to each age between zero and 49. To adopt a conservative view, we assume that AIDS deaths after age 50 are equal to zero.

The income variable used is real GDP per capita, adjusted for terms of trade in 1996 international prices. This is the RGDPTT (real gross domestic income adjusted for terms of trade changes) variable from the PWT 6.1 database. We use GDP per capita as the average for the period between 1995 and 2000, or years available in this interval.

All sub-Saharan countries for which UNAIDS estimates on the number of AIDS deaths exist are included in the sample. This leaves us with the main 34 sub-Saharan countries, out of a total of 48 (see the list in the appendix).

We calculate the survival probabilities that would be observed in the absence of AIDS in the following way. By definition, the survival probability between ages t and $t+1$ can be calculated as

$$S(t+1,t) = 1 - \frac{N(t+1,t)}{P(t+1,t)}, \tag{11}$$

where $N(t+1,t)$ is the number of deaths between ages t and $t+1$, and $P(t+1,t)$ is the population between ages t and $t+1$. The counterfactual survival probabilities in the absence of AIDS are constructed as:

$$SNA(t+1,t) = 1 - \frac{N(t+1,t) - NA(t+1,t)}{P(t+1,t)}, \tag{12}$$

where $NA(t+1,t)$ is the number of AIDS deaths between ages t and $t+1$, and $SNA(t+1,t)$ is the non-AIDS survival rate between ages t and $t+1$. This rate gives the survival probability that would be observed between ages t and $t+1$ if no deaths caused by AIDS were registered.[5]

These single-period survival probabilities can be immediately transformed into cumulative survival probabilities. By definition, $S(t,a) = \prod_a^{t-1} S(i+1,i)$ and $SNA(t,a) = \prod_a^{t-1} SNA(i+1,i)$.

Life expectancy at birth is the integral under the survival function evaluated from the perspective of age 0 ($S(t,0)$). In this discrete setting, life expectancy at birth is $L = \sum_{t=1}^{\infty} S(t,0)$, and the life expectancy at birth that would be observed in the absence of AIDS is $LNA = \sum_{t=1}^{\infty} SNA(t,0)$. With the cumulative survival probabilities, the counterfactual change in survival probabilities that would be brought about by the eradication of AIDS is calculated as

$$S_\theta(t,a) = SNA(t,a) - S(t,a). \tag{13}$$

Finally, $S_\theta(t,a)$ allows us to calculate an interesting descriptive statistic, which will be discussed in the next section: the expected years of life lost to AIDS. Since life expectancy at birth is simply the integral of

$S(t, 0)$ from zero to infinity, the expected years of life lost to AIDS can be defined as

$$L_\theta = \sum_{t=1}^{\infty} S_\theta(t, 0) = \sum_{t=1}^{\infty} SNA(t, 0) - \sum_{t=1}^{\infty} S(t, 0) = LNA - L, \qquad (14)$$

which is simply the reduction in life expectancy at birth that can be attributed to AIDS deaths. Or, in terms of survival functions, the difference that arises when we calculate life expectancy using, respectively, $SNA(t, 0)$ and $S(t, 0)$.

The $S_\theta(t, a)$ constructed according to equation (13) is the one used, together with equations (10) and (7), to estimate individual and social costs of AIDS for the 34 countries included in the sample. The next section presents and discusses the results.

3   Results

3.1   Descriptive Analysis

Table 12.1 presents a series of descriptive statistics for the sub-Saharan countries in the sample. These include life expectancy at birth, estimated number of AIDS deaths, AIDS gross mortality rate, estimated life expectancy without AIDS, and income per capita.

The numbers for AIDS are staggering. In the 34 countries listed in the table, it is estimated that 2.2 million people died of AIDS in 2001. This corresponds to a 0.38 percent gross mortality rate for the overall population, which, given the age profile of AIDS mortality, generates a reduction in life expectancy at birth of roughly 7 years.

But a word of caution regarding the quality of AIDS mortality data for sub-Saharan Africa should be placed here. The estimated number of AIDS deaths for some countries is so large that it is hard to believe that they are accurate. For Botswana and Zimbabwe, for example, it is estimated that more than 1.5 percent of the population dies every year from AIDS. More than that, for these two countries, plus Lesotho, South Africa, Swaziland, and Zambia, the estimated number of adult AIDS deaths is larger than the total number of adult deaths estimated by the World Health Organization. It is also true that the World Health Organization data may underestimate overall mortality for the sub-Saharan area, as is commonly thought to be the case for developing countries.

In any case, this implies that the strategy for calculating survival functions outlined in the previous section would generate survival rates above 1 in certain age groups between 15 and 49, for the countries mentioned in the previous paragraph. For these cases, we substitute the calculated value by the upper bound of 1, which gives a flat survival function in certain ranges. But mortality rates within this age interval are usually very low, even for poor countries, so this is not such a serious problem as it may seem at first. Even in the cases of Botswana, Lesotho, South Africa, Swaziland, Zambia, and Zimbabwe, our estimates are consistent with data from other sources. For example, for all of these cases except Zambia, our estimates of life expectancy without AIDS are very close to and slightly below the estimates of life expectancy without AIDS from the United Nations' *World Population Prospects* (2002, p. 79). Also, the numbers are consistent with the life expectancies observed in these same countries before the AIDS epidemic hit.[6] We think, therefore, that despite the limitations, the data do convey a reasonable approximation to the mortality changes due to AIDS in the different countries.

Figure 12.1 presents the estimated change in the survival function due to AIDS for the cases of Botswana, Kenya, Mozambique, and Nigeria. The area between the two curves is the loss in life expectancy at birth implied by AIDS, and it corresponds to, respectively, 22, 13, 4, and 3 years. The flat portion of the non-AIDS survival function for Botswana reflects the limitation of the data discussed above.

One of the most salient aspects of AIDS mortality is illustrated in this figure: its high incidence during adult life. Survival functions from age zero $(S(t,0))$ for human populations are typically concave between ages 10 and the very end of life (70 or above). AIDS is introducing a convexity in this function, starting in the prime years of reproductive life, just after age 20. This has several implications in terms of educational and fertility decisions, which can be understood in light of recent theories of human capital investment and fertility choice (see, e.g., Meltzer 1992; Soares 2004a). In addition, this increase in mortality at ages usually associated with very low mortality rates has a devastating direct effect in terms of welfare. This is the focus of our application of the methodology discussed in section 1.

The figure also illustrates that, despite being widespread throughout sub-Saharan Africa, AIDS seems to have affected the different countries to different degrees. The estimated life expectancy loss due to

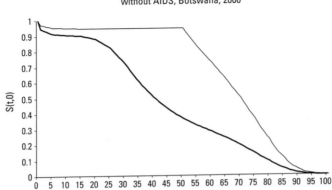

Figure 1(a): Cumulative Survival Function with and without AIDS, Botswana, 2000

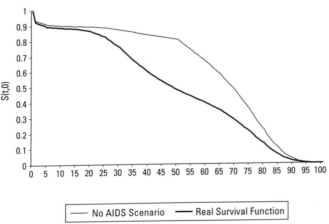

Figure 1(b): Cumulative Survival Function with and without AIDS, Kenya, 2000

——— No AIDS Scenario   ——— Real Survival Function

Figure 12.1
Cumulative survival functions with and without AIDS, selected sub-Saharan countries, 2000.

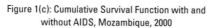

Figure 1(c): Cumulative Survival Function with and without AIDS, Mozambique, 2000

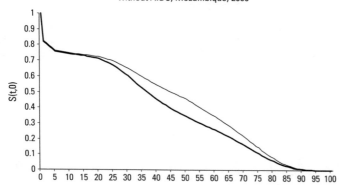

Figure 1(d): Cumulative Survival Function with and without AIDS, Nigeria, 2000

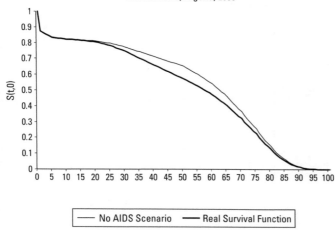

No AIDS Scenario   Real Survival Function

Figure 12.1
(continued)

Table 12.1
AIDS mortality and welfare cost, sub-Saharan Africa, 2000.

Country	Life Exp*	AIDS Deaths**	AIDS Gross Mort Rate	Life Exp Without AIDS	Life Exp Reduction	GDP per capita*	Value of AIDS Eradication for 18 Year Old Individual		Social Value of AIDS Eradication	
							Money Value	% of GDP per capita	Money Value (millions)	% of GDP
Angola	44.2	24,000	0.18%	47.7	3.4	1,310	432	33%	3,788	22%
Benin	51.2	8,100	0.13%	54.0	2.8	1,113	226	20%	999	14%
Botswana	43.7	26,000	1.69%	66.2	22.5	6,202	19,895	321%	22,973	240%
Burkina Faso	41.2	44,000	0.38%	48.3	7.1	909	464	51%	3,627	35%
Burundi	39.5	40,000	0.63%	50.1	10.6	647	320	49%	1,402	34%
Cameroon	48.4	53,000	0.36%	55.8	7.4	1,957	1,522	78%	15,895	55%
Central African Republic	40.4	22,000	0.59%	50.1	9.7	955	645	68%	1,675	47%
Chad	47.5	14,000	0.18%	51.0	3.5	902	205	23%	1,109	16%
Congo	50.3	11,000	0.36%	58.4	8.0	1,706	1,254	74%	2,603	51%
Cote d'Ivoire	45.9	75,000	0.47%	54.8	8.8	1,954	1,801	92%	20,706	66%
Dem. Rep. of the Congo	40.9	120,000	0.24%	44.8	3.9	306	(15)	-5%	(513)	-3%
Equatorial Guinea	53.4	370	0.08%	55.2	1.8	3,844	899	23%	285	16%
Eritrea	48.8	350	0.01%	48.9	0.2	775	7	1%	19	1%
Ethiopia	42.2	160,000	0.25%	46.2	4.0	598	100	17%	4,384	12%
Gambia	56.2	400	0.03%	56.8	0.6	1,123	48	4%	45	3%
Ghana	55.3	28,000	0.15%	58.6	3.2	1,293	305	24%	4,317	17%

Guinea-Bissau	43.7	1,200	0.10%	45.4	1.6	747	72	10%	60	7%
Kenya	47.9	190,000	0.62%	60.6	12.8	1,262	1,236	98%	27,973	72%
Lesotho	40.8	25,000	1.23%	59.2	18.4	1,408	2,334	166%	3,344	117%
Malawi	35.7	80,000	0.71%	46.1	10.4	747	517	69%	3,990	47%
Mali	41.5	11,000	0.10%	43.1	1.6	870	101	12%	780	8%
Mozambique	36.9	60,000	0.33%	41.1	4.3	929	343	37%	4,352	26%
Namibia	41.7	13,000	0.74%	53.9	12.2	4,419	7,825	177%	9,879	127%
Nigeria	49.2	170,000	0.15%	52.2	3.0	827	145	18%	11,552	12%
Rwanda	37.7	49,000	0.64%	47.6	9.8	848	573	68%	3,151	49%
Senegal	53.7	2,500	0.03%	54.3	0.6	1,523	73	5%	496	3%
Sierra Leone	35.1	11,000	0.25%	38.3	3.2	816	211	26%	629	17%
South Africa	49.9	360,000	0.83%	65.6	15.6	7,385	17,106	232%	561,979	176%
Swaziland	44.0	12,000	1.30%	62.2	18.2	4,792	12,122	253%	8,112	183%
Togo	50.6	12,000	0.27%	56.1	5.6	912	302	33%	970	24%
Uganda	42.7	84,000	0.36%	48.9	6.2	899	370	41%	6,020	29%
United Rep. of Tanzania	45.2	140,000	0.40%	52.4	7.2	450	58	13%	1,455	9%
Zambia	38.1	120,000	1.15%	58.0	20.0	801	943	118%	6,892	83%
Zimbabwe	44.7	200,000	1.58%	65.0	20.4	2,662	5,766	217%	53,141	158%
Sub-Saharan Africa***	45.4	2,166,920	0.38%	52.1	6.7	1,451	1,867	129%	788,089	96%

Notes:

*Life Expectancy is calculated with the 2000 World Health Organization estimated Life Tables. GDP per capita is the RGDPTT variable from the Penn World Tables 6.1 (PPP in 1996 international prices).

**2001 estimate from the UNAIDS, for children and adults (between ages 0 and 49). Gross mortality rate calculated with population from the 2000 World Health Organization estimated Life Tables.

***Refers only to countries included in the table. Life Expectancy variables, GDP p. capita, and values for an 18-year-old are cross-country averages weighted by population. Other variables are sum for the region.

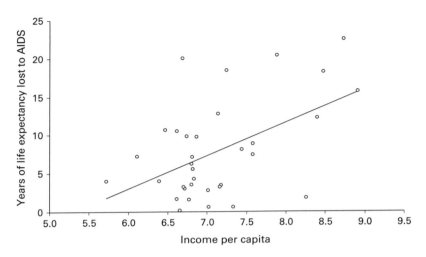

Figure 12.2
Relationship between life expectancy lost to AIDS and income per capita, sub-Saharan
Africa, 2000.

AIDS, which has an average of 7 years, varies from 22 years in Botswana to 0.2 years in Eritrea.

This variation in AIDS incidence has a curious correlation with income per capita. Sub-Saharan Africa is the world's poorest area, with
an average income equal to $1,451 in PPP terms. But there is still con-
siderable income heterogeneity across the different countries in the region. South Africa has an income per capita comparable to the richest
Latin American countries ($7,385), whereas the Democratic Republic
of the Congo and Tanzania have incomes per capita below $500.

In the data, the level of income is significantly related to years of life
expectancy lost to AIDS, or to the AIDS gross mortality rate. Figure
12.2 plots the cross-sectional relationship between the logarithm of income and years of life expectancy lost to AIDS, and fits a regression
line to it. The regression equation displayed in the figure shows an R^2
above 0.25, and a coefficient significant at any conventional significance level.

It is possible that urbanization and demographic density, both associated with income per capita, increase the ease of contamination and
hence spread of the AIDS epidemic. Nevertheless, it is also likely that
the number of AIDS deaths is underestimated in the poorest areas.
Becker, Philipson, and Soares (2004) show that deaths attributed to

"ill-defined causes" are more common in developing countries, and Soares (2004b) shows that reporting rates of different types of crime are strongly related to income per capita. It would be surprising if something similar was not happening also in relation to the reporting of AIDS deaths and the surveys used in the construction of the UNAIDS estimates. If that is the case, our results will underestimate the true welfare cost of AIDS for the poorest countries in the sample.

3.2 The Welfare Cost of AIDS

The last four columns in table 12.1 present the results for the welfare cost of AIDS. Results are presented for an individual just entering adulthood (18 years old) about to face the highest levels of AIDS mortality, and for the society as whole. For an 18-year-old individual, numbers are presented in monetary units (1996 international prices) and as a percentage of income per capita. For the social cost, numbers are presented as monetary units and as a percentage of aggregate GDP.

The average welfare cost of AIDS for an 18-year-old individual in sub-Saharan Africa is $1,867, which corresponds to 129 percent of the average per-capita income in the region. In the case of Botswana, one of the richest countries in the area and the one most affected by AIDS—where income per capita is $6,202 and the AIDS gross mortality rate is 1.69 percent—the welfare cost of AIDS equals $19,895, corresponding to 321 percent of the income per capita. In some other cases, values are very low, either because of extremely low income levels, or because of not-so-high AIDS mortality.

In the case of the Democratic Republic of the Congo, the value for an 18-year-old individual is virtually equal to zero, although it is actually negative. As mentioned before, this happens because of the extreme poverty in the country (income per capita equal to $306). According to the calibration of the parameters, individuals in the Democratic Republic of the Congo would not be willing to pay anything in order to increase life expectancy. In reality, they should be willing to sacrifice life expectancy in order to increase consumption. This is how this negative number for the welfare cost of AIDS should be interpreted, and not as saying that welfare is increased because of AIDS.

Figure 12.3 plots the age profile of the welfare cost of AIDS for an individual in the case of Kenya. The general shape of the profile is virtually identical for the other countries, with differences being mostly related to the scale. Typically, the profile is increasing between ages 5 and 30, when it peaks. The cost of AIDS is calculated to be zero after

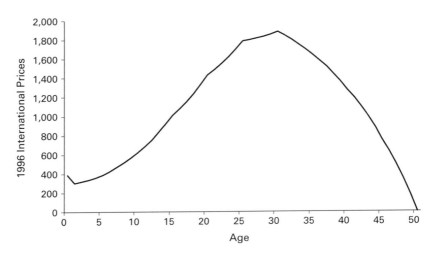

Figure 12.3
Age profile of the welfare cost of AIDS for an individual, Kenya, 2000.

age 50 because our data does not contain the number of AIDS deaths after that age. The highest overall cost of AIDS is registered for age 30 in the case of Botswana, when it reaches $30,603.

The last two columns of table 12.1 present the results for the social costs of AIDS. The social cost is obtained by aggregating individual age-specific marginal willingness to pay according to equation (7). The result for the region as a whole is staggering: the loss of welfare caused by the reduction in life expectancy due to AIDS has an aggregate value of approximately $800 billion, which corresponds to virtually all the production of the region during one year.

This number eclipses any available estimate of the financial cost of AIDS. For example, a recent UNICEF evaluation report (2000) estimated that the direct economic cost of AIDS in Africa in 2000 was around 5 percent of the GDP. An annual cost of 5 percent of the GDP, even if incurred forever and discounted at the interest rate used here, would imply a lifetime present value equal to 55 percent of the GDP. Based on these numbers, the report claimed that "Emergency widespread mobilization of governments and populations, even at a cost of 1 percent of GDP, is an appropriate, indeed essential, response level." Our results suggest that this response would be timid. The direct economic cost of AIDS is relatively modest in face of the total welfare cost, once reduced life expectancy is also taken into account. Nevertheless, even our results should be seen as a lower bound for the overall welfare cost of AIDS. The long-term costs of AIDS should also take into account its impacts on human capital investments and growth, along the lines discussed in some of the papers cited here and the other chapters of this book.

For Botswana and Swaziland, the welfare cost of AIDS corresponds roughly to two full years of gross national product. In several other cases, the welfare cost is above 50 percent of annual production. It seems obvious that any reaction that does not place AIDS as an absolute emergency and priority will be insufficient.

4 Conclusions

In this chapter, we used the value-of-life methodology to evaluate the full cost of AIDS in sub-Saharan Africa, not only the effects of AIDS on marketed goods (as measured by GDP statistics). Africa is the area most affected by AIDS in the world, with an average reduction in life expectancy of 7 years due to AIDS mortality. This chapter used AIDS death statistics from UNAIDS, and life tables from the World Health Organization, to estimate counterfactual mortality rates that would be observed if AIDS did not exist. It then used the marginal willingness-to-pay approach to estimate the welfare loss from the changes in mortality rates brought about by the AIDS epidemic. This number summarizes how much the population would be willing to pay in order to experience the counterfactual survival rates without AIDS rather than those observed with AIDS. The results indicate that the welfare cost of AIDS in sub-Saharan Africa is of the order of $800 billion, or the equivalent to one year of aggregate production for the whole region. This value is at least one order of magnitude larger than any available estimate of the partial economic cost of AIDS due to its direct impact on consumption and growth, as measured in previous studies. The full economic cost of AIDS, taking into account nonmarketed goods, is overwhelmingly larger than the cost measured by considering only the effects on marketed goods.

Notes

1. In Rosen's words (1988, p. 286): "Valuing risks to life requires some unusual normalizations of preferences because utility is inherently state-dependent in this problem.... When preferences are state dependent, any increasing linear transformation is acceptable

as long as the same transformation is consistently applied to the utility function of each state."

2. Cultural differences may be another concern in this matter. But not much can be done in this direction until country or region-specific studies allow the identification of parameters for each particular case.

3. The formula used in the calculations is a discrete-time version of equation (7).

4. The data set is the *Life Tables for 191 Countries: World Mortality in 2000*, which forms the basis of the WHO mortality estimates. When this chapter was written, these data were available online at the WHO Web site: http://www3who.int/whosis/life_tables/life_tables.cfm. The WHO database contains data for each 5-year age interval. To calculate life expectancy and survival probabilities, we assume constant mortality rates within these 5-year intervals.

5. We switch to a discrete setting for ease of exposition and to match the discrete nature of the data.

6. According to the World Bank Development Database, the maximum life expectancy observed in each one of these countries and its respective year of occurrence was: 61 for Botswana in 1987, 58 for Lesotho in 1992, 65 for South Africa in 1997, 60 for Swaziland in 1990, 51 for Zambia in 1982, and 57 for Zimbabwe in 1987. These all seem to be consistent with our 2000 estimates for the non-AIDS survival rate.

Appendix

Appendix 1: Countries Included in the Sample
Angola; Benin; Botswana; Burkina Faso; Burundi; Cameroon; Central African Republic; Chad; Congo; Côte d'Ivoire; Democratic Republic of the Congo; Equatorial Guinea; Eritrea; Ethiopia; Gambia; Ghana; Guinea-Bissau; Kenya; Lesotho; Malawi; Mali; Mozambique; Namibia; Nigeria; Rwanda; Senegal; Sierra Leone; South Africa; Swaziland; Togo; Uganda; United Republic of Tanzania; Zambia; Zimbabwe.

Appendix 2: Data
Income per capita: RGDPTT from the Penn World Tables version 6.1. Real GDP per capita adjusted for terms of trade, in 1996 international prices. The value is the average for all years available between 1995 and 2000.

Age-Specific Population and Number of Deaths: From the World Health Organization Life Tables, 2000.

Number of AIDS Deaths and Number of Children and Adults Infected by HIV: Number of AIDS deaths between ages 0 and 49, and number of people infected by HIV between ages 0 and 14, and 15 and 49, from the Joint United Nations Program on HIV/AIDS, 2001.

References

Becker, G. S., and J. J. Elias. 2003. Introducing Incentives in the Market for Live and Cadaveric Organs. Unpublished manuscript, University of Chicago.

Becker, G. S., T. J. Philipson, and R. R. Soares. 2004. The Quantity and Quality of Life and the Evolution of World Inequality. *American Economic Review*, in press.

Bloom, D. E., and A. S. Mahal. 1995. Does the AIDS Epidemic Really Threaten Economic Growth? Working paper no. 5148, National Bureau of Economic Research, Cambridge, Mass.

Browning, M., L. P. Hansen, and J. J. Heckman. 1999. Micro Data and General Equilibrium Models. In *Handbook of Macroeconomics*, vol. 1A, edited by J. B. Taylor and M. Woodford. Amsterdam: Elsevier Science B.V., pp. 543–636.

Cutler, D., and E. Richardson. 1997. Measuring the Health of the U.S. Population. *Brookings Papers on Economic Activity: Microeconomics*, pp. 217–271.

Dixon, S., S. McDonald, and J. Roberts. 2001. AIDS and Economic Growth in Africa: A Panel Data Analysis. *Journal of International Development* 13 (4): 411–426.

Dow, W. H., T. Philipson, and X. Sala-i-Martín. 1999. Longevity Complementarities under Competing Risks. *American Economic Review* 89 (5): 1358–1371.

Garrett, A. M. 2001. Health Improvements and the National Income and Product Accounts: 1880 to 1940. Ph.D. dissertation. Chicago: University of Chicago.

Grossman, M. 1972. On the Concept of Health Capital and the Demand for Health. *Journal of Political Economy* 80 (2): 223–255.

Heston, A., R. Summers, and B. Aten. 2002. Penn World Table Version 6.1. Center for International Comparisons at the University of Pennsylvania.

MEDLINKS. 2003. *HIV/AIDS in Africa.* 2002. Available at http://medilinkz.org/healthtopics/statistics/hivaids2003.asp.

Meltzer, D. 1992. Mortality Decline, the Demographic Transition, and Economic Growth. Ph.D. dissertation, Department of Economics, University of Chicago.

Murphy, K. M., and R. Topel. 2001. Black–White Differences on the Economic Value of Improving Health. Unpublished manuscript. University of Chicago.

———. 2003. The Economic Value of Medical Research. In *Measuring the Gains from Medical Research: An Economic Approach*, edited by Kevin M. Murphy and R. H. Topel. Chicago: University of Chicago Press, pp. 41–73.

Nordhaus, W. D. 2003. The Health of Nations: The Contribution of Improved Health to Living Standards. In *Measuring the Gains from Medical Research: An Economic Approach*, edited by Kevin M. Murphy and R. H. Topel. Chicago: University of Chicago Press, pp. 9–40.

Philipson, T. J., and R. R. Soares. 2002. World Inequality and the Rise in Longevity. In *Annual World Bank Conference on Development Economics 2001/2002*, edited by B. Pleskovic and N. Stern. New York: The World Bank and Oxford University Press, pp. 245–259.

Rosen, S. 1988. The Value of Changes in Life Expectancy. *Journal of Risk and Uncertainty* 1: 285–304.

Schelling, T. C. 1968. The Life You Save May Be Your Own. In *Problems in Public Expenditure Analysis*, edited by S. B. Chase, Jr. Washington, D.C.: Brookings Institution, pp. 127–161.

Soares, R. R. 2003. The Welfare Cost of Violence. Unpublished manuscript. University of Maryland.

———. 2004a. Mortality Reductions, Educational Attainment, and Fertility Choice. *American Economic Review*, in press.

———. 2004b. Development, Crime, and Punishment: Accounting for the International Differences in Crime Rates. *Journal of Development Economics* 73 (1): 155–184.

Thaler, R., and S. Rosen. 1975. The Value of Saving a Life. In *Household Production and Consumption—National Bureau of Economic Research Studies in Income and Wealth*, vol. 40, edited by N. Terleckyj. Cambridge, Mass.: National Bureau of Economic Research, pp. 265–298.

UN, Population Division. 2002. *World Population Prospects: The 2002 Revision*. New York: United Nations.

UNICEF. 2000. Evaluation of the Financial Implications of HIV/AIDS for Africa. Evaluation report, ESARO region, 2002. New York: UNICEF.

Usher, D. 1973. An Imputation of the Measure of Economic Growth for Changes in Life Expectancy. In *The Measurement of Economic and Social Performance*, Studies in Income and Wealth, vol. 38, edited by Milton Moss. New York: National Bureau of Economic Research and Columbia University Press, pp. 193–225.

Viscusi, W. K. 1993. The Value of Risks to Life and Health. *Journal of Economic Literature* 31 (4): 1912–1946.

Viscusi, K. W., and J. E. Aldy. 2003. The Value of a Statistical Life: A Critical Review of Market Estimates Throughout the World. Working paper no. 9487, National Bureau of Economic Research, Cambridge, Mass.

13

Profits and People: On the Incentives of Business to Get Involved in the Fight against AIDS

David Bloom and Jaypee Sevilla

AIDS and business: it would be an immeasurable benefit to humankind to put the two together. The former is the most tragic public health predicament of our time. The latter is the most successful organizational engine for innovation and the satisfaction of human needs ever devised. Many of the virtues required to solve the AIDS crisis are among those eminently possessed by modern business: the ability to mobilize great amounts of financial, material, and human resources; to innovate and solve problems creatively; to affect consciousness, perceptions, knowledge, and behavior; to distribute goods and services. The range of activities to which these abilities can be applied is great. They include those focused on the workforce, such as workplace education, access to condoms, and HIV treatment and counseling. They could focus on the customer base through consumer education and social marketing, or on clients and business partners by creating financial incentives for these partners to address AIDS issues in their own workplaces. And they may be focused on broader involvement in society through advocacy and lobbying, awareness campaigns, or involvement in local community projects.[1]

This insight is not new, and it is shared by many others who have remarked on the complementarity between the needs of a worldwide effort against AIDS, and the abilities modern businesses have to meet these needs. But many who believe this also believe in another view; that firms have strong incentives to employ these abilities in the battle against AIDS. Or at least firms would realize they do, if they became sufficiently enlightened or forward looking. It is this further view that we would like to reflect on in this chapter.

Doubtless, the good of the world would be served by the active involvement of business in anti-AIDS efforts. If they were to educate populations about health risks, and disseminate condoms and information about safe-sex practices with as much zeal and efficacy as they market soft drinks, fast food, sneakers, and automobiles, we would likely make serious progress against this epidemic. But it seems fair to say that two decades into the epidemic, the global campaign against AIDS continues to be led by national governments and some very vigorous and innovative not-for-profit organizations. With some exceptions, modern business is conspicuous in this campaign mainly because of its absence. What is the cause of this absence, and what is its remedy?[2]

We apply standard economic reasoning to account for the absence of significant business involvement. We believe, perhaps in contrast to many who have written on the subject, that the reason business ingenuity and energy are not forthcoming is that there are not sufficient incentives to elicit that ingenuity. There is what economists call an externality, or a gap between the benefit to businesses and the benefit to society of business involvement in AIDS prevention and treatment, resulting in an underinvolvement relative to the degree that is socially desirable.

This does not imply that firms have no incentives to act. They certainly do, for reasons pointed out by many, and we review these reasons below.[3] Neither does this imply that the moral suasion performed by governments, multilateral institutions, and nongovernmental organizations (NGOs) is entirely ineffectual in stimulating greater business involvement. But we emphasize that the externality is real and large. When we try to imagine the potential of firms to contribute to solving the problem of AIDS, and compare that potential to their current efforts, we see a great chasm separating the two. This chasm is not likely to be bridged by existing incentives facing firms, nor by repeated attempts at moral suasion by many members of the world community. It certainly has not as we enter the epidemic's third decade.

Can this externality gap be bridged by other means? Since we rely on standard economic approaches to frame the problem, we also rely on them for ideas about possible solutions. Externalities have been much studied, so we describe traditional solutions to them, and discuss the potential relevance of these solutions to the problem of binding business incentives more closely to the needs of the war against AIDS.[4] Finally, and most significantly, we suggest that a system of government contracting to businesses, with the explicit goal of harnessing their innovative and organizational capacities, may be the best way of involving business in the fight against AIDS.

1 The Traditional Economic Approach

Economics is fundamentally concerned with the allocation of resources, especially with the way markets perform this function and the conditions under which they do it well. While the dimensions of the AIDS tragedy are human, many considerations related to its solution are economic. How much of our resources do we devote to vaccine research, to education for prevention, and to treatment with antiretrovirals? Who bears the costs of these efforts? These are questions about resource allocation and therefore economic questions. The question we discuss in this chapter is also economic: what role can businesses play in society's battle against the epidemic?

Businesses are market actors. They exist to participate in markets: buying inputs and producing and selling outputs in order to make a profit.[5] To understand what potential role businesses might have in the crisis, we need to understand the logic of markets and of business participation in them.

We prize markets because they are an incredibly good mechanism for satisfying a plethora of human wants within the constraints of our finite resources. They are better at this than any other institution humanity has ever devised. But if markets are truly good at satisfying human wants, should not they also be good at satisfying society's needs for mobilizing resources effectively against AIDS? Here we come to an important point: markets are good at satisfying some social needs but bad at satisfying others. In this chapter, we elaborate on this basic observation in an attempt to shed light on the possible role that markets and market actors such as businesses might have to play in addressing one of the major social issues of our time.

Adam Smith (1776) said, "It is not from the benevolence of the butcher, the brewer, or the baker that we expect our dinner, but from their regard to their own interest. We address ourselves, not to their humanity but to their self-love, and never talk to them of our necessities but of their advantages." Smith tells us a central truth: markets are effective in providing for social needs as long as these needs express themselves as profit-making opportunities.

Modern economic theory has developed this insight considerably beyond Adam Smith's original formulation. Now we know that a system of purely self-interested economic actors will do what is desirable from a social point of view if the net private benefits of actions are equal to their net social benefits. When the gains to individuals from performing actions are equal to the gain to society from those actions being performed, actions that benefit society would also yield benefits to any self-regarding private actors who perform them. This is Smith's invisible hand: self-regarding actions collectively bringing about the social good.

We also know that reality is not always so favorable to the social good. Sometimes a gap, perhaps very wide, can exist between the social desirability of acts and the net private benefits to actors from undertaking those acts. When these gaps occur, it is said that an externality exists. Under such conditions, there is no reason to expect self-regarding behavior to bring about socially desirable outcomes. If net private benefits are smaller than net social benefits, these acts will not be performed often enough, and vice versa.

There are many examples of these externalities in the field of public health. One classic example is vaccinations. The benefits from an individual getting vaccinated against a particular disease include the reduced risk of that person getting the disease, as well as the reduced risk to society of the disease being passed on to someone else. Individuals presumably care mainly about the first benefit, and only care about the second to the extent that they prevent infections in family members, friends, and others to whom they are altruistically linked. On the whole, they are likely to care relatively little about many of the other secondary infections that their vaccinations could prevent; thus their incentives to get vaccinated are too weak from society's point of view. Society would want the individual to take full account of the latter benefit as well.[6] On the other hand, externalities may be negative as well. Excessive use of antibiotics encourages the spread of drug-resistant strains of disease. From society's point of view, our private incentive to use antibiotics is too strong because we do not incorporate the negative effects our acts confer on everyone else.

We think these considerations provide an appropriate framework for mobilizing resources for the prevention and treatment of AIDS, and in particular for overcoming the difficulties of getting business involved in the effort. There is a gap between the financial incentives firms have to get involved, and the social benefit that would come from their doing so. Some would question this. In fact many have argued that firms have quite powerful incentives to involve themselves. These arguments usually fall into four categories: efficiency wages, the customer base, enlightened self-interest, and cost-benefit calculations.

Efficiency wages   Traditional economic theory holds that firms have an incentive to keep wages as low as possible in order to economize on costs. By contrast, the efficiency wage theory (Solow 1979) argues that firms may have an incentive to raise wages beyond what is strictly necessary because by doing so, one can gain the loyalty and commitment of one's workers. This can in turn result in higher profits because workers exert more effort, are less likely to shirk their responsibilities, have improved morale, and go through less turnover. When a firm supports AIDS prevention and treatment for its workforce, these same kinds of efficiency wage benefits could result.

While we have no a priori reasons to rule out this argument, we think its validity is limited in labor surplus economies where a large amount of labor is performed doing relatively unskilled tasks. Under these conditions, the mere possession of a job is incentive enough to work hard in order to keep it, and few additional incentives will be required to make the workforce work efficiently. When the labor required is relatively unskilled, it is also easily replaced and will not require much training. This implies that efficiency wage arguments may matter depending on two conditions: whether a firm requires skilled labor, and whether the labor pool is large. Where the required labor is unskilled and in large supply, efficiency wages are unnecessary. Where the required labor is skilled and scarce, we may see stronger firm incentives to invest in prevention and treatment.

"Dead customers don't buy"   According to Daly (2000), "The lifeblood of business is its customers. HIV/AIDS threatens not only present consumer markets but also future markets if education and prevention campaigns are not extended to a wider audience." Although this is undoubtedly true of the world as a whole, we are more skeptical of the relevance of this customer-based argument to particular businesses in specific countries with specific clientele. Many firms sell their outputs on foreign export markets and would be indifferent to the health of local populations. Many others sell their outputs to other firms. And many firms that sell their outputs to households do so only to well-defined demographic and socioeconomic categories. A high prevalence rate among the poor, unemployed, commercial sex workers, miners, soldiers, and long-haul truck drivers may be of limited interest to producers who find these categories of purchasers marginal. Supporters of this argument have not presented any evidence that aggregate consumer expenditures are being threatened by the epidemic.[7] If we assume that wealthy and more educated house-holds are more likely over time to take precautions against AIDS, these potential customers will be in less need of firms' contributions to prevention.

In addition, it is not clear that even if firms cared about these effects, they would have sufficient incentive to do anything about it. There is a classic free-rider problem: any firms that expended resources to reduce HIV incidence would be conferring a benefit on all other firms. This gives each firm an incentive to sit back and depend on the efforts of others.

"A penny saved is a penny earned" Some authors, Rosen et al. (2000) in particular, argue that given current benefit structures, the present value of the costs of HIV prevention are much smaller than the present value of the foreseeable AIDS-related costs that this prevention eliminates, hence yielding a net benefit to firms from prevention activities. They measure these net benefits through an incidence approach where they assume that firms become responsible for the stream of future costs foreseeable when an employee becomes infected while employed at the firm. These costs include paid sick leave due to increased absenteeism, pension benefits, and recruitment and training costs. They assume in a baseline scenario that the average time from infection to death is 7 years, that half of the costs of paid sick leave occur in year 6, and that all other costs occur in year 7. They discount costs at 10 percent a year, and simulate the reduced HIV/AIDS costs to firms that would result from three intervention scenarios that extend working life by 1, 3, and 5 years respectively. They find that the savings of intervention as a percentage of baseline costs range from a low of 9 percent to a high of 38 percent. They conclude that these cost savings provide an incentive for firms to implement these interventions.

Although this research is remarkable for the detailed empirical data set on which the calculations are performed, we feel that these cost savings calculations are irrelevant to firms because they misspecify the counterfactual. The choice faced by firms is not to treat workers or not treat them. There is another alternative, made very easy and attractive in labor surplus settings, and that is simply to replace the ill worker with a healthier one, thereby avoiding both the costs of prevention and the costs of AIDS treatment, and shifting them onto society.

The main reason we think firms do not have a sufficiently strong incentive is the long lag between the moment at which a firm's actions may lead to preventing HIV, and the moment that such an action could result in any saved labor costs. If there is on average an 8-year lag between contracting HIV and experiencing AIDS-related illnesses, a business would have no incentive to prevent the HIV unless it could foresee the worker staying on for longer than those 8 years. And this incentive would not be very strong if, instead of maintaining the employment of the HIV-infected worker and coping with AIDS-related labor costs, firms could simply replace that worker from a pool of surplus labor that often characterizes AIDS-stricken economies. The discounting of costs that arise far off into the future reduces this incentive even more: the present discounted value of a $1 cost 8 years into the future, when discounted at 10 percent annually, amounts to only 46 cents.

We do not dispute that firms—depending on circumstances surrounding the kind of labor they employ, the pool of labor from which they hire, the kinds of consumers purchasing their products, the norms governing the societies in which they operate, and their responsiveness to moral suasion by civil society and government—may have some incentives to devote resources to prevention and treatment activities. Our point is not that these incentives do not exist. There are numerous examples of firms that have devoted considerable resources to HIV prevention and AIDS care, and with demonstrable success in terms of worker health and public goodwill. Many of these initiatives are summarized in Bloom, Mahal, and River Path Associates 2001. Nothing here is intended to belittle those initiatives. Our point is simply that they are probably not nearly big enough to realize the full potential of business involvement. We do not claim that it is optimal for firms to do no prevention; we claim simply that what they find optimal is likely to be considerably below what is desirable and necessary from a social point of view. For every firm that can be held up as an example of active involvement, there are many more who do nothing, little, or not nearly enough to make a difference.

Enlightened self-interest   Finally, it seems plausible that firms could sharpen their image and potentially generate a fair amount of public goodwill by identifying themselves with a social issue like HIV/AIDS. According to Daly (2000), "The benefits to ... business of social investment initiatives are less immediate and usually less measurable than actions designed to protect employees; nevertheless, they can be substantial. Sustained involvement not only helps reduce the risk to employees, but also promotes a healthy community, which in turn can enhance the company's reputation for social responsibility with public officials, local customers and other community members ... [building] a company's reputation as a good corporate citizen." But it is equally plausible that such activities could provoke the opposite response. In some societies, AIDS and sex remain unsavory topics, and a social-activist approach could backfire and stigmatize the firms who adopt it. A firm wishing to contribute to the larger common good may prefer to contribute to less controversial objectives, like education, the arts, public amenities like parks and museums, and charities.

In sum, given the usual market milieu in which firms exist, the incentives that firms have to get involved in anti-AIDS efforts will fall considerably short of the incentives they have to penetrate markets, develop innovative products, and serve the needs of their customers; precisely those features of private enterprise that we wish to harness in the fight against the disease. If the nature of capitalism, firms, and labor markets implies this, can a government policy compelling business involvement make a difference, in the same way that governments can mandate employer-provided pensions or health insurance? This is an important question, but before answering it, we wish to try a different line of argument first. We will find that the issues it raises shed light on the potential for government regulation.

Returning to our elaboration of Adam Smith's observation about the nature and consequences of rational individual behavior, in order to get firms involved enough, what is needed is to align their in-centives with society's good so that the larger the benefits to society from certain actions, the larger the pecuniary benefits to firms from performing them. This is known to economists as finding a way for firms to internalize the externality, since it requires bridging the gap between social benefits and private incentives.[8] Economic theory pro-vides some traditional ways of accomplishing this. We discuss each briefly.

Pigouvian subsidy The first is through a Pigouvian subsidy, named after the early twentieth-century English economist Arthur Pigou who first formalized the argument. The idea is that if the government could subsidize firms for performing certain otherwise unprofitable activ-ities, the private benefits from these activities could be raised until they equaled the social benefits. If firms do not have sufficient in-centives to perform AIDS prevention and treatment, government subsidies for carrying out these activities could make them cheaper and raise incentives to do them.

Although this reasoning is attractive, it should be recognized that the traditional Pigouvian logic may be inapplicable to the case of HIV prevention and AIDS treatment. The subsidy consists of a fixed amount per unit of activity performed, and so in order for the subsidy to do its work, the government must be able to verify the level of the activity it is subsidizing. This is relatively easy where the output is a marketed good or service whose quantity can be recorded and observed by the government, perhaps at the point of sale. It may not be easy, if at all possible, to subsidize the performance by firms of a worker education program if the government cannot inexpensively verify that such a program has in fact taken place, or that substantive AIDS-related education occurred at such an event.

So in order for the subsidy to work, there would need to be some kind of government mechanism to verify that the activities being subsidized actually took place. This may require setting minimum standards for an acceptable worker education program, for example.

But then, if giving a subsidy does not eliminate the need for government verification of firm compliance, we see that it is really not the subsidy that gets the job done, it is government imposition and verification of regulations. All that the subsidy does is minimize the burdens on the firm of complying with the regulations. This is not a trivial function since in the absence of subsidies, firms could transfer the costs of compliance to its workers through lower wages, or to its customers through higher prices. But still, it limits the role of subsidies to affecting the distribution of the burdens of prevention, rather than being the motivating force behind prevention.

In fact, this argument about the role of subsidies being limited to affecting the distribution of the burdens of prevention has another implication: a government mandate that firms undertake certain HIV prevention strategies does not necessarily imply that these firms will bear the costs of these strategies. There is a traditional lesson in public finance that when a tax is imposed on the production of a good, who ends up paying the tax does not usually depend on who the tax is levied on. The true incidence of the tax depends on, among other things, the relative elasticities of supply and demand, both of the product itself and of the labor needed to produce it. A producer who must pay the tax may be able to completely escape it by charging its customers more or paying its workers less. The same thing will be true here. Mandating that firms contribute to prevention activities does not mean that firms will ultimately pay for these programs. They may instead reduce wages—a real possibility in labor surplus settings—or raise prices.

Selling the river   The second solution gets its odd name from a famous application of its principle to the problem of the commons, or the use of collectively owned resources. When fishermen fail to consider the effect that their collective harvests may have on fish populations in a communally owned river, they may overfish, resulting in the collapse of fish stocks. The socially optimal remedy is to limit aggregate harvests so that this does not happen, but this is difficult to accomplish since each individual fisherman has an incentive to catch as many fish as possible. The overfishing problem can be remedied if the river is either sold or given to any private individual in the community. The logic of the solution is simple. If the river belongs to someone, that person will have a direct pecuniary interest in maintaining the fish population, and would be willing to let fishermen fish, but only to an extent that does not threaten the fish population with collapse.

As with the Pigouvian subsidy, the point of the solution is to give a private actor an incentive scheme under which it is in that actor's own interest to act in the best interests of the community. It differs from the Pigouvian subsidy in that the subsidy focuses on changing the incentives of each individual firm, whereas this option puts the responsibility for carrying out all the socially desired actions on one or a small set of firms whose incentives have been specially designed to mimic those of society.

But what would it mean to "sell the river" in the case of AIDS prevention? The analogy between AIDS prevention and selling the river is inexact in the sense that in the river example, the aggregate level of sustainable fishing is maintained by limiting the amount of fishing each fisherman is allowed to do, usually through the sale of "rights to fish" that do not exceed unsustainable levels. It is hard to see what the counterpart to this sale of rights would be in the AIDS example. What the analogy does point out is that society needs a private actor, or a small number of actors, whose incentives have been designed so that it is in their interest to ensure that the desired aggregate level of AIDS prevention and treatment is taking place in society. This would entail structuring a financial contract between society and a firm so that the firm's profitability is maximized when it is undertaking the socially optimal amount of AIDS prevention and treatment. Can such a contract be designed?

One might consider the idea of government contracts that firms could bid for, as at an auction. The winner gets to design an AIDS prevention strategy through social marketing, condom distribution, company-based educational programs, and so on, and receives a payment that depends on some predetermined and independently verifiable standards of performance such as HIV or STD incidence, or population-based measures ascertainable by phone and household surveys of AIDS-related knowledge, attitudes, and practices (KAP). In principle, such contracts could be designed so that different firms specialize in different constituencies such as schools, industrial sectors, geographic regions, age groups, types of firm, and so on. These contracts could have payments based on independently verifiable performance so that firms have a profit motive to lower HIV/STD incidence, or increase AIDS-related KAP. Since payments are not related to costs, firms have an incentive to innovate in order to produce as much prevention as possible at the least cost.

The government The third solution is to rely on government to provide the service.[9] Governments are a natural choice for dealing with externalities since they are, by most normative and democratic theories, the guardians of the social good. Although private actors may not have the incentives to perform socially optimal actions, government incentives are theoretically defined by them. In fact, this is probably the most widespread view of how AIDS prevention and treatment in developing countries ought to be implemented, through vigorous government action.

But what is true in theory all too often fails in practice. Although externalities are an example of what is referred to as market failures, their existence should not automatically lead to the conclusion that governments can succeed in their stead. Governments can be as prone to failure as markets, with respect to bringing about socially optimal outcomes. Regimes may have a mistaken view of what the social good is, either through lack of information or a refusal to acknowledge the gravity of particular social problems, the latter fault being one to which nondemocracies may be prone as pointed out by Amartya Sen (1984) in his study of famines. Or regimes may have a grasp of the problem and yet be hobbled in their efforts by poor infrastructure, or a corrupt and inefficient bureaucracy. It is precisely firms' comparative advantage over governments in innovation and getting things done that makes our question about the role of business so important.

In addition, although governments may recognize the severity of the AIDS problem, they may, because of peculiarities of the political process, systematically underinvest. The importance of maintaining political power may cause governments to discriminate in its efforts, investing more heavily on geographic and demographic constituencies that reward it with political support. It may also encourage a myopic approach in which short-term investments yielding benefits to current voters could displace those with long-term benefits that do not yield political dividends in the present.

Our view should not be interpreted as meaning that "governments always fail." This would be as unreasonable a claim as "markets always succeed." Also there are some, unfortunately fewer than we would like, examples of governments that have taken decisive and effective action against the epidemic. One thinks of Thailand, Brazil, Senegal, and Uganda. We only wish to claim that governments, like markets, have their limits.

These are three solutions that standard economic thought proposes for solving the problem of externalities: subsidies, selling the river, and leaving it to government. These solutions are informed by one of the deepest methodological principles of economics: private actors act out of self-interest. The first two depend on changing the incentives of firms in order to induce them to take socially optimal actions. The last recognizes that when it is simply not feasible to give firms sufficient incentives, governments will need to go at it themselves. Wherein lies the solution?

There is not going to be an unambiguous and universally valid answer to this question. But our three options do highlight some principles that ought to help define nation-specific solutions. Governments and businesses have their respective advantages and disadvantages. Governments have, in theory, the requisite social incentives. Business is usually better at getting things done, and getting them done cheaply. So we have the following options. The first is to continue the task of trying to convince businesses to step up to the plate. This is not without its effectiveness, although we doubt it can come close to making business fulfill its full potential. The second is to use government policy to make firms implement AIDS-related programs at the firm level. Since the costs of such a policy may be shifted by firms to either customers or workers, subsidies may be necessary to avoid such cost shifting. The third is to design financial contracts with firms so that the service they produce and for which they are rewarded is a reduction in societywide markers for disease incidence, or improvements in AIDS-related KAP. The fourth is government performance of the necessary activities, with its concomitant greater focus on the inputs to prevention and treatment than the outputs forthcoming from those activities.

Current thinking on the role of business focuses on the first of these options. The third option, although new in our minds, may have the potential for an even larger role for business, in which the relative advantages of government and businesses are harnessed. Government designs the contract in accordance with its guardianship role of the social good. Firms, under the terms of the contract, do what they do best: innovate, minimize costs, and get things done, this time in the service of our battle against AIDS.

2 Conclusions

Our argument can be recapitulated simply. If we think seriously of how much businesses can contribute to the world's efforts against AIDS, we find a large gap between potential and reality. This gap is not due to a short-sightedness in business. It comes from an externality, an inherent difference between the interests of businesses (making profits), and society (combating AIDS). Although it is likely that businesses have some incentives to do something about the epidemic, and although it is likely that moral suasion by the international community will have some efficacy in improving business participation, these measures are unlikely to bridge the externality gap sufficiently. In order to accomplish this, one must attack the question of the incentives facing firms directly. Economic theory provides a way of thinking about possible solutions. The general principle is that one ought to build a public-private partnership that capitalizes on the relative strengths and comparative advantages of governments and business enterprises. In the realm of financial contracts that convert social benefits into corresponding profit opportunities, governments are the natural designers. And because of their comparative advantage in mobilizing resources, innovation, marketing, and distribution, businesses are the natural adopters.

Acknowledgments

The authors thank the editors for helpful comments. They also thank the Merck Foundation for underwriting this project by providing financial support to Pompeu Fabra University.

Notes

1. Businesses' perceptions of the HIV/AIDS crisis, the effects on their operations, and a review of some businesses' responses appear in Bloom, Mahal, and River Path Associates 2001. More recently, Bloom et al. (2003) provided a full description and analysis of HIV/AIDS questions asked in a survey of executive opinion conducted via mail in 2003 by the World Economic Forum (WEF). The main goal of the Executive Opinion Survey (EOS) was to gather information about attitudes and practices related to the business environment in which firms operate. The inclusion of questions on HIV/AIDS in a general business survey allows one to examine opinion on HIV/AIDS, and to explore the social, economic, and political correlates of those opinions. Survey responses were received from nearly 8,000 business executives in 103 countries. A set of technical issues related to the nature of the survey instrument and the paucity of information concerning the sampling frame used limit the inferences one can make from the results. Nevertheless, the EOS reveals a number of coherent and reasonable patterns in the data. These patterns bear on three fundamental issues: are businesses aware of the economic and human impacts of HIV? Are they acting? And are they comfortable with the situation and their actions?

With respect to the first issue, the results of EOS 2003 indicate that HIV appears to be of concern among one-half of the executive respondents (i.e., the fraction indicating that they have at least some concern about the impact of HIV on the current or future operation of the firm; a similar estimate is obtained with respect to the impact of HIV on the current or future operation of the community in which the firm operates, with the estimates ranging from 15 percent among executives in the Middle East and North Africa to 60 percent among executives in sub-Saharan Africa). One in five executive respondents expressed a high level of concern about the current or future impact of HIV on their firm and community. The levels of concern about HIV exceed those for malaria or tuberculosis. Moreover, the intensity of concern about HIV is positively associated with UNAIDS HIV-prevalence estimates for the country in which the executive works, and with the executive respondent's estimate of HIV prevalence among their workforce. It is negatively associated with the per-capita income level of the country in which the firm is located, and with firm size. Other things equal, the less confidence the firm has in the government's ability to get things done, the more concern they express about the impact of HIV. Executive respondents, however, are generally unable to identify specific impacts of HIV/AIDS on their operating costs or revenue.

Notwithstanding these fairly high levels of concern, relatively few firms reported having formal policies for safeguarding workers' HIV status and affirming nondiscriminatory treatment. Moreover, even among those firms with policies, the policy apparatus in place appears relatively weak. Fewer than 6 percent of the executive respondents report that their company has a written policy. Only 2 percent have a committee that meets regularly to ensure policy implementation, monitoring, and review. Firms who report a serious current or future impact from the epidemic are only twice as likely to have a written policy in place. Firms in countries with high prevalence, meanwhile, are only slightly more likely to have a written policy than firms in low-prevalence countries. Among firms with HIV/AIDS policies and programs, the provision of information about risks is the most common feature (showing up in 60% of programs). Less than 40 percent of the programs offer voluntary testing or condoms as part of their programs. Around a quarter, meanwhile, offer antiretrovirals to all HIV-positive employees, and one-sixth continue to offer care even after an employee has retired.

Finally, there is a fairly strong sense that private HIV policies are sufficient to handle the problem. One-third of executive respondents revealed that they are satisfied with the nature and efficacy of their company's HIV policies. By contrast, only 20 percent expressed the view that their company policies are inadequate. Businesses in countries in which there is a perception of good governance are generally more optimistic about the capacity to cope with HIV/AIDS.

2. See Bendell 2003, Greener 1997, Rau and Roberts 1996, Rosen and Simon 2003, Rosen et al. 2002, Rugalema, Weigang, and Mbwika 1999, Simon et al. 2000, and USAID 2001.

3. Previous research has clarified the impacts of AIDS on businesses. This research bears on their incentive to act. See Aventin and Huard 2000, Biggs and Shah 1997, Forsythe 2002, International Labour Office 2003, and Smith and Whiteside 1995.

4. We will focus on issues that face businesses in general. We will therefore ignore the obviously important fact that the impact of AIDS can vary systematically by industry. For example, the long-distance trucking and mining industries in Africa suffer much more significantly from the epidemic than others. This will clearly imply that the incentives businesses face to get involved in the AIDS issue will vary by sector as well.

5. We will ignore, for this chapter, nonprofits.

6. The idea of externalities in public health can also blur the distinction between prevention and treatment. For example, antiretroviral (ARV) treatment of HIV/AIDS lowers the amount of tuberculosis (TB) bacteria in the human reservoir. Since TB is spread randomly, AIDS treatment confers a positive externality by cutting back on TB transmission to seronegative individuals.

7. We recognize that the well-being of a firm's customers may also depend on the well-being of other individuals with whom those customers are economically linked. These links introduce some second-order incentives for firms to care about HIV/AIDS beyond their immediate customer base.

8. We note here that the ideal private actor whose self-interest is overwhelmingly identical to the social interest is the individual himself or herself. The private benefit from practicing safe sex is presumably much larger than its cost for most people. But we know that the problem is often a lack of awareness of self-interest in prevention, due to a paucity of information and feelings of helplessness. On the other hand, in populations in which non-AIDS mortality is high, fatalism may indeed be rational for some segment of the population (see O'Flaherty 1998).

9. This option stands in contrast to a Pigouvian subsidy that depends on government action but rests the responsibility for providing the services with business.

References

Aventin, L., and P. Huard. 2000. The Cost of AIDS to Three Manufacturing Firms in Côte d'Ivoire. *Journal of African Economies* 9 (2): 161–188.

Bendell, J. 2003. Corporate Responses to HIV/AIDS in the Workplace: Findings from a Global Survey of Transnational Corporations and Three Surveys of Corporations in "Developing" Countries. Working paper no. 12. Geneva: United Nations Research Institute for Social Development.

Biggs, T., and M. Shah. 1997. The Impact of the AIDS Epidemic on African Firms. Discussion paper, Africa Regional Program on Enterprise Development (RPED), The World Bank, Washington, D.C.

Bloom, D., L. R. Bloom, and River Path Associates. 2001. Business, AIDS, and Africa. In *The Africa Competitiveness Report 2000–2001*. World Economic Forum, Harvard Center for International Development. Oxford: Oxford University Press.

Bloom, D., L. R. Bloom, D. Steven, and M. Weston. Business and HIV/AIDS: Who Me? A Global Review of the Business Response to HIV/AIDS 2003–2004. Paper presented at World Economic Forum, December 2003, Geneva Switzerland. Available at http://www.weforum.org/pdf/Initiatives/GHI_BusinessAIDSWhoMe_All.pdf.

Bloom, D., A. Mahal, and River Path Associates. 2001. *HIV/AIDS and the Private Sector: A Literature Review*. Washington, D.C.: American Foundation for AIDS Research.

Daly, K. 2000. *The Business Response to HIV/AIDS: Impact and Lessons Learned*. Geneva and London: Joint United Nations Programme on HIV/AIDS (UNAIDS), The Prince of Wales Business Leaders Forum (PWBLF), and the Global Business Council on HIV and AIDS.

Forsythe, S. 2002. How Does HIV/AIDS Affect African Businesses? In *State of the Art: AIDS and Economics*. Washington, D.C.: International AIDS Economics Network (IAEN).

Greener, R. 1997. Impact of HIV/AIDS and Options for Intervention: Results of a Five Company Pilot Study. Working paper no. 10, Botswana Institute of Development Policy Analysis.

International Labour Office. 2003. *Projected Labour Force Losses Due to AIDS for 2005 and 2020, by Region*. Geneva: International Labour Office. Available at http://www-ilo-mirror.cornell.edu/public/english/protection/trav/aids/facts/stats_page.htm.

O'Flaherty, B. 1998. Why Repeated Criminal Opportunities Matter: A Dynamic Stochastic Analysis of Criminal Decision-Making. *Journal of Law, Economics, and Organization* 14: 232–255.

Rau, B., and M. Roberts. 1996. *Private Sector AIDS Policy: Businesses Managing HIV/AIDS*. Arlington, Va.: AIDSCAP/Family Health International.

Rosen, S., and J. L. Simon. 2003. Shifting the Burden: The Private Sector's Response to the AIDS Epidemic in Africa. *Bulletin of the World Health Organization* 81: 131–137.

Rosen, S., J. Simon, D. Thea, and J. Vincent. 2000. Care and Treatment to Extend the Working Lives of HIV-Positive Employees: Calculating the Benefits to Business. *South African Journal of Science* 96 (6): 300–334.

Rosen, S., J. R. Vincent, W. MacLeod, D. M. Thea, and J. Simon. 2002. What Makes Nigerian Manufacturing Firms Take Action on HIV/AIDS? *World Bank Findings* 199: 1–4.

Rugalema, G., S. Weigang, and J. Mbwika. 1999. *HIV/AIDS and the Commercial Agricultural Sector of Kenya: Impact, Vulnerability, Susceptibility and Coping Strategies*. Rome: Food and Agriculture Organization of the United Nations and the United Nations Development Programme (FAO).

Sen, A. 1984. *Poverty and Famines: An Essay on Entitlement and Deprivation*. New York: Oxford University Press.

Simon, J., S. Rosen, A. Whiteside, J. R. Vincent, and D. M. Thea. 2000. The Response of African Businesses to HIV/AIDS. In *HIV/AIDS in the Commonwealth 2000/01*. London: Kensington Publications.

Smith, A. 1776 (1937). *An Inquiry into the Nature and Causes of the Wealth of Nations*. New York: Random House.

Smith, J., and A. Whiteside. 1995. The Socioeconomic Impact of HIV/AIDS on Zambian Businesses. London: The BEAD Group and the Commonwealth Development Corporation.

Solow, R. 1979. Another Possible Source of Wage Stickiness. *Journal of Macroeconomics* 1: 79–82.

United States Agency for International Development (USAID). 2001. *The HIV/AIDS Crisis: How Are African Businesses Responding?* Washington, D.C.: U.S. Agency for International Development. Available at http://www.usaid.gov/pop_health/aids/Publications/pubarchives.html.

Conclusion

Guillem López-Casasnovas,
Berta Rivera, and Luis Currais

1 Summary

How can we explore the way and the extent to which health affects economic growth? The answer, by necessity, is rather complex. There are multiple factors constantly interacting that create difficulties when it comes to estimating the causal effects between improved health status and variations in income. This complexity may be captured from different perspectives, both empirical and theoretical, that take in a variety of methodologies that combine microeconomic and macrodynamic analysis. The main objective here has been to provide results that demonstrate the economic benefits of improved health and link these results to policy issues.

We might reformulate our initial question thus: how, and to what degree do health conditions affect a country's per-capita GDP over time? Some chapters in this volume look at the health variable through the optic of growth theories that model the multiple effects of health when considered as a form of human capital. These models share the idea that technological progress is endogenous, although their approaches are different. These approaches presuppose different mechanisms via which health status affects the long-term growth performance of a country.

On a theoretical level, the relationship between technological progress and human capital occupies a prominent place in the relevant literature. Different theories of economic growth consider technological progress to be either endogenous or exogenous depending on the model. Although endogenous growth theories assume that technological progress can vary from country to country, neoclassical theory assumes that technical progress is exogenous and occurs at a rate that is constant across countries.

An empirical approach estimates the effects of health on long-term economic growth by using an aggregate production function and considers health as a component of human capital in line with the augmented Solow model used by Mankiw, Romer, and Weil. One way of escaping from the limitations that exogenous long-term economic growth presupposes is by relaxing the assumption of homogeneity in long-term rates of technical progress across countries. This allows the model to be considered as partially endogenous, which is achieved by using multilevel modeling techniques in order to estimate the extent to which the rate of technical progress differs across countries. Human capital, public policy, and geographical location are considered as potential determinants of these differences and special emphasis is placed on the role of health. In this case, changes in health status, or adult survival rate, may legitimately be considered as important determinants of the income growth rate in the long term. Further, these changes constitute a more important stimulus to growth in countries with initially low levels of survival rates.

A second approach uses theoretical models that assume economic growth to be endogenous. One framework traditionally used in the relevant literature adopts the generally accepted model of Lucas. This conceptualization envisages health as playing a quite different role in the way it affects economic growth, and emerges by modeling the health status of a population as a determinant of the supply of a healthy labor force. Health, therefore, influences the accumulation of knowledge by improving learning capacities and is incorporated within the model through three different channels. First, it is assumed that when a population's health levels get worse there is a consequent reduction in the effective labor supply. Second, there is the logical supposition that the resources spent on health will not be available for other uses. Third, good health also influences utility in a direct way through the net growth rate of the population and the endogenously determined level of health activities. This approach also takes into consideration the fact that health resources are used not only for curing, but also for caring.

The analysis, which demonstrates a variety of effects, clearly shows that good health is a prerequisite to the optimization of productive potential and that growth performance appears to be highly sensitive to changes in the productivity of human capital accumulation activities. The results obtained are particularly relevant when it comes to weighing up economic policy analysis, which should take into account not only the effects of health spending on welfare, but also the intertemporal effects that potentially influence long-term economic growth.

A further approach using endogenous growth models is based on the Schumpeterian perspective that considers technological progress to be the main driving force behind economic growth in the long term. This approach draws an important distinction between increases in physical capital and increases in innovation or intellectual capital. Even the technology spillovers and transfers that arise as a result of innovation taking place in other countries are dealt with using recent versions of this theory. In focusing on the health variable, it is found that the aggregate improvements in health levels produce positive effects in long-term economic growth through a variety of channels such as productivity efficiency, life expectancy, learning capacity, creativity, coping skills, and inequality. Basically, in every case, productivity and per-capita GDP increase in any country whose growth rate is the same as, or below that, of a technologically leading country. At the same time, these effects reduce the relative differences between the living standards that separate these countries from technological leaders. Changes in levels of life expectancy, on the other hand, have the opposite effect. This is true, however, only when these changes come about through reductions in infant mortality as opposed to prolonging the life span of productive workers who have already acquired and assimilated most of their skills.

Another way of approximating the relationship between health and economic growth is by assuming that bad health is a direct source of costs, both on an individual and household level. In this sense, bad health gives rise to a reduction in the number of hours worked due to illness or infirmity, lower productivity in the workplace, and reduced access to the labor market.

The idea that the healthiest individuals are also the most productive has normally been analyzed from a microeconomic point of view, via the relationship between health status and wage levels. The studies contained in this book have attempted to explore the relationship between health and labor outcomes by focusing on developing countries in which inequalities, both with respect to income and health levels, are evident within their respective populations. The fundamental objectives of these studies are to analyze the effects of changes in health conditions on the productive capacity of the individual and, to discover what the individual or social conditions are that might favor such changes. To this end it becomes possible to evaluate the costs and benefits of distinct programs aimed at achieving such improvements.

Carrying out these kinds of studies involves certain problems derived from the intangible nature of some of the components of human capital. As with education, health status is a nonobservable variable that must be estimated by proxy using imperfect indicators. These indicators are not always objective, do not represent a full range of conditions, or are linked to just one facet of health. In this sense, we find ourselves faced with measurement errors in the explanatory variables due to the heterogeneous sources of variation and problems with causal feedback between health and income or productivity. These difficulties have, of course, been taken into consideration when carrying out the empirical analyses. The tools honed to cope with this problem have been used as a variety of survey indicators; as instrumental variables that facilitate the prediction of health human capital, and as methods that make it possible to capture individual heterogeneity in returns to health.

The magnitude of the results obtained differs depending on the type of indicator chosen or on the technique used, although almost all of the studies would appear to capture an important link between health and productivity. This relationship would appear to be stronger as the levels of individual income decrease. Thus improvements in the health status of the less well off stimulate a reduction in the inequalities in income or wage levels, and this, in turn, tends to improve access to better quality goods and services improving the general quality of life, and thus further enhancing levels of human capital.

Health also affects economic growth through its impact on demography. For decades, researchers have noted systematic shifts in cause-of-death patterns as mortality levels change. The "epidemiologic transition" consists of the passage from a situation in which infectious and parasitic diseases are the main causes of death in a high-mortality setting to a situation in which chronic and degenerative diseases such a heart disease, cancer, or diabetes become the main causes of death. This change in the order of importance of the causes of death runs in parallel with declines in mortality rates.

The study of the epidemiologic transition, which looks at the way in which the evolving health status of different societies is linked to economic growth, may be undertaken from a range of perspectives. These approaches combine many of the skills specific to the analysis of economic growth theory with an emphasis on health through the epidemiologic transition. These approaches may normally be divided into either empirical or theoretical studies that usually analyze longevity and long-term growth. From a theoretical point of view the endogenous growth model given in this volume assumes physical and human capital to be determinants of economic growth while also introducing health investments that allow the agents to improve health status, proxied by improving levels of life expectancy.

The available evidence points to the fact that, beyond a specific threshold, health improves as income rises. The analysis uncovers three basic patterns that the transition tends to follow. These correspond to the three stages of the epidemiological transition: the classical model, the accelerated transition, and the delayed transition.

Low levels of life expectancy inhibit educational investment together with other forms of investment in human capital. This is quite simply because there is an increased risk that each individual will not survive long enough to enjoy the benefits of such investment. Healthier individuals with longer life expectancies have greater incentives to invest in the development of their abilities, since they expect to obtain the benefits of that investment over longer periods of time. A higher scholarization rate promotes higher productivity and higher incomes. The effects of health and demographic variables on economic growth, therefore, will prove to be especially relevant in developing countries, countries that are particularly sensitive to prohealth economic policy.

Empirical models provide a further means of unraveling the thread of economic growth and economic transition. Long-term demographic and economic data corresponding to developed countries show that the increase in human capital during the transition influences the rhythm of economic growth permanently. This empirical evidence adds further support to human-capital-based growth theory, which offers an important framework for analyzing the various stages of the transition.

The evidence presented shows that improving health may result in sustained increases in skilled labor only in the presence of skill-based technological change. In the very long run, progress in food production may be considered as a determinant of improved social health conditions. Further, public intervention with respect to the creation of infrastructures that facilitate the containment of communicable and parasitic diseases would seem to be indispensable in the face of market failures. These fixed investments have been key components of epidemiologic transitions and have generated important social returns.

Health-related changes during the epidemiologic shifts of the nineteenth century have therefore influenced the slope of the growth path permanently, and this phenomenon has had far-reaching social consequences that have swelled the pool of health-related externalities over successive generations.

One of the most readily accepted relationships in economic literature is the positive link between health and per-capita income. The higher a country's per-capita income the more likely its population is to be long living and healthy. Higher incomes provide greater access to goods and services that favor improved health such as more nutritious food, drinking water and sewage facilities, health services, better quality information, and education. The reverse may also be true however; when levels of GDP stagnate or fall, this tends to prevent improvements in health, and this lack of health human capital feeds a relative degeneration in a country's economic capacity. This vicious circle is known as the poverty trap.

The concept of the poverty trap is especially useful when it comes to trying to understand the growth dynamic in sub-Saharan Africa when compared to parts of East Asia. At the beginning of the 1960s, the two areas had similar levels of per-capita GDP, but the costs of illness and disease in Africa have been much greater, and birth rates and ratios of juvenile dependency much higher since then. Some studies attribute more than half of the difference in the annual growth rate between sub-Saharan Africa and East Asia to differences in life expectancy and in the inherent differences in the way their respective populations have evolved.

According to the results presented in this volume, health is an important factor when it comes to avoiding or escaping the poverty trap, where aggregate levels of health and income are considered and the relationship between them analyzed. This effect may be captured through the multiple channels suggested above, such as improved productivity, education levels, and mortality rates.

In this sense, improvements in health levels in less developed countries have effects that, at first glance, might appear to be somewhat strange. Improved health in underdeveloped countries does not give rise to population growth, but rather a contraction in that growth in the medium and long term. Population-related issues come into play, and development follows the pattern traced by the demographic transition, through which lower mortality rates, especially among the young, lead to reduced birth rates. In a scenario in which individuals are at a high risk from disease, families opt to have large numbers of children given that the probability of survival is low. When the effects of disease are reined in, numbers of children per family tend to be checked or planned. The higher the number of children, in any given family, the lower will be the investment that each child receives. This leads to very low levels of human capital, a dynamic that is transmitted from one generation to the next over relatively short periods of time. The main result is that per-capita growth rates decline, springing the poverty trap.

Increases in longevity, on the other hand, create the need for individuals to save for their retirement. The fact that increased savings leads to greater investment means that workers have greater access to capital and higher incomes. These effects are discernible not only with respect to private investment, but also in terms of public funds. This tendency toward capital accumulation has a direct impact on the economy's levels of aggregate efficiency, which are, in turn, directly related to the region's level of economic activity.

There is much evidence, too, that suggests that poverty and malnutrition are linked directly, with almost one billion people suffering from malnutrition in developing countries. The relationship that exists between health and the creation of human capital through nutritional improvements and the resultant increases in physical and mental capacity has been touched on by different studies in this book and dealt with in depth by some. Thus, there are different channels via which nutrition favors economic growth. Improved nutrition leads to better health, which means that resources that would otherwise be used in coping with problems derived from nutritional deficiencies are saved. These savings are achieved as the result of physiological changes affecting characteristics such as height and weight, and also those indirect savings that come about as a consequence of improved learning capacities and the development of future skills.

On establishing a direct relationship between nutrition and productivity one discovers that malnutrition reduces the physical and mental capacity of workers, and this leads to lower rates of productivity and less leverage when it comes to finding a job and negotiating a salary, which in turn leads to lower wages. Individual height and strength in adults depends on nutrient intake and general good health during infancy through to adolescence. In this sense, there is considerable evidence that there is a direct positive relationship between the physical stature of a population and the probability that these individuals belong to the workforce. Tall people are more likely to have jobs. Even in developed countries such as the United States there would seem to be evidence of a direct positive relationship between size and salary. Further, deficiencies in nutrition can have important long-term costs in the way they prejudice the development of an individual's cognitive abilities. Research suggests that malnourished adults whose diets change in favor of a higher calorie and protein intake become more productive.

Another way of analyzing the effects of health on economic growth is by estimating the cost of an illness or group of illnesses. It is possible to consider the costs incurred by households or by individuals directly; these come in the form of the expenses a family must pay for the prevention or medical treatment of illnesses; or the economic value or willingness to pay due to pain, suffering, and the reduction in life expectancy.

The above approach has been used as a way of gauging the costs of AIDS in sub-Saharan Africa, where the majority of sufferers are to be found, by trying to capture the economic value of reductions in mortality rates measured in terms of improvements in wellbeing. That is, an estimation is carried out, both individual and social, based on a willingness to pay, with respect to the changes in mortality rates that would occur if the disease were to be eradicated. This approach is especially useful for analyzing the gains in wellbeing that the eradication or reduction of a particular disease create for a society.

An individual survival function is posited, and this may be affected by exogenous factors such as technological changes or the outbreak of new diseases or epidemics, in this particular case, AIDS. The reductions in physical and human capital caused by AIDS are considerable given that the majority of those affected are "working-age" individuals, and this tends to throttle economic growth in the worst hit regions.

The empirical implementation of this methodology provides results that are more incisive than those derived from estimations of the direct economic costs of illness. Findings show that in those African countries with relatively high levels of per-capita income the prejudicial economic effects of AIDS are greater. These results would seem to reconfirm the lack of resources and adequate investment policy aimed at bringing AIDS under control, the beneficial effects of which would go far beyond the purely economic, creating important gains in wellbeing.

In this sense, when talking about policy designed to combat AIDS, we think of public policy or the intervention of non-profit-making organizations, and tend to dismiss any notion of business involvement. However, given the effects of AIDS, the relative difficulty of procuring a healthy workforce has a direct negative impact on industrial and business performance. If, on the other hand, the population is healthy, this generates positive externalities that attract investment, boost commerce and tourism, and generate additional economic activity.

Commercial involvement in arresting the advance of AIDS has been analyzed from a traditional economic approach in which firms are modeled as market agents that aim to maximize profits. However, even when firms have incentives to participate actively in the fight against AIDS, if it is outweighed by the opportunity cost of alternative investment we should not expect definitive tide-turning intervention on the part of firms in the fight against AIDS. In short, there is a gap between the financial incentives that firms have for preventing and treating AIDS, and the social benefits that would come from their doing so.

From this perspective, economic theory provides four reasons why firms do not get involved in the fight against the disease: efficiency wages, the customer-based argument, enlightened self-interest, and cost-benefit calculations. These barriers to involvement might be rather more flimsy than we might, at first, suppose. In the case of efficiency wages for example, the incentives for a firm's positive intervention would grow if the labor required was both skilled and scarce. Traditional ways of motivating firms to take an active role in the prevention and treatment of AIDS are not exempt from difficulty. A more workable alternative must surely be available in a public–private partnership capable of maximizing both the opportunities available to the state for converting social benefits into profit opportunities, and the advantages available for firms in mobilizing resources, innovation, or marketing.

2 Final Thoughts

The line of research that attempts to analyze the relationships between health and economic growth, which has become firmly established as a rich field of study in recent years, is steadily becoming a fertile area that may help us to know more about the links between health human capital and economic and social development. Research alone, however, will be of little value unless there are coherent policies based on these investigations capable of putting into practice, planning, and orientating specific programs aimed at maximizing the potential of health as a dynamic motor of human capital in the future.

The difficulties, doubts, or reflections that have been aired in these studies echo just how much research still needs to be carried out in this field and the need to develop new methodologies, specific tools, and data in order to improve analytical capacity. The potential agenda for future research includes the ways in which increases in longevity affect health status, public finance, and productivity; the benefits of preventative action with respect to specific diseases; sexual and reproductive health and their demographic implications; or the possibilities of incentives that would reduce the opportunity costs of investing in health. The benefits of pharmacological alternatives that reduce the cost of treating certain diseases, as is the case of generic medicines in the treatment of AIDS, would also be found within the planning of programs destined for poor countries. A field of research that remains fertile studies the way income inequalities, poverty, and health affect income dynamics, and the possibility of reverse causation. The way health influences social capital and community cohesion and their impact on economic growth is also embraced by this approach.

If one considers the benefits derived from health investment it would seem logical that social agents should try to take advantage of the opportunities provided by new technologies, improvements in infrastructures, the results of research and, in general, the positive potential generated by global development as a means of improving the health of underprivileged populations. The reduction in these inequities with respect to health status is a prerequisite to the successful deployment and enacting of sustained development and investment policy, both economic and social.

Contributors

Adriaan van Zon is Senior Research Fellow at MERIT, the Maastricht Economic Research Institute on Innovation and Technology, and Associate Professor in Economics at the Faculty of Economics and Business Administration, Maastricht University. He obtained his Ph.D. in Economics at Groningen University on a multisectoral macromodel of the Dutch economy. His research interests are macroeconomic model building with special emphasis on the links between technology and employment issues, technology and environmental issues, and technology and health issues. He has helped to compile European Commission reports and has published articles in various journals of prestige such as the *Journal of Health Economics* and the *Journal of Health Management Sciences*.

Berta Rivera is Associate Professor of Economics at the University of A Coruña in Spain. She received her Ph.D. from Universitat Pompeu Fabra. She is also a research associate of the Economics and Health Research Center at Universitat Pompeu Fabra University. Her main areas of research are health economics, economic development, and fiscal policy. She has taken part in health-related research projects for the central government, the Spanish Health Ministry, and for the regional governments, the Generalitat de Cataluña and the Xunta de Galicia. Her doctoral thesis received a special award by the Spanish Economic Ministry and she has numerous articles in relevant journals including *World Development, Applied Economics, The Review of Development Economics,* and *Applied Economic Letters*.

David Bloom is Clarence James Gamble Professor of Economics and Demography, and Chairman of the Department of Population and International Health, at the Harvard School of Public Health. After receiving a Ph.D. in Economics and Demography from Princeton University, he served on the public policy faculty at Carnegie-Mellon University and in the economics departments at Harvard University and Columbia University. He was subsequently Deputy Director of the Harvard Institute for International Development. Bloom has carried out extensive research in the areas of population, health, labor, and HIV/AIDS, and has advised the UN Development Programme, the World Bank, the International Labour Organization, and UNAIDS.

David Mayer-Foulkes studied for his Ph.D. in Mathematics at the University of California, Berkeley and UNAM, Mexico. He has worked in research in economics at CIDE in Mexico City since 1991, concentrating mainly on health and economic growth as well as on economic growth at the cross-country level. His interests focus on the existence of different kinds of human capital and technology development traps from both the empirical and theoretical points of view. He has carried out a series of projects in health and economic growth for the Pan American Health Organization, as well as projects on economic growth for the World Bank.

Dean T. Jamison is a Fellow at the Fogarty International Center of the National Institutes of Health where he is seconded from his position as a Professor of International Health Economics, University of California, Los Angeles. Before joining the UCLA faculty in 1988, Jamison spent many years at the World Bank where he was a senior economist in the research department, task manager for projects and sector work in China and Gambia, division chief for education policy, and division chief for population, health, and nutrition. In 1992–1993 he temporarily rejoined the World Bank to serve as lead author for the Bank's 1993 World Development Report, *Investing in Health*. Jamison studied at Stanford (A.B., Philosophy; M.S., Engineering Sciences) and at Harvard (Ph.D., Economics, under K. J. Arrow). In 1994 he was elected to membership in the Institute of Medicine of the U.S. National Academy of Sciences, and he currently chairs the Institute's Board on Global Health.

Edward Miguel is Assistant Professor of Economics at the University of California, Berkeley and also works for the Center for Health and Wellbeing at Princeton University. He obtained his Ph.D. from Harvard University. He is also a consultant to the Vice President of Development Economics for the World Bank. He is a Faculty Research

Associate of the National Bureau of Economic Research, a Junior Fellow of the Bureau for Research and Economic Analysis of Development and Co-organizer of the UCLA Working Group in African Political Economy. He has written for the *Journal of Monetary Economics* and the *East African Medical Journal*. His interests include the analytics of economic development and planning and African economic development.

Guillem López-Casasnovas is Professor of the Economics and Business Faculty of Pompeu Fabra University. He is Director of the Economics and Health Research Center (CRES) at Universitat Pompeu Fabra. He received his Ph.D. from the University of York. López-Casasnovas was the second economist to be appointed to the Royal Academy of Medicine of Catalonia. He has been the Vice Chancellor of the Universitat Pompeu Fabra responsible for International Relations and Economic Affairs. He is the author of numerous articles and publications about public economy, social policy, fiscal policy, public management, and health economics. He is a member of the Health Ministry's Advisory Council, and of the Spanish Medicines Agency, which is part of the Catalonian government's Health Department.

Harold Alderman received his Ph.D. in economics from Harvard University in 1984 and a M.S. in Nutrition from Cornell University. He is currently the Lead Human Development Economist in the Africa Regional Vice-Presidency of the World Bank where he works on issues of social protection and nutrition policy. Prior to joining the World Bank in 1991 he had spent ten years with the International Food Policy Research Institute. His main research interests are food policy and nutrition as well as the economics of education and of targeted poverty programs. He has published important contributions to the *Journal of Public Economics, Journal of Human Resources, Journal of African Economies, Demographic Research,* and *Economics of Education Review,* among others.

Jaypee Sevilla is an Assistant Professor of International Health Economics at the Harvard School of Public Health. He received his Ph.D. in Economics from Harvard in 1999. His research interests include ethical issues in health sector resource allocation, the socioeconomic impact of HIV/AIDS in South Africa, and cohort crowding effects in developing countries.

Jere R. Behrman (Ph.D., Massachusetts Institute of Technology, 1966) is the William R. Kenan, Jr. Professor of Economics and Director of the Population Studies Center at the University of Pennsylvania, where he has been on the faculty since 1965. His research interests are in empirical microeconomics, economic development, labor economics, human resources, economic demography, and household behaviors. He has published over 230 professional articles and 30 books and monographs on these topics. He has worked as a research consultant with numerous national and international organizations, including the World Bank, the Asian Development Bank, and the Inter-American Development Bank. He has been the principal investigator or coprincipal investigator on over 40 research projects funded by organizations including the U.S. National Institutes of Health, the U.S. National Science Foundation, the Rockefeller Foundation, and the Ford Foundation. He has received various honors, including being selected as a Fulbright Fortieth Anniversary Distinguished Fellow, a Fellow of the Econometric Society, a Guggenheim Foundation Faculty Fellow, and a Ford Foundation Faculty Fellow.

Jia Wang   is a Senior Research Associate at the Center for the Study of Evaluation, University of California, Los Angeles (UCLA). She received her doctorate in social research methodology from UCLA. Wang uses advanced methodology in her research into public health that focuses on how the levels of a country's income, education, and technical progress affect its health performance. She has ongoing contracts with the National Institutes of Health and the World Bank to provide statistical consultation.

Joan Muysken   is Professor of Economics at the Faculty of Economics and Business Administration, Maastricht University. He studied quantitative economics and obtained his Ph.D. on the aggregation of production functions from the University of Groningen. He has been a visiting researcher at the University of Oslo, State University of New York, Buffalo, Catholic University of Louvain-la-Neuve in Belgium, and the University of Newcastle in Australia. He is Director of CofFEE-Europe. His research interests are wage formation, labor demand, matching problems, analysis of unemployment, and the relationship between endogenous growth and the diffusion of technologies. He has published articles in prestigious journals such as the *Journal of Health Economics, Scandinavian Journal of Economics*, and *Applied Economics*, and has contributed to several books in his field.

John Hoddinott   is Associate Professor of Dalhousie University. He was research economist in the Ontario Ministry of Treasury and Economics and acting divisional director in the International Food Policy Research Institute. He has worked in the University of Nairobi, Oxford University, Princeton University, and the University of Toronto. His current lines of research focus on poverty, health, intrahousehold resource allocation, and labor markets, with particular reference to developing countries. He has published important research in the *Journal of Development Studies, Journal of Epidemiology and Community Health, World Development,* and *Economic Development and Cultural Change.* He is also the author of numerous chapters in various books published by Oxford University Press, Johns Hopkins University Press, and Macmillan, among others.

Lawrence J. Lau   holds a B.S. in Physics and Economics from Stanford University and a Ph.D. in Economics from the University of California, Berkeley. He joined the Department of Economics at Stanford University in 1966, and was promoted to Professor of Economics in 1976. In 1992, he was named the first Kwoh-Ting Li Professor of Economic Development at Stanford University. His many honors include serving as a fellow of the Econometric Society and being an academician of the Academia Sinica. His research interests include economic theory, economic development, economic growth, applied microeconomics, econometrics, and the economies of East Asia and other transition economies. He has published over 200 articles, book chapters, and monographs in the most prestigious of economics' publications. Lawrence Lau is currently the Vice-Chancellor of the Chinese University of Hong Kong.

Luis Currais   is Associate Professor of Economics at the University of A Coruña. He obtained his Ph.D. degree from A Coruña University where he modeled the incorporation of health into neoclassical growth models. He was awarded a European Doctorate. Currais was a visiting researcher at the Universitat Autonoma de Barcelona in Spain and the Universidade Federal Fluminense in Brazil. He is also a research associate of the Economics and Health Research Center at Universitat Pompeu Fabra. His main areas of research are economic growth, macroeconomics, and health economics. He has taken part in health-related research projects for the Spanish Ministries of Health, and of Technology and Science. He has numerous articles in relevant journals such as the *Review of Development Economics, Applied Economics Letters,* and *World Development*.

Olivier F. Morand   is Assistant Professor of Economics at the University of Connecticut. He obtained his Ph.D. at Arizona State University. He is an expert in dynamic macroeconomics, general equilibrium, and economic growth. He has taken part and contributed to various professional meetings and associations such as the Research Group on Income Distribution and Growth of NBER. He has also published articles in prestigious journals such as the *Journal of Economic Growth, Journal of Macroeconomics, Annals of Operation Research,* and the *Journal of Monetary Economics*.

Peter Howitt   is Professor of Economics and the Lyn Crost Professor of Social Sciences at Brown University. Most of his research has been in the areas of macroeconomics and monetary economics. Together with Philippe Aghion of Harvard University, the coauthor of his book, *Endogenous Growth Theory,* he has developed the new "Schumpeterian" approach to the theory of economic growth. He was the editor of the *Journal of Money, Credit, and Banking* and associate editor of *Econometrica, Journal of Economic Growth,* and *Macroeconomic Dynamics*. He has also been active in the search for new foundations to macroeconomics and monetary theory, and has written extensively on the subject of Canadian monetary policy.

Rodrigo R. Soares   is an assistant professor in the Department of Economics at the University of Maryland at College Park and Catholic University of Rio de Janeiro. He received his Ph.D. in Economics from the University of Chicago in 2002, and has held visiting positions at Catholic University and the Graduate School of Economics at the Getúlio Vargas Foundation, both in Rio de Janeiro, Brazil. Soares's research focuses on the economic consequences of changes in health and mortality, and on the relationship between crime, institutions, and economic development. His dissertation on the economic impacts of mortality reductions won the 2003 Brazilian National Award for best Ph.D. dissertation in economics ("Prêmio Haralambos Simeonidis"). Soares is affiliated with the Maryland Population Research Center, the American Economic Association, and the Latin American and Caribbean Economic Association.

Suchit Arora   is an international economist in the State Teachers Retirement System of Ohio. He completed his doctorate in Economics under the supervision of Paul D. Evans, Richard H. Steckel, and Peter W. Howitt at Ohio State University. A keen interest in health and macroeconomic phenomena has led him to research the relationship between health and long-term economic growth, and in particular the links between the transmission of epidemics and short-term business fluctuations, the epidemiologic transition, the nature of aging during the transition and its implications for pension costs, and the reasons for cross-country differences. He is also a consultant to the Pan American Health Organization.

T. Paul Schultz received his Ph.D. from MIT in 1966, started and directed the population research program at Rand from 1966 to 1972, and was Director of the Economic Growth Center at Yale University from 1983 to 1996, where he has been the Malcolm K. Brachman Professor of Economics since 1975. He has contributed to two National Academy of Sciences panels assessing the implications of the demographic transition, the first, Rapid Population Growth (1971) and the second, Population Growth and Economic Development (1987), and has written chapters for the Handbooks in Economics series: "Education" (1988), "Fertility" (1997), and "Women's Roles and Bargaining in the Household" (2001). He has also studied the economic and demographic behavior of the family using microeconomic models and econometric methods.

Tomas J. Philipson is a professor in the Irving B. Harris Graduate School of Public Policy Studies and a faculty member in the Department of Economics and the Law School at the University of Chicago. He received his Ph.D. in Economics from the University of Pennsylvania, and has held positions at Yale University, the World Bank, and the Food and Drug Administration. His research has been published in leading academic journals such as *American Economic Review, Journal of Political Economy, Quarterly Journal of Economics, Journal of Economic Theory*, and *Econometrica*. He is affiliated with the National Bureau of Economic Research, the George J. Stigler Center for the Study of the Economy and the State, the Robert Wood Johnson Clinical Scholars Program, the Northwestern/University of Chicago Joint Center for Poverty Research, the National Opinion Research Center, and the American Economic Association.

Xavier Sala-i-Martín is Professor of Economics at the Universities of Columbia and Pompeu Fabra. He received his Ph.D. in economics from Harvard University. His various professional posts include that of research fellow at the National Bureau of Economic Research, the Center for European Policy Research, and the Institute of Policy Research. Sala-i-Martín is also a research associate at the Rochester Center for Economic Research and a consultant for the International Monetary Fund. He is the editor of many relevant publications and is one of the most frequently cited active economists in the world. His research interests include poverty and income inequality, empirical growth and convergence, growth theory, technology and technological diffusion, human capital and investment, public finance and social security, money and inflation, international economics and health and population economics. He is the author of numerous articles published in journals of repute, and his books run to numerous editions worldwide.

Index